Introduction to Archaeology

A Selection of Readings
Organized and Introduced

By

David A. Walsh
Rochester University

Linus
Publications, Inc.

Published by Linus Publications, Inc.

Deer Park, NY 11729

ISBN 0-9777197-1-X

Printed in the United States of America.

10 9 8 7 6 5 4 3 2 1

Table of Contents

Introduction

I have chosen a series of readings taken from archaeological writings in the service of anthropology and history and art history to introduce the student to a variety of archaeological activity from field work to the more theoretical interpretation of culture. The authors of these secondary sources deal with material studied from the point of view of more than one discipline, and I have intentionally tried to include works over a substantial range of time. Additionally, the writings are organized into three groups: the history of archaeological activity through the nineteenth century (chapters 1-3); the development of field techniques, scientific material analysis, recording, chronology and syntheses of site data (chapters 4-14); and interpretation of culture in the twentieth century (chapters 15-18).

The Birth of Archaeology

Introduction

The text is taken from Glyn Daniel's *Short History of Archaeology*, one of a number of writings by this author on the historiography of the field. Daniel (1914-1986) was distinguished for his work on prehistoric sites (*The Megalith Builders of Western Europe* of 1958, *The Idea of Prehistory* of 1961) and, notably, his interest in interpretation of a wide range of cultures as editor, from 1955-1986, for the series, *Ancient People and Places*.

In the reading from *A Short History* reproduced here, we are introduced to the problem of defining archaeology, not only for its early exploration of ancient remains *following* historical writings, but the development of cultural study seen through its material remains, along with strategies of both excavation and interpretation. Citing early examples of excavation such as that of the Babylonian king Nabonitus at Ur in Mesopotamia, artifacts and especially inscriptions were understood as belonging to the distant past and even brought together as a collection. The Greeks and Romans were also interested in the cultures of their ancestors, and they could, on occasion, appreciate the distinct characteristics of artifactual material and speculate about the development of culture; but their theories of evolutionary development were not based on a systematic study of artifacts. The recovery of material of antiquity in the Renaissance was stimulated by the admiration for classical culture in the fifteenth and especially sixteenth centuries C.E., in which focus was on the art and architecture still visible or fortuitously uncovered. Enthusiasm for classic remains continued to stimulate seventeenth- and eighteenth-century collecting of antiquities, and from this would emerge a growing organization and critical discussion of material, characteristic of the new societies of antiquarians and of lavishly illustrated treatments of buildings and sites or areas. The eighteenth century saw a growing appreciation and knowledge of Greek remains, and, in Italy, the excavation of ancient Roman sites of Herculaneum and Pompeii provided vast quantities of antiquities. Although excavation merely sought to recover works of art for collections, such material began to be organized, notably by Joachim Winkelmann, in order to develop an account of art related to history. At this time also, remains from the great civilizations of Mesopotamia and Egypt attracted attention, although it would not be until the nineteenth century that texts were decoded that would enable a leap in the understanding of these ancient peoples.

Northern European antiquarians from the sixteenth through the eighteenth centuries were largely committed to the study of their own cultural backgrounds. In England, antiquities were surveyed in the sixteenth century by John Leland and William Camden; their work, along with Edward Lhwyd and John Aubrey in the next century, not only made comparative studies of prehistoric sites, but initiated enquiries into the date and nature of monuments such as Avebury and Stonehenge and the cultures that produced them. This constituted a movement in the direction of identifying cultures and their practices that might be seen in standing remains and the fruits of archaeological investigation; the colonization of the New World stimulated reflections on the earlier stages of the development of humankind, and at this time a pan-European interest in ancient culture was evidenced by figures such At Ole Worm in Holland, Thomas Bartholin and Erik Pontoppidan in Denmark, and Olof Verelius in Sweden, as well as private and state-sponsored societies.

Archaeology is that branch of the study of history which deals with the material remains of man's past. The study of history in its widest sense deals with all sources: literary, epigraphic and material and the historian aims to create as complete and true a picture of the human past as it is reasonably possible to do. The archaeologist deals with man's artifacts: his tools and weapons, his houses, tombs, temples. Written sources existed for the first time about five thousand years ago, and so there are, very broadly speaking, two kinds of archaeology. There is the archaeology that deals with human history before writing and this is called prehistory. It goes back to the first hominids in East Africa which are now dated to two and a half million years ago and more. The other archaeology deals with the material remains of societies that are documented by writing: at first the material remains are as important as or more important than the written sources : this is the time generally referred to as protohistory. Then as the written sources become common and important we move out of protohistory into history *sensu stricto,* and the study of man's material remains becomes, as has often been said, 'the handmaiden of history'.

The *Oxford English Dictionary* tells us the origin of the word archaeology: it comes from a Greek word *arkhaiologia* meaning 'discourse about ancient things'; and also tells us how it has been used first to mean ancient history generally, secondly to mean a systematic description or study of antiquities, and thirdly 'the scientific study of the remains and monuments of the prehistoric period'. The first usage is no longer in common parlance, and the third is a restricted use of the term—prehistory and prehistoric archaeology are very important aspects of our study of the past but prehistory, though much the longest period studied by the archaeologist, is only a part of archaeology which, in the correct second statement, is the 'systematic description or study of antiquities'.

What the *OED* definition does not make clear is that this 'systematic description or study' is not primarily concerned with the antiquities themselves but with using them to explain and illumine man's prehistoric, protohistoric and historic past.

Georges Daux, in his admirable short history of archaeology entitled *Les Étapes de l Archéologie* (1942) in the *Que-sais-je?* series, tells US that the term archaeology was re-created in the modern world of scholarship in the seventeenth century by Jacques Spon (1647-85), a German doctor in Lyons who was forced to leave France by the revocation of the Edict of Nantes. He traveled widely accompanied by a Sir George Wheeler (d. 1723) who published in 1682 *A Journey into Greece . . . in the company of Dr. Spon.* Spon himself published his *Voyage d'ltalie, de Dalmatie, de Gr»ce et du Levant fait aux ann»es 1675-1676* in Amsterdam in 1689 and his *Miscellanea eruditae antiquitatis* in Lyons between I 689 and 1713.

So when did archaeology begin? And who was the first archaeologist. The last native kings of Babylon carried out very active building schemes in several of the ancient cities of Sumer and Akkad. Both Nebuchadrezzar and Nabonidus, the last king of Babylon, dug and restored Ur Nabonidus was delighted to find at Ur 'the inscriptions of former ancient kings', and his daughter En-nigaldi Nanna (her name was formerly transcribed incorrectly as Belshalti Nanner) had dug for years at the temple of Agade. When a heavy downpour of rain opened a great gallery revealing the temple it is recorded that this discovery 'made the king's heart glad and caused his countenance to brighten'. The princess seemed to have a room in her house for her collection of local antiquities. For an account of these early Babylonian archaeological activities see Joan Oates, *Babylon* (1979, 162).

But of course these early activities were not archaeology properly Speaking and in the classical world of Greece and Rome there was no archaeology as a deliberate way of finding man's early history by studying his material remains. Herodotus and other Greeks made remarkable ethnographical observations and came into contact with surviving prehistoric barbarians: they were ethnologists or anthropologists but not archaeologists, although they saw ancient people whose remains were later rediscovered by archaeology.

The Greeks and Romans had ideas about man's past but they were not based on archaeology. The Greeks knew of their Mycenaean past when iron was not in use: and both Greeks and Romans speculated on the technological evolution of man. They had ages of stone, bronze and iron just as they had golden ages. And there were speculations about the origins of civilization and the spread of culture. In the time of Diodorus Siculus some Egyptians or Graeco-Egyptians maintained that mankind spread from Egypt, and, in later ages, all civilization as well. This was probably local pride and not an anticipation of the Egyptocentric hyperdiffusionist doctrines of the early twentieth century.

Curiously enough a Chinese compilation of AD 52 set out a sequence of the past of man based on an age of stone, then bronze, then iron. Professor R. H. Lowie, in his *The History of Ethnological Theory* (1937), said 'this is not a case of genius forestalling science by two thousand years: an alert intelligence is simply juggling possibilities without any basis of facts or any attempt to test them': but I think that the Chinese scheme probably preserved a folk memory of the technological succession of stone, bronze and iron which was to be established as historical fact and the cornerstone of modern archaeology in the early nineteenth century.

The Chinese compilation and the Greek and Roman speculations did not affect thought in Western Europe in post-Roman times. Archaeology did not exist and the past was invented in terms of the Bible and classical writers. In *A History of the Kings of Britain* (1508) Geoffrey of Monmouth brought Brutus, son of Acneas, to England in 1125 BC to start British history. This was the invented past –a past of myth and legend, but it was all people could do before the nature of archaeological evidence was appreciated.

The Mediterranean World and Egypt

The decay of the ancient world of Greece and Rome meant the loss of the notions about early man that the classical world had set out. The schemes of Hesiod and Lucretius were replaced by the story of the creation of the world and man and of a Universal Flood as set out in Genesis. The renaissance of learning in the fifteenth and sixteenth centuries, however, brought back an interest in the classical period: Lucretius, Aristotle, Hesiod and Herodotus were read again and so were Caesar's *Commentaries on the Gallic War* and Tacitus's *Agricola* and the *Germania.* Here was a description of the barbarians of central and northern Europe—the Celts, Gauls, Germans, Britons, and Goths—and a description of that remarkable class in Celtic society—the Druids, who were teachers, priests and judges.

The classical civilization of the ancient world survived to the sixteenth century in its material remains. Scholars in Italy and travellers from other countries to Italy, Greece, Asia Minor and Egypt began to discover, describe and admire classical and Near Eastern antiquities. Popes and cardinals began collecting antiquities and made their villas into private museums. It was this age in Italy that produced the word *dilettanti*—those who delighted in the arts.

In England the Society of Dilettanti was founded by learned men in 1732: it met in London to bring together those who had done Italy and the Grand Tour. In the preface to his *Ionian Antiquities* Richard Chandler wrote of the origin of the Dilettanti, 'Some Gentlemen who had travelled in Italy, desirous of encouraging, at home, a taste for those objects which had contributed so much to their entertainment abroad, formed themselves into a Society under the name of the DILETTANTI.'

It was during the period 1750-1880, the second renaissance of Greek scholarship, that the antiquities of the classical world were discovered by French, English and German scholars. The great age of English collectors began with the travels of the painter James Stuart (1712-86) and the architect Nicholas Revett (1720-1804) in Athens in the three years 1751-53. They spent those years measuring, drawing, recording. Their great work, *The Antiquities of Athens,* was long delayed: the first volume appeared in 1762 but the fourth not until 1816. The Society of Dilettanti had financed the publication of *The Antiquities of Athens:* in 1764 they financed their 'first Ionic expedition' consisting of Revett, Chandler and William Pars. The results were published between 1769 and 1797 in the volumes entitled *The Antiquities of Ionia.* At the same time as Stuart and Revett were working in Athens, two other Englishmen, Robert Wood and James Dawkins, toured Asia Minor and the Near East publishing their results in two volumes by Robert Wood, *Ruins of Palmyra* (1753) and *Ruins of Baalbec* (1757).

Figure 1   Engraving of the Temple of Artemis from Stuart and Revett, *The Antiquities of Athens.*

Figure 2   Capitals and pilasters from the Temple of Apollo at Dedyma, from *The Antiquities of Ionia* by chandler, Revett and Pars. The Sketches and studies of Engish travellers in Greece and Turkey during the mid eighteenth century brought about a revival of interest in ancient Greek civilization.

During the eighteenth century the collecting zeal of Italians was waning and much of the Roman collections had been dispersed to Paris, Madrid, Munich and Prague. Yet when Joachim Winckelmann, in the middle of the eighteenth century, wrote his famous *History* of *Art* (1763-68), it was Rome that provided him with his main material. Winckelmann has been called 'the father of archaeology': he was certainly the first scholar to study ancient art historically—but art history is only one facet of archaeology.

Figure 3

Portrait of J. J. Winckelmann (1717-68).

Excavation in classical lands had begun early together with collecting and describing. The ancient cities of Pompeii and Herculaneum, south-east of Naples, owe their fame in history and in the history of archaeology to their sudden destruction when Vesuvius erupted on 24 August AD 79. When the eruption ceased the next day, Pompeii was covered with lapilli and ashes to a depth of twenty feet (six metres). At Herculaneum the volcanic material was carried along by torrents of water and mud which solidified into lava that covered the city with a hard tufa up to sixty-five feet (twenty metres) thick. An eye- witness account of these strange happenings is given in letters by Pliny the Younger to Tacitus.

The ruins of Pompeii were discovered in the late sixteenth century during tunnelling to build a conduit. Excavation of these buried cities began in 1709 at Herculaneum during the Austrian occupation. Workmen found three marble statues of young women and these excited the imagination of the wife of King Charles IV of Naples. In 1738 the king began excavations at Herculaneum: ten years later excavation began at Pompeii and in 1763 an inscription *rei publicae Pompeianorum* was found which identified the site as Pompeii.

Figure 4   **Excavations at Herculaneum from** *voyages pittoresques de Naples et de Sicile* (1782).

Excavation at Herculaneum were carried on by sinking shafts and driving tunnels until 1765 by which time the theatre, the Basilica and the Villa of the Papyri were found and a plan of the city made. In the neighbourhood of Stabia and Gragnano, excavations between 1749 and 1782, organized by King Charles IV of Naples (later Charles III of Spain), uncovered a dozen villas.

The discovery and appreciation of classical antiquity had an effect on taste and design in eighteenth-century Europe. An important collection of painted Greek vases

Figure 5

Engraving of theTemple of Isis at Pompeii by Piranesi the Younger. The Discovery and excavation of Pompeii and Herculaneum had a profound impact on taste in eighteenth-century Europe.

formed by Sir William Hamilton, the man who was cuckolded by Nelson, British ambassador at Naples in 1772, was acquired by the British Museum and his *Antiquit»s Etrusques, Grecques et Romaines* (1766-67) inspired Josiah Wedgwood to fashion Greek, Etruscan and Pompeian vases. The Wedgwood Works at Staffordshire in England still bear the name Etruria in recognition of this inspiration.

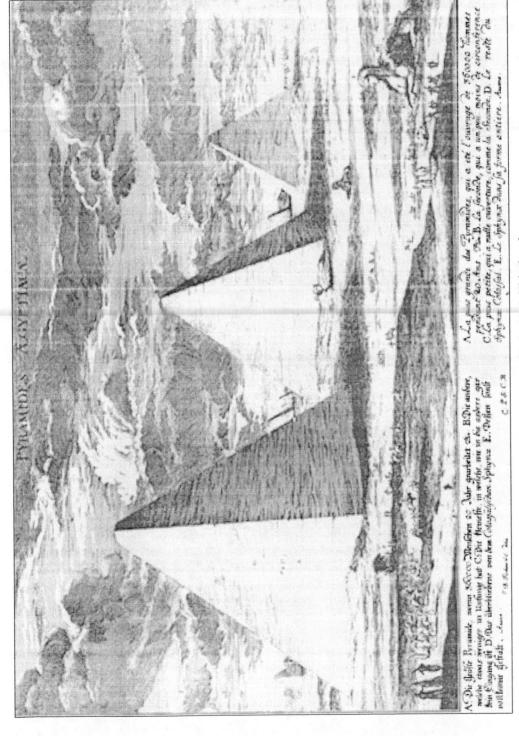

Figure 6   John Greaves of Oxford visited the Egyptian pyramids in 1638. This drawing from his *pyramidographia* is the first accurate one of the Great Pyramid

Many of the dramatic surface antiquities of Egypt were known to early Greek and Arab travellers. Herodotus, 'the Father of History' as he has been called, travelled in Egypt as far south as Aswan and wrote about mummification and the pyramids. Diodorus Siculus, Strabo, Pausanias and Pliny the Elder all visited Egypt. The great seated statues of Amenhotep III at Thebes were mistakenly named the Colossi of Memnon after the Homeric hero Memnon. The Greeks also called the mortuary temple of Ramesses I1 the Memnonium: but Diodorus called it the tomb of Ozymandias (the Greek for the real name of Ramesses) and quotes an inscription found on one of the statues, 'My name is Ozymandias, king of kings : if any would know how great I am and where I lie, let him surpass me in any of my works.' (This is probably the source of Shelley's poem *Ozymandzias.)*

The First PYRAMID

A Descrpition of the Inside of tbe first PYRA M I D.

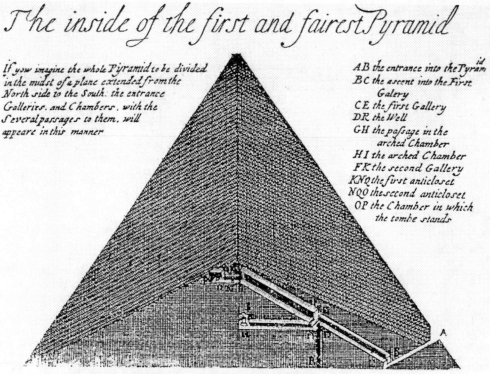

The inside of the first and fairest Pyramid

If you imagine the whole Pyramid to be divided in the midst of a plane extended from the North side to the South. the entrance Galleries. and Chambers. with the several passages to them. will appeare in this manner

AB the entrance into the Pyramid
BC the ascent into the First Galery
CE the first Gallery
DR the Well
GH the passage in the arched Chamber
HI the arched Chamber
FK the second Gallery
KNQ the first anticloset
NQO the second anticloset
OP the Chamber in which the tombe stands

Figure 7   **The pyramids at Giza caught the imagination of travellers from Herodotus on wards, and were often fancifully interpreted as in this engraving by Fischer von Erlach of 1721**

Arab travellers exploring Egypt in the Middle Ages were mainly concerned with the pyramids at Giza: they were interested above all in finding treasure. European travellers in the sixteenth, seventeenth and eighteenth centuries seldom travelled further from Cairo than the Giza pyramids. In 1610 an Englishman called Sandys, in his *Travels,* described how he entered the First pyramid and declared it was not a treasure store but a king's tomb. John Greaves of Oxford was in Egypt in 1638 and later wrote *Pyramidographia*. He produced the first true measurements of the Great Pyramid, argued that its purpose was to act as a royal tomb and a symbol of immortality, and produced the first accurate drawing of the interior entitled 'The Inside of the First and Fairest Pyramid.'

Richard Pococke, whose *Travels in Egypt* appeared in 1755, went beyond Giza: he described the pyramids at Sakkara and Dahshur, gave probably the earliest account of the stepped pyramid of Zoser and described the mastabas at Giza which he correctly said were the tombs of princes and nobles.

Napoleon Bonaparte deliberately equipped his great expeditionary force to Egypt, that left Toulon on 19 May 1798, with skilled draftsmen and scientists to investigate the geography, resources and antiquities of Egypt. These savants—the 'donkeys' as they were called by the soldiers—included Dolomieu, the mineralogist, and Dominique Vivant, Baron Denon (1747-1825) (see p. 64). It is said that Napoleon even used the pyramids for a pep talk to his troops, and he is supposed to have addressed them with these words: 'Soldiers: forty centuries of history look down upon you from the top of the Pyramids.' Despite the destruction of the French fleet in Aboukir Bay by Admiral Nelson, the army lasted on for a while until in August 1799 Napoleon sailed back to France. Meanwhile the French Egyptian Institute was set up, and it continued through to the twentieth century. The archaeological work of the Institute did not involve excavation; was concerned with the recording of field monuments and the collection of portable antiquities.

Figure 8

The Rosetta stone, now in the British museum, was discovered in the Nile Delta near Alexandria in 1799.

Among these was the famous Rosetta stone. In 1799 a French soldier found quite by chance, while digging for a fort near Alexandria, a black basalt slab 3 feet 9 inches (1114 centimetres) in height, 2 feet 4½ inches (72 centimetres) in width, and 11 inches (28 centimetres) thick bearing an inscription in three different scripts. An officer named Boussard or Bouchard thought this stone might be of great importance and had it taken to Cairo. Plaster casts were made of the Rosetta Stone and sent to Paris. In 1802, when the British took possession of Egypt, all the antiquities collected by the French were taken over by the British including, after some difficulty, the Rosetta Stone. This is why this priceless antiquity is in the British Museum—one of the spoils of war!

European travellers from the sixteenth century onwards journeyed in Mesopotamia: they visited the two large tells near Hillah in Babylonia and near Mosul in Assyria which were described, correctly, in Jewish and Arab traditions as the sites of Babylon and Nineveh, and they collected potsherds, brickbats and fragments of tablets covered with cuneiform writing such as was found in old Persian monuments. In 1765 the Danish scholar, Carsten Niebuhr, visited the ruins of Persepolis and made copies of many cuneiform inscriptions: he observed that the inscriptions seemed to be of three different kinds and these were later deciphered as Old Persian, Elamite and Babylonian.

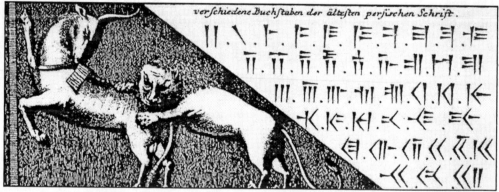

Figure 9   **Carsten Niebuhr visited Persepolis in 1765 and recorded the carvings and Persian cuneiform inscriptions there.**

Antiquarianism in Northern and Western Europe

But not all European antiquaries could find time and money to take themselves to study the antiquities of classical lands and Egypt. Dr William Borlase, who published his *Antiquities of Cornwall* in 1754, says that he conducted his Cornish researches as a substitute for foreign travels.

A brief survey of British antiquaries may serve to illustrate what was going on. John Leland (1506-52) was appointed, in 1533, King's Antiquary by Henry VIII, and toured Britain describing things of antiquarian interest, mainly libraries, monasteries and buildings.

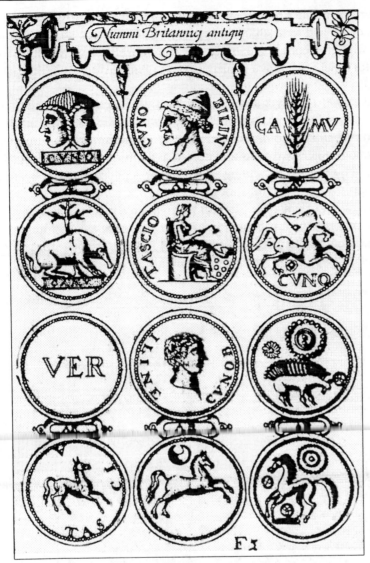

Figure 10

One of the earliest illustrations of British antiquities. Roman coins from the 1600 edition of Camden's *Britannia*.

William Camden (1551-1623), first a master of Westminster School, then Clarenceux King of Arms in the College of Heralds, travelled extensively studying the visible antiquities of Britain. He defended the study of antiquities which he called 'the back-looking curiosity'; he recognized that there were some 'which wholly contemne and avile this Study of Antiquity' but he was of quite another view: he wrote, 'In the Study of Antiquity (which is always accompanied with dignity and hathe a certain resemblance with eternity) there is a sweet food of the mind well befitting such as are of honest and noble disposition.' When he was only 35, in 1586, he produced his *Britannia*, the first general guide to the antiquities of Britain. It went through several editions, being reproduced and revised during two hundred years. In the original edition there appeared the first illustration in an English antiquarian book: it was of a re-used Saxon chancel arch in a church at Lewes in Sussex. In 1600, when he produced a new edition of the *Britannia*, he added illustrations of Stonehenge and of Roman coins. Camden was a very careful observer and noted what we now call cropmarks, which are most easily picked up by air photography. Writing of the Roman city of Richborough he said: 'By now age has erased the very tracks of it : and to teach us that cities dye as well as men, it is at this day a corn-field, whereas when the corn is grown up, one may observe the draughts of streets crossing one another for where they have gone the corn is thinner.'

Robert Plot and Edward Lhwyd, among others in Britain, carried on the traditions of Leland and Camden. Plot (1640-96) was the first curator of the Ashmolean Museum in Oxford. His *Natural History of Staffordshire and of Oxfordshire* were published in the 1670s: he was a topographer as well as a historian and antiquary. He, like his contemporaries, worked by field visits and by questionnaires addressed to the landed gentry, clergy and schoolmasters. One of Plot's questions was, 'Are there any ancient sepulchres hereabout of Men of Gigantic Stature, Roman Generals, and others of ancient times?' and a contemporary, Machell, in his questionnaire asks for answers to these questions: 'What memorable places where Battles have been fought? Round heaps of stone or earth cast up in Hills, trench'd round about or otherwise? What fortifications, camps?'

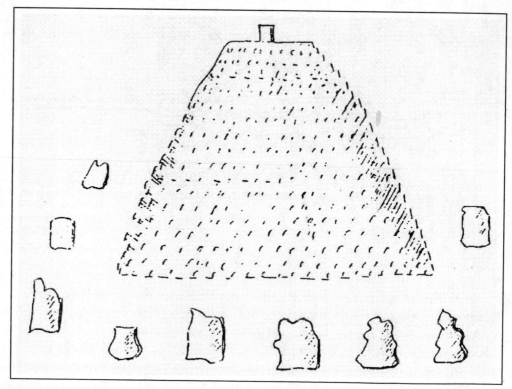

Figure 11   New Grange, a great chambered tomb north of Dublin in Ireland, was discovered in 1699. Edward Lhwyd visited it soon afterwards and had this drawing made.

Edward Lhwyd (1660-1708) succeeded his old tutor Plot as Keeper of the Ashmolean. A polymath, he wrote about geology, Celtic languages and antiquities. He travelled extensively in England, Wales, Scotland, Ireland and briefly in Brittany. The great chambered tomb of New Grange, north of Dublin, was discovered by accident in 1699 and Lhwyd visited it and was most impressed by it and the carved stones. A

Roman coin was found near the top of the barrow which he said 'might bespeak it Roman: but that the rude carving at the entry and in the cave seems to denote it a barbarous monument. So, the coin proving it ancienter than any Invasion of the Ostmans or Danes : and the carving and rude sculpture barbarous : it should follow that it was some place of sacrifice or burial of the ancient Irish . . . the monument was never Roman, not to mention that we want History to prove that ever the Romans were at all in Ireland.' This is one of the earliest and clearest examples of good archaeological reasoning: Lhwyd was arguing from material remains and not from classical writers.

John Aubrey (1626-97), author of the famous *Brief Lives*, was a friend of Lhwyd's and a keen field archaeologist. His great *Monumenta Britannica* lay unpublished till recently (1980) in the Bodleian Library at Oxford. Writing of North Wiltshire in the 1660s he says,

Let us imagine then what kind of countrie this was in the time of the Ancient Britons. . . . a shady dismal wood and the inhabitants almost as savage as the Beasts whose skins were their only rayment. . . . Their religion is at large described by Caesar. Their priests were Druids some of their temples I pretend to have restored, as Avebury, Stonehenge etc as also British sepulchres. Their way of fighting is lively sett down by Caesar. . . . They knew the use of iron.

Figure 12   Portrait of Edward Lhwyd *(1660-1708)*, from a decorated initial capital in the Ashmolean Book of Benefactors, Ashmolean Museum, Oxford.

Figure 13   Portrait of John Aubrey *(1626-97)*, from John Britton's *Memoir of Aubrey*.

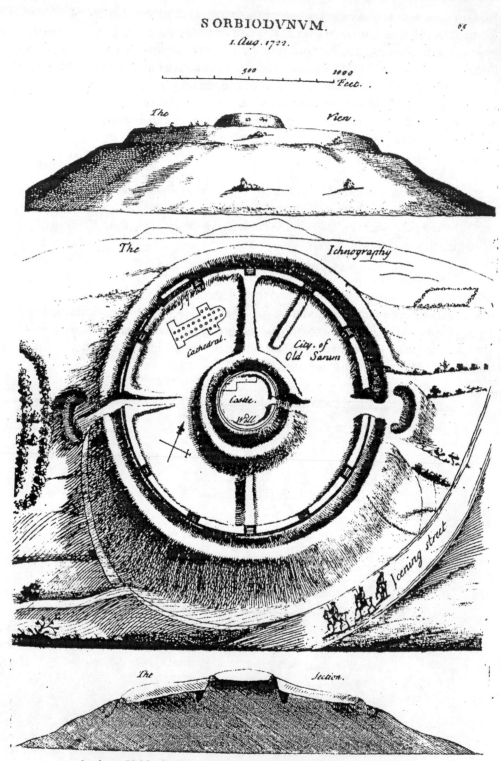

SORBIODVNVM.

1. Aug. 1722.

The View.

The Ichnography

Cathedral.

City of Old Sarum

Castle.
Well.

Icening street

The Section.

Antique Urbis Cadaver Æ s tranflulit Johes Pine Chalcographus

Figure 14   Plan and section of Old Sarum, near Salisbury, by
               William Stukeley, from his *Itinerarium Curiosum*,
               Centuria *I(1725)*.

Figure 15

Stukeley's drawing of Stonehenge, from his *Stonehenge, a Temple Restored to the British Druids (1740).*

. . . They were two or three degrees I suppose less savage than the Americans. . . The Romans subdued and civilized them.

Aubrey was using classical writers to interpret antiquities. He it was who first attributed stone circles to the Druids. The literary movement known as the Romantic Revolt, with its interest in the picturesque in the landscape, made it easy to make the Ancient Britons and their Druids attractive.

The finest example of the romantic British archaeologist was William Stukeley (1687-1765), who is sometimes mainly remembered for his Druidomania, but he was a good and careful field archaeologist and his *Itinerarium Curiosum* (1725), *Abury* (1743) and *Stonehenge* (1740) are very fine for their time. His intentions were clear: he says his purpose was 'to oblige the curious in the Antiquities of Britain: [to give] an account of places and things from inspection, not complete from others' labours, or travels in one's study.'

The eighteenth century saw not only field archaeologists but those who speculated philosophically about the early past of man. Such was Thomas Pownall (1722-1805), who was Governor of Massachusetts from 1757 to 1760: 'The face of the earth', he wrote in 1733, being originally everywhere covered with wood, except where water prevailed, the first human beings of it were *Woodland-Men* living on the fruits, fish and game of the forest. To these the land-worker succeeded. He *settled* on the land, became a fixed inhabitant and increased and multiplied. Where-ever the land-worker came, he, as at this day, ate out the thinly scattered race of Wood-Men.

Here was a different way of looking at the past: it looks forward, in a way, to economic prehistory and is akin to the views of the Scottish primitivists of the eighteenth century like Thomas Blackwell and James Burnett, later Lord Monboddo (1714-99), who took their ideas from the medieval notion of an ordained universe of purposeful and unfolding plan: the concept of the Great Chain of Being in which everything from the lowliest object to man had a place in the framework. Monboddo's great work *On the Origin and Progress of Language* was published in six volumes between 1773 and 1792, and his *Ancient Metaphysics* in another six volumes between 1779 and 1799. He argued that the orang-utan was a variety of man and its want of speech accidental; man was born with a tail and it was the work of midwives that had prevented this fact from being generally known.

Dr Samuel Johnson (1709-84) did not approve of Monboddo's speculations. 'Other people have strange notions,' he wrote, 'but they conceal them. If they have tails, they hide them :Lord Monboddo is as jealous of his tail as a squirrel.' Neither did Johnson approve of antiquarian speculations based on field monuments and surface antiquities. 'All that is really known of the ancient state of Britain is contained in a few pages,' he wrote. 'We can know no more than what old writers have told us.' This negative attitude to archaeology was very widespread in the late eighteenth century.

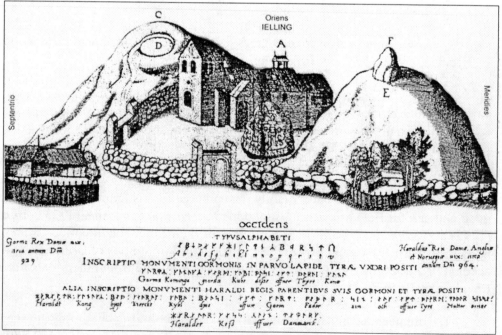

Figure 16   In Denmark, the recording of field monuments began as early as the late sixteenth century. This drawing of the two royal tumuli and large rune stone (with transcription) at Jelling, East Jutland, was published in 1591.

The development of archaeology in Renaissance Scandinavia presents a pattern parallel to that of Britain, but there was some early excavation. In 1588 the long 'dolmen' north of Roskilde, known as the Langben Rises Høj, was excavated in the hope of proving that these tombs were the tombs of giants and warriors as folklore alleged: but there were only meagre finds of pottery and other artifacts. During the late sixteenth century the famous field monuments of Jelling in Jutland were depicted on the orders of the governor of Holstein and some other runic inscriptions were copied and deciphered. King Gustavus Adolphus II of Sweden and King Christian IV of Denmark encouraged the study of antiquities. John Bure, or Johannes Bureus as he was known in his latinized form (1568-1652), was for a time tutor to Gustavus Adolphus. He studied rune-stones, travelling all round Sweden and publishing his results in *Monumenta Sveo-Gothica Hactemus Exsculpta* and an unpublished corpus entitled *Monumenta Runica*. The king established the post of Riksantikvariat or Royal Antiquary to which Bure was appointed.

Ole Worm, or Olaus Wormius to give him his latinized name (1588-1654), was the son of the mayor of Aarhus but came of a family of refugees from religious persecution in Holland. Trained as a doctor he was a true polymath, being successively professor of humanities, then Greek, then medicine at the University of Copenhagen. He collected many types of objects, especially flora and fauna and human artifacts, which he very carefully arranged and classified according to a rigorous system he had invented. He prepared a detailed catalogue which was published as *Museum Wormianum* in 1655 after his death by his son William. His museum, which was a great attraction in Copenhagen, included an assortment of bizarre and exotic objects, antiques and stuffed animals. Worm was very interested in Danish antiquities, particularly runic monuments, and published *Monumenta Danica* and *Fasti Danici* (1643). In 1626 he organized a royal circular to be sent round to all clergy to report on all rune-stones, burial sites and other historical remains in their parishes. In 1639 a gold horn was found at Gallehus in south Jutland, and Worm, with his great knowledge of runes and antiquities, was asked to describe it, which he did in *De aureo cornu* in 1641. This gold horn, and another discovered a hundred years later, were stolen from the royal collections in 1802 and destroyed. Worm's account of the horn and the runes and designs on it are therefore of great importance still, over three hundred years later.

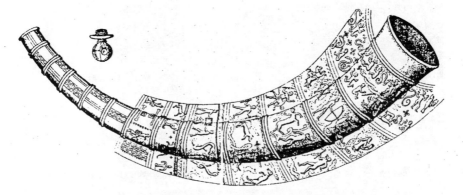

Figure 17   **The gold horn found at Gallehus. South Jutland, in 1639 was subsequently stolen from the Danish royal collections, and this drawing of it by Ole Worm, published in 1641, is therefore of great importance over three hundred years later.**

Thomas Bartholin, a professor of history, was appointed Danish Royal Antiquary in 1684. In 1689 he published, together with his assistant, the Icelander Arni Magnusson, a three-volume work entitled *Antiquitatum Danicarum de causis contemptae a Danis adhuc gentilibusmortis,* in which he used written sources as well as antiquities to explain the scornful attitude of the heathen Danes to death.

In 1662 in Sweden a Chair of Antiquities was created in the University of Uppsala: Olof Verelius was the first holder. In 1666 he was appointed Royal Antiquary and an Antiquities College was created affiliated to the University of Uppsala. The College was the brain child of Johan Hadorph, Secretary of the Museum. He also drafted a royal proclamation protecting the ancient monuments of the Kingdom of Sweden and Finland: a few years later a second royal proclamation added protection to portable antiquities. With its Antiquities College and these royal proclamations, Sweden led all Europe in pioneering archaeological studies. In 1692 the College was transferred to Stockholm and called the Antiquities Archive.

In Denmark Erik Pontoppidan (1698-1764), then court chaplain, and the crown prince, later Frederik V, excavated a megalithic passage grave at Jaegerspris in 1744. It was perhaps the first such excavation properly carried out; the report was published in the first (1744) issue of the proceedings of the Danish Royal Society. Pontoppidan argued that this monument was the burial place of ordinary human beings not giants as had been thought previously: 'built', he said, 'by our pious, though heathen, forefathers at least 1,800 years ago.' In 1763 he summarized his researches on Danish antiquity in his great work *Den danske Atlas I.* The achievements of the antiquaries of Denmark and Sweden in the seventeenth and eighteenth centuries are truly remarkable.

Figure 18

The Neolithic chambered tomb at Cocherel, near Dreux, in northern France, found by chance in 1685 and excavated. It was one of the earliest excavations to be published in Western Europe.

In France a megalithic tomb was discovered and excavated in 1685 at Cocherel near Dreux in the Eure. It was obviously a good example of what we would now call an *allée couverte*. The records present one of the earliest accounts of the excavation of a chambered tomb in Western Europe : they were published in Bernard de Montfaucon's *L'Antiquité expliquèe et reprsentèe en figures* (1719) and Le Brasseur's *Histoire Civile et Ecclèsiastique du Comtè d' Èvreux* (1722).

Southern Brittany with its great number and variety of megalithic monuments was bound to attract the early attention of antiquaries. In the decade 1727-37 de Robien described the megalithic monuments of Carnac and Locmariaquer and employed an artist to record them. The Comte de Caylus (1692-1765) in the last volume of his *Recueil d'antiquitès égyptiennes, Etrusques, grecques et gauloises* (1767) illustrates many prehistoric monuments. Legrand d' Aussy (1738-1800) was elected a member of the Institut in 1795 and read a paper called 'Les anciennes sépultures nationales' :he quoted with approval the book of La Tour-d'Auvergne-Coret *Origines gauloises celles des plus anciens peuples de I'Europe* (1796), who correctly assigned Breton megaliths to the pre-Roman Gauls.

CHAPTER 2

Classical Archaeology and Antiquarianism

Introduction

Chapters 2-5 are taken from Trigger's *The History of Archaeological Thought*. Bruce Trigger (1937-2006) was a Canadian anthropologist, ethnohistorian and archaeologist. His principal anthropological studies were of the Hurono and other native peoples of Canada, but his expertise and interest extended far beyond the area temporally and geographically, exemplified by his study of the Nubians in ancient Egyptian culture. He also wrote extensively on archaeological theory, situating archaeology as a discipline in its own social/ideological context.

Chapter 2 covers some of the same history discussed by Daniel, but we may note here an account of the generation after Daniel characteristic for its greater awareness of the context of archaeological analysis *itself* which led to the choices of cultures and sites to be examined and motivated those who researched ancient cultures. As to the motivations for an interest in a culture's past, Trigger sites anthropological evidence for the collection of artifacts of many peoples with some examples of objects preserved very far removed from the people collecting them; further, there is presumed veneration of such objects and use in religious practices. Such may well have been the case of the "archaeology" of King Nabonitus cited by Daniel in Chapter 1. The material gathered from levels beneath a temple floor likely represented more than remnants of a past; it could have constituted a link to earlier practices, to a heroic past both in terms of being from a time closer, and therefore more perfect, relation with the time of Creation. They could also be a relation to a past that substantiated the legitimacy of the king's position of power.

Oral and then written histories in Greece show a significant interest in ancestors, and we see occasional comments on the material objects uncovered that they believed to have been used in the heroic past; especially important was the observation that bronze rather than contemporary iron was used for weapons, noted by Pausanius. From the Classic period on, we see that the objects as works of art were gathered as collections. But, despite the enthusiasm for objects for the past, this material was not organized or studied in a systematic way and certainly was not used as evidence for the age system that was characterized in terms of metals (gold silver iron) hypothesized the Greeks and Romans. For the Middle Ages, all history was Bible history, and ancient artifacts, if objects of interest at all, were interpreted within the narratives of the Bible, which featured events such as the flood, and genealogies since the Creation. Growing secularization, changing society and economy and especially interest in reviving things from ancient Rome during the later Middle Ages and the Renaissance set the stage not only for the enthusiasm for classical Latin and then Greek among intellectuals and a taste for classical art of antiquity among collectors (who could often be the intellectuals), but also led to a new discipline of specifically classical studies, which included the cultures Greece and Rome, but also the extension of interest and approach to other civilizations of Egypt and Mesopotamia (called Egyptology and Assyriology).

Europeans were exposed to cultures different from their own with exploration, trade and colonization. The physical characteristics of such people along with articles of their material culture was food for speculation about the development of societies, the idea, present since the classical world, of progress or degeneration keynoted by the form and material of artifacts, especially tools. New world peoples, who used stone tools, might be, it was thought, an "early stage" of developing society, not yet having made the discovery of metal.

An important contribution to the history of archaeology is Trigger's linking of developing archaeological analysis in the eighteenth century with the systematic analysis of society and its relation to the natural world represented by the Enlightenment. Here evolutionary ideas, were supported by the types of tools and the materials from which they were made was now seen as supportive of theories of the nature of humankind and its societies. Human potential was viewed as universal, cultural progress characteristic, even inevitable, and that there was progress not only in tool making and the like, but in the organization of society, the systems of power and moral and religious beliefs. In this optimistic view, progress is possible and there might be change for the better by the application of rationality to the problems of society.

Hand in hand with rationalistic studies of society are developments in technology and science in the study of material remains, allowing resulting in closer observation of the material under analysis, the systems of its organization, the rethinking of older interpretations of features and artifacts, and the dissemination through societies and publications. Trigger also gives importance to Romanticism which might be thought at odds with rational studies of the earlier eighteenth century; the new outlook did, however, stimulate a closer identification with the past and an increase of excavation which began to be more systematic.

Knowing. the past is as astonishing a performance as knowing the stars.

George Kurler, *The Shape of Time* (1962), p. 19

Some recent treatments of the history of archaeology have suggested that the current concern with explanation is a modern development (Willey and Sabloff 1980: 9-10). It is alleged that prior to the 1960s there was no established body of theory. Instead each scholar was free to build his discipline anew on the basis of his own ideas. Yet general beliefs about human origins and development that are potentially testable using archaeological data long antedate any recognizable discipline of archaeology. It is concepts such as these that either implicitly or explicitly constituted the earliest high-level theories that gave purpose and direction to the collection and study of archaeological data. Hence archaeology, no more than any other scientific discipline, passed through a stage in which data were collected entirely for their own sake or in the hope that in the future enough would be known for serious questions to be asked. From the time when archaeological data became an object of serious study, scholars examined them in the hope that they would shed light on problems that were significant from a philosophical, historical, or scientific point of view.

The ancient world

All human groups appear to have some curiosity about the past. For much of human history, however, this interest has been satisfied by myths and legends concerning the creation of the world and of humanity, and by traditions chronicling the adventures of individual ethnic groups. Among tribal peoples these accounts frequently refer to a continuing supernatural realm and serve as a mythical charter for present-day social and political relations, as is the case with the Australian Aborigine concept of dream-time (Isaacs 1980). In other cases oral traditions claim to preserve accurate accounts of human activities over many generations (Vansina 1985).

A different approach developed in those early civilizations where written records provided a chronological framework and information about what had happened in the past that was independent of human memory. Even so, the compiling of annals did not give rise to the writing of detailed histories of the past or narratives of current events either in the Mediterranean region or in China until after 500 B.C. (Van Seters 1983; Redford 1986). Moreover, the development of history as a literary genre did not ensure the concurrent growth of a disciplined interest in the material remains of earlier times.

Artifacts from an unknown past have been collected by at least some tribal societies. Projectile points, stone pipes, and native copper tools made thousands of years earlier are found in Iroquoian sites of the fifteenth and sixteenth centuries A. D. in eastern North America. These objects must have been discovered in the course of everyday activities and kept by the Iroquoians (Tuck 1971: 134), just as 'thunderstones' (stone celts) and 'elf-bolts' (stone projectile points) were collected by European peasants in the medieval period (European stone celts were also sold to goldsmiths who used them for burnishing [Heizer 1962a: 63]). While we have no direct record of how the Iroquoians regarded these finds, they may have treated them as charms, as they are said to have done various types of peculiarly shaped stones, which they believed belonged to spirits who had lost them in the woods (Thwaites 1896-1901, 33: 211). In many cultures such artifacts were believed to have a supernatural rather than a human origin and were credited with magical powers, which may have been the main reason they were collected.

The remains of the past were also used in the religious observances of the early civilizations. In the sixteenth century the Aztecs performed rituals at regular intervals in the ruins of Teotihuacan, a city that had been inhabited in the first millennium A. D. and which was believed to be where the gods had re-established the cosmic order at the beginning of the most recent cycle of existence (Heyden 1981). They also included much older Olmec figurines, as well as valuable goods from many parts of their empire in the ritual deposits that were periodically buried in the walls of their Great Temple in Tenochtitlan (Matos 1984). Yet to identify such activities as archaeology, even 'indigenous archaeology', is to dilute the meaning of the word beyond useful limits.

In later stages of the ancient civilizations artifacts came to be valued both as the relics of specific rulers or periods of national greatness and as sources of information about the past. In Egypt, conscious archaism was already displayed in the construction of royal tombs beginning in the Twelfth Dynasty (1991-1786 B.C.) (Edwards 1985: 210-17). In the Eighteenth Dynasty (1552-1305 B.C.) scribes left graffiti to record their visits to ancient and abandoned monuments, while a fragmentary predynastic palette has been found inscribed with the name of Queen Tiye (1405-1367 B.C.). In the Nineteenth Dynasty (1305-1186 B.C.), Khaemwese, a son of Ramesses II whose fame as a sage and magician was to last into Greco-Roman times, carefully studied the cults associated with ancient monuments near the capital city of Memphis as a basis for restoring these observances (Kitchen 1982: 103-9) and by the Saite Period (664-525 B.C.) knowledge of Old Kingdom relief carving was sufficiently detailed for an attempted stylistic revival (W. Smith 1958: 246-52). A collection of ancient Babylonian artifacts, including inscriptions, amassed by Bel-Shalti-Nannar, a daughter of King Nabonidus, in the sixth century B.C. has been described as the first known museum of antiquities (Woolley 1950: 152-4). This growing interest in the physical remains of the past was part of a heightened preoccupation with former times among the literate classes. Such interests had a strong religious component. It was believed that the gods or a series of culture heroes had established civilization in a perfect form at the beginning of time. Later generations of human beings had failed to maintain this ideal form. The monuments as well as the written records of the past therefore constituted tangible links to eras that were closer to the time of creation and hence were the means by which the sacred prototype of civilization could be more nearly approximated. Because of their greater proximity to the cosmic drama of creation these artifacts were probably also thought to be endowed with unusual supernatural power.

In the classical civilizations of Greece and Rome the production of substantial narrative histories based on written records and oral traditions, as well as an interest in ancient religious practices, local customs, and civil institutions, were accompanied only by a sporadic interest in the physical remains of the past. The Greek historian Thucydides noted that some of the graves dug up on Delos, when that island was purified in the fifth century B.C., belonged to Carians, since they contained armour and weapons resembling those of the Carians of his day. In his opinion this confirmed a tradition that Carians had once lived on the island (Casson 1939: 71). In his *Description of Greece*, written in the second century A.D., the physician Pausanias systematically described the public buildings, art works, rites, and customs of different regions of that country, together with the historical traditions associated with them. Yet, while he briefly described the celebrated Bronze Age ruins at Tiryns and Mycenae, for him and other classical writers of guide books, ruined buildings were 'hardly worth mentioning' (Levi 1979, 1: 3). The Greeks and Romans preserved valued relics of the past as votive offerings in their temples and graves were sometimes opened to recover the relics of 'heroes'. In support of literary evidence that the warriors of the Homeric age had all used bronze weapons, Pausanias noted that the blade of the alleged spear of Achilles in the temple of Athena at Phaselis was made of bronze (Levi 1979, 2: 17). Yet such historical inferences are notable for their rarity. Ancient bronzes and pottery vessels that were accidentally unearthed or plundered by dealers sold for high prices to wealthy art collectors (Wace 1949). Nevertheless, scholars made no effort to recover such artifacts in a systematic fashion, nor, despite some classicists' claims to the contrary (Weiss 1969: 2), did these artifacts become a special focus of study. There was absolutely no awareness that the material remains of the past could be used to test the numerous conflicting philosophical speculations about human origins and the general outlines of human history that characterized classical civilization.

Si-ma Qien, the first great Chinese historian, who wrote in the second century B.C., visited ancient ruins and examined relics of the past as well as texts when compiling material for the *Shi Ji,* his influential account of ancient Chinese history. The systematic study of the past was valued by Confucian scholars as a guide to moral behaviour and, by stressing a common heritage going back at least to the Xia Dynasty (2205-1766 B.C.), it played a powerful role in unifying Chinese cultural and political life (Wang 1985). Yet for almost a millennium Chinese historians continued to base their books on written records, while bronze vessels, jade carvings, and other ancient works of art only were collected as curiosities or heirlooms, as they were in the classical civilizations of the Mediterranean region.

While a few scholars of the ancient world occasionally used artifacts to supplement what could be learned about the past from written records, they did not develop specific techniques for recovering or studying such artifacts and utterly failed to establish a tradition of such research. Nothing resembling a discipline of archaeology can be said to have existed in any of these civilizations. Although philosophers replaced religious beliefs with various static, cyclical, and even evolutionary explanations for the origins of human beings and civilization, these remained purely speculative.

The medieval paradigm of history

In medieval Europe prehistoric tumuli and megalithic monuments were objects of local interest and priests occasionally recorded the folk tales that surrounded them. Few of these monuments escaped plundering by lords or peasants who believed them to contain treasure (Klindt-Jensen 1975: 9). Ancient buildings were also plundered in search of building material, holy relics, and treasure (Kendrick 1950: 18; Sklenár 1983: 16-18). The only certain knowledge of past times was thought to be what was recorded in the Bible, the surviving histories of Greece and Rome, and historical records incorporating traditions going back into the Dark Ages. On this basis a medieval Christian view of the past was evolved that in certain ways has continued to influence the interpretation of archaeological data to the present. This view can be summarized in terms of six propositions:

1. The world was thought to be of recent, supernatural origin and unlikely to last more than a few thousand years. Rabbinical authorities estimated that it had been created about 3700 B.C., while Pope Clement VIII dated the creation to 5199 B.C. and as late as the seventeenth century Archbishop James Ussher was to set it at 4004 B.C. (Harris 1968: 86). These dates, which were computed from biblical genealogies, agreed that the world was only a few thousand years old. It was also believed that the present world would end with the return of Christ. Although the precise timing of this event was unknown, the earth was generally believed to be in its last days (Slotkin 1965: 36-7).

2. The physical world was in an advanced state of degeneration and most natural changes represented the decay of God's original creation. Since the earth was intended to endure for only a few thousand years there was little need for divine provision to counteract depletions resulting from natural processes and human exploitation of its resources. The biblical documentation of greater human longevity in ancient times provided a warrant for believing that human beings as well as the environment had

Figure 1

Merlin erecting Stonehenge, from a fourteenth-century British manuscript .

been deteriorating physically and intellectually since their creation. The decay and impoverishment of the physical world also bore witness to humanity of the transience of all material things (Slotkin 1965: 37; Toulmin and Goodfield 1966: 75-6).

3   Humanity was created by God in the Garden of Eden, which was located in the Near East, and spread from there to other parts of the world, first after the expulsion of the original humans from the Garden of Eden and again following Noah's flood. The second dispersal was hastened by the differentiation of languages, which was imposed on humanity as divine retribution for their presumption in building the Tower of Babel. The centre

of world history long remained in the Near East, where the Bible chronicled the development of Judaism and from where Christianity was carried to Europe. Scholars sought to link Northern and Western Europe to the recorded history of the Near East and the classical world by constructing fanciful pedigrees that identified biblical personages or individuals known from other historical accounts as the founders of European nations or early kings in that region (Kendrick 1950: 3). These claims, which were often based on folk etymologies, had the Goths descended from Gog, one of Noah's grandsons (Klindt-Jensen 1975: 10), and Brutus, a Trojan prince, becoming the first king of Britain after he defeated a race of giants who had previously lived there. Pagan deities were often interpreted as deified mortals who could be identified with minor biblical figures or their descendants (Kendrick 1950: 82). Continuing links were sought with the Near East, such as the claim first made by the monks of Glastonbury in A.D. 1184 that Joseph of Arimathea had brought the Holy Grail there in A.D. 63 (Kendrick 1950: 15).

4   It was believed to be natural for standards of human conduct to degenerate. The Bible affirmed that Adam and his descendants had been farmers and herdsmen and that iron working had been practised in the Near East only a few generations later. The earliest humans shared in God's revelation of himself to Adam. Knowledge of God and his wishes was subsequently maintained and elaborated through successive divine revelations made to Hebrew patriarchs and prophets. These, together with the revelations contained in the New Testament, became the property of the Christian Church, which henceforth was responsible for upholding standards of human conduct. On the other hand, groups who had moved away from the Near East and failed to have their faith renewed by divine revelation or Christian teaching, tended to degenerate into polytheism, idolatry, and immorality. The theory of degeneration was also used to account for the primitive technologies of hunter-gatherers and tribal agriculturalists when they were encountered by Europeans. When applied to the spheres of technology and material culture, the concept of degeneration found itself in competition with the alternative view, promoted by Roman historians such as Cornelius Tacitus, that material prosperity encouraged moral depravity. Medieval scholars were primarily concerned with explaining moral and spiritual rather than technological progress and decay.

5   The history of the world was interpreted as a succession of unique events. Christianity encouraged a historical view of human affairs in the sense that world history was seen as a series of happenings that had cosmic significance. These events were interpreted as the results of God's predetermined interventions, the final one of which would terminate the struggle between good and evil. There was therefore no sense that change or progress was intrinsic to human history or that human beings, unaided by God, were capable of achieving anything of historical significance (Kendrick 1950: 3; Toulmin and Goodfield 1966: 56). Between God's interventions, human affairs continued in a static or cyclical fashion.

6   Finally, medieval scholars were even less conscious of historical changes in material culture than ancient Greek and Roman ones had been. A few

popes and emperors, such as Charlemagne and Frederick Barbarossa, collected ancient gems and coins, reused elements of Roman architecture, and imitated Roman sculpture (Weiss 1969: 3-15). Yet, in general, there was no explicit awareness that in classical and biblical times human beings wore clothes or lived in houses that were significantly different from those of the Middle Ages. When statues of pagan deities were discovered, they were often destroyed or mutilated as objects of devil worship or indecency (Sklenár 1983: 15). Almost universally, biblical times were viewed as culturally, socially, and intellectually identical to those of medieval Europe.

During the Middle Ages an interest in the material remains of the past was even more restricted than it had been in classical times; being largely limited to the collection and preservation of holy relics. This did not encourage the development of a systematic study of the material remains of the past. Yet the view of the past that was held at this time formed the conceptual basis on which the study of archaeology was to develop in Europe as social conditions changed.

Development of historical archaeology

By the fourteenth century A.D., the rapid social and economic changes that marked the end of feudalism in northern Italy led scholars to try to justify political innovations by demonstrating that there were precedents for them in earlier times. Renaissance intellectuals turned to the surviving literature of the classical era to provide a glorious past for the emerging Italian city states and to justify the increasing secularization of Italian culture (Slotkin 1965: x). Their views generally reflected the interests of the rising nobility and bourgeoisie upon whose patronage they depended. While the use of historical precedents to justify innovation had its roots in medieval thinking the expanding search for these precedents slowly led to a realization that contemporary social and cultural life did not resemble that of classical antiquity. As a result of growing familiarity with the historical and literary texts of ancient Greece and Rome, which had remained unknown or unstudied in Western Europe since the fall of the Roman Empire, scholars came to realize that the past was separate from the present and different from it, that each period in the past had to be understood on its own terms, and that the past should not be judged by the standards of the present (Rowe 1965). The cultural achievements of ancient Greece and Rome were interpreted as evidence of cultural degeneration since that time, which in turn reinforced the traditional Christian view of human history. The aim of Renaissance scholars was to understand and try to emulate as best they could the glorious achievements of antiquity. At first there was little belief that in their present degenerate state human beings could ever hope to excel those achievements. Only in its possession of a religion based on divine revelation could the modern age be viewed as unambiguously superior to ancient times.

The appreciation of classical antiquity was not restricted to literature but rapidly extended into the fields of art and architecture. These were of particular concern to the Italian nobility and wealthy merchants, who were rivalling each other as patrons of the arts. Gothic styles were rejected and an effort was made to emulate the art and architecture of ancient Rome. This development gradually made it clear that not only the written word but also material objects surviving from the past could be important sources of information about classical civilization.

Both currents of interest are expressed in the work of Cyriacus of Ancona (Ciriaco de' Pizzicolli, A.D. 1391-1452), whose research entitles him to be considered the first archaeologist. He was an Italian merchant who travelled extensively in Greece and the eastern Mediterranean over a period of 25 years, often specifically in order to collect data about ancient monuments. In the course of his travels he copied hundreds of inscriptions, made drawings of monuments, and collected books, coins, and works of art. His chief interest, however, was public inscriptions. While his six volumes of commentaries on these inscriptions were destroyed in a fire in 1514, some of his other works survive (Casson 1939: 93-9; Weiss 1969: 137-42).

By the late fifteenth century, popes, such as Paul II and Alexander VI, cardinals, and other members of the Italian nobility were collecting and displaying ancient works of art. They also began to sponsor the systematic search for and recovery of such objects (Taylor 1948: 9-10). As early as 1462 Pope Pius II passed a law to preserve ancient buildings in the papal states and in 1471 Sixtus IV forbade the export of stone blocks or statues from his domains (Weiss 1969: 99-100). For a long time there was no excavation in the modern sense but merely digging in search of objects that had aesthetic and commercial value. The excavations that began at the well-preserved Roman sites of Herculaneum and Pompeii in the first half of the eighteenth century were treasure hunts of this sort, although a desire to recover statues and other works of art gradually came to be accompanied by an interest in Roman domestic architecture. There was, however, little concern for understanding the context in which finds were made. The owners of the land under which Pompeii was buried rented the right to entrepreneurs to dig there by the cubic yard (Leppmann 1968).

Figure 2   Digging at Herculaneum, 1782

An interest in classical antiquity gradually spread throughout the rest of Europe. In due course members of the nobility became avid collectors of Greek and Roman art, which their agents purchased for them in the Mediterranean region. Early in the seventeenth century Charles I , the Duke of Buckingham, and the Earl of Arundel were friendly rivals in importing such works into England. In 1734 a group of English gentlemen who had travelled in Italy formed a Society of Dilettanti in London to encourage a taste for classical art. Over the next 80 years this society sponsored archaeological research in the Aegean region (Casson 1939: 202-5). Classical inscriptions, monuments, and works of art found in England, France, West Germany, and other lands that had been part of the Roman Empire were being studied systematically by local antiquarians, such as William Camden (1551-1623) in England, as early as the sixteenth century. Yet the great monetary value placed on high-quality works of art tended to restrict the investigation of such material and of the classical archaeology of the Mediterranean region to the nobility or those scholars who enjoyed their patronage (Casson 1939: 141).

The establishment of art history as a distinct branch of classical studies was the work of the German scholar Johann Winckelmann (1717-68). His *Geschichte der Kunst des Altertums (History of Ancient Art)* (1764) and other writings provided the first periodization of Greek and Roman sculptural styles, as well as meticulous descriptions of individual works and discussions of factors influencing the development of classical art, such as climate, social conditions, and craftsmanship. He also attempted to define ideal, and in his opinion eternally valid, standards of artistic beauty. Winckelmann's work shaped the future development of classical studies, which until modern times have continued to be based on the dual investigation of written documents and art history. Written records were viewed as providing an indispensable account of the history and development of thought of ancient Greece and Rome. Art history, while depending upon written records to provide the chronological and contextual data required to study changes in art styles, extended the study of the past into a sphere of material culture that could not be systematically investigated using only literary sources. While it was not an independent discipline, art history, as a properly constituted branch of classical studies, did more than illustrate what was already understood from written records.

Classical studies provided a model for the development of Egyptology and Assyriology. In the late eighteenth century almost nothing was known about the ancient civilizations of Egypt and the Near East except what had been recorded about them in the Bible and by the ancient Greeks and Romans. Their scripts could not be read and their writings and works of art were unstudied and largely remained buried in the ground. The systematic investigation of ancient Egypt began with observations by the French scholars who accompanied Napoleon Bonaparte's invasion of Egypt in 1798-9 and produced the multi-volume *Description de l'Egypte* beginning in 1809. Another result of this military campaign was the accidental discovery of the Rosetta Stone, a bilingual inscription that played a major role in Jean-Francois Champollion's (1790-1832) decipherment of the ancient Egyptian scripts, which began to produce substantial results by 1822. Egyptologists, such as Champollion and Karl Lepsius (1810-84), visited Egypt recording temples, tombs, and the monumental inscriptions associated with them. Using these inscriptions, it was possible to produce a chronology and skeletal history of ancient Egypt, in terms of which Egyptologists could study the development of Egyptian art and architecture. At the same time adventurers, including the circus performer and strong man Giovanni Belzoni and the agents of the French Consul-General Bernardino Drovetti, were locked in fierce competition to acquire major collections of Egyptian art works for public display in France and Britain (Fagan 1975). Their plundering of ancient Egyptian tombs and temples was halted only after the French Egyptologist Auguste Mariette (1821-81), who was appointed Conservator of Egyptian Monuments in 1858, took steps to stop all unauthorized work. Even his own excavations were designed to acquire material for a national collection rather than to record the circumstances in which it was found.

Although reports of cuneiform inscriptions reached Europe as early as 1602, the first successful attempt to translate such writing was made by Georg Grotefend (1775-1853) in 1802. It was not until 1849 that Henry Rawlinson (1810-95) succeeded in publishing a thorough study of the Old Persian version of the long trilingual text that the Achaemenid king Darius I (reigned 522-486 B.C.) had carved on a cliff at Bisitun in Iran. By 1857 he and other scholars had deciphered the version of the text that was composed in the older Babylonian language, thereby providing the means to unravel the history of ancient Babylonia and Assyria. Sporadic digging in search of treasure in Iraq gave way in the 1840s to Paul-Emile Botta's (1802-70) excavations in the ruins of Nineveh and Khorsabad and Austen Layard's (1817-94) at Nimrud and Kuyunjik. These excavations of elaborate neo-Assyrian palaces yielded vast amounts of ancient sculpture and textual material. The latter aroused great interest because some of them paralleled early stories in the Bible. Eventually, as for Egypt, an outline chronology was established for Mesopotamian civilization that allowed scholars to study changes in the styles of art and monumental architecture from the earliest stages of writing onward.

The development of Egyptology and Assyriology in the course of the nineteenth century added 3,000 years of history to two areas of the world that were of particular interest in terms of biblical studies, but for which no direct documentation had been available. Both disciplines modelled themselves on classical studies. They relied on written records to supply chronology, historical data, and information about the beliefs and values of the past, but also were concerned with the development of art and monumental architecture as revealed by archaeology. Both Egyptology and Assyriology depended even more heavily on archaeology than classical studies did, since the vast majority of texts they studied had to be dug out of the ground. Thus, while the investigation of art history continued to depend on written records for the chronological ordering of its data, the extension of this method to earlier periods made a growing number of archaeologists more aware of the extent to which archaeologically recovered objects constituted important sources of information about human achievement. To this degree the development of classical archaeology, which began in the Renaissance, helped to point the way towards a more purely archaeological study of prehistoric times. Nevertheless, classical archaeologists, such as D. G. Hogarth (1899: vi), continued to regard prehistoric archaeology as greatly inferior to the archaeological study of periods that can be illuminated by written texts.

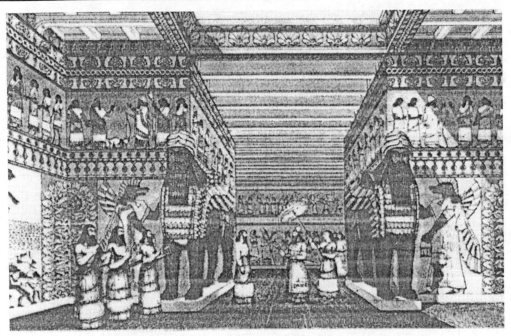

Figure 3   Layard's reconstruction of an Assyrian palace, from *Monuments of Nineveh, 1853*

In China, as we have already noted, the writing of history had emerged as a significant literary genre with the work of Si-ma Qien early in the Han Dynasty. In the Song Dynasty (A.D. 960-1279) a new interest in antiquity was stimulated by the unearthing of bronze vessels of the Shang Dynasty, following a displacement in the course of the Yellow River. These vessels formed the nucleus of an imperial collection of antiquities still preserved in Beijing (Elisseeff 1986: 37-9). Song scholars began to publish detailed descriptions and studies of ancient bronze and jade objects, especially ones bearing inscriptions. The earliest surviving work of this sort, *Kaogutu* by Lu Dalin, describes in words and line drawings 210 bronze and 13 jade artifacts dating from the Shang to the Han Dynasties which were kept in the Imperial collection and in 30 private ones. The inscriptions on these objects were studied as sources of information about ancient epigraphy and historical matters and the artifacts themselves were minutely categorized in an effort to acquire information about early forms of rituals and other aspects of culture that was not supplied by ancient texts. Inscriptions, decorative motifs, and the general shapes of objects were also used as criteria for dating them and assuring their authenticity and in due course scholars were able to assign dates to vessels on the basis of formal criteria only. Although traditional antiquarianism suffered a severe decline after the Song Dynasty, systematic studies of this sort revived in the late Qing Dynasty (A.D. 1644-1911) and are viewed as providing an indigenous basis for the development of archaeology in modern China. This included early studies of inscriptions on Shang oracle bones that were unearthed at Anyang beginning in 1898 (Chang 1981). Until the 1920s, however, Chinese scholars made no effort to recover data by carrying out excavations, and antiquarianism remained a branch of traditional historiography rather than developing into a discipline in its own right, as classical studies, Egyptology, and Assyriology had done in the West.

In Japan, during the prosperous Tokugawa period (A.D. 1603-1868) gentleman-scholars of the samurai (warrior) and merchant classes collected and described ancient artifacts and recorded burial mounds and other ancient monuments as data relating to local and national history. By the end of the Tokugawa period these scholars were engaged in careful surveys of sites and artifacts even in areas that were remote from the urban centres of learning where such studies had begun (Ikawa-Smith 1982). Michael Hoffman (1974) has suggested that these activities were a response to European influence but this is by no means certain. It is possible that in Japan, as in China and Italy, an interest in material remains of the past developed as an extension of historical studies beyond the use of written texts.

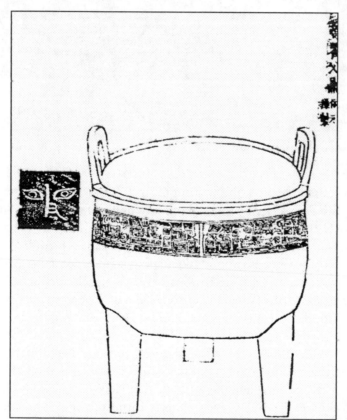

Figure 4

Shang cast bronze ritual vessel, illustrated with rubbing of inscriptions and their transcription into conventional characters, from twelfth-century A.D. catalogue *Bogutu*

On the other hand, systematic antiquarianism did not develop in India prior to the colonial period. Despite impressive intellectual achievements in other fields, Indian civilization did not evolve a strong tradition of historical studies (Chakrabarti 1982), perhaps because the Hindu religion directed efforts to understand the meaning of life and of historical events more towards cosmology (Pande 1985). Antiquarianism also failed to develop in the Near East, where Islamic peoples lived in the midst of impressive monuments of antiquity. Yet in that region there was a strong interest in history and efforts had been made to explain history in naturalistic terms, especially by Abu Zayd Abd ar-Rahman ibn Khaldun (A.D. 1332-1406), that modern historians judge to have been in advance of historical research anywhere else in the world (Masry 1981). The failure of antiquarianism to develop in the Arab world may be attributed to its rejection of pagan pre-Islamic civilizations and their works as an Age of Ignorance, to a tendency to view many features of Islamic history as cyclical, and to a religiously based disdain for works of art that involved the portrayal of human forms. India and the Arab world indicate the highly particularistic factors that must be taken into account in explaining the origins of archaeological research in any specific culture.

Nevertheless the parallels between Europe, China, and Japan suggest that, where traditions of historiography are well established, the chances are good that studies of written documents will come to be supplemented by systematic research on palaeography and art history. The much more extensive and systematic development of such studies in Europe, although they began there later than in China, can at least partly be attributed to the particular importance that medieval Christian thought attached to schemes of human history as a basis for understanding the human condition. The rediscovery of classical antiquity was seen as providing information about the glorious past of Italy, which received little attention in traditional biblical accounts, while the study of Egypt and Mesopotamia in the nineteenth century was largely motivated by a desire to know more about civilizations that had featured prominently in the Old Testament. A sense of the discontinuity and diversity of origins of European civilization encouraged research that relied ever more heavily on archaeology as a source of textual data as well as artifacts. This situation, which contrasted with the greater continuity in Chinese and Japanese history, may have helped to stimulate the development of archaeology as major source of information about the literate civilizations of ancient times.

Antiquarianism in Northern Europe

Yet what did the development of text-aided archaeology signify for most of Central and Northern Europe, where historical records usually did not antedate the Roman period and in some areas began only after A.D. 1000? As long as people believed that the world had been created about 4000 B.C. and that the Bible provided a reliable chronicle of events in the Near East for the whole of human history, relatively little appeared to lie beyond the purview of written records or folk traditions. In the course of the Middle Ages chroniclers, who were often priests, had constructed a colourful picture of the remote past for each of the peoples of Europe. These accounts were based on legends and sheer invention as well as documents. In an uncritical climate of scholarship even written records were often successfully forged (Sklenár 1983: 14) English scholars proudly claimed that Arthur and before him king Brutus had conquered much of the world (Kendrick 1950: 36-7). Individual chronicles were frequently composed to support or oppose particular ruling groups. For example, Geoffrey of Monmouth, who wrote in the twelfth century, stressed England's earlier British, rather than its Anglo-Saxon past in order to please his Norman masters (ibid. 4). Prehistoric monuments were sometimes mentioned in these chronicles. Geoffrey of Monmouth associated Stonehenge wth Arthurian legend, while in Germany megalithic graves and tumuli were often ascribed to the Huns, who had invaded Europe in the fifth century A.D. (Sklenár 1983: 16).

The stirrings of patriotism in Northern Europe, which led to the Reformation, stimulated a new and more secular interest in the history of these countries that was already evident by the sixteenth century. This Patriotism was especially strong among the urban middle class, whose growing prosperity, whether based on royal service or professional training, was linked to the decline of feudalism and the development of national states. In England the Tudor dynasty was glorified by renewed historical studies of Arthurian legends that reflected the family's British, as opposed to narrowly English, origins. There was also a marked increase of interest in the history of England before the Norman Conquest as scholars combed early records in an attempt to prove that Protestantism, rather than engaging in innovation, was restoring elements of true Christianity that had been destroyed or distorted by Roman Catholicism (Kendrick *1950:* 115).

Yet T. D. Kendrick (1950) has interpreted the growth of historical scholarship in England during the sixteenth century as a slow triumph of Renaissance over medieval thought. Historians, such as Polydore Vergil, rejected the uncritical approach of medieval chroniclers and sought to base their work on reliable documentary sources. This involved denying the historicity of many national legends that could not sustain careful comparison with the historical records of other countries (ibid. 38).

In England already by the fifteenth century John Rous (1411-91) and William of Worcester (1415-82) were aware that the past had been materially different from the present. William was working on a description of Britain that involved measuring and describing old buildings (Kendrick 1950: 18-33). This concern with the material remains of the past was strengthened by the destruction of the monasteries in the reign of Henry VIII. The dismantling of these familiar landmarks and the dispersal of their libraries spurred scholars to record what was being destroyed as well as monuments of the more remote past. In this way the study of physical remains began to supplement that of written records and oral traditions, giving rise to a new tradition of antiquarian, as distinguished from purely historical, scholarship. These leisured, although not rich, antiquarians were drawn from the professional and administrative middle class, which was expanding and prospering under the more centralized rule of the Tudors (Casson 1939: 143). For these patriotic Englishmen local antiquities were an acceptable substitute for those of Italy and Greece. They visited monuments dating from the medieval, Roman, and prehistoric periods and described them as part of county topographies and histories. They also recorded the local legends and traditions relating to these sites. In addition, some antiquarians made collections of local (as well as exotic) curiosities. John Twyne, who died in 1581, collected Romano-British coins, pottery, and glass, as well as studying earthworks and megaliths (Kendrick 1950: 105). A more varied and extensive, but less archaeological, collection of curiosities by the royal gardener John Tradescant was to become the nucleus of the Ashmolean Museum, established at Oxford in 1675. Hitherto collections containing antiquities had consisted either of church relics or the family heirlooms of the nobility.

At first no clear distinction was drawn between curiosities that were of natural and those that were of human origin. Scholars, as well as uneducated people, believed stone celts to be thunderstones (a view endorsed by the Roman naturalist Pliny [Slotkin 1965: x]) and stone projectile points to be elf-bolts, while in Poland and Central Europe it was thought that pottery vessels grew spontaneously in the earth (Abramowicz 1981; Sklenár 1983: 16). In a world unaware of biological evolution, it was not self-evident that a prehistoric celt was man-made while a fossil ammonoid was a natural formation. Most of these curios were found accidentally by farmers and manual labourers and there was as yet no tradition of excavating for prehistoric remains.

John Leland (1503-52) was appointed King's Antiquary in 1533. He played an important role in rescuing books following the dispersal of monastic libraries. He also toured England and Wales recording place-names and genealogies as well as objects of antiquarian interest, including the visible remains of prehistoric sites. Although he was only vaguely aware even of major changes in architectural styles in medieval times, his great innovation was his desire to travel to see things rather than simply to read about them (Kendrick 1950: 45-64). William Camden, the author of the first comprehensive topographical survey of England, concentrated mainly on Roman and early medieval remains. His *Britannia,* first published in 1586, was to go through many posthumous editions. Camden was also a founding member, in 1572, of the Society of Antiquaries, a London-based association for the preservation and study of national antiquities. This society was suppressed by James I in 1604, presumably because the Scottish-born monarch feared that it was encouraging English nationalism and hence opposition to his

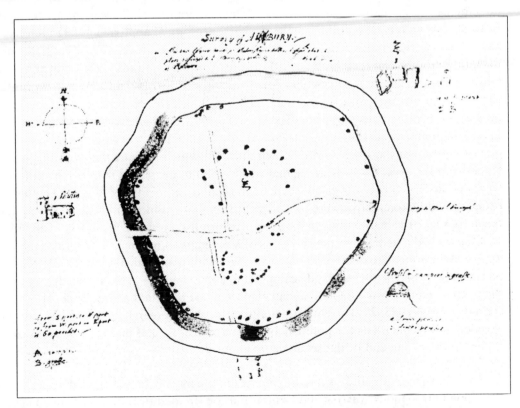

Figure 5   **Aubrey's plan of Avebury, from his *Monumenta Britannica, c.* 1675**

rule (Taylor 1948: 10; Joan Evans 1956: 14). John Aubrey (1626-97), the most famous of the seventeenth-century English antiquarians, worked mainly in Wiltshire. He prepared descriptions of Stonehenge and Avebury, arguing that these great prehistoric monuments were probably druidical temples (Hunter 1975). The research of these early antiquarians was continued by a succession of historians and topographers, most of whom worked at the county level. They did little deliberate digging and had no sense of chronology apart from what was known from written records. Like classical archaeologists, they sought to explain ancient monuments by associating them with peoples mentioned in historical accounts. This meant that what we now recognize as prehistoric remains were generally ascribed quite arbitrarily either to the Britons, whom the Romans encountered when they first invaded England, or to the Saxons and Danes, who had invaded Britain after the fall of the Roman Empire.

Systematic antiquarian research developed somewhat later in Scandinavia than in England, as part of the political and military rivalry that followed the separation of Sweden and Denmark in 1523. Renaissance historians soon became as fascinated with their respective national heritages as were those in England. They were encouraged by Kings Christian IV of Denmark (reigned 1588-1648) and Gustavus II Adolphus of Sweden (reigned 1611-32) to draw from historical records and folklore a picture of primordial greatness and valour that was flattering to their respective nations. This interest quickly extended to the study of ancient monuments. Royal patronage enabled leading antiquaries to record these monuments in a thorough and systematic fashion. Johan Bure (1568-1652), a Swedish civil servant, and Ole Worm (1588-1654), a Danish medical doctor, documented large numbers of rune stones. The inscriptions on these stones, which dated from the late Iron Age, permitted a classical archaeological approach to late prehistoric and early historical times. These antiquaries also collected information about much older megalithic tombs and rock drawings. Bure and Worm learned from each other despite the tense political relations between their countries and their own commitment to promoting patriotic sentiments (Klindt-Jensen 1975: 14-21). Some of their work was carried out by means of questionnaires that were distributed nationwide. Museums were also established in which humanly fabricated objects and natural curiosities were assembled. In Denmark one of the first of these was Worm's own museum which became the basis for the Kunstkammer, or Royal Collection, that was opened to the public in the 1680s. In Sweden an Antiquaries College was established at Uppsala in 1666 in order to pursue antiquarian research and national laws were passed to protect ancient monuments. These required the surrender of valuable finds to the king in return for a reward. Olof Rudbeck (1630-1702) trenched and drew vertical sections of Vikingage tumuli at Old Uppsala, and in this way he determined the relative age of the burials within individual mounds. He also believed that the thickness of sod accumulated above a grave could be used to indicate to the nearest century how much time had elapsed since a burial had been placed in it (Klindt-Jensen 1975: 29-31). Unfortunately, antiquarian research tended to languish in Sweden and Denmark as the political ambitions of these states and their economies faltered toward the end of the seventeenth century.

A similar, although less intense, interest in the physical remains of the past developed throughout Western and Central Europe. In medieval France, Roman and prehistoric ruins alike were ascribed to heroes, such as Charlemagne and Roland, and to

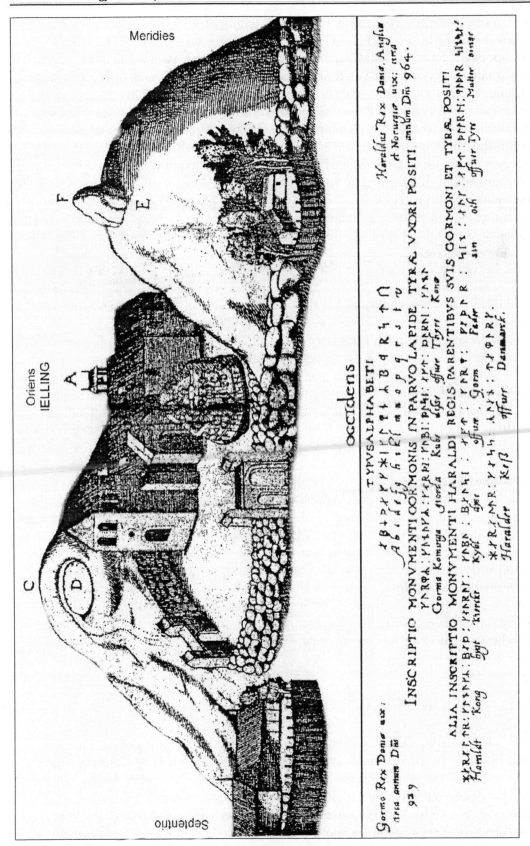

Figure 6   Engraving of tumuli and rune stones at Jelling, Denmark, 1591

local saints. With the Renaissance, Roman antiquities were soon identified for what they were and Francis I (reigned 1515-47) and Henri IV (reigned 1589-1610) built up substantial collections of local and imported classical marble statues and bronzes. Much scholarship was concentrated on Roman inscriptions, while for a long time pre-Roman antiquities were little valued. Only in the eighteenth century did an interest develop in the earlier Celtic inhabitants of France and their origins. This led to the excavation of some prehistoric monuments. In the latter part of the eighteenth century a growing desire to demonstrate the cultural achievements of the Celts, who were recognized as the ancestors of the French, encouraged the study of pre-Roman times to develop independently of classical archaeology. This movement, which continued into the nineteenth century, was linked to growing nationalism. Like early English studies of pre-Roman remains, it encouraged more fanciful speculation than sober investigations and ultimately contributed little to the development of archaeology (Laming-Emperaire 1964).

In Germany the rediscovery in 1451 of the Roman historian Cornelius Tacitus' (c. A.D. 56-120) *Germania,* which contained a detailed description of the customs of the ancient Germans, led scholars to use classical sources rather than medieval legends to study their early history. This trend laid the basis for the first general historical study of ancient Germany, Philip Klüver's *Germaniae Antiquae* (Ancient Germany), published in 1616 (Sklenár 1983: 24-5). As happened elsewhere, this research led to a growing interest in the material remains of the past. The excavation of barrows at Marzahna in Saxony in 1587 was one of the first in Europe that sought to answer a specific question (whether the vessels found in such structures were manufactured or formed naturally) rather than to find treasure or enrich a collection (ibid. 38). A few efforts were also made to classify megaliths and funerary vessels according to shape and use (ibid. 33).

Analogous developments occurred in Hungary and the Slavic countries. Political figures, churchmen, and scholars incorporated archaeological finds into their collections of curiosities. In some princes' collections local discoveries considered to have artistic merit were displayed alongside statues and painted vessels imported from Italy and Greece. Some digging was carried out to recover artifacts and occasionally laws were passed to protect antiquities and secure new finds for national collections (Sklenár 1983: 32-3). While archaeological discoveries were often fancifully associated with historically known peoples, no system was devised for dating prehistoric artifacts anywhere in Europe. Indeed, in the absence of written inscriptions, it was not even clear which finds dated prior to earliest written records in any particular area and which did not.

Recognition of stone tools

The sixteenth and seventeenth centuries marked the beginning of worldwide Western European exploration and colonization. Mariners started encountering large numbers of hunter-gatherers and tribal agriculturalists in the Americas, Africa, and the Pacific. Descriptions of these peoples and their customs circulated in Europe and collections of their tools and clothing were brought back as curiosities. At first the discovery of groups who did not know how to work metal and whose cultures bounded with practices that were contrary to Christian teaching seemed to confirm the traditional medieval view that those who had wandered farthest from the Near East and lost contact with God's continuing revelation had degenerated both morally and technologically. Gradually, however, an awareness of these people and their tools gave rise to an alternative view, which drew a parallel between modern 'primitive' peoples and prehistoric Europeans. Yet it took a long time for this comparison to be generally accepted and even longer for all of its implications to be worked out.

The first step in this process was the realization by scholars that the stone tools being found in Europe had been manufactured by human beings and were not of natural or supernatural origin. Until the late seventeenth century crystals, animal fossils, stone tools, and other distinctively shaped stone objects were all classified as fossils. In 1669 Nicolaus Steno (1638-86) compared fossil and modern closely than either did inorganic crystals. Hence he argued that fossil shells were the remains of once living animals. Ethnographic analogies played a similar role in establishing the human origin of stone tools (Grayson 1983: 5). The possibility that people had once lived in Europe who did not know the use of metal tools was implicitly raised early in the sixteenth century by Pietro Martire d'Anghiera when he compared the native peoples of the West Indies with classical traditions of a primordial Golden Age (Hodgen 1964: 371).

The Italian geologist Georgius Agricola (1490-1555) expressed the opinion that stone tools were probably of human origin (Heizer 1962a: 62); while Michel Mercati (1541-93), who was Superintendent of the Vatican Botanical Gardens and physician to Pope Clement VI1, suggested in his *Metallotheca* that, before the use of iron, stone tools might have been 'beaten out of the hardest flints, to be used for the madness of war' ([1717] Heizer 1962a: 65). He cited biblical and classical attestations of the use of stone tools and was familiar with ethnographic specimens from the New World that had been sent as presents to the Vatican. Ulisse Aldrovandi (1522-1605) also argued that stone tools were human fabrications in his *Museum Metallicum*, published in 1648. In 1655 the Frenchman Isaac de la Peyrère, one of the first writers to challenge the biblical account of the creation of humanity, identified thunderstones with his 'pre-Adamite' race, which he claimed had existed prior to the creation of the first Hebrew, which was described in the Book of Genesis.

In Britain increasing knowledge of the native peoples of the New World resulted in a growing conviction that stone tools were made by human beings. In 1656 the antiquarian William Dugdale (1605-86) attributed such tools to the ancient Britons, asserting that they had used them before they learned how to work brass or iron. Robert Plot (1640-96), Dugdale's son-in-law and the Keeper of the Ashmolean Museum, shared this opinion to the extent that in 1686 he wrote that the ancient Britons had used mostly stone rather than iron tools and that one might learn how prehistoric stone tools had been hafted by comparing them with North American Indian ones that could be observed in their wooden mounts. In 1699 his assistant Edward Lhwyd drew specific comparisons between elf-arrows and chipped flint arrowheads made by the Indians of New England. Similar views were entertained by the Scottish antiquarian Sir Robert Sibbald as early as 1684. Around 1766 Bishop Charles Lyttelton speculated that stone tools must have been made before any metal ones were available and therefore that they dated from some time prior to the Roman conquest (Slotkin 1965: 223). A decade later the writer Samuel Johnson ([1775] 1970: 56) compared British stone arrowheads with tools made by the modern inhabitants of the Pacific Islands and concluded that the former had been manufactured by a nation that did not know the use of iron. By the eighteenth century such observations had encouraged a growing realization in the United Kingdom that antiquities could be a source of information about the past as well as curiosities worthy of being recorded in county topographies.

In France in 1719 Dom Bernard de Montfaucon (1655-1741), who 24 years earlier had published an account of the excavation of a megalithic stone tomb containing polished stone axes, ascribed such tombs to a nation that had no knowledge of iron. In reaching this conclusion he was influenced by knowledge of archaeological research in England and Scandinavia (Laming-Emperaire 1964: 94). Five years later the French scholar Antoine de Jussieu (1686-1758) drew some detailed comparisons between European stone tools and ethnographic specimens brought from New France and the Caribbean. He stated that 'the people of France, Germany, and other Northern countries who, but for the discovery of iron, would have much resemblance to the savages of today, had no less need than they—before using iron—to cut wood, to remove bark, to split branches, to kill wild animals, to hunt for their food and to defend themselves against their enemies' ([1723] Heizer 1962a: 69). In 1738 Kilian Stobeus, Professor of Natural History at the University of Lund, argued that flint implements antedated metal ones in Scandinavia and compared them with ethnographic specimens from Louisiana, an opinion echoed in 1763 by the Danish scholar Erik Pontoppidan (Klindt-Jensen 1975: 35-9). As late as 1655, as distinguished an antiquarian as Ole Worm had continued to think it likely that polished stone axes were of celestial origin rather than fossilized iron tools or stone ones, even though he had ethnographic examples of stone tools from the New World in his collection (ibid. 23). Nevertheless, by the seventeenth century both the human fabrication of stone tools and their considerable antiquity in Europe were widely accepted.

Yet a growing realization that stone tools had probably been used prior to metal ones in Europe and elsewhere did not necessitate the adoption of an evolutionary perspective (cf. Rodden 1981: 63), since stone tools could be seen in use alongside metal ones in the contemporary world. Noting that according to the Bible iron working was practised from early times, Mercati argued that knowledge of metallurgy must have been lost by nations that migrated into areas where iron ore was not found ([1717] Heizer 1962a: 66). Similar degenerationist views were widely held. Other antiquarians maintained that stone tools were used at the same time as metal ones by communities or nations that were too poor to own metal. As late as 1857 it was argued in opposition to the theory that stone tools antedated metal ones that stone tools must be imitations of metal originals (O'Laverty 1857; 'Trevelyan' 1857). Without adequate chronological controls and any archaeological data from many parts of the world, it remained possible that iron working and lack of such knowledge had existed side by side throughout most of human history. Prior to the nineteenth century there was no factual evidence to make an evolutionary view of human history more plausible than a degenerationist one. The strong religious sanctions enjoined by the degenerationist position also made many antiquarians reluctant to challenge it.

The Enlightenment paradigm

The development of an evolutionary view of the past was encouraged far less by a growing body of archaeological evidence than by a gradual transformation in thought that began during the seventeenth century in northwestern Europe, the region which was rapidly emerging as the economic hub of a new world economy (Wallerstein 1974; Delâge 1985). This view was based on rapidly increasing confidence in the ability of human beings to excel and to develop both economically and culturally. Early in the century the English philosopher and statesman Francis Bacon protested against the idea that the culture of classical antiquity was superior to that of modern times. A similar theme was echoed in France in the late seventeenth-century Quarrel between the Ancients and the Moderns, in which the 'moderns' argued that the human talents were not declining and hence present-day Europeans could hope to produce works that equalled or surpassed those of the ancient Greeks or Romans (Laming-Emperaire 1964: 64-6). While Raleigh and many other Elizabethan writers had continued to believe, in the medieval fashion, that the world was hastening toward its end, by the second half of the seventeenth century many Western Europeans were confident about the future (Toulmin and Goodfield 1966: 108-10). The reasons for this growing optimism included the scientific revolutions of the sixteenth and seventeenth centuries, as manifested above all in the work of Galileo and Newton, the application of scientific discoveries to the advancement of technology, and a widespread appreciation of the literary creations of English writers in the reign of Elizabeth I and of French ones under Louis XIV. Especially among the middle classes, these developments encouraged a growing faith in progress and a belief that to a large degree human beings were masters of their own destiny. They also inclined Western Europeans to regard the ways of life of the technologically less advanced peoples that they were encountering in various parts of the world as survivals of a primordial human condition rather than as products of degeneration.

Neither the Renaissance discovery that the past had been different from the present nor the realization that technological development was occurring in Western Europe led directly to the conclusion that progress was a general theme of human history. In the seventeenth century successive historical periods were viewed as a series of kaleidoscope variations on themes that were grounded in a fixed human nature, rather than as constituting a developmental sequence worthy of study in its own right (Toulmin and Goodfield 1966: 113-14). The Italian philosopher Giambattista Vico (1668-1774) viewed history as having cyclical characteristics and argued that all human societies evolve through similar stages of development and decay that reflect the uniform actions of providence. He prudently stressed, however, that this view of human history as governed by strict laws did not apply to the Hebrews, whose progress was divinely guided. Although he was not an evolutionist, his views helped to encourage a belief that history could be understood in terms of regularities analogous to those being proposed for the natural sciences (ibid. 125-9).

An evolutionary view of human history that was sufficiently comprehensive to challenge the medieval formulation not only on specific points but also in its entirety was formulated by the Enlightenment philosophy of the eighteenth century. This movement began in France, where it is associated with leading philosophers, such as Montesquieu, Turgot, Voltaire, and Condorcet, but it also flourished in Scotland in the school of so-called 'primitivist' thinkers, which included John Locke, William Robertson, John Millar, Adam Ferguson, and the eccentric James Burnett, who as Lord Monboddo remains notorious for his claim that human beings and orangutans belong to a single species (Bryson 1945; Schneider 1967).

The philosophers of the Enlightenment combined a more naturalistic understanding of social processes with a firm belief in progress to produce an integrated set of concepts that purported to explain social change. They also created a methodology that they believed enabled them to study the general course of human development from earliest times. In England and the Netherlands, where political power was already in the hands of the mercantile middle class, intellectual activity was directed towards assessing the practical political and economic significance of this change. The continuing weakness of the French middle class in the face of Bourbon autocracy appears to have encouraged French intellectuals to engage in broader speculations about the nature of progress. The great impact that these ideas had on scholars in Edinburgh reflected not only the close cultural ties between France and Scotland but also the greater power and prosperity suddenly acquired by the Scottish middle class following Union with England in 1707.

The following are the most important tenets of the Enlightenment that were to become the basis of popular evolutionary thinking among the European middle classes:

1   Psychic unity. All human groups were believed to possess essentially the same kind and level of intelligence and to share the same basic emotions, although individuals within groups differed from one another in these features. Because of this there was no biological barrier to the degree to which any race or nationality could benefit from new knowledge or contribute to its advancement. All groups were equally perfectable. In its most ethnocentric form this constituted a belief that all human beings were capable of benefitting from European civilization. Yet it also implied that an advanced technological civilization was not destined to remain the exclusive possession of Europeans. Cultural differences were generally either ascribed to climatic and other environmental influences or dismissed as historical accidents (Slotkin *1965:* 423).

2   Cultural progress as the dominant feature of human history. Change was believed to occur continuously rather than episodically and was ascribed to natural rather than supernatural causes. The main motivation for progress was thought to be the desire of human beings to improve their condition, principally by gaining greater control over nature (Slotkin 1965: 441). Many Enlightenment philosophers regarded progress as inevitable, or even as a law of nature, while others thought of it as something to be hoped for (ibid. 357-91; Harris 1968: 37-9).

3   Progress characterizes not only technological development but all aspects of human life, including social organization, politics, morality, and religious beliefs. Changes in all of these spheres of human behaviour were viewed as

occurring concomitantly and as following, in a general fashion, a single line of development. As a result of similar ways of thinking, human beings at the same level of development tended to devise uniform solutions to their problems and hence their ways of life evolved along parallel lines (Slotkin 1965: 445). Cultural change was frequently conceptualized in terms of a universal series of stages. Europeans were viewed as having evolved through all of these stages, while technologically more primitive societies had passed only through the first ones.

4   Progress perfects human nature, not by changing it but by progressively eliminating ignorance, passion, and superstition (Toulmin and Goodfield 1966: 115-23). The new evolutionary view of cultural change did not negate either the traditional Christian or the Cartesian notion of a fixed and immutable human nature. Yet human nature as it was now conceived was far removed from the medieval preoccupation with sinfulness and individual dependence on divine grace as the only means of achieving salvation.

5   Progress results from the exercise of rational thought to improve the human condition. In this fashion human beings gradually acquired greater ability to control their environment, which in turn generated the wealth and leisure needed to support the creation of more complex societies and the development of a more profound and objective understanding of humanity and the universe. The exercise of reason had long been regarded as the crucial feature distinguishing human beings from animals. Most Enlightenment philosophers also viewed cultural progress teleologically, as humanity's realization of the plans of a benevolent deity. A faith that benevolent laws guided human development was long to outlive a belief in God among those who studied human societies.

The Scottish philosopher Dugald Stewart labelled the methodology that Enlightenment philosophers used to trace the development of human institutions 'theoretic' or 'conjectural' history (Slotkin 1965: 460). This involved the comparative study of living peoples whose cultures were judged to be at different levels of complexity and arranging these cultures to form a logical, usually unilinear, sequence from simple to complex. These studies were based largely on ethnographic data derived from accounts by explorers and missionaries working in different parts of the world. Despite disagreement about details, such as whether agricultural or pastoral economies had evolved first, it was believed that these sequences could be regarded as historical ones and used to examine the development of all kinds of social institutions. In the writings of the historian William Robertson and others, the apparently similar sequences of cultures in the eastern hemisphere and the Americas were interpreted as proof of the general validity of the principle of psychic unity and of the belief that human beings at the same stage of development would respond to the same problems in the same way (Harris 1968: 34-5).

It is generally acknowledged that a cultural-evolutionary perspective was widely accepted for explaining human history long before the publication of Darwin's *On the Origin of Species*. Glyn Daniel (1976: 41) doubts the importance of Enlightenment philosophy for the development of archaeology since Enlightenment scholars, with few exceptions (see Harris 1968: 34), ignored archaeological data in their own writings. That they did so is scarcely surprising since, in the absence of any established means for dating prehistoric materials, archaeology had little to contribute to their discussions of cultural evolution. This does not mean, however, that the writings of the Enlightenment did not influence the thinking of antiquarians. On the contrary, their advocacy of an evolutionary view of human development from primitive beginnings encouraged a more holistic understanding of prehistoric times.

In particular the Enlightenment encouraged renewed interest in the materialistic and evolutionary views of cultural development that had been expounded by the Roman Epicurean philosopher Titus Lucretius Carus (98-55 B.C.) in his poem *De Rerum Natura* (On the Nature of Things). He argued that the earliest implements were hands, nails, and teeth, as well as stones and pieces of wood. Only later were tools made of bronze and then of iron. While his scheme was supported by various classical writings that referred to a period when bronze tools and weapons had not yet been replaced by iron ones, it was based largely on evolutionary speculations, which postulated that the world and all living species had developed as a result of irreducible and eternal particles of matter, which he called atoms, combining in ever more complex ways. Neither Lucretius nor any other Roman scholar sought to prove his theory and it remained only one of many speculative schemes known to the Romans. A popular alternative postulated the moral degeneration of humanity through successive ages of gold, silver, bronze, and iron.

Early in the eighteenth century French scholars were familiar both with the ideas of Lucretius and with the growing evidence that stone tools had once been used throughout Europe. They were also familiar with classical and biblical texts which suggested that bronze tools had been used prior to iron ones. In 1734 Nicolas Mahudel read a paper to the Academie des Inscriptions in Paris, in which he cited Mercati and set out the idea of three successive ages of stone, bronze, and iron as a plausible account of human development. Bernard de Montfaucon and many other scholars repeated this idea throughout the eighteenth century. In 1758 Antoine-Yves Goguet (1716-58) supported the Three-Age theory in a book that was translated into English three years later with the title *The Origin of Laws, Arts, and Sciences, and their Progress among the Most Ancient Nations*. He believed that modern 'savages set before us a striking picture of the ignorance of the ancient world, and the practices of primitive times' ([1761] Heizer 1962a: 14). Yet to square this evolutionary view with the biblical assertion that iron working had been invented before the flood, he claimed, like Mercati and some other contemporary evolutionists, that this process had to be reinvented after 'that dreadful calamity deprived the greatest part of mankind of this, as well as of other arts'. Glyn Daniel (1976: 40) correctly warned against exaggerating the influence that the Three-Age theory exerted on antiquarian thought during the eighteenth century. Yet, as an interest in cultural progress grew more pervasive, the Three-Age theory gained in popular esteem. In Denmark this idea was expounded by the historian P. F. Suhm in his History of Norway, Denmark, and Holstein (1776) and by the antiquarian Skuli Thorlacius (1802), as well as by L. S. Vedel Simonsen in his textbook of Danish history published in 1813. Yet, despite a growing number of supporters, the Three-Age theory remained as speculative and unproved as it had been in the days of Lucretius. By comparison, the observation that sometime in the remote past at least some Europeans had made and used stone tools was far more widely accepted.

Scientific antiquarianism

The study of prehistoric antiquities was also influenced by the general development of scientific methodology, which in turn was intimately related to the growing ability of Europeans to manipulate their environment technologically. The philosopher René Descartes (1596-1650), as part of his efforts to account for all natural phenomena in terms of a single system of mechanical principles, expounded the idea that the laws governing nature were universal and eternal. God was viewed as existing apart from the universe, which he had created as a machine that was capable of functioning without further intervention (Toulmin and Goodfield 1966: 80-4). Descartes' views, together with Francis Bacon's emphasis on inductive methodology and the exclusion of negative cases, produced a new spirit of scientific inquiry that was reflected in the importance that the Royal Society of London, founded by Charles II in 1660, placed on observation, classification, and experimentation. The members of the Royal Society rejected the authority that medieval scholars had assigned to the learned works of antiquity as the ultimate sources of scientific knowledge and devoted themselves to studying things rather than what had been written about them. Yet even some of these researchers were pleased when they thought they found their most recent discoveries anticipated in the great scientific writings of ancient times. Antiquarians were elected fellows of the Royal Society and their work was encouraged and published by the society, except when Isaac Newton was its president between 1703 and 1727. Although Newton was a great physical scientist, his interests in human history were decidedly mystical and medieval in character.

Members of the Royal Society provided accurate and detailed descriptions of archaeological finds. They identified animal bones from archaeological sites and sought to determine how tools had been made and used. They also tried to work out how large stones might have been moved and monuments constructed in ancient times. The kinds of research that the Royal Society encouraged are exemplified by the early work of William Stukeley (1687-1765). Like Camden before him (Daniel 1967: 37), he realized that the geometrical crop marks that farmers had noted in various parts of England since the medieval period (and which they had interpreted as supernatural phenomena) outlined the buried foundations of vanished structures (Piggott *1985: 52).* He grouped together as types monuments of similar form, such as linear earth-works or different kinds of burial mounds, in hopes of interpreting them in the light of the meagre historical evidence that was available. Stuart Piggott (1985: *67)* has noted that Stukeley was one of the first British antiquarians to recognize the possibility of a lengthy pre-Roman occupation, during which distinctive types of prehistoric monuments had been constructed at different times and different peoples might have successively occupied southern England. Even this, however, was suggested by Julius Caesar's documentation of a Belgic invasion of southeastern England shortly before the Roman conquest. At the same time, Stukeley and other antiquarians took the first steps towards trying to ascertain relative dates for archaeological finds for which there were no historical records. He observed construction layers in barrows and argued that Silbury Hill, the largest artificial mound in Europe, had been built prior to the construction of a Roman road, which curved abruptly to avoid it (Daniel 1967: 122-3). He also noted that Roman roads cut through Bronze Age disc ('Druid') barrows in several places (Piggott 1985: 67) and used the presence of bluestone chips in some burial mounds near Stonehenge to infer that these burials were contemporary with the building of the temple (Marsden 1974: 5).

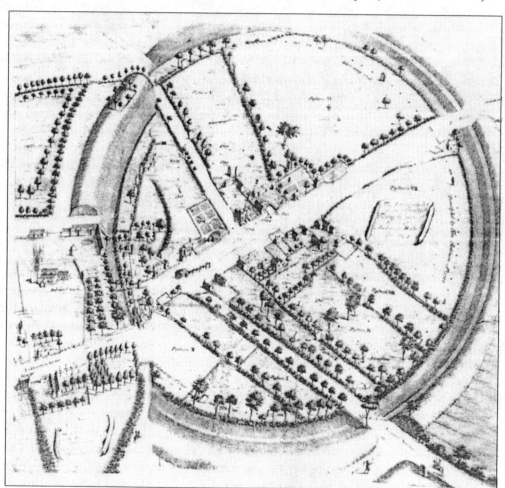

Figure 7 Stukeley's view of Avebury, published in *Abury*, 1743

In 1758 his daughter Anna dated the White Horse cut in the chalk at Uffington, and which had been thought to be a Saxon memorial, to the pre-Roman period on the basis of its stylistic similarity to horses portrayed on pre-Roman British coins (Piggott 1985: 142). In 1720 the astronomer Edmund Halley estimated that Stonehenge might be 2,000 or 3,000 years old, following an examination of the depth of weathering of its stones; while a later comparison of relative weathering convinced Stukeley that Avebury was much older than Stonehenge (Lynch and Lynch 1968: 52). In Denmark Erik Pontoppidan carefully excavated a megalithic tomb on the grounds of a royal palace in northwest Sjaelland, the main Danish island, in 1744. He reported on the structure and the finds it contained in the first volume of the *Proceedings of the Danish Royal Society,* concluding that cremation burials found near the top of the mound dated from a more recent era than the stone chamber below them and the mound itself (Klindt-Jensen 1975: 35-6) When three megalithic tombs opened in 1776 were found to contain stone and bronze artifacts but not iron ones, O. Hoegh-Guldberg, the excavator, assumed that they were very ancient (ibid. 42-3).

Studies of these sorts helped to advance the investigation of prehistoric times by encouraging more accurate observations and descriptions of ancient artifacts and monuments, more disciplined thought about them, and efforts to date a few of them in either relative or calendrical terms. Although this research was too fragmentary and the results too disconnected to constitute a discipline of prehistoric archaeology, it helped to lay the groundwork for the eventual development of such a discipline. Noting similar trends in the antiquarian researches of the eighteenth century in continental Europe, Karel Sklenár (1983: 59) observed that 'the very fact that archaeologists in Central Europe preferred analytical description of the facts to the formation of a synthetic picture of the past' shows how small was the contribution that the new scientific approach made to the development of a better knowledge of prehistory. This statement cannot be applied to England and Scandinavia, where antiquarians were making substantial progress in conceptualizing the problems confronting the study of prehistoric times and tentative steps were being taken to resolve these problems.

Antiquarianism and romanticism

The growing influence of cultural-evolutionary thought during the eighteenth century spawned a conservative reaction that at that time had even greater influence on antiquarian research than did evolutionism. In 1724 the French Jesuit missionary Joseph-Francois Lafitau (1685-1740), who had worked among the Indians of Canada, published his *Moeurs des sauvages ameriquains comparées aux moeurs des premiers temps.* Although this book has often been described as an early contribution to evolutionary anthropology, Lafitau argued that the religions and customs of the Amerindians and the ancient Greeks and Romans resembled each other because both were corrupt and distorted versions of the true religion and morality that God had revealed to Adam and his descendants in the Near East. These views, which revived the doctrine of degeneration, were similar to those held by Stukeley, who in later life was obsessed by the belief that the religion of the ancient Druids was a relatively pure survival of primordial monotheism and therefore closely akin to Christianity. Stukeley associated all of the major prehistoric monuments in Britain with the Druids and based extravagant interpretations of them on this premise. His writings were directed against the Deists, who believed that reasonable people could apprehend God without the help of revelation, a view that had much in common with the Enlightenment.

Stukeley's thinking also reflected a growing trend towards romanticism. This intellectual movement, which began in the late eighteenth century, was anticipated in the back-to-nature philosophy of Jean-Jacques Rousseau. Although he believed in the importance of reason, he emphasized emotion and sensibility as important aspects of human behaviour. He also stressed the inherent goodness of human beings and attributed greed and envy to the corrupting influences and artificiality of civilization. In Germany and England romanticism flourished ill part as a revolt against French cultural domination and the literary and artistic restrictions of neo-classicism. In its championing of strong emotions, romanticism mingled a preoccupation with horror and evil with a delight in natural beauty. Romantically inclined individuals developed a strong interest in ruined abbeys, graves, and other symbols of death and decay, including human skeletons grinning 'a ghastly smile' (Marsden 1974: 18). They also treated 'primitive' or 'natural' societies and the 'spirit' of European nations as preserved in their monuments and folk traditions, especially those of the medieval period, as the ideal inspiration for arts and letters (K. Clark 1962: 66). In this fashion romanticism became closely linked to nationalism. It appealed to the more conservative members of the middle class, who identified neo-classicism with the values of the aristocracy and equated rationalism with atheism and political radicalism. Significantly, the Society of Antiquaries of London, which was founded in 1717 and received its charter in 1751, was far more interested in medieval England than in Roman or prehistoric Britain (Piggott 1985: 43-4). The romantic movement was strengthened in conservative circles in the years following the French revolution, when the Enlightenment was denounced for encouraging popular liberty and republicanism. In the conservative restoration that followed the defeat of Napoleon Bonaparte, a concerted effort was made to suppress Enlightenment ideas in Central and Western Europe.

The late eighteenth century has been viewed as a period of intellectual decline in historical and antiquarian studies in Britain (Piggott 1985: 108, 115-17, 154-5). Yet, romanticism appears to have been instrumental in encouraging a growing emphasis on excavation, and especially the excavation of graves, that contributed to the development of antiquarianism in the later part of the eighteenth century. Between 1757 and 1773 the Reverend Bryan Faussett (1720-76) excavated more than 750 Anglo-Saxon burial mounds in southeastern England. James Douglas (1753-1819), in his *Nenia Britannica, or Sepulchral History of Great Britain,* which was published in parts between 1786 and 1793 and based on a massive compilation of information derived from barrow excavations throughout Britain, assumed that graves containing only stone artifacts were earlier than those that also contained metal ones (Lynch and Lynch 1968: 48). Some of the best work done during this period was by William Cunnington (1754-1810) and his wealthy patron Sir Richard Colt Hoare. They surveyed a large area in Wiltshire, locating ancient village sites and earthworks and excavating 379 barrows. They recorded their observations carefully, divided barrows into five types, and employed stratigraphy to distinguish between primary and secondary interments. They used coins to date some barrows from the historical period and, like Douglas, thought it possible that graves containing only stone artifacts might be earlier than prehistoric burials accompanied by metal ones. Yet, despite these tentative advances, they were unable to demonstrate to 'which of the successive inhabitants' of Britain various classes of monuments were to be ascribed or even whether they were the work of more than one people. Moreover, Cunnington could not discover enough regularity in types of grave goods associated with particular barrow styles to implement the antiquary Thomas Leman's suggestion that stone, bronze, and iron weapons could be used to distinguish three successive ages (Chippindale 1983: 123). Thus, in Glyn Daniel's (1950: 31) words, they 'failed to find any way of breaking down the apparent contemporaneity of pre-Roman remains'. Even at the most elementary level, there were always antiquarians prepared to argue that graves containing only stone tools were not necessarily older than the rest but merely belonged to ruder tribes or poorer social groups. As yet there was no satisfactory rebuttal for this claim.

The New World

The first historical questions that Europeans asked about the native inhabitants of North and South America were who they were and from where they had come. Between the sixteenth and eighteenth centuries scholars speculated that the Indians might be descended from Iberians, Carthaginians, Israelites, Canaanites, and Tartars. Still more imaginative writers claimed that they came from the vanished continent of Atlantis. Most of these speculations reflected the pretensions or biases of particular groups of settlers. Some early Spanish colonists denied that the Indians had souls, which meant they were not human beings. They sought to be free to exploit them as they could animals. The Spanish Crown, however, wanted recognition from the Church that the Indians had souls, since that allowed the Spanish government to assert its right to govern them and to curb the independence of its colonists. When the Roman Catholic Church proclaimed native people to be human beings, it also meant that Christians were required to recognize that they were descended from Adam and Eve and hence had originated, like other peoples, in the Near East (Hanke 1959).

Some of the leaders of the seventeenth-century Massachusetts Bay Colony liked to think of their own colonists as constituting a New Israel and the Indians as Canaanites, whose possessions God was delivering into their hands as he had given Palestine to the ancient Hebrews. This was interpreted as giving the Puritans the right to seize land and enslave the Indians. As recently as 1783, Ezra Stiles, the President of Yale University, was promoting the idea that the Indians of New England were literally descended from Canaanites who had fled from Palestine at the time of Joshua's invasion, as recorded in the Bible (Haven 1856: 27-8).

Over time, however, there was growing support for the theory, first expounded in 1589 by the Jesuit priest José de Acosta in his *Historia natural y moral de las Indias* that the Indians had crossed the Bering Strait as wandering hunters from Siberia (Pagden 1982: 193-7). Although Acosta believed that the Indians had lost all knowledge of sedentary life in the course of their migrations, later proto-evolutionists saw in America evidence of what the childhood of all humanity had been like. In the late sixteenth century it was being suggested that in ancient times the native inhabitants of Britain had been as primitive as the modern Indians of Virginia (Kendrick 1950: 123). On the other hand, degenerationists viewed native cultures as the corrupt remnants of the divinely revealed patriarchal way of life described in the Book of Genesis and also saw amongst them evidence of the half-remembered teachings of early Christian missionaries. In the seventeenth century the technological inferiority and alleged cultural degeneracy of native American cultures by comparison with European ones were interpreted in theological terms as manifestations of divine displeasure (Vaughan 1982). During the next century some leading European scholars advanced the more naturalistic argument that the New World was climatically inferior to Europe and Asia and that this accounted for the inferiority of its indigenous cultures as well as of its plant and animal life (Haven 1856: 94).

In Mexico and Peru archaeological monuments were frequently effaced or destroyed during the sixteenth and seventeenth centuries in an attempt to eliminate the memories native people had of their pre-Christian past (Bernal 1980: 37-9). A particular effort was made to destroy symbols of Aztec sovereignty and national identity. Only a small number of European travellers discussed the great pre-Hispanic monuments of Mexico and Peru prior to the nineteenth century.

Before the late eighteenth century almost no notice was taken of prehistoric remains in North America apart from occasional references to rock carvings and rock paintings which were usually thought to be the work of modern native peoples. Few collections of artifacts recovered from the ground were assembled in North America and the excavation of sites was rarely attempted. Among the exceptions is a splendid collection of polished stone tools from the late Archaic period found near Trois-Rivières, in Quebec, in 1700 and preserved in a convent from that time to the present (Ribes 1966). Equally exceptional were Thomas Jefferson's carefully reported excavation of an Indian burial mound in Virginia in 1784 (Heizer 1959: 218-21) and the alleged exploration of a burial mound in Kansas a decade earlier (Blakeslee 1987). Throughout this period a pervasive ethnocentrism caused Europeans to doubt that anything significant could be learned about the history of peoples whom they viewed as savages fit only to be swept aside, or in rare cases assimilated, by the advance of European civilization. Because of the paucity of archaeological data, most discussions of native history had to be based on oral traditions (often garbled in transmission and not understood in their cultural context), comparative ethnology, and physical resemblances. A notable exception to this was the naturalist and explorer William Bartram, who in 1789 used contemporary ceremonial structures belonging to the Creek Indians of the southeastern United States as a basis for interpreting prehistoric mound sites in that region. Ian Brown (n.d.) has pointed out that this is one of the earliest known examples of the employment of the direct historical approach to interpret archaeological remains in North America.

The impasse of antiquarianism

In North America no less than in Europe antiquarians who were interested in what are now recognized to be prehistoric remains looked to written records and oral traditions to provide a historical context for their finds no less than did classical archaeologists. Yet in the case of prehistoric remains there were no adequate written records. In his book on the antiquities of the island of Anglesey published in 1723 the Reverend Henry Rowlands noted that 'in these inextricable recesses of antiquity we must borrow other lights to guide us through, or content ourselves to be without any' (Daniel 1967: 43). He went on to declare that 'analogy of ancient names and words, a rational coherence and congruity of things, and plain natural inferences and deductions grounded thereon, are the best authorities we can rely upon in this subject, when more warrantable relations and records are altogether silent in the matter'. Generally the explanation of a monument consisted of trying to identify what people or individual mentioned in ancient records had constructed it and for what purpose. This approach left Camden to speculate whether Silbury Hill had been erected by the Saxons or the Romans and whether it had served to commemorate soldiers slain in a battle or was erected as a boundary survey marker. While Stukeley demonstrated stratigraphically that this mound was older than the nearby Roman road, his conclusion that it was the tomb of the British king Chyndonax, the founder of Avebury, was a mere flight of fantasy (Joan Evans 1956: 121). Stonehenge was alternatively attributed to the Danes, Saxons, Romans, and either generically to the ancient Britons or specifically to the Druids.

As a result of their dependence on written records, throughout the eighteenth and into the early nineteenth centuries antiquarians generally despaired of ever learning much about the period before such records became available. In 1742 Richard Wise commented 'where history is silent and the monuments do not speak for themselves, demonstration cannot be expected; but the utmost is conjecture supported by probability' (Lynch and Lynch 1968: 57). Colt Hoare concluded 'we have evidence of the very high antiquity of our Wiltshire barrows, but none respecting the tribes to whom they appertained, that can rest on solid foundations'. Later in his *Tourin Ireland* he added: 'Alike will the histories of those stupendous temples at Avebury and Stonehenge . . . remain involved in obscurity and oblivion' (Daniel 1963a: 35-6). In 1802 the Danish antiquarian Rasmus Nyerup expressed a similar despair: 'everything which has come down to us from heathendom is wrapped in a thick fog; it belongs to a space of time we cannot measure. We know that it is older than Christendom but whether by a couple of years or a couple of centuries, or even by more than a millennium, we can do no more than guess' (ibid. 36). The English essayist and lexicographer Samuel Johnson, who had little patience with antiquarians, pressed the case against a future for their research even more trenchantly: 'All that is really known of the ancient state of Britain is contained in a few pages. We can know no more than what old writers have told us' (ibid. 35). Even J. Dobrovsky, 'the father of Czech prehistory', who in 1786 argued that archaeological finds were 'speaking documents' that by themselves might illuminate as yet unknown periods of national history (Sklenár 1983: 52), was not very successful in determining how this could be done.

Antiquarians continued to believe that the world had been created about 4000 B.C. They also thought that reliable written records were available as far back as the time of creation for the most crucial region of human history. If humanity had spread from the Near East to the rest of the world, in most regions there was likely to have been only a brief period between the earliest human occupation and the dawn of history. Antiquarians were uncertain whether the general course of human history had been one of development, degeneration, or cyclical change.

Yet the situation was not as stagnant as it is often represented. Between the fifteenth and eighteenth centuries European antiquaries had learned to describe and classify monuments and artifacts, to excavate and record finds, and to use various dating methods, including stratigraphy, to estimate the age of some finds. Some of them had concluded on the basis of archaeological evidence that there had probably been an age when only stone tools had been used in Europe prior to the use of metal and that the use of bronze might have preceded that of iron. These developments represented genuine progress and carried the study of prehistoric remains beyond what had been accomplished in China, Japan, and other parts of the world prior to Western influence. The most serious stumbling-block to the establishment of a relative chronology of prehistoric times and hence to acquiring a more systematic knowledge of early human development was the assumption that artifacts and monuments merely illustrated the historically recorded accomplishments of the past. This was based on the belief shared with classical archaeologists that historical knowledge can be acquired only from written documents or reliable oral traditions and that without these there can be no connected understanding of earlier times. The creation of prehistoric archaeology required that antiquarians find the means to liberate themselves from this restricting assumption.

The Beginnings of Scientific Archaeology

Introduction

In this chapter, Trigger discusses the importance of dating and a history of its employment in archaeology, as well as some of the strategies of determining chronology. In his narrative of the eighteenth and nineteenth centuries, we see a struggle to establish a dating of objects and cultures in Northern Europe without the benefit of written sources from the classical world, and, for earlier prehistory, an attempted rationalization with the time frames calculated from Biblical chronologies. Establishing a relative sequence for objects was first put on a firm basis and given a consistently applied method in Denmark by Christian Thomsen, who related types of objects and their material as criteria for putting them in a relative chronology (seriation). From Thomsen's fundamental work, Scandinavia saw the development of more refined methods and theory exemplified by Jens Worsaae, who also took on extensive work in the field where excavation provided much needed information about the context of objects. The Danish pioneers, stimulated by their own prehistory and social theories of the development of society generated during the Enlightenment, came to develop a method and approach for the study of material culture contributing to archaeology's distinction as a discipline.

By the early nineteenth century there was serious study of prehistory and the central question of the age of humankind. This was the time of the emerging fields of geology and zoology (and paleontology), and the contexts of human remains and stone tools; coupled with the growing evidence of a very long period of geological time hypothesized by Charles Lyell and others, there was closer study of processes of change, resulting in vast and detailed chronology of the period named at this time 'Paleolithic.' It remained for Darwin's concept of evolution, which he could only imagine to happen very slowly, that it became possible to have a wider view of prehistoric time, although Darwinian concepts continued to have opponents, particularly those archaeologists working in the biblical lands of the Near East.

Within no very distant period the study of antiquities has passed,
in popular esteem, from contempt to comparative honour.

E. Oldfield, Introductory Address, *Archaeological Journal* (1852), p. I

The development of a self-contained and systematic study of pre-history, as distinguished from the antiquarianism of earlier times, involved two distinct movements that began in the early and middle parts of the nineteenth century respectively. The first originated in Scandinavia and was based on the invention of new techniques for dating archaeological finds that made possible the comprehensive study of the later periods of prehistory. This development marked the beginning of prehistoric archaeology, which was soon able to take its place alongside classical archaeology as a significant component in the study of human development. The second wave, which began in France and England, pioneered the study of the Palaeolithic period and added a vast, hitherto unimagined time depth to human history. Palaeolithic archaeology was concerned with questions of human origins that had become of major concern to the entire scientific community and to the general public as a result of the debates between evolutionists and creationists that followed the publication of *On the Origin of Species* in 1859.

Relative dating

The creation of a controlled chronology that did not rely on written records was the work of the Danish scholar Christian Jürgensen Thomsen (1788-1865). The principal motivation for Thomsen's work, like that of many earlier antiquaries, was patriotism. The antiquarian research of the eighteenth century and the evolutionary concepts of the

Enlightenment were indispensable preconditions for his success. Yet these accomplishments would have been of little value if Thomsen had not developed a powerful new technique for dating archaeological finds without recourse to written records. Unfortunately, because Thomsen wrote little, the importance of what he accomplished has been underrated by historians and detractors. It is therefore necessary to clarify what he actually accomplished.

Thomsen was born in Copenhagen in 1788, the son of a wealthy merchant. As a young man he studied in Paris and, after he returned home, he undertook to arrange a local collection of Roman and Scandinavian coins. Collecting coins had become a popular gentleman's hobby during the eighteenth century (McKay 1976). From the inscriptions and dates they bore it was possible to arrange them in series according to the country and reign in which they had been minted. It was also often possible to assign coins on which dates and inscriptions were illegible to such series using stylistic criteria alone. Working with this coin collection may have made Thomsen aware of stylistic changes and their value for the relative dating of artifacts.

The beginning of the nineteenth century was a period of growing nationalism in Denmark, which was greatly strengthened when the British, who were fighting Napoleon and his reluctant continental allies, destroyed most of the Danish navy in Copenhagen harbour in 1801 and bombarded Copenhagen again in 1807. Worsaae later argued that these calamities encouraged Danes to study their past glories as a source of consolation and encouragement to face the future. Yet he also noted that the French Revolution, by encouraging greater respect for the political rights of a broader spectrum of the population everywhere, awakened in Denmark a new popular, as opposed to dynastic, interest in the past (Daniel 1950: 52). Many middle-class Western Europeans who lacked political rights saw in the Revolution, and later in Napoleon, hope for their own political and economic improvement; while those who enjoyed a measure of political power viewed them as a threat to their interests.

Denmark was at that time politically and economically less evolved than Western Europe. Hence the ideals of the French Revolution appealed to many middle-class Danes. These same Danes were also receptive to the teachings of the Enlightenment, which in popular thinking were closely associated with the Revolution (Hampson 1982: 251-83). Denmark had a strong antiquarian tradition, although it had not been as flourishing in recent decades as that in England. Most English antiquaries were conservatives who had rejected the ideals of the Enlightenment and taken refuge in romantic nationalism. By contrast, Scandinavian archaeologists were inspired to study the past for nationalistic reasons but these interests did not exclude an evolutionary approach. For them history and evolution were complementary rather than antithetical concepts.

In 1806 Rasmus Nyerup, the librarian at the University of Copenhagen, published a book protesting against the unchecked destruction of ancient monuments and advocating the founding of a National Museum of Antiquity modelled on the Museum of French Monuments established in Paris after the Revolution. In 1807 a Danish Royal Commission for the Preservation and Collection of Antiquities was established, with Nyerup as its secretary. It began to amass a collection of antiquities from all over Denmark. This collection soon became one of the largest and most representative in Europe. In 1816 the Commission invited Thomsen to catalogue and prepare it for exhibition. His chief qualifications for this post, which was not a salaried one, were his knowledge of numismatics and his independent means. For the rest of his life Thomsen was to divide his time between his family business and archaeological research.

The main problem that Thomsen faced was how the material in the collection could be exhibited most efficiently. Very early he decided to proceed chronologically by subdividing his prehistoric or heathen period into successive ages of stone, bronze, and iron. Presumably he knew of Lucretius' Three-Age scheme through the work of Vedel Simonsen, if not the writings of French antiquarians such as Montfaucon and Mahudel. He also appears to have been aware of archaeological evidence suggesting an era when stone but not metal tools had been used and of the classical and biblical texts, which suggested that bronze had been used before iron. The notion of three successive ages of stone, bronze, and iron therefore was not mere speculation (as often has been maintained) but a hypothesis for which there was already some evidence.

In attempting to sort the prehistoric material in the collection into three successive periods, Thomsen faced a daunting task. He recognized that even for the stone and metal objects a mechanical sorting would not work. Bronze and stone artifacts had continued to be made in the Iron Age, just as stone tools had been used in the Bronze Age. The challenge was therefore to distinguish bronze tools made during the Iron Age from those made during the Bronze Age and to differentiate which stone tools had been made in each period. There was also the problem of assigning objects made of gold, silver, glass, and other substances to each period. Individual artifacts were no help in beginning this work. Yet in the collection there were sets of artifacts that had been found in the same grave, hoard, or other contexts and that one could safely assume had been buried at the same time. Thomsen called these 'closed finds' and believed that by carefully comparing the various items from each such discovery it would be possible to determine the sorts of artifacts that were characteristic of different periods (Gräslund :1974: 97-118, 1981).

Thomsen sorted and classified his artifacts into various use categories, such as knives, adzes, cooking vessels, safety pins, and necklaces. He further refined each category by distinguishing the artifacts according to the material from which they were made and their specific shapes. Once types had been defined, he began to examine closed finds in order to determine which types were and were not found together. He also examined the decorations on artifacts and found that these varied systematically from one closed find to another. On the basis of shape and decoration it became possible for Thomsen to distinguish bronze artifacts made in the Bronze Age from ones made in the Iron Age. He was also able to demonstrate that large flint knives and spearpoints that had similar shapes to bronze ones had been made in the Bronze Age. Eventually he could assign single artifacts to his sequence on the basis of stylistic similarities. In this fashion he worked out a rough chronological sequence for the whole of Danish prehistory.

Thomsen did not stop at that point but proceeded to examine the context in which artifacts were recorded as having been found. Ultimately this process yielded a developmental sequence of five stages. The first was the early Stone Age, when only stone tools were used. This was followed by a later Stone Age, which he described as the period when metal first came into use. At this time the dead were buried, uncremated, in megalithic tombs, accompanied by crude pottery vessels with incised decoration. In the full Bronze Age, weapons and cutting tools were made of copper or bronze, the dead were cremated and buried in urns under small tumuli, and artifacts were decorated with ring patterns. In the Iron Age, tools and weapons were made of tempered iron, while bronze continued to be used for ornaments and luxury goods. The Iron Age was divided into two stages, the earlier characterized by curvilinear serpent designs and the later by dragons and other fantastic animals. The latter forms of ornamentation continued into the historical period ([1837] Heizer 1962a: 21-6).

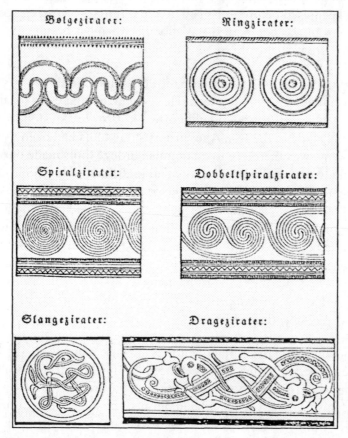

Figure 1

Successive styles of ornamentation, from Thomsen's *Guidebook* **(older forms at top)**

In the past a few archaeologists had attempted to subdivide prehistoric materials into various temporal segments. Possibly the most elaborate of these efforts was Pierre Legrand d'Aussy's (1737- 1800) six-period classification of burial practices from earliest times to the Middle Ages (Laming-Emperaire 1964: 100-1). These schemes were based largely on intuition and failed to convince many people. Thomsen overcame this impasse by developing a crude but effective form of seriation, which provided scientific evidence to support the historical validity of his chronological series. For this scheme to work, it was insufficient that only one class of data formed a sequence. Instead, all the characteristics of individual artifacts and of those found together in closed finds had to be arranged in a sequence in which material, style, decoration, and the context of discovery formed a coherent pattern of variation. Discrepancies in any part of the pattern (such as the discovery of iron tools decorated with Bronze Age ring patterns) would have caused the entire scheme to fall apart. Thomsen's assumption that his sequence had evolved from stone to iron, rather than moved in the opposite direction, was confirmed by decorative continuities between his late Iron Age and the early historical period. Although some antiquarians mocked him for not adding ages of glass, wood, and gold to his sequence and others tried to ascribe his stone, bronze, and iron objects to different economies that had existed alongside one another, these critics failed to recognize that his phases were not the result of a mechanical sorting of artifacts but instead were based on the concurrent analysis of style, decoration, and context, which reinforced each other to produce a rough but effective chronology.

Figure 2   Thomsen showing visitors around the Museum of Northern Antiquities

Thomsen's Museum of Northern Antiquities, with its collection arranged in accordance with his new system, was opened to the public in 1819, but the first written account of his research appeared only in 1836 in the *Ledetraad til Nordisk Oldkyndighed* (Guide Book to Scandinavian Antiquity), which was available in a German translation the next year but not in English until 1848. At least part of the appeal of Thomsen's work was that it offered independent support for an evolutionary view of early human development, which slowly became more popular, especially in England, as fear of the French Revolution and of Napoleon receded. It is true that neither Thomsen nor his successors regarded the Three Ages as constituting an evolutionary sequence within Scandinavia. Instead they argued that knowledge of bronze and iron working was brought into the region either by successive waves of immigrants from the south or as a result of 'intercourse with other nations' (Daniel 1967: 103). They did, however, assume that somewhere in Europe or the Near East an evolutionary development had taken place. Nineteenth-century archaeology did not view diffusion and migration as concepts that were antithetical to evolution but as factors that helped to promote evolutionary change (Harris 1968: 174).

The development and spread of Scandinavian archaeology

Even in his earliest work Thomsen was interested not merely in artifacts and their development over time but also in the contexts in which they had been found and what this might reveal about changing burial customs and other aspects of prehistoric life. During the first half of the nineteenth century archaeology continued to develop in Scandinavia as a discipline concerned with the evolution of ways of life throughout prehistoric times. This development was powerfully assisted by the work of Sven Nilsson (1787- 1883), who had studied under the leading French palaeontologist Georges Cuvier and for many years was Professor of Zoology at the University of Lund. Nilsson strongly believed in cultural evolution but, unlike Thomsen, he was mainly interested in the development of subsistence economies rather than technology. Like some eighteenth-century philosophers, he believed that increasing population had been the principal factor compelling Scandinavian hunter-gatherers to become first pastoralists and then agriculturalists. His most important contribution to the study of prehistory was his systematic effort to determine the uses made of stone and bone artifacts by means of detailed comparisons with ethnographic specimens from around the world. Since many Scandinavian artifacts had been parts of compound tools now decayed, inferring the sort of implements to which they had belonged was often far from easy. As an exponent of unilinear evolution, he believed that ethnographic specimens from North America, the Arctic, and the Pacific Islands could shed light on prehistoric Scandinavian cultures that were at the same level of development. He also advocated that ethnographic parallels should be verified through the study of wear patterns on prehistoric artifacts, which could help to confirm what they had been used for (Nilsson 1868: 4). In these ways he sought to infer prehistoric patterns of hunting and fishing directly from archaeological data. His most important study of the Stone Age was published in four parts between 1836 and 1843 and was translated into English as *The Primitive Inhabitants of Scandinavia* in 1866.

Figure 3   **Worsaae boring into one of the large tumuli at Jelling; he explains the procedure to King Frederik VII of Denmark**

An even more influential contributor to the development of Scandinavian archaeology was Jens J. A. Worsaae (1821-85). He became the first professional prehistoric archaeologist and was the first person to be trained in the discipline, albeit informally as a volunteer working with Thomsen. He was appointed Denmark's Inspector for the Conservation of Antiquarian Monuments in 1847 and the first Professor of Archaeology at the University of Copenhagen in 1855. Unlike Thomsen, who remained a museum researcher, Worsaae became a prolific field worker. His excavations helped to confirm Thomsen's chronology by providing more closed finds and also by means of stratigraphic excavations, which offered a more concrete demonstration of cultural change over time than did seriation. Major stratigraphic evidence in support of the Three-Age theory was provided by the excavations that the biologist Japetus Steenstrup carried out in the peat bogs of Denmark in his efforts to trace changes in the patterns of flora and fauna since the end of the last Ice Age. Many artifacts were found in the course of these excavations. These showed that the initial pine forests corresponded with the Stone Age occupation, while the Bronze Age was roughly coeval with the succeeding period of oak forests, and the Iron Age with beech forests. Steenstrup's findings were confirmed as archaeologists sought to relate their own discoveries to these environmental changes (Morlot 1861: 309-10).

Worsaac was a prolific writer and in his first book *Danmarks Oldtid* (The Primeval Antiquities of Denmark), published in 1843 (English translation 1849), he used Thomsen's findings as the basis for a prehistory of Denmark. In 1846-7, with financial support from King Christian VIII, he visited Britain and Ireland, mainly to study Viking remains there. His observations of prehistoric finds in these countries convinced him that Thomsen's Three-Age scheme was applicable to large parts, if not all, of Europe.

Worsaae also played an important role in developing interdisciplinary research related to archaeology. As early as 1837 on Sjaelland, mounds of oyster and cockle shells containing numerous prehistoric artifacts had been observed a short distance inland from the present coastline. As the result of a desire to learn more about geological changes, in 1848 the Royal Danish Academy of Sciences established a commission to study these shell middens. The commission was headed by Worsaae, the biologist Steenstrup and J. S.

Forchhammer, the father of Danish geology. In the early 1850s these scholars published six volumes of reports on their studies of these 'kitchen middens'. Their interdisciplinary research demonstrated that the middens were of human origin and traced the patterns of their accumulation. They also determined that, when the middens had formed, the palaeo-environmental setting had consisted of fir and pine forests and some oak, that the only animals likely to have been domesticated were dogs, and that the middens had been occupied during the autumn, winter, and spring but not during the summer. The distributions of hearths and artifacts within the middens were also studied to learn more about human activities at these sites. Experiments, which involved feeding animal bones to dogs, were carried out in order to explain the numerical preponderance of the middle part of the long bones of birds over other parts of their skeleton (Morlot 1861: 300-1). The one issue Worsaae and Steenstrup did not agree about was the dating of the middens. Steenstrup maintained that they were Neolithic, and hence contemporary with the megalithic tombs, but, because they contained no ground or polished stone implements, Worsaae correctly believed them to be earlier (Klindt- Jensen 1975:71-3).

The archaeology that was developing in Scandinavia provided a model for work elsewhere. Contacts with Worsaae inspired the Scottish antiquarian Daniel Wilson (1816-92) to use the Three-Age system to reorganize the large collection of artifacts belonging to the Society of Antiquaries of Scotland in Edinburgh. This work provided the basis for his book *The Archaeology and Prehistoric Annals of Scotland* published in 1851. In this first scientific synthesis of prehistoric times in the English language, Wilson assigned archaeological data to the Stone (Primeval), Bronze (Archaic), Iron, and Christian eras. Yet his study was not merely a slavish imitation of Scandinavian work. He demonstrated that, while Scotland and Scandinavia had passed through the same stages of development in prehistoric times, Scottish artifacts differed stylistically from their Scandinavian counterparts, especially in the Iron Age. In this work Wilson also coined the term prehistory, which he defined as the study of the history of a region prior to the earliest appearance of written records relating to it. He stressed that the understanding of the past that could be derived from artifacts alone was very different from the kind of understanding that could be derived from written records. Yet he expressed the hope that in due course archaeologists would be able to learn about the social life and religious beliefs of prehistoric times. In his ready commitment to an evolutionary perspective Wilson showed himself to be a true product of the Scottish Enlightenment. Among English antiquarians there was much more resistance to accepting the Scandinavian approach (Daniel 1963a: 58-9) and Wilson's call to reorganize the collections of the British Museum in accordance with the new system long fell on deaf ears. Unfortunately for British archaeology, Wilson, although honoured for his accomplishments with a doctorate from the University of St Andrews, failed to find satisfactory employment in Scotland. In 1855 he left to teach English and history at University College in Toronto, Canada.

Scandinavian archaeology also provided a model for significant research in Switzerland. There, as the result of a drought in the winter of 1853, lake levels fell unprecedentedly low, revealing the remains of ancient settlements preserved in waterlogged environments. The first of these sites, a Bronze Age settlement at Obermeilen, was studied the following summer by Ferdinand Keller (1800-81), a Professor of English and President of the Zurich Antiquarian Society. His initial report led to the identification of several hundred such sites, including the Neolithic village at Robenhausen, which was excavated by Jakob Messikommer beginning in 1858 (Bibby 1956: 201-19). These so-called 'Lake Dwellings' were interpreted as settlements built on piles driven into lake bottoms on the basis of the traveller C. Dumont d'Urville's descriptions of villages of this sort in New Guinea (Gallay 1986: 167). They are now believed to have been constructed on what would have been swampy ground around the edge of lakes.

These excavations yielded the remains of wooden piles and house platforms, stone and bone tools still mounted in their wooden handles, matting, basketry, and a vast array of foodstuffs. Villages dating from both the Neolithic and Bronze Ages provided Swiss archaeologists with the opportunity to study changes in the natural environment, economies, and ways of life of these people. The Swiss finds not only revealed many sorts of perishable artifacts not usually found in Scandinavia and Scotland but also verified the reconstructions of stone and bone tools by Nilsson and others. Switzerland was already a major centre of tourism and the continuing study of these prehistoric remains attracted wide interest. It played a major role in convincing Western Europeans of the reality of cultural evolution and that ancient times could be studied using archaeological evidence alone (Morlot 1861; 321-36).

Prehistoric archaeology had thus developed as a well-defined discipline in Scandinavia, Scotland, and Switzerland prior to 1859. The basis for this new discipline was the ability to construct relative chronologies from archaeological data alone using seriation and stratigraphy. Thomsen had pioneered seriation using a large and representative museum collection, while Worsaae had employed stratigraphy to confirm his findings. For the first time relative chronologies were offered into which all known prehistoric data could be fitted. This demonstrated that artifacts from reasonably well-documented archaeological contexts could be used as a basis for understanding human history.

The development of prehistoric archaeology has long been ascribed to the influence of geological and biological evolution. It has been assumed that the stratigraphically derived chronologies of geological time constructed by geologists and palaeontologists provided a model for the development of archaeological chronologies of prehistory. Yet in Thomsen's pioneering work we see a seriational chronology of human prehistory inspired by social-evolutionary theories of the Enlightenment combining with the data collected by earlier antiquarians and with an implicit knowledge of stylistic change probably derived from the study of numismatics. Prehistoric archaeology did not begin as the result of borrowing a dating device from other disciplines. Instead it started with the development of a new technique for relative dating that was appropriate to archaeological material.

The kind of history produced by Scandinavian archaeology also made sense only in terms of the cultural-evolutionary perspective of the Enlightenment. History had traditionally been concerned with recounting the thoughts and deeds of famous individuals. Even classical archaeology and Egyptology, insofar as they were interested in material culture rather than epigraphy, were concerned with works of fine art understood in relation to recorded history. Yet Worsaae pointed out that in many cases prehistoric archaeologists could not even determine what people had made the implements they were studying. He and Wilson protested against the idea that the earliest people to be mentioned in recorded history were the original inhabitants of Europe (Daniel 1950: 50). A chronology offering independent confirmation of the development of European society from Stone Age beginnings was only of interest to people who were already predisposed to regard cultural evolution as a worthwhile topic. The groundwork for such an interest had been established by Enlightenment views of human nature. By the early nineteenth century, and despite periods of economic contraction such as the one that lasted from 1826 to 1847 (Wolf 1982:291), many members of the expanding and now increasingly entrepreneurial middle class imagined themselves to be the spearhead of developments that were creating a new and better life for everyone. By identifying moral and social progress as concomitants of technological development and the latter as a fundamental characteristic of human history, Enlightenment theories reassured the middle classes of Western Europe of the cosmic significance and hence of the inevitable success of their role in history and portrayed their personal ambitions and those of their class as promoting the general good of society. Technological progress was also attributed to the initiative of individual human beings who used their innate intellectual capacities to control nature better. This was an optimistic view appropriate to the middle classes at the dawn of an era that was to see their power and prosperity increase throughout Western Europe. Thus, by providing what appeared to be material confirmation of the reality of progress throughout human history, Scandinavian-style archaeology appealed to those who were benefitting from the Industrial Revolution. While Danish archaeology continued to be strongly nationalistic and to enjoy the patronage of successive generations of the royal family, its innovators and increasingly its audience were members of a growing commercial middle class (Kristiansen 1981), for whom nationalism and evolutionism were both attractive concepts. By contrast, in the politically reactionary environment of post-Napoleonic Germany, archaeologists, while inspired by nationalism, tended to reject the Scandinavian approach partly because its evolutionism was too closely aligned with Enlightenment philosophy (Böhner 1981; Sklenár-1983:87–91)

Scandinavian and Scandinavian-style archaeologists did not, however, limit their efforts to demonstrating the reality of cultural evolution. They also sought to understand the technologies and subsistence economies of prehistoric peoples and the environments in which they had lived, as well as something about their social life and religious beliefs. Their aim was to learn as much as the archaeological evidence would permit not only about the patterns of life at any one period but also about how those patterns had changed and developed over time. In order to understand the behavioural significance of archaeological finds they were prepared to make systematic comparisons of archaeological and ethnographic data, to carry out replicative experiments to determine how artifacts had been manufactured and used, and to perform experiments to explain the attrition patterns on bones found in archaeological sites. They also learned how to cooperate with geologists and biologists to reconstruct palaeoenvironments and determine prehistoric diets.

What archaeologists of this period did not do was to challenge the traditional biblical chronology, which allowed a total of about 6,000 years for the whole of human history. For Thomsen, Worsaae, and others, several thousand years appeared long enough to encompass the past that was being revealed by the archaeological record. Worsaae dated the first arrival of human beings in Denmark around 3000 B.C. and the beginning of the Bronze Age between 1400 and 1000 B.C. By an ironic coincidence Scandinavia, Scotland, and Switzerland had all been covered by glaciers during the Würm glaciation and to this day have produced little evidence of human habitation prior to the Holocene era. Hence the absolute chronology imagined by the Scandinavians, Scots, and Swiss for their finds was not significantly out of line with reality as we currently understand it.

The antiquity of humanity

The prehistoric archaeology pioneered by the Scandinavians influenced archaeology in some of the smaller countries of Western and Northern Europe. Yet it was largely ignored by the antiquarians of France and England, who, although some of them were prepared to translate the writings of Thomsen and Worsaae into their languages, were unwilling to follow the example set by colleagues from a peripheral country such as Denmark. Their conservative attitude ensured that the scientific study of prehistory did not begin in these countries before the late 1850s and that it developed largely independently of Scandinavian-style archaeology. Unlike Scandinavia, early scientific archaeology in England and France was concerned primarily with the Palaeolithic period and ascertaining the antiquity of humanity. The presence in France and southern England of caves and glacial deposits containing traces of human activities going back into Lower Palaeolithic times provided archaeologists in these countries with an opportunity to study early phases of human existence that was wholly lacking in Scandinavia, Scotland, and Switzerland.

The development of Palaeolithic archaeology depended on the emergence of an evolutionary perspective in geology and also of some knowledge of palæontology. Progress in these fields was necessary for a scientific study of human origins to replace reliance on the traditional biblical accounts. While the major archaeological breakthroughs in studying the antiquity of humanity slightly preceded the first major statement of Darwinian evolutionism, Palaeolithic archaeology was quickly drawn into the controversies that surrounded Darwin's work and was strongly influenced by concepts derived from biological evolution.

When a flint handaxe was found near the skeleton of what was probably a mammoth beneath a street in London towards the end of the seventeenth century, the antiquary John Bagford interpreted the find as that of a war elephant brought to Britain by the Roman emperor Claudius in A. D. 43 and slain by an ancient Briton armed with a stone-tipped spear (Grayson 1983: 7-8). This interpretation was clearly in the tradition of text-aided archaeology. On the other hand, in 1797 John Frere described a collection of Acheulean handaxes that were found together with the bones of unknown animals at a depth of four metres in eastern England. He argued that the overlying strata, which included a presumed incursion of the sea and the formation of half a metre of vegetable earth, could only have been built up over a long period and concluded that 'the situation in which these weapons were found may tempt us to refer them to a very remote period indeed; even beyond that of the present world' ([1800] Heizer 1962a: 71). By this he meant that they were probably more than 6,000 years old. The Society of Antiquaries thought his paper worthy of publication but it aroused no contemporary discussion. While the intellectual climate was clearly opposed to assigning a great antiquity to humanity, Donald Grayson (1983: 58) has pointed out that Frere's failure to identify either the animal bones or the shells in his stratigraphy did not demand agreement with his claims.

Figure 4

Acheulean handaxe found by Frere at Hoxne, published in *Archaeologia,* **1800**

In the course of the eighteenth century scientists such as Georges Buffon began to propose naturalistic origins for the world and to speculate that it might be tens of thousands or even millions of years old. This in turn suggested the need for a symbolic rather than a literal interpretation of the biblical account of the seven days of creation. The French zoologist Georges Cuvier (1769-1832), who established palaeontology as a scientific discipline, used his knowledge of comparative anatomy to reconstruct complete skeletons of hitherto unknown fossil quadrupeds. In this fashion he was able to assemble evidence that numerous species of animals had become extinct. He also observed that older geological strata contained animal remains that were increasingly dissimilar to those of modern times. Since he assumed a relatively short span since the creation of the world, he concluded that a series of natural catastrophes had destroyed entire species of animals and shaped the modern geological configuration of the planet. While he believed that devastated areas were repopulated by migrations of animals from areas that had been spared, other geologists, such as William Buckland (1784-1856), an Anglican priest and Professor of Mineralogy at Oxford University, viewed many catastrophes as universal ones that had wiped out most species. This required God to create new ones to replace them. The increasing complexity of plant and animal life observed in successive geological strata was therefore not viewed as a developmental sequence but rather as a series of ever more complex creations. He conceived of evolution as having occurred in God's mind rather than in the natural world.

In the first half of the nineteenth century naturalists and antiquarians encountered human physical remains and stone tools associated with the bones of extinct animals in stratified deposits in cave sites in many parts of Western Europe. The most important work was that of Paul Tournal (1805-72) near Narbonne and Jules de Christol (1802-61) northeast of Montpellier, both in France, Philippe-Charles Schmerling (1791-1836) near Liège in Belgium, and the Reverend John MacEnery (1796-1841) at Kent's Cavern in England. Each of these men believed that his finds might constitute evidence of the contemporaneity of human beings and extinct animal species. Yet their techniques of excavation were not sufficiently developed to rule out the possibility that the human material was intrusive into older deposits. MacEnery's finds were sealed beneath a layer of hard travertine that must have taken a long time to form. Buckland maintained that ancient Britons had dug earth ovens through the travertine and that their stone tools had found their way through these pits into much older deposits containing the bones of fossil animals. While MacEnery denied this claim, he accepted that the human bones, while old, need not be contemporaneous with the extinct animals. It was argued that deposits elsewhere contained mixtures of animal bones and artifacts from diverse periods that had been washed into caves and mixed together in fairly recent times (Grayson 1983: 107). It became obvious that caves were not going to be conclusive. Their deposits were notoriously difficult to date and it was hard to rule out the possibility that human remains had become mixed with the bones of extinct animals as a result of human or geological activity in recent times.

A much-debated question was whether traces of human beings and their works should be found associated with extinct mammals. The bones of mammoth and woolly rhinoceros were encountered frequently in the glacial deposits that covered France and southern England. At the beginning of the nineteenth century these were generally believed to have resulted from Noah's flood, the last great catastrophe to convulse the earth's surface. Since the Bible recorded the existence of human beings prior to that time, it seemed possible that human remains might be found in these diluvial deposits. Yet fundamentalist Christians believed that the Bible implied that as a result of divine intervention all animal species had survived the flood; hence the presence of extinct species in these levels indicated that they dated before the creation of humanity rather than simply before the last flood. Even those palaeontologists who were inclined to interpret the Bible less literally believed that a beneficent God would have brought the earth to its modern state prior to creating the human species. By the 1830s it was generally accepted that all the diluvium had not been deposited at the same time. It was also believed to be older than the flood and therefore should not contain human remains (Grayson 1983: 69).

The intellectual problems of this period art clearly exemplified in the work of Jacques Boucher de Crèvecoeur de Perthes (1788-1868), who was the director of customs at Abbeville, in the Somme Valley of northwestern France. In the 1830s Casimir

Picard, a local doctor, reported discoveries of stone and antler tools in the region. Boucher de Perthes began studying these finds in 1837. Soon after, in the canal and railway excavations of the period, he started to find Lower Paleolithic handaxes associated with the bones of extinct mammoth and rhinoceros, deeply buried in the stratified gravel deposits of river terraces that predated the local peat formations.

Boucher de Perthes' sound stratigraphic observations convinced him that the stone tools and extinct animals were equally old. Yet, as a catastrophist, he decided that these tools belonged to an antediluvian human race that had been completely annihilated by a massive flood 'prior to the biblical deluge'. After a lengthy period of time God had created a new human race—that of Adam and Eve and their descendants (Grayson 1983: 126-30). It is scarcely surprising that when these fanciful ideas were published in the first volume of his *Antiquitès celtiques et antédiluviennes* in 1847, they were dismissed by French and English scholars alike. Yet even when his field observations were duplicated by the physician Marcel-Jérôme Rigollot (1786-1854) at St. Aucheul and another site near Amiens, 40 kilometres upstream from Abbeville, and these deposits were confirmed to be of 'diluvial age' by geologists, including Edmond Hébert from the Sorbonne, geologists and antiquarians continued to express concern that the artifacts might be intrusive. Grayson (1983: 207) has concluded that the rejection of Rigollot's sound evidence 'stemmed from the sheer belief that such things could not be' and Rigollot's status as an outsider with respect to the scientific elite of his day.

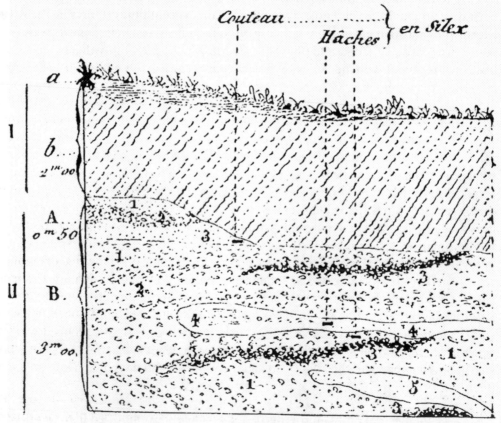

Figure 5   Profile showing location of Palaeolithic material from Boucher de Perthes'
              Antiquities celtiqués et antediluviennes, 1847

The resolution of such controversies concerning the antiquity of humanity required an improved understanding of the geological record. In 1785 the Edinburgh physician James Hutton (1726-97) proposed a uniformitarian view of geological history in which the slow erosion of rocks and soil was balanced by the uplifting of other land surfaces. He believed that all geological strata could be accounted for in terms of the forces currently at work operating over very long periods of time. In the years that followed William (Strata) Smith (1769-1839) in England and Georges Cuvier and Alexandre Brongniart in France, recognized that strata of different ages each possessed their own characteristic assemblage of organic fossils and concluded that such assemblages could be used to identify coeval formations over large areas. Smith, unlike Cuvier, accepted the principle of the orderly deposition of rock formations over long periods of time.

Between 1830 and 1833 the English geologist Charles Lyell (1797-1875) published his *Principles of Geology*, in which he assembled an overwhelming amount of data, much of it based on his observations around Mount Etna in Sicily, to support the uniformitarian assumption that geological changes had occurred in the past as a result of the same geological agencies acting over long periods and at approximately the same rate as they do at present. Lyell's book quickly won support for the principle of uniformitarianism in geology. Contrary to catastrophism, it indicated the past to have been a long and geologically uninterrupted period in which other events could have happened. This provided a setting for scholars to consider the possibility of biological evolution, a concept that Lyell rejected, although Jean-Baptiste Lamarck (1744-1829) had already argued in favour of it.

This new view of geological history also left the question of the antiquity of humanity as one that required an empirical answer. The favourable reception given to Lyell's geology reflected the increasing openness of British scholars and the public to evolutionary ideas. By the middle of the nineteenth century, Britain had become the 'workshop of the world' and the growth of industrialism had greatly strengthened the political power and self-confidence of the middle classes, who had come to view themselves as a major force in world history. This new attitude was reflected in the writings of Herbert Spencer (1820-1903), who in the 1850s began to champion a general evolutionary approach to scientific and philosophical problems. He argued that the development of the solar system, plant and animal life, and human society was from simple, uniform homogeneity to increasingly complex and differentiated entities. By emphasizing individualism and free enterprise as the driving forces behind cultural evolution, he rescued the latter from its former revolutionary associations and helped to make it the ideology of a substantial portion of the British middle class, whose faith in progress had already been expressed in the Great Exhibition held in London in 1851 (Harris 1968: 108-41). In so doing he inclined all but the religiously most conservative members of the middle classes to be sympathetic to arguments favouring biological evolution and the antiquity of humanity.

In 1858 William Pengelly (1812-94) excavated in Brixham Cave near Torquay in southwestern England. This was a newly discovered site known to contain fossilized bones. His work was sponsored by the Geological Society of London and was carefully supervised by a committee of prestigious scientists, including Charles Lyell. In the course of his excavations stone tools and fossil animal bones were found beneath an unbroken layer of stalagmitic deposit 7.5 cm thick, which suggested considerable antiquity (Gruber 1965). As a result of growing interest in the antiquity of humanity, in the spring and summer of 1859, first the geologist John Prestwich and the archaeologist John Evans and then a number of other British scientists, including Charles Lyell, visited the sites in the Somme Valley. All of these scientists were convinced of the validity of the finds Boucher de Perthes and Rigollot had made there and the geologists also recognized that the strata in which these finds occurred must have been deposited long before 4000 B.C. In their reports to leading British scientific associations, including the British Association for the Advancement of Science, the Royal Society of London, and the Geological Society of London, they agreed that there was now solid evidence that human beings had coexisted with extinct mammals at some time that was far removed from the present in terms of calendar years (Chorley *et al.* 1964: 447-9; Grayson 1983: 179-90). This new view of the antiquity of human beings won what amounted to official approval in Lyell's *The Geological Evidences of the Antiquity of Man* (1863).

Charles Darwin's *On the Origin of Species* was published in November 1859. This book, which summarized the results of almost 30 years of research that had been inspired by uniformitarian geology, accomplished for evolutionary biology what Lyell's *Principles* had done for geology. Darwin's concept of natural selection was accepted by many scientists and members of the general public as providing a mechanism that made it possible to believe that a process of biological evolution accounted for modern species and explained the changes observed in the palaeontological record. The obvious implication that humanity had evolved from some ape-like primate not only made the antiquity of the human species a burning issue that had to be empirically studied but also made this investigation a vital part of the broader controversy that was raging concerning Darwin's theory of biological evolution. Palaeolithic archaeology therefore quickly acquired a high-profile role alongside geology and palaeontology in the debates concerning a question of escalating public interest.

Palaeolithic archaeology

The subject-matter of Palaeolithic archaeology was first given its name in 1865 when, in his book *Pre-historic Times,* the English banker and naturalist John Lubbock divided the Stone Age into an earlier Palaeolithic or Archaeolithic (Old Stone) and a more recent Neolithic (New Stone) period. He was, however, merely formally labelling a distinction that was already obvious between an initial period, when all tools had been chipped from stone, and a later period, when some stone tools, such as axes and gouges, had been ground and polished (Daniel 1950: 85). After 1860 the main advances in Palaeolithic archaeology took place in France, where the river terraces of the north and the rock shelters of the south provided better evidence than was available in England. The principal goals of these studies were to determine how long human beings had been in the area and whether evolutionary trends could be detected within the Palaeolithic period. Evolutionary theory predicted that over time human beings would have become both morphologically and culturally more complex. The first goal of Palaeolithic archaeologists was therefore to arrange their sites in chronological order.

The leading figure in early Palaeolithic research was Edouard Lartet (1801-71), a magistrate who had turned to the study of palaeontology and had publicly acknowledged the importance of Boucher de Perthes' discoveries in 1860. Supported by the English banker Henry Christy, he began to explore cave sites in the Dordogne in 1863. He quickly realized that the Palaeolithic was not a single phase of human development but a series of phases that could be distinguished according to artifacts and associated prehistoric animals. He preferred a classification based on palaeontological criteria and distinguished four ages or periods, which from most recent to oldest were: (I) Aurochs or Bison, *(2)* Reindeer, of which the cave sites at Laugerie Basse and La Madeleine were typical, (3) Mammoth and Woolly Rhinoceros, and (4) Cave Bear, although he gradually recognized that the last two periods could not be temporally separated. The Le Moustier site was designated as typical of a new Cave Bear and Mammoth period. To Lartet's three periods Félix Garrigou added a still earlier Hippopotamus one when human beings had inhabited mainly open sites and which was not represented in the caves of southern France (Daniel 1950: 99-103).

Lartet's work was continued by Gabriel de Mortillet (1821-98), a geologist and palaeontologist who turned to the study of archaeology. He was assistant curator at the Museum of National Antiquities at Saint-Germain-en-Laye for seventeen years before becoming Professor of Prehistoric Anthropology at the School of Anthropology in Paris in 1876. Although he admired Lartet's work, he believed that an archaeological subdivision of the Palaeolithic had to be based on cultural rather than palaeontological criteria. In this respect he chose to follow the example of Lubbock and Worsaae.

In spite of this, his approach to archaeology was greatly influenced by his knowledge of geology and palaeontology. He sought to distinguish each period by specifying a limited number of artifact types that were characteristic of that period alone. These diagnostic artifacts were the archaeological equivalent of the index fossils that geologists and palaeontologists used to identify the strata belonging to a particular geological epoch. Mortillet also followed geological practice in naming each of his subdivisions of the Palaeolithic after the type site that had been used to define it. Like palaeontologists he relied on stratigraphy to establish a chronological sequence. In the Palaeolithic research of the nineteenth century, seriation played only a minor role as a means of establishing chronology. This was no doubt partly because technological and stylistic sequences were harder to recognize in Palaeolithic stone tools than in later artifacts and also because the issues being discussed were so controversial that only the clearest stratigraphic evidence was universally agreed to be able to provide conclusive temporal sequences. The reliance on stratigraphy also reflected Lartet's and Mortillet's training as natural scientists.

Lartet's Hippopotamus Age became the Chellean Epoch, named after a site near Paris, and most of Lartet's Cave Bear and Mammoth Age became the Mousterian, although Mortillet assigned finds from Aurignac that Lartet had placed late in his Cave Bear and Mammoth Age to a separate Aurignacian Epoch. Lartet's Reindeer Age was divided into an earlier Solutrean Epoch and a later Magdalenian one. Mortillet was uncertain about the date of the Aurignacian. He later placed it after the Solutrean and finally dropped it from his classification of 1872. He also added a Robenhausian Epoch to represent the Neolithic period and in later studies, such as *formation de la nation française* (Development of the French Nation) (1897), he added still more epochs to incorporate the Bronze and Iron Ages into his system. It is doubtful, however, that he was ever serious about the universality of these highly distinctive Western European periods (Childe 1956a: 27).

TEMPS	AGES	PÉRIODES	ÉPOQUES
Quaternaires actuels	Nisioriques / du Fer.	Mérovingienne	Webenienne (Waben, Pas-de-Calais
		Romane.	Champdolienne. (Champdolent, Seine-el-Oise.)
			Lugdunienne. (Lyon, Rhone)
	Prolohisloriques.	Galatienne.	Beuvraysienne. (Monl-Beuvray, Niévre,)
			Marnienne. (Départment de la Marne).
			Hallstallienne. (Hallstall, haute Autriche.)
	du Bronze	Tsignienna.	Larnaudienne. (Larnaad, Jura)
			Morgienne. (Morges, canlon de Vaad, Suisse.)
		Nélithique.	Robenhausienne. (Robenhausen, Zurich)
			Campignyenne. (Campigny, Seine-Inferieure.)
			Tardenoisienne (Fère-en Tardenois, Aisne)
Quaternaies anciens.	Prébisloriques. / de la Pierre.	Paléolithique.	Tourassienne. (La Tourasse, Haute-Garonne.) Ancien Hiatus.
			Magdalénienne. (La Madeleine, Durdogne)
			Solutéenne. (Solutré, Saone-el-Loire.)
			Moustérienne. (Le Mouslier, Dordogne)
			Acheuléenne. (Chelles, Seine-el-Marne).
			Chelléenne, (Chelles, Seine-et-Marne).
Tertiaires		Éolithique.	Puyeournienne. (Puy-Courny, Contal)
			Thenaysienne. (Thenay, Loir-el-Cher)

Figure 6   **Mortillet's epochs of prehistory, from** *Formation de la nation) francaise, 1897*

Mortillet also invented a Thenaisian Epoch and later a Puycournian one to cover pre-Chellean finds. Between 1863 and 1940 archaeologists discovered eoliths, or presumed artifacts of exceptionally crude manufacture, in early Pleistocene as well as still earlier Pliocene and Miocene deposits in France, England, Portugal, and Belgium. Evolutionary theory implied that the earliest tools would be so crude that they could not be distinguished from naturally broken rocks; hence in the absence of human bones or other convincing proofs of human presence the authenticity of these finds was challenged. In the late 1870s Mortillet and others who supported the artifactual status of eoliths began to develop a set of criteria that might be used to distinguish intentional stone working from natural breakage. Challenges to these criteria alternated with efforts to elaborate new and more convincing tests. Comparative studies were made of eoliths and rocks from formations hundreds of millions of years old and experimental work was carried out, including S. H. Warren's (1905) observations of striations on flints broken by mechanical pressure, Marcelin Boule's (1905) study of flints recovered from a cement mixer, and A. S. Barnes' (1939) quantitative analysis of edge angles fabricated by human hands and by natural processes. In the course of these studies much was learned about stone working and many sites were disqualified as evidence of human antiquity (Grayson 1986). Either as a result of direct influence or by coincidence, this research carried on the traditions of archaeological experimentation established by Scandinavian investigators in the 1840s.

Mortillet's training in the natural sciences was reflected in more than his classificatory approach. He and most other Palaeolithic archaeologists were primarily concerned with establishing the antiquity of humanity. Within their evolutionary framework, this meant trying to trace evidence of human presence back as far as possible in the archaeological record and demonstrating that older cultures were more primitive than later ones. The sequence that Lartet and Mortillet established stratigraphically and palaeontologically carried out this task admirably. Comparing later with earlier stages of the Palaeolithic, there was evidence of a greater variety of stone tools, more stages and greater precision in their preparation, and an increasing number of bone tools. This demonstrated that the technological progress that Thomsen and Worsaae had documented from the Stone to the Iron Ages could also be found within the Palaeolithic period.

While archaeologists discussed what Palaeolithic populations had eaten at different stages and it was debated whether certain art work might indicate that horses had been domesticated in the Magdalenian period (Bahn 1978), Palaeolithic archaeologists were far less interested in studying how people had lived in prehistoric times than Scandinavian archaeologists had been. In this respect Palaeolithic archaeologists resembled palaeontologists, who at that time were more concerned to demonstrate evolutionary sequences than they were to study ecological relations within rock formations from individual periods. The main units of archaeological excavation were strata, although even these were often recorded in surprisingly rudimentary fashion. Sites were frequently excavated with minimal supervision, which meant that detailed cultural stratigraphy and features within major levels went unrecorded. Particularly in rock shelters where living floors had been preserved, this resulted in a severe loss of information concerning how people had lived. The artifacts that were kept for study in museums were often only those recognized as being of diagnostic value for ascertaining the age and cultural affinities of sites. Debitage and artifacts that were not thought to have diagnostic significance were frequently discarded. This encouraged a non-cultural view of artifacts as dating devices and evidence of progress, which was very different from the Scandinavian approach to archaeological data. Even Boyd Dawkins, who criticized Mortillet for his preoccupation with evolutionary development and his failure to allow that some differences between Palaeolithic assemblages might reflect tribal or ethnic variation as well as varying access to different types of stone, did not produce any satisfactory alternative analyses (Daniel 1950: 108-9).

Mortillet, like the geologists and palaeontologists of the mid nineteenth century, was caught up in the evolutionary enthusiasm that characterized scientific research at that time. He viewed his Palaeolithic sequence as a bridge between the geological and palaeontological evidence of biological evolution prior to the Pleistocene era and the already established documentation of cultural progress in Europe in post-Palaeolithic times. As Glyn Daniel (1950: 244) has noted, one of the keynotes of evolutionary archaeology was the idea that humanity's cultural development could be represented in a single sequence and read in a cave section, just as the geological sequence could be read in stratified rocks.

Mortillet was also influenced by a strong ethnological interest in cultural evolution during the second half of the nineteenth century. In 1851 the German ethnologist Adolf Bastian (1826-1905) began a series of voyages around the world in order to build up the collections of the Royal Museum of Ethnology in Berlin. Impressed by the cultural similarities that he encountered in widely separated regions, he emphasized the Enlightenment doctrine of psychic unity by arguing that as a result of universally shared 'elementary ideas' *(Elementargedanke)* peoples at the same level of development who are facing similar problems will, within the constraints imposed by their environments, tend to develop similar solutions to them.

After 1860 there was a great revival of theoretic history, as ethnologists sought, by comparing modern societies assumed to be at different levels of development, to work out the stages through which European societies had evolved in prehistoric times. These researches ranged from studies of specific issues, such as Johann Bachofen's (1861) theory that all societies had evolved from matrilineal beginnings and John McLennan's (1865) arguments that the oldest human societies had been polyandrous, to general delineations of development from savagery to civilization by E. B. Tylor (1865) and Lewis H. Morgan (1877). Unlike the 'theoretic' histories of the eighteenth century, these ethnological formulations were presented as scientific theories rather than as philosophical speculations. While reflecting the general vogue for evolutionary studies in the mid-nineteenth century and usually addressing questions that archaeological data were ill equipped to handle, these works derived much of their self-confidence from growing archaeological evidence that technological advances had been an important feature of human history. Reciprocally these ethnographic formulations encouraged archaeologists to interpret their data in a unilinear perspective.

In his guide to the archaeological displays at the Paris Exposition of 1867 Mortillet declared that prehistoric studies revealed human progress to be a law of nature, that all human groups passed through similar stages of development, and the great antiquity of humanity (Daniel 1967: 144). The first two concepts had their roots in the philosophy of the Enlightenment and the third had been recognized as a result of research carried out prior to the publication of *On the Origin of Species*. Yet, while Palaeolithic archaeology had vindicated an evolutionary origin for humanity, Mortillet's first two laws were far from validated. Not enough work had been done outside of Western Europe to determine whether or not human groups everywhere had developed—insofar as they had developed at all—through the same Palaeolithic sequence. While some scholars were prepared to accept the multiple invention of simple artifacts, such as spears or calabash containers, they suspected that more complex ones, such as boomerangs or bows and arrows, were more likely to be traced to a common origin (Huxley [1865] 1896: 213). Likewise, overly rigid applications of notions about what constituted progress led many archaeologists, although not Mortillet (Daniel 1950: 131), to reject the authenticity of cave paintings on the ground that they were too advanced to have been produced at an early stage of human development. This view was only overcome as fresh discoveries of bone carvings and cave paintings were made in contexts that clearly dated this art to the Upper Palaeolithic period (ibid. 131-2). Once validated, however, European cave art was largely interpreted in terms of the totemism associated with the Australian aborigines (Reinach 1903; Ucko and Rosenfeld 1967: 123-8).

Palaeolithic archaeology was scientifically important and aroused great public interest because it revealed the hitherto unexpected antiquity of humanity and the gradual evolution of European civilization from very primitive beginnings. It also set new standards for stratigraphic analysis in archaeology. Palaeolithic archaeology enjoyed great prestige because of its close ties with geology and palaeontology, which were both sciences in the forefront of creating a new vision of the history of the world. All three of these disciplines were valued because they were viewed as demonstrating the reality of progress in prehistoric times. Palaeolithic archaeology also was respected because it had evolved in France and England, which were the centres of political, economic, and cultural development in the world at that time. Because of its prestige Palaeolithic archaeology provided a model for studying post-Palaeolithic prehistory in Western Europe. Yet its view of artifacts mainly as dating devices and evidence of cultural evolution was a very narrow one by comparison with Scandinavian prehistoric archaeology, which was concerned with studying cultural evolution but also sought in a more rounded fashion to learn as much as possible about how human beings had lived in prehistoric environments. The interdisciplinary cooperation of Scandinavian archaeologists with geologists and biologists in their pursuit of these objectives contrasts with the wholesale modelling of archaeological research upon often inappropriate natural science methods by Palaeolithic archaeologists. As a result the prehistoric archaeology that developed in France and England was limited in the range of its interests just as it was enhanced in its time depth by comparison with Scandinavian archaeology.

Reaction against evolution

Those who objected to evolutionary accounts of human origins or the denial of biblical accounts of human history fought back in various ways. During the 1860s creationists who accepted current interpretations of the archaeological record could still hypothesize that human beings had been created much earlier than had previously been thought and hope that early hominid skeletons, when discovered, would resemble those of modern human beings rather than the 'pithecoid forms' predicted by the Darwinians (Grayson 1986: 211). Yet not everyone accepted an evolutionary interpretation of the archaeological record. As early as 1832 Richard Whately, Archbishop of Dublin (1787-1863), had breathed new life into the doctrine of degenerationism. He argued that there was no evidence that savages, unaided, had ever developed a less barbarous way of life. It followed that humanity originally must have existed in a state 'far superior' to that of modern savages, a view which he felt was in accord with the Book of Genesis (Grayson 1983: 217-20). This position became increasingly popular among conservatives in the 1860s, although not all degenerationists denied the great antiquity of humanity or attributed its earliest cultural achievements to divine revelation. One of the most eminent degenerationists was the Canadian geologist and amateur archaeologist John William Dawson, who was Principal of McGill University in Montreal from 1855 to 1893. Dawson accepted the association between human remains and extinct mammals but argued that these associations confirmed the recency of the Pleistocene gravels in which they were found. On a trip to Europe in 1865 he inspected the geological deposits of the Somme Valley and described his mentor Charles Lyell as taking 'very good-naturedly' his opinion that evidence was lacking 'of the excessive antiquity at that time attributed to [these formations] by some writers' (Dawson 1901: 145). He also maintained that North American ethnographic evidence revealed that the peoples who used the best-made stone implements also used the rudest and that the developmental sequence found in Europe might represent idiosyncratic local trends or the accidental interdigitation of neighbouring, contemporary groups with different cultures. From this he concluded that there was no evidence that cultures at different levels of complexity had not coexisted throughout human history (Dawson 1888: 166-7; 214; Trigger 1966). While in retrospect Dawson can be seen as defending a lost cause, in the nineteenth century it was easier for his opponents to ignore his objections than to refute them. Not enough was yet known about prehistoric sequences outside Europe to establish evolution as a general trend in human history.

Still more links existed between Near Eastern archaeologists and those who sought to prove the literal truth of the Bible. Interest in Mesopotamian archaeology was revived in the 1870s after George Smith published a clay tablet from Nineveh containing a Babylonian account of the deluge. The Daily Telegraph offered 1,000 pounds sterling to send an expedition to Iraq in search of the missing portions of this tablet, which were duly found (Daniel 1950: 132-3). Much of the early work of the Egypt Exploration Society was directed towards sites in the Delta, such as Tell el-Muskhuta, that were associated with biblical accounts. In 1896 W. M. F. Petrie was quick to identify the ethnic name *I. si. ri. ar?*, which appeared on a newly discovered stela of the Pharaoh Merneptah (reigned 1236-1223 B.C.), as the first known mention of Israel in Egyptian texts (Drower 1985: 221). As late as 1929 Leonard Woolley excited great interest by claiming that the thick silt deposits that he had found in his excavations of prehistoric levels at Ur attested a great flood in Mesopotamia that had given rise to the biblical account of the deluge (Woolley 1950: 20-3). While Egypt and Mesopotamia produced spectacular archaeological discoveries that excited the public in their own right, those that related to the Bible and appeared to confirm scriptural accounts ensured widespread support for archaeological research carried out in these countries as well as in Palestine. Individual archaeologists were on both sides in the struggle between the supporters of revealed religion and of evolutionism during the late nineteenth and early twentieth centuries (Casson 1939: 207-8).

The Development of Excavation Techniques

Introduction

Philip Barker (1920-2001) was an English archaeologist who directed large projects of excavation, notably Hen Domen in Montgomeryshire and Wroxeter in Shopshire, and also acted as architect for Worcester Cathedral. His organized and meticulous process of excavation and analysis of remains set a high standard for field work in England after the mid-twentieth century, and his philosophy of archaeological activity and the everyday practice of excavation are set down with exceptional clarity in his *Techniques of Archaeological Excavation*.

In this chapter, Barker surveys some of the modern methods of excavation, citing a number of projects of innovative importance. His commentary begins with the late nineteenth century with the extraordinary work of Pitt-Rivers at Cranbourne Chase, where, one may say, the origins of modern attitudes and techniques are seen clearly for the first time. The excavator dug large areas with unprecedented care, but, more importantly, he produced a record of unprecedented detail. He realized that the record of the excavation should include more than the excavator might have understood or thought relevant to record, since his record of the excavation might be interrogated in the future for such data. Such record-keeping would set a high standard, followed by many progressive excavators of the twentieth century.

The next topic is the approach to excavation in which the levels/layers recorded are best understood horizontally or vertically, that is in plan or vertical section. It was thought that particularly large sites might only be recorded in sections (of a grid imposed upon the site). Barker cites the work of Sir Mortimer Wheeler in creating enormous grids with resulting boxlike excavated parts in which, however, the sections left between the units of the grid would be carefully examined, compared and recorded, in effect comparing and combining horizontal and vertical views. Such a double approach could lead to a fully three-dimensional recording and understanding of the site as existing over time. Further refinements in recognizing features, particularly ephemeral ones such as timber structures, were made possible by this approach, and by the 1960s work such as that of Brian Hope-Taylor at Yeavering in Yorkshire, Philip Rahtz at Cheddar, two large Anglo-Saxon sites consisting mainly of timber buildings requiring extensive open area excavation, and Martin Biddle at Winchester, an urban site which was flexibly extended from 1962 to 1975.

T
he growth of archaeology, and with it the techniques of excavation, have been
outlined, with many contemporary quotations and a bibliography, by Professor Glyn
Daniel (1950 and 1967) and its more recent aberrations castigated by Sir Mortimer
Wheeler (1954). Our modern techniques stem from the fifteen years between 1881 and
1896 during which Lieut. - General Pitt Rivers carried out a series of masterly
excavations on Cranborne Chase (Pitt Rivers, 1887-98) where he had inherited estates,
and was therefore able to work with unhurried care, with adequate finances and labour,
but, above all, to publish with a lavishness which we can now rarely hope to emulate. As
he tells us (Vol. 1, 1887, xix), his first lessons as an excavator were derived from Canon
Greenwell, the opener of Yorkshire barrows, but he far transcended his tutor, and dug with
a breadth of vision and a grasp of detail which were quite unprecedented. It was this
meticulous attention to detail that was, and is, important, together with his realisation that
all the observed evidence should be recorded, even if its meaning is not understood at the
time. Two short quotations will put his point of view:

> Excavators, as a rule, record only those things which appear to them important
> at the time, but fresh problems in Archaeology and Anthropology are
> constantly arising, and it can hardly fail to escape the notice of anthropologists
> . . . that on turning back to old accounts in search of evidence, the points
> which would have been most valuable have been passed over from being
> thought uninteresting at the time. Every detail should, therefore, be recorded
> in the manner most conducive to facility of reference, and it ought at all times
> to be the chief object of an excavator to reduce his own personal equation to a
> minimum. (Pitt Rivers, vol I, 1887, xvii)
>
> I have endeavoured to keep up in the present volume the minute attention to
> detail with which the excavation commenced. Much of what is recorded may
> never prove of further use, but even in the case of such matter, superfluous
> precision may be regarded as a fault on the right side where the arrangement
> is such as to facilitate reference and enable a selection to be made. A good

deal of the rash and hasty generalization of our time arises from the unreliability of the evidence on which it is based. It is next to impossible to give a continuous narrative of an archaeological investigation that is entirely free from bias; undue stress will be laid upon facts that seem to have an important bearing upon theories current at the time, whilst others that might come to be considered of greater value afterwards are put in the background or not recorded, and posterity is endowed with a legacy of error that can never be rectified. But when fulness and accuracy are made the chief subject of study, this evil is in a great measure avoided . . . (Pitt Rivers, preface to Vol.11, 1888)

As a result of his 'fulness and accuracy', the General's excavations can be reinterpreted in the light of our much more extensive background knowledge (eg. Hawkes, 1948). Similarly, a large-scale excavation of his assistant's, Harold St George Gray, has recently been fully published for the first time by Richard Bradley (Bradley, 1976). This was only possible because Gray kept detailed records in the manner of Pitt Rivers. The General also realised that area excavation was the only way to understand the structures and sequences of settlement sites (see front endpapers). His chief weakness was his summary treatment of layers above the natural chalk. They tended to be ignored except in ramparts, ditches and pits, so that only major features cut into the subsoil were seen and recorded. It may be a platitude to say that the General was in advance of his time, but it is true that the lessons implicit in his work were not fully appreciated for many years. Even Flinders Petrie, writing in *Methods and Aims in Archaeology*, published in 1904 (quoted in Daniel, 1967, 233-6), betrays a complete lack of understanding of Pitt Rivers' example. And Sir Leonard Woolley modestly describes his first experience of digging when, in 1907, the great Haverfield agreed to supervise an excavation at Corbridge on behalf of the authors of the *Northumberland County History*. It was considered that 'a small-scale dig' would 'settle the character of the site' and Woolley, with an assistant, some volunteers and labourers, taught himself by trial and error.'...we were all', he says, 'happily unconscious of our low performance, nor did anyone from outside suggest that it might have been better. ..'British field archaeology was at a low ebb. (ibid, 246)

In the years leading up to the First World War Harold St George Gray modelled his own excavations on the General's. In fact, as Richard Bradley says, 'His actual digging was cleaner and more orderly than his mentor's, and some of his photographs must rank among the best of all time' (Bradley, 1976). But the publication of Maumbury Rings has had to wait until 1976, and, as a result, Gray's work did not have the influence on British excavation techniques that it deserved.

Since the late nineteenth century there have been significant shifts of emphasis in excavation techniques, first towards horizontal, then to vertical, and now again towards horizontal methods. The earliest excavators of our Roman towns, such as Caerwent, Silchester and Wroxeter, excavated horizontally in large areas, attempting to see the sites as a whole, but failing to observe the subtleties of stratification which are necessary not only for the understanding of the chronology of the site but even for the recognition of more tenuous evidence (e.g. fig. 18). One result was that these sites, among many others, appeared to contain only stone buildings, whereas we now know that almost all have long sequences of timber buildings, some earlier, some contemporary with and some later than the stone buildings. Thus the chronological and structural sequences were distorted by this summary digging, which, though fundamentally the right method, was crudely applied. The plan was dominant. In both the Silchester and the earlier Wroxeter reports for example there are large diagrammatic plans but very few sections (Fox and Hope, 1891; Fox, 1892; Fox and Hope, 1893; Bushe-Fox, 1913, 1914, 1916).

In Britain, reaction came in the 1930s, mainly under the powerful influence of Sir Mortimer Wheeler, when the section, the grid system and three-dimensional recording became paramount, and as a result the importance of the plan decreased.

Sir Mortimer, like many innovators, transcended the limitations of his innovations. This is perhaps because he worked on the grand scale, and because he was aware of the need to see the evidence horizontally as well as vertically (Wheeler, 1956, 149, 246), so that he usually finished up with a large open area. His followers— that is, nearly all excavators working in Britain between the 1930s and the 1960s— usually worked on a much smaller scale. As a result the *sample* was too small, often no more than one or two trenches or a small grid of boxes, even, on occasions, tiny trenches leap-frogging in a line across large and complex sites.

Sections were now drawn in the greatest detail, whereas plans, even of totally excavated features, were recorded much more summarily, and where structures disappeared under the frequent baulks, they were completed with conjectural dotted lines. The section seemed to offer an economical, swiftly obtained microcosm of the site's development and this led to the trial trenching of hundreds of sites, with the results being used as the basis for generalised statements about the whole site, and often of other, unsampled sites.

These techniques were used particularly on Romano-British sites. Because it is possible to separate the four centuries of Roman rule from the rest of our history there have been, and are, a considerable number of 'Romano-British archaeologists' both professional and amateur, whose interest waxes *c.* AD 43 and wanes *c.* AD 410. Archaeologists in the countries of north-west Europe outside the Roman Empire are fortunate in that they are much freer of these period divisions, so that their archaeology is seen as a continuum to be studied naturally as a whole.

The Roman occupation was a period of building in stone and timber sandwiched between periods of timber building in the prehistoric period and the immediate post-Conquest years and again in the so-called sub-Roman period. Since stone buildings can more easily be dug in trenches and boxes, it can reasonably be argued that the isolation of the Roman period by scholars, coupled with the widespread use of stone buildings in Roman times, led to the general adoption of the grid system, even on sites where it was unsuitable.

Prehistorians were the first to become aware of the limitations of this method (eg. Case, 1952), chiefly because they were more often dealing with structures which simply cannot be understood in trenches or boxes, if they are seen at all.

Pioneer work, notably by Dr van Giffen in Holland (van Giffen, 1958), Professors Gudmund Hatt and Axel Steensberg in Denmark (Hatt, 1957, Steensberg, 1952, 1974) and Professor Gerhard Bersu in Britain (Bersu, 1940, 1949), showed that the only way to elucidate the intricate patterns of the timber buildings found on by far the majority of ancient sites is to combine highly detailed observation of the layers in plan with a study of their composition in depth; a fully three-dimensional approach in which every cubic centimeter of soil is made to yield the maximum information.

Professor Hatt's last excavation, that of the Iron Age village of Nørre Fjand in Jutland, carried out between 1938 and 1940 (Hatt, 1957), was his most highly developed and influential (figs. 1 and 2).

Professor Steensberg has described, in a letter to me, the evolution of Hatt's technique in the 1920s. He writes:

However, Hatt realized – being a geographer – that in the case of indistinct sites it would be necessary to uncover bigger areas in order to follow the edge of the houses. The break came in 1927 when he had to excavate a house site in Tolstrup, Himmerland (south of Alborg). The local archaeologist, S. Vestergaard Nielsen, who had found the site, could not be present all the time, because he was a school teacher. He told me later on, that the following day he came out to the site and found that Hatt made use of wheelbarrows and uncovered a considerable area before he started the real digging. This amused Vestergaard Nielsen, and he threatened Hatt saying: 'I am going to write a letter to the National Museum's First Department telling C. Neergaard, that you are excavating like a peasant's servant!' The method proved, however, to be very profitable. But as can be seen from Hatt's publications in *Aarboger for nordisk Oldkyndigbed*, 1928 and 1930, he still made use of the traditional measuring tapes from two main points A and B. Therefore the features had a rather awkward outline which irritated Hatt. He wished to uncover the features according to their real shape, and what is very important he wished to remove layers just as they had been deposited, not taking away a layer of 5 or 10 cm. everywhere. This must have been due to his geological training. And he did not use sections where it was not necessary, though in his investigations of pre-historic fields he dug sections through the low division walls and analysed them as other geologists would have done.

Hatt realized that sections cut across the very flimsy and discontinuous floors and superimposed hearths of Iron Age houses would destroy them unseen, so in order to keep vertical records he levelled-in layers, features and finds on the assumption that a notional section could subsequently be drawn across the site wherever required. This method was adopted and refined by Steensberg, who had assisted Hatt at Nørre Fjand, in a series of excavations on farm sites in Denmark (Steensberg, 1952), and reached its fullest development at Store Valby, (Steensberg 1974). Fig. 3 shows the successive buildings of Farm 3 at Store Valby.

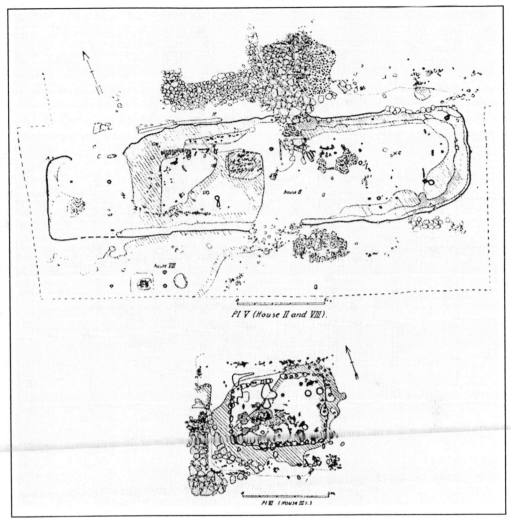

PI V (House II and VIII).

PI VI (House III 1.)

Figure 1   Nørre Fjand: this is the plan of two houses from this Iron Age site in Jutland.
                 Each stone is drawn to scale and the outlines of layers of burnt and unburnt
                 clay show the positions of the clay walls.

The internment of Professor Gerhard Bersu in the Isle of Man during the War was
an ill wind which blew good for British archaeology, for while there Bersu dug a number
of sites (Bersu, 1949 and 1977). Outstanding among them, technically, was the excavation
of a Viking camp at Vowlan (Bersu, 1949) where it is clear from the plan along (fig. 4)
that a system of grids with intervening balks would seriously have hampered the
understanding of the site (op. cit., 67). Though Bersu's section drawing has sometimes
been criticized for its excessive naturalism and over-elaboration, the naturalistic technique
of the plan of Vowlan is there most appropriate, showing, as it does, the soil-changes
which were the sole evidence for the buildings.

The lessons implicit in excavations such as Vowlan were slow to be understood but
are now the basis for the very large investigations of sand and gravel sites which form a
great proportion of the rescue excavations in the lowlands of Britain.

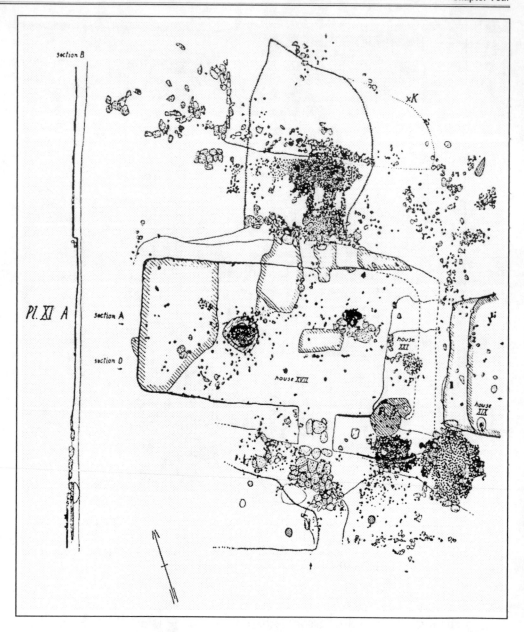

Pl. XI A

section B

section A

section D

house XVII

house XII

house III

xK

Two crucial excavations of this type were carried out by Brian Hope-Taylor from 1953-58 at Yeavering (Hope-Taylor, 1977) and by Philip Rahtz in 1960-62 at Cheddar (Rahtz, 1964, and in press). Both as it happens, were on the sites of Anglo-Saxon palaces. The excavation of Yeavering, though only recently published, has had a profound influence on the standards of excavation in Britain, due to the exceptional acuteness of the observation, the precision of the recording and the beauty of the draughtsmanship, which led to a depth of interpretation beyond the capacity of most previous excavators. Rahtz, working on the grand scale at Cheddar, demonstrated conclusively that very large sites cannot be understood unless they are excavated totally.

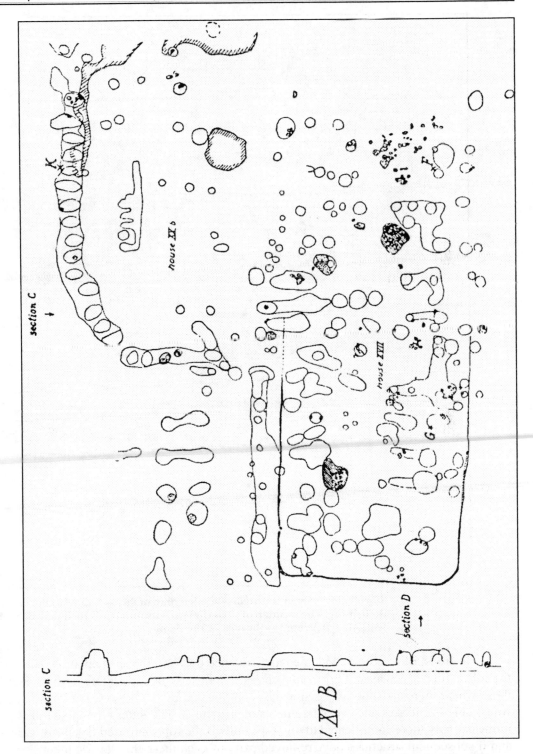

Figure 2   Nørre Fjand: this drawing shows the plan of a series of houses, XVII, XXI,
              XIX, as first discovered, and, right, the pattern of underlying post-holes
              revealed when the uppermost layers were removed. At this point house XXb
              was revealed.

Figure 3   Store Valby: part of the highly detailed plan of farms 3 and 4 at the medieval
                  Danish site. The position of each find with its number is included. Schematic
                  sections are printed at the side of the plan.

There is, of course, a fundamental difference between those excavations in which
the sole evidence consists of horizontal changes in the colour and texture of the soil and
those where there are superimposed levels, complicated by the presence of vestigial stone
walls, pebble surfaces and other fragments of structures. The latter type of site is
immeasurably more complicated to dig, especially if the superimposed layers are very thin,
and if subsequent structures have removed parts of even these thin layers, their
discontinuity making them yet more difficult to trace and interpret.

In England, research in the 1950s on the peasant houses of deserted medieval villages
faced just this sort of problem. The excavation of the now classic site of Wharran Percy,
begun by Professor Beresford, was continued in 1955 by J. G. Hurst and J. Golson, using

techniques derived from those of Steensberg. The account of the development of the excavation (Hurst, 1956, 271-3 and 1979), with its cautious beginnings, using balks which were abandoned when they proved to mask vital evidence, records a turning point in British archaeology. The methods used at Wharram have since been further modified, the leveling in of all finds being discarded in favour of the recording of finds within their layers. This continuous modification of techniques during the course of long-term excavations is one of the principal ways in which the science, or art, of excavation advances. In addition, techniques developed on one type of site have been tested on other sites of quite different character. It is now clear that the methods used at Wharram Percy are equally valid on sites containing major stone buildings and that if such sites, which once might have been thought to contain only the stone buildings, are excavated horizontally and in great detail, the plans of unsuspected timber buildings may well emerge.

During the 1950s and '60s urban excavation was developing in parallel with the rural excavations of prehistoric and medieval sites. Professor Sheppard Frere's excavations at Verulamium in 1955-61 (Frere 1959 and 1971) pointed the way towards Martin Biddle's rapidly expanding excavations at Winchester in the early 1960s. It is very instructive to follow the development of Biddle's techniques through the series of interim reports which began in 1962 and continued until 1975 (Biddle, 1962-1975).

On many sites timber and stone buildings were intermixed or followed one another in varying sequences. It is in those areas and periods in which timber buildings follow stone that the elusive evidence of wooden structures is most vulnerable, either to later disturbance, or to the excavator's desire to get at the underlying stone buildings. How many Roman villas have been dug with the possibility in mind that later occupants of the site might have used the destruction rubble as foundation rafts for timber buildings? Similarly, the final phases of Roman towns and the 'Dark Age' layers of our cities have been neglected in the past partly because they require the uncovering of large areas if they are to be understood, but partly also because they require a different attitude of mind, one that is open to any form of structural evidence which presents itself, and does not look simply for preconceived features, such as walls and post-holes, and ignores the unexpected.

We are only just beginning to realise the potential of excavated evidence, especially the wealth of information which might be revealed by a really detailed analysis of every aspect of the soil removed in the dissection of the structures we are excavating.

Techniques in the past have often been too panoramic, too clumsy to reveal more than the broadest outlines of the more obvious structures. The excavation of the Roman town of Silchester is an often-quoted example, where it is suspected that the published plan, showing, as it does, only a scatter of stone buildings in a sort of garden city, may be quite misleading, the gaps being filled by undiscovered timber buildings. This is an old and obvious example; what is much more worrying is that it is at least possible that the majority of all published (or, for that matter, unpublished) excavations may be misleading in that, either by taking too small a sample of the site in boxes or trenches, or by digging too insensitively, especially in the upper levels, whole periods of the site's occupation have been lost, ignored or distorted.

The consequences for the history and prehistory of Britain are far-reaching. If I am right, the syntheses made from these excavation reports and integrated with other forms of evidence will be falsified because the distortions and missing phases, being unknown, cannot be taken into account.

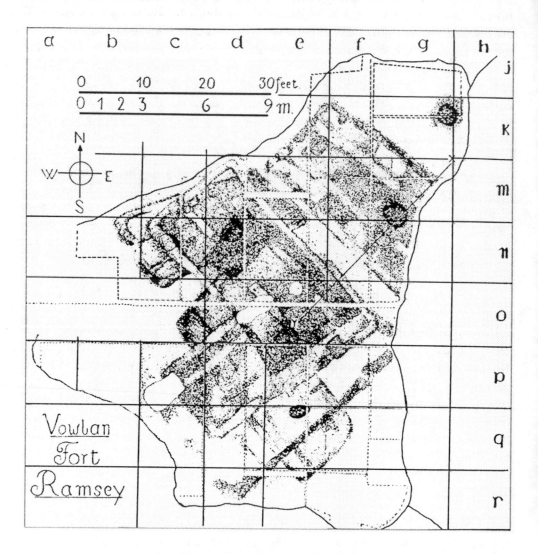

Figure 4   Vowlan, Isle of Man: excavated area inside the promontory fort at the level of the untouched soil. The drawing indicates, by means of differential shading, the varying colours and shades of the surface of the sand revealed when the turf and topsoil were removed.

It is sometimes argued that, if an excavation is published as fully as possible, the evidence should be sufficient for re-interpretation by future workers in the light of their greater background experience. However, if the evidence from the original excavation was mistakenly observed or inadequately recorded in the field, the inadequacies will lie further back than the published drawings and lists of finds, however plausible they may seem; and the more skilful the drawings, the more convincing they will be. There is no absolute safeguard against this since excavation can never be completely objective, but we must be constantly aware that all interpretation is, in a sense, a personal opinion, and be careful, as far as possible, to keep the interpretation separate from the evidence on which it is based. Naturally, the more detail there is in the publication, the more confidence the reader will have that the losses of evidence are minimal; although this in its turn brings further difficulties. In an age of larger and more complex excavations drawings must now be published at a much greater scale if the mass of significant detail is not to be lost, and here the problems of ever-increasing printing costs become a major factor in the adequate publication of excavations (see below p. 222). Yet it may well be that greatly increased attention to detail is the key to all improvements in excavation techniques.

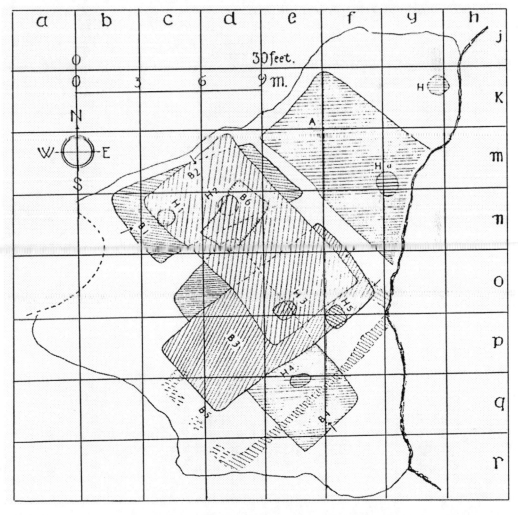

Figure 5   Vowlan: diagram of houses inside the promontory fort. This drawing is a simplification and interpretation of the plan shown in fig. 4. It is clear from both plans that a system of trenches or grids cut across the site would not have uncovered an understandable pattern. If the reader doubts this, he can play a salutary game by taking a piece of cardboard and cutting in it holes to represent any desired system of trenches or grids (to scale), laying it over the plan, and then attempting an interpretation from the visible areas. A similar game can be played with any of the other area excavations here reproduced e.g. figs 1, 2, 3, 17, 19, 38, 70, 71, 76, 82, 83 and 84.

The archaeological dilemma of our age is that just as it is becoming necessary for us to excavate more slowly, and in much greater detail, we are beginning to realise the full extent and speed of destruction of sites and whole settlement areas which is going on around us. How can we justify months spent on the *minutiae* of part of a small site when the hearts of great cities, such as London, Lincoln, York and Gloucester, are being torn out in a matter of weeks and when square miles of prehistoric settlement are being totally removed in a matter of months? There is no single, simple answer, but the dilemma must be faced and a solution attempted.

s useless for the field archaeologist to try to work in isolation from the
, the geographer, the pedologist, the climatologist or the ecologist. It is, on the
d, depressing to read settlement studies by geographers or historians which
ly fail to take into account the work of archaeologists in the same region.
xcavation should ideally be the work of a team of specialists, so should
minary fieldwork. It is becoming more and more necessary for the field
ogist to be an *entrepreneur*, an intermediary between a whole range
lines which can be brought to bear on the problems posed by archaeol-
vestigation.

lthough the complex discipline of fieldwork in archaeology is dealt with at length
me in this series (Taylor, 1974), and has an exemplary introduction in Aston and
, 1974, it cannot here be passed over without mention since sites must be dug in
ntext as part of the landscape, not as isolated detachable phenomena. In addition,
lication of the excavation must include location and area maps, and at least one
ich relates the site to its immediate surroundings. This will usually require
rk more detailed than that to be found on Ordnance Survey maps, so that the
becomes the excavator's responsibility.

There is no doubt that some archaeologists have a better 'eye' for the ground than
but fieldwork is an art which can be transmitted by experienced and perceptive
rs, and developed by practice. Often only long acquaintance with a site and the
which it is set will reveal the subtle indications of former earthworks, roads or
ngs. A well-known field, seen daily under all conditions of light and shade, damp and
ht, will quite suddenly, on a day of thawing snow, reveal for the first time, and for a
urs only, that it is full of the most ephemeral traces of ridge and furrow. On other
ions a summer of exceptional drought will bring out the parch-marks of a totally
pected building.

The slight undulations of ploughed-out or eroded earthworks are concealed by
grass and weeds, so that the winter and early spring are the optimum seasons for
-walking. Even with conditions at their best, with the grass short and with
cing light, one can often only sense very slight earthworks by walking across
in different directions; and when one stands still they seem to vanish. The
nced three-dimensional sense which movement gives, revealing these subtleties,
es oblique stereo-photography, taken from the optimum angle to the earthworks,
best way of recording them pictorially. Aerial or terrestrial photogrammetry, if the
ours are drawn at small enough intervals, would be the most satisfactory way of
rding large areas; but for smaller areas ordinary contour surveys, drawn at
rvals of 20cm. or less, will not only reveal the earthworks but enable them to be
erstood in a way impossible on the ground, just as the aerial photograph draws
ether the visible evidence within the compass of a glance. The aerial
otogrammetric surveys carried out in advance of major developments can often be
de available to the archaeologist, especially if he is engaged in rescue excavation
or to the development.

CHAPTER

5

Fieldwork

Introduction

Barker believed that, "Excavation must be seen as the culmination of the investigation
of the site." (p. 87) This simple statement characterizes his attitude toward the whole
archeological enterprise: excavation of a site is a part of a larger study that is carried
on before and after digging. The nature of the setting must be considered carefully,
and include studies such as geography, geology, soils, climate, and the like that
usually require specialist input. Specific techniques in the pre-excavation of a site are
described: use of the Ordinance Survey maps, survey on the ground; photography
from the air (including oblique, vertical and stereoscopic) as an aid to creating
topographical maps for identifying features in the planning stage of excavation;
geophysical study to understand the nature of the surface, and, using the scientific
techniques of measuring soil resistivity and magnetic scanning that may suggest
subsurface character; sampling soil and surface material by field walking; and
research into any previous work on the site.

The site's setting

I t is a platitude worth repeating that the landscape is a pa
man's activities have left some trace. The earth's surfac
intensively occupied countries such as Britain, is a floor
carved and scratched a mesh of superimposed *graffiti*. The
patterns take is not accidental; it is the resultant of convergin
shape of the land surface, the underlying geology, the soil cov
the evolution of agriculture, as well as the expansion and cont
and the necessities of defence. Recognition of meaningful seq
patterns can be intensely gratifying, so that for some archaeolo
becomes an end in itself. However, archaeological conclusion.
inspection of earthworks or crop-marks can be very misleading
excavation has shown that previous assumptions have been wro
when dug, almost always prove to be much more complex than
indications suggest.

Excavation must be seen as the culmination of the investigati
only resort to surgery after intensive preoperative examination. The
investigation must be complete—an amalgam of fieldwork (that is, th
examination of the site and its surroundings), excavation, the study o
on the site but in the region, and, in the case of sites of the historic pe
specialised study of the documentary evidence.

The site must be seen in its setting. The geology of the region is
metaphorically fundamental. From it the landscape has evolved. It has
nature of the soil and thus the nature of the primal vegetation, and ultim
pattern of agriculture.

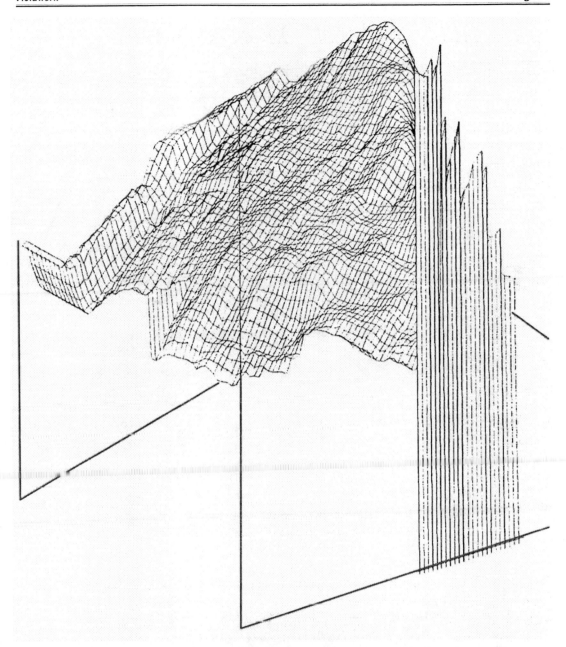

Figure 6   Hen Domen, Montgomery: three dimensional computer print-out of contour survey of pre-Norman field system (by Susan Laflin, University of Birmingham). The vertical scale is exaggerated to emphasise the very slight ridges, which were only a few centimeters high.

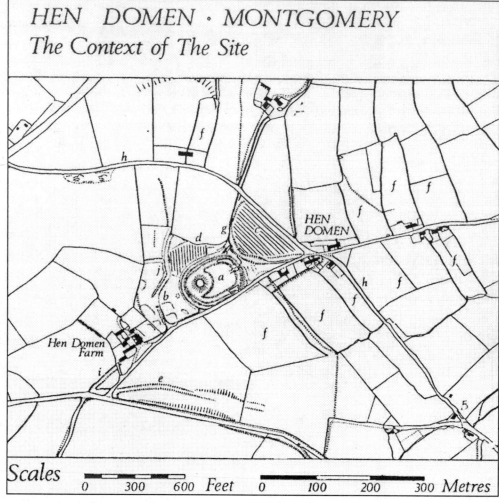

HEN DOMEN · MONTGOMERY
The Context of The Site

HEN
DOMEN

Hen Domen
Farm

Scales

0   300   600 Feet   0   100   200   300 Metres

Figure 7   Hen Domen, Montgomery: the Context of the Site.

Key:
a.   The Motte and Bailey Castle
b.   Earthworks of settlement possibly connected with pre-Norman
     field system
c.   And d. Pre-Norman ridged fields
e.   Former road to Montgomery
f.   Medieval strips (notice reversed S shape)
g.   and j. Pre-Norman hollow ways
h.   An early road leading to the ford at Rhydwhyman
i.   An earlier alignment of the present lane

Not only is the stereoscopic mosaic of photographs (usually of the highest quality) likely to be full of information but the contoured maps derived from the mosaic will often reveal slight earthworks, such as eroded ridge and furrow, which cannot be seen on the photographs. It is now possible to feed the raw data of a grid of levels into a computer programmed to provide a three-dimensional print-out in which earthworks or other remains are viewed from any desired angle. This has been done for the survey of the pre-Norman ridged field system at Hen Domen, Montgomery (Barker and Lawson, 1971). A grid of levels was taken at 1-metre horizontal intervals over the field, and the resulting contours were interpolated by eye. At the same time a three-dimensional computer plot was made to provide a more objective interpretation (fig. 6).

The more rapid type of survey, based on a series of measurements made at points chosen by the surveyor along the tops of banks or in the bottoms of hollows and then drawn as a series of hachures or 'tadpoles', is more easily 'read'; it is, however, inevitably simplified and runs the risk of being subjective, since some surveyors will have a more acute awareness of the subtleties of earthworks than others. The accuracy of this kind of survey is very considerably reduced by long grass and weeds, but on the other hand it may be the only practicable method in wooded scrub country where the theodolite or the level cannot be used. Aston and Rowley, 1974, fig. 46, p. 156 shows a fine survey of this kind, of the earthworks surrounding the Cistercian Abbey of Bordesley in Redditch, Worcestershire. They show how such a plan can reveal the fact that the earthworks are of many periods. The surveyors have distinguished four phases in the development of the site and the exploitation of the water resources provided by the nearby River Arrow. While this interpretation may be modified by the long-term excavations now being carried out there, it provides a good example of this comparatively rapid method of planning complex earthworks. Clearly surveys of this or any other kind will be more accurate if carefully measured with tape or chain, but if speed is necessary because of the imminent destruction of the site, a paced survey is better than nothing. However, there is no need here to describe surveying methods in detail, since a number of good textbooks are available (e.g. Fryer, 1966 and 1971; Coles, 1972; Taylor, *op. cit.* 1974).

The basis of the site fieldwork will, of course, be the Ordnance Survey maps of the region and the immediate locality. Contemplation of the 2½-inch or 6 inch maps will very often reveal patterns of field boundaries, roads or tracks, which are the fossilised remnants of deserted settlements or superseded field systems. For example, fig. 7, prepared as part of the publication of a long-term excavation, shows the area round the small castle at Hen Domen, Montgomery, Powys. On this old superseded road lines (g, j, e and i) can be seen together with curving field boundaries (f) which are almost certainly the result of enclosing strips in the open fields. 'This example could be paralleled in differing forms almost anywhere in rural Britain, and often (except where development is total) in urban areas as well—in cities such as Lincoln or Gloucester where the skeletal remains of their Roman ancestry can still be seen, or in Ludlow, where eighteenth-century streets preserve a twelfth-century plan.

The older editions of the Ordnance Survey, beginning with the first edition of 1801-05, are invaluable, and many public libraries have sets of the 1:2500 sheets published in the nineteenth century, which show a great deal of information that has since been lost. The 1:500 sheets of towns are a unique record which is a necessary tool for the urban archaeologist, as are the early town maps of Speed, Roque and others. The splendid collection of the King's maps in the British Museum is also invaluable. The Public Record Office and, most libraries and county archive collections have estate maps, terriers and tythe maps which may contain a scrap of information about a long-vanished site, trapped like an insect in amber. Field names from early sources may lead to the discovery of lost sites, or to sites peripheral to the one under excavation. Many collections of documents in libraries and museums include topographical drawings of the sort popular in the eighteenth and nineteenth centuries. These are often the only record of prehistoric monuments, castles, churches and other subjects suitable for the Romantic pencil, showing them in less weathered or damaged condition than they are today.

As more county and regional archaeological units are formed the cumulative storage of all known information about the archaeology of the district concerned is becoming normal practice. Many of these site and monument records are designed to be compatible one with another and the information, stored on cards or tape, with accompanying maps, is readily retrievable, and is normally available to the public for consultation.

Except in the case of the most unexpected emergency excavation, the area in which the site lies should be intensively examined by field-walking and the study of maps and aerial photographs, as well as in discussion with the local farmers and other residents who may remember earthworks now ploughed out, or finds adorning mantelpieces. The results of this examination should, as far as possible, be incorporated into the area map published with the excavation report. More than this, the study of the surrounding landscape inevitably illuminates the excavation and brings greater understanding to the interpretation of the site in its wider sense.

Too many excavators in the past have treated sites almost as though they were portable objects which just happened to be in the field where the excavation was to take place. It is obviously insufficient to dig a deserted medieval village without identifying and examining the field system on which its economy depended; or to dig a Roman fort without attempting to trace the roads which sewed it, temporary camps which may have preceded it or the civil settlements attached to it which may have continued in existence. Barrows, perhaps more than any other monument, have been dug in isolation, probably because they are small and seem self-contained. Only rarely has the archaeologist widened the excavation to include the surrounding area with its possibly related structures or peripheral burials, or attempted to identify the settlement site from which the buried people came. Happily, one of the benefits of the large-scale destruction caused by mineral extraction and ploughing is that in a few cases whole ancient landscapes are being examined by excavation (e.g. Jones, 1968; Cunliffe, 1973). Much more often, excavation is confined to a single site or even to part of site. In these cases the results of digging will be stultified if the surrounding landscape is not studied as fully as possible, both by fieldwork and, as described below, by the environmental sciences.

Aerial photography

It is of the greatest value to have access to aerial photographs of a site and its surrounding landscape as a complement to the study of maps and to fieldwalking.

The major collections of archaeological aerial photographs are held by the National Monuments Record and the Committee for Aerial Photography at Cambridge, though large collections are held by some of the major museums and universities, and by a number of private flyers. Not all of these collections are easily available for inspection, even to scholars, and there is no doubt that an immense amount of information, much of it unique and unprecedented, awaits assessment. Unfortunately, one might almost say, disastrously, many of the sites newly revealed from the air will have been destroyed before their existence is known to more than a very few. The problem, which is primarily one of man-power and money in storing, cataloguing and making available the prints, is beyond the scope of this book, but is under active consideration by a Committee of the Council for British Archaeology. The papers read at a symposium entitled 'Aerial Reconnaissance for Archaeology' have been published by the C.B.A. under that title (Wilson, ed., 1975). This volume forms an excellent summary of recent developments, while the realization of the importance of aerial photography has led to the founding, in 1971, of the *Journal of Aerial Photography*.

The Royal Air Force cover is an invaluable source of high-level photographs, though not, of course, taken with archaeology in mind. Sometimes it happens, however, that the circumstances are favourable. For instance, part of the second world war Royal Air Force cover for Shropshire was taken when light snow covered the ground—the conditions could not have been better for the definition of earthworks and the series has produced much new evidence. Many Development Corporations and Road Construction Units have commissioned photogrammetric surveys made from vertical mosaics of photographs. Both the surveys and the photographs are usually available if an approach is made through the proper channels.

Aerial photographs, vertical, oblique or stereoscopic, may reveal earthwork or crop-mark sites related to the site to be excavated. The site itself, if it has been, or can be, photographed from the air before excavation, may reveal details of earthworks within it not otherwise visible, and there is no need to say that very many archaeological investigations are carried out on sites which would not be known without aerial photography. If aerial photography can be arranged during or immediately after the excavation, the resulting photographs will greatly enhance the published report. By giving a panoramic view, they may also reveal patterns in the excavated surface not readily seen from the ground.

This is not the place to discuss either the techniques of aerial photography or its specialised interpretation. The best introductions to the subject are: J.K.S. St Joseph, *The Uses of Aerial Photography* 1966, and Wilson, *op. cit.*, together with M.W. Beresford and J.K.S. St Joseph *Medieval England, An aerial survey*, 2nd ed., 1979 and J. Bradford, *Ancient Landscapes,* 1957.

Geophysical prospecting

The various forms of geophysical prospecting (for an introduction to geophysical prospecting see Brothwell and Higgs, 1969, Chap. 60 and 61, and see also the volumes of the Journal *Archaeometry)* give, under optimum conditions, a broad picture of the potential of the site before excavation, a picture comparable with that given by crop-mark photographs. Geophysical prospecting shares the limitations of aerial photography in that a negative result does not mean that archaeological features are not present. On the positive side, however, the evidence provided by a magnetometer or resistivity survey may be invaluable in planning the excavation in those cases where the whole site cannot be dug. Where it is intended to dig the whole site, geophysical surveys may be of value to the scientists involved in developing the equipment and interpreting its results when, ultimately, the survey is compared with the excavated evidence. Obviously a total excavation should be conducted as methodically as possible, and the temptation to divert the excavation on to some massive magnetic or other anomaly must be avoided, allowing the excavation to reach it in due course. In cases such as this it will be of great interest to see how the excavated results compare with the plot of anomalies. But, in the case of a rescue excavation, which is working against time, or where a site is so large that total excavation cannot be contemplated, geophysical surveys can be of great use in planning the course and size of the excavation. An excellent account of the use of geophysical evidence to determine the areas to be excavated within a large site will be found in Alcock, 1972, 54ff. and the use of a magnetometer to determine the strategy of excavation of a small site in Barker, 1966.

Geophysical prospecting will always be more useful on sites without deep stratification, since on stratified sites not only may deep structures escape detection, but with a whole sequence of structures and occupation levels lying one below another, the geophysical record will inevitably be confused. Nevertheless, even under these circumstances, over a large site the general areas of occupation may be very clearly defined, even if the details are not clear (Alcock, 1972, figs. 6 and 8).

The apparatus used in both resistivity and magnetic prospecting is continually being modified and techniques refined. An account of recent developments will be found in Vol. **II** of the *Journal of Archaeological Science*. Experiments are at present being carried on applications of radar and sonar scanning which may be able to scan to successive depths (at, say, 10 cm. intervals) in the hope of detecting major stratigraphic changes.

Many small groups have constructed their own resistivity meters, which often give remarkably accurate results, and the Department of Physics at Bradford University has developed and marketed the Bradphys, which is a compact resistivity machine costing £595 plus VAT (in 1980). Some C.B.A. groups and other confederations of societies own a magnetometer which enables individuals or groups to carry out independent surveys while the Department of the Environment Laboratory has a geophysics section which carries out major surveys on threatened sites in advance of their excavation. Magnetic scanning with a fluxgate gradiometer has proved the most successful in surveying large areas in a comparatively short time, and is undoubtedly the most useful technique for rescue work.

Field-walking and soil sampling

A good deal of thought has been given recently to the problems of field-walking, to evolving methods which will minimize the effects of the weather, the light and the varied abilities of the walkers on the recovery of finds. A most useful booklet, Fasham *et al., Fieldwalking for Archaeologists* (1980) has been published by the

Hampshire Field Club and Archaeological Society, while the Department of the Environment has published a series of papers arising from a seminar held in 1976, under the title of *Fieldwalking as a method of Archaeological Research*, Occasional Paper No. 2, 1980.

Both of these publications describe and assess the various methods of field-walking, though detailed guidelines for standardized methods have not yet been agreed, the variables being so numerous and difficult to assess. In spite of this, field-walking is an essential supplement to all the other methods of site discovery and assessment.

If the site or sites to be excavated are under the plough intensive field-walking for pottery, tile or burnt daub scatters may limit the likely occupation areas, particularly if these coincide with areas of darker soil or burning.

Field walking in times of drought will often discover areas of parching, revealing former roads or stone buildings, sometimes in great detail, or, alternatively, the darker green lines of ditches, pits and wells can be seen as distinctly from the ground as from the air. For example, the ripe corn over the Roman fort at Duncot in Shropshire grows three to four inches higher over the silted-up ditches than it does elsewhere, an effect which can be clearly seen from ground level, and enables the site to be plotted with great accuracy.

Farmers often know a good deal about earthworks and cropmarks on their land, and will equally often be interested to hear archaeological explanations for them. Conversely, they may explain the real origins of earthworks which wishful thinking archaeologists might otherwise make into ancient sites. I was once saved by a farmer from considerable embarrassment when showing two eminent field workers round the site of a deserted medieval village. A splendid platform close to the farm house promised to be the site of one of the major buildings of the abandoned settlement until the farmer told me, *sotto voce*, that it was the platform for a long-disused tennis court, leveled-up by terracing.

A grid of soil samples tested for phosphates may also delimit occupation areas, though this method has had only variable success, probably because it is dependent on a number of other factors apart from ancient occupation, factors such as intensive fertilising which may obscure or eliminate the detectable chemical differences.

Previous work on the site

It is essential, before beginning the excavation, to discover if possible, the extent and nature of any previous work on the site. Search should be made in national and local journals, in the records of local museums (where chance finds from the site may also be encountered), in bibliographies both general and specialist (see Grinsell, Rahtz and Price Williams, 1974, 31 for a list) and the topographical and subject card catalogues of the Society of Antiquaries of London.

Too often, however, earlier work is not recorded at all, or, if it is, the location of the trenches is not illustrated, and the excavator has to discover the earlier trenches during the course of the excavation, and treat them simply as recent features. It should be observed that many earlier excavators did not take their trenches down to the undisturbed subsoil but stopped when they reached floors or similar levels. It should not, therefore be assumed that a pattern of early trenches or areas has necessarily been totally destructive.

The positions of earlier excavations should be shown on the general plan of the excavation included in the final report. In addition, finds from earlier work may still be available in museums, or in private possession, for illustration in the report, when they can be integrated with more recent material.

CHAPTER

6

Problems and Strategies

Introduction

Barker points out the necessity of creating a strategy for excavation, starting with the fundamental question of what is to be gained, what may be proved or disproved. He considers, in particular, the "problem oriented" approach, in which the archaeologist focuses on a particular question in the way a scientist might develop an experiment to test hypotheses. He reminds us that, while many kinds of scientific analyses are used by the archaeologist, the data contained within the site are never uniform, never the same, and investigation with a narrow focus runs the risk of ignoring other valuable aspects of the site, an idea expressed generations earlier by Pitt-Rivers. An extreme case of narrow focus would be the removal of layers of little interest to the investigator or the setting of a substantial "test trench" which might destroy features of interest and value. Barker also considers the value of "random sampling" in either dense or extensive areas, suggesting that the strategy "…should include intensive site evaluation by all the non-destructive methods possible…" (p. 99).

What follows in this chapter is a guide to useful investigative practices before large-scale excavation is undertaken. The function test trenches are again brought up as having value, but mainly in relation to geophysical survey and determining the nature of the site. The kind of excavation is determined, as far as possible, by considering the kind of features likely to be encountered: earthwork, timber or masonry, and Barker sets out the special problems of dealing with stone walls and the evidence of their construction and destruction as well as the consequences of such elements as dividing areas of the site.

T here is a continuing debate on the strategies to be adopted when designing an excavation. Some archaeologists, using the parallel of scientific experiments set up to prove hypotheses, would advocate specifically problem-orientated excavations designed to throw light mainly, or sometimes only, on the questions which are uppermost in their minds at the time. The danger of this procedure is that, by investigating one period or aspect of a site single-mindedly, other periods or aspects will be ignored, or given scant treatment, and any remains belonging to them may well be destroyed in the course of the excavation. The grossest examples of this approach were the unconsidered bulldozing or summary digging of the medieval and post-medieval levels of towns in order to get at the underlying Roman levels.

Apart from the problems of the size of the excavated samples of a site, discussed below, p. 54, archaeological excavation differs from other scientific research in that postulated theories cannot be proved by the setting up of duplicate experiments. Each part of every site is unique, so that the results obtained on one part of a site cannot, except in the broadest sense, be demonstrated to be correct by reference to work on another part of the same, let alone a different, site. Moreover, archaeological experiments cannot be set up to investigate isolated problems, since every site is not only unique but complicated and above all unpredictable. An excavation designed to answer a specific question will almost certainly run into completely unexpected evidence, in all probability tangential to, or even entirely unconnected with, the problem to be solved, evidence which is likely to raise more questions than it answers and which should certainly not be ignored.

It may be useful to cite some examples of mistakenly conceived problem-orientated digs. A long trench was dug, under my direction, across the ditch and part of the inner bailey of a castle in Shropshire not otherwise threatened (Barker, 1961). This excavation was specifically planned to recover a pottery sequence dating from between 1115-1225, dates suggested by the documentary evidence.

It not only produced a plausible and entirely misleading pottery sequence (Barker, 1961, 76, 77) but, though care was taken to do as little damage as possible, the trench destroyed parts of timber and stone buildings of the inner bailey without producing enough evidence to understand them. When eventually the castle is properly excavated the missing evidence may prove to have been vital, and I shall rightly be castigated.

I also directed a limited excavation on the castle mound at Hastings (Barker and Barton). The work was initiated principally to prove whether or not the mound was that built by William I and which appears in a famous scene on the Bayeux Tapestry. The excavation showed, among other things, that the primary mound was probably of near-Conquest date (it contained a large unabraded sherd of c. 1050-1100, which strictly only gives a *terminus post quem* of that date), but it is now clear that it is impossible to prove by excavation that this is the mound depicted in the Tapestry. Even if coins of William I were found in the mound, or its make-up proved to be banded like that shown on the Tapestry, it could still be the castle said to have been built at Hastings by the Count of Eu a year or so after the Conquest. It is extremely improbable that any dating methods capable of a precision of ± one year will be evolved, methods moreover which would date the construction of a mound and not simply the objects or other material found in it. There is some reason to believe that William's castle was sited on the beach to protect his ships, in which case the present mound on the cliff-top cannot be the one shown on the Tapestry. But there is now no way of establishing this, especially as the coastline on which William landed has long been eroded away. In retrospect this was a piece of problem-orientated excavation, which, although producing interesting results, did not, and I believe could not, have satisfactorily answered the question posed.

Trenching the ramparts and ditches of a series of individual classes of earthworks, such as Roman forts or medieval moats, in order to obtain a sequence of dated periods of occupation, will almost certainly fail to produce reliable information, either because the whole sequence is not present at the point or points, chosen, or, if it is, it cannot be shown to be so without very much more extensive excavation. Such trenches are also notoriously liable to destroy other unsought for and unexpected evidence.

A dig which aims to shed light on a particular problem or period in a town's history is also liable to run into similar difficulties since towns are probably the most complicated and unpredictable of all archaeological sites. A long-buried castle ditch, of great interest to the student of the Norman period, may be overlain by a series of seventeenth-century industrial buildings, unique in the region and of great importance to the industrial archaeologist. The Roman and medieval town nuclei may sandwich between them the much more elusive evidence of the immediate post-Roman centuries. In the past, holes carefully sited to determine the extent of the forum or the *principia* or other monuments of Roman town or forts have been dug oblivious of a host of overlying problems.

What questions can be asked about a deserted medieval village which do not require virtually the total excavation of the village? Sampling trenches will certainly not give answers relevant to dates or structures except in a purely general sense. Such trenches may show that occupation extended beyond the period suggested by the documentary evidence, or that the village overlay an earlier sequence of settlements, that the houses were of wood, or clay or stone; but the price paid for this information may be the mutilation of the site to the extent that the structures trenched may never be subsequently understood. Even the total excavation of one or two house sites will only give answers which relate to those houses, which may be, for some reason, anomalies in the village, either in date or function, and cannot, in any case, be *proved* to be typical without further excavation. For example, at Abdon in Shropshire, R.T. Rowley excavated two house sites at opposite ends of the complex of earthworks which filled the large field in which stood an isolated church. One house proved to date from the thirteenth century, the other from the late eighteenth. Without extensive excavation it would be hazardous to assign a date to any of the other houses which may be there (personal communication).

Such examples could be multiplied tenfold. What questions therefore should we ask of our sites and what sampling units might be considered valid? No-one, presumably, plans an excavation without some inkling of what he is likely to find and some reason for digging this, rather than another site. Even under emergency conditions, or perhaps especially under emergency conditions, excavation is selective, dependent on the predicted richness of the site in structural or material evidence, or its importance in the area, or its rarity, its availability, its degree of preservation or the particular interests of the excavator or a controlling academic committee. In the absence, as yet, of any planned and coordinated strategy of investigation of our sites on a national scale all these factors may, or may not, be considered before digging, but usually some of them are.

M.O. Carver has admirably expounded the problem and suggested solutions in 'Sampling Towns, an optimistic strategy' in Clack and Haselgrove, 1981. He argues that one should concentrate on those areas of a town where the archaeological deposits are deeper, or more intact, and preferably waterlogged, especially if these coincide with good documentary and architectural evidence. Thus, the effectiveness of the excavation will be at its maximum at these points. This strategy is in contrast to that which advocates either digging wherever opportunity occurs within a town, or digging only in those places where one expects to solve specific, often isolated, problems.

Such an approach, can, of course, be extended into the countryside. If it is, it follows that untouched earthworks will take precedence over crop-mark sites, that, by definition, have been damaged by the plough, which, in many cases, will have churned up or removed all the superficial layers. Again, Hen Domen, Montgomery illustrates this point. One nine-inch ploughing of that site would have destroyed the last two periods of occupation, leaving only the deeper, posthole structures (which may well have appeared as marks in a subsequent crop). Clearly, therefore, if there is a choice between a ploughed and an unploughed site of the same type, excavation of the second will be likely to be more productive. It follows that, in general, intact earthworks deserve more protection than crop-mark sites, as they are likely to embody more (and more reliable) evidence.

Any excavation strategy should therefore include intensive site evaluation by all the non-destructive methods available. The decision to excavate one rather than another site can then be made on more strictly archaeological grounds than has often been the case in the past. Such site evaluation may, of course, result in the site's preservation rather than its excavation, since the best and richest of our sites (in terms of surviving evidence) should be protected from destruction by excavation and should be conserved as part of a rapidly diminishing resource.

Nevertheless, we seem to be moving towards a more coherent research/rescue policy, in which non-archaeological factors, such as individual interests, local availability of funds or manpower, as well as the patterns of destruction are minimized. The question has recently been discussed in relation to the Anglo-Saxon period (Wade, 1974) where, after the very great practical difficulties of statistically random sampling of sites are acknowledged, cogent arguments are put forward for a mixed strategy of large-scale excavations together with small-scale sampling based on extensive fieldwork. It is an open question whether fieldwork on the scale needed, particularly the assessment of the vast back-log of aerial photographs, can be made before a large proportion of the sites here have disappeared or been deeply damaged. It is also open to question whether one should pursue the study of settlements of a particular period, since unless they happen to be founded on virgin territory, and to have had no successors, other periods of occupation will be drawn into the enquiry, and may receive less than their due from the single-minded worker. So we are brought back to the relationships of sites to their setting and the concept of landscape archaeology, in which it is the landscape which is sample, rather than a series of sites; Wade's discussion of sampling criteria and strategies is therefore as applicable to the landscape as to Anglo-Saxon settlement research (*ibid*.p. 88).

There are two levels of sampling: since all known or suspected sites cannot be sampled, some must be selected for large-scale work, some for small-scale sampling, and others either left to be eroded by natural processes or destroyed by development or ploughing, or preserved intact for future investigation. The difficulties of making such a selection are formidable and liable to the grossest errors of judgement, especially if the only criteria are crop-mark photographs, scatters of pottery (with their bias toward ceramic periods in regions which have long aceramic periods), field names and other imponderables. To this must be added the complication that many village, town and city sites overlie sites of the period or period under consideration. The Deserted Medieval Village Research Group changed its name and its objectives to the Medieval Village Research Group because by definition it had been studying failed settlements. The successful villages had flourished and are now under expanded settlements. Beormasingham is a notable example.

To all the difficulties of statistical sampling of the population of sites must be added the continuing distortions due to the fact that they are not a static, fossilized entity but a rapidly changing and diminishing asset, disappearing, like the expanding universe, at a rate faster than we can overtake.

If we can envisage an Ideal Excavation, in which every scrap of the evidence which survives is recovered, from complete plans of major buildings to the total pollen count (and if it is remembered that all of this will only be a small fraction of what existed during the occupation of the site), then it will be clear that this ideal level of recovery would give us the best chance of interpreting the site most fully and that anything less than this ideal situation would give us progressively less information down to the point where much of the structural and stratigraphic evidence could not be understood. Since the Ideal Excavation is unattainable we have to decide what the acceptable levels of recovery are. In the case of structures and buildings I believe that total recovery should be the aim.

Only in a very few special cases, where the structures are known beforehand to be repetitive and the stratification simple (as, for example, at Trelleborg or Fyrkat) can sampling provide valid and satisfying evidence. The case of Chalton may here be cited. Champion (1978) has shown that a 20 percent random sample using 8 m. quadrats covering no more than 30 percent of the site gave a fair estimate of the total number of buildings (60 against an observed total of 57) and some information about the nature of the structures. However, Chalton is an exceptional site consisting of many buildings of roughly similar size, and with little, if any, superimposed stratification. In addition, this exercise was retrospective and sampled an excavation rather than an untouched field. The difficulty is to know beforehand what the size and variety of the structures present are likely to be, so that a sampling strategy can be devised. Aerial photographs and geophysical surveys are notoriously deceptive, detecting the major structural features such as walls, floors and large post-holes, but failing to detect those more tenuous sorts of evidence such as pebble spreads, lines of stones, shallow post-sockets and discolorations of the soil which may, nevertheless, indicate the presence of major buildings. In addition, a large proportion of sites are vertically stratified, with the sizes and distribution of structures changing through time and the nature of the occupation. The writer knows of no sampling strategies which would be adequate for the excavated evidence illustrated in figures 1, 2, 3, 4, 15, 18,70,76,82, 83, 84 and the end papers of this book.

Nevertheless, it would be patently ludicrous to take a total sample of every type of evidence. A total soil sample would mean keeping the whole spoil heap, while the labour involved in recording a total seed or pollen sample can be demonstrated statistically to be pointless. The problem then resolves itself into a determination of the size of sample of each type of evidence which is valid. For example, at Wroxeter all pottery sherds are kept, as are all animal bones, because specialist opinion is currently divided on the validity of sampling such assemblages, and we are only at the beginning of a very long-term investigation of the site. It may well be that, when this pottery is well known and a large collection has been made, sampling strategies will be initiated. Similarly, it may one day be considered unproductive to keep and examine all the animal bones, and sampling strategies for these will be devised. However, sampling for organic remains like seeds and charcoals, insects, snails etc. is based on criteria such as the apparent importance of the feature, e.g. a buried soil, a hearth, the filling of a pit, or a waterlogged context, together with a horizontal distribution which covers the various areas of the site with their varied structures and uses. Here the sampling is carried out within the context of a total excavation.

The case is different if the site is to be destroyed and a rescue excavation is mounted. Here, a whole range of sampling techniques may be deployed, aimed at the site's subsistence, economy, diet and industry, technology, trading links as evidenced by pottery and other artefacts, animal bones and other faunal remains, together with the evidence for the natural and man-made environment. Such sampling is, however, less likely to answer questions of the site's structures and their inter-relationships, nor to relate the sampled evidence to the structures.

Faced with the destruction of a large and complex site a number of interrelated decisions have to be made. These will be based on the expected survival (or not) of the structural remains and their nature, the likely survival of organic material, the expected density of artefacts such as potsherds (a Roman site as opposed to a Bronze Age site, for example), and the amount of information already available about this type of site in the region—an early Anglo-Saxon site is proportionately more important in the West Midlands than in East Anglia (see Ellison, 1981, p. 11, for a suggested rank order of sites in Wessex).

Intensive and extensive sampling should be preceded by site evaluation which uses all means of archaeological prospection. (See Carver, 1981, for a discussion of the problem in the context of a town, and Cherry, Gamble and Shennan eds., 1978 for a comprehensive discussion of sampling methods and strategies.)

Nevertheless, when a site has been selected for excavation, whether total or partial, I believe that the questions should be widened as far as is possible to include all aspects of the site which might be recovered.

I am becoming more and more convinced that the only valid questions to ask of a site are 'What is there?' and 'What is the whole sequence of events on this site from the beginnings of human activity to the present day?' Any other question must only be a part of this all-embracing one. (See Collingwood, 1939, Chap. V, and particularly the example of the non-starting car and the spark-plug.) If one asks, 'Was there prehistoric occupation here?', an excavation designed merely to answer this question will probably do so fairly quickly but perhaps at the expense of later occupation levels. Or if one asks 'What is the date range of the occupation of the site?' then a series of cuttings through the whole sequence of deposits may answer this but only for those parts of the site tested; there may be other periods of occupation in the untested areas. One might ask 'Does this site contain a sequence of imported pottery?', or 'Is it a deserted medieval village?', or 'Was it a ring-work before it achieved a motte?', or 'What is the extent of the suspected mesolithic occupation area?'. In obtaining answers to all these perfectly reasonable questions, other aspects of the site may, and probably will, be ignored and perhaps irretrievably damaged. If, however, while keeping firmly in mind the questions which prompted the excavation in the first place, together with all the myriad subsidiary questions which are posed by the emerging evidence, we are alert to the possibility of the unexpected —the medieval cottage built into the Roman fort, the motte encapsulating a bronze-age barrow—we shall avoid finding only what we set out to find rather than what is there. On this point Collingwood's advice is less than sound (ibid.p. 124) and runs counter to the considerations that prompted this book.

If a trial excavation is required for some overriding reason, to produce evidence of dating of the structures rather than simply the fact that they are there and something of their nature, it will be necessary to empty features, and remove floors, foundations and other structural remains in the hope of recovering stratified datable material. In such a case, the recording must be especially rigorous. Only if each surface, layer or feature is precisely levelled and drawn with an accuracy of ± 1cm. will it be possible for a subsequent excavator to be certain of correlating his results with those from the trial trench.

However, no excavation can be totally neutral in its approach. We inevitably enter a site with some preconceptions as to what we hope to find and we constantly formulate questions and as constantly abandon them. The evidence as it emerges will pose new questions of tactics, and may even alter the course or strategy of the whole excavation. Whatever major problems we may have upper- most in our minds we must always be prepared to encounter entirely unexpected (perhaps unwanted) evidence, which must be treated comprehensively, and not given scant attention or even swept away as irrelevant. What is more important is that the unexpected evidence may present itself in an unexpected form, one with which we are not familiar or which does not fit in with our preconceptions of what might or should be there.

The scale and complexity of all but the smallest sites may deter us from total excavation, especially when the increasing refinement of excavation techniques can turn the study of one quite small site into a lifetime's work. Almost always in the past, research by means of excavation has been aimed at solving the problems of a site as quickly as possible, within a year or two, or at least within the lifetime of the excavator. Now, however, complete excavation is necessarily such a slow process that we shall not know within our own lifetimes the answers to many of the questions we ask about single sites, let alone complexes of related sites. Research excavations, therefore, must be planned for posterity, eschewing the quick answer and setting up a framework of excavation and recording which can be handed over, extended, modified and improved over decades, and in some cases, centuries.

I have in mind particularly the case of the Roman City at Wroxeter, where some 150 acres are being preserved for the nation. Total excavation of the city, spreading out from the central area which has been the focus of most previous excavation, would occupy at least two centuries even if the present rate of progress were to be doubled. Since all previous work has shown that each area of the city is radically different from its neighbour, the results of the work at present being carried out there cannot be extrapolated to any other part of the site. The whole will have to be dug in the greatest detail if the rise, heyday and decline of the city are to be fully understood. The same applies to many other complicated and comparatively unthreatened sites, such as deserted medieval villages, hill forts, and motte and bailey castles. We must be patient and work for the future, so that we do not leave our prospective colleagues a legacy of mutilated indecipherable monuments.

Sample trenching and gridding

To dig holes, however well recorded, in an ancient site is like cutting pieces out of a hitherto unexamined manuscript, transcribing the fragments, and then destroying them, a practice which would reduce historians to an unbelieving stupor, but whose counterpart is accepted by the majority of archaeologists as valid research. A single section, even of a ditch, can be grossly misleading, as anyone who has cut multiple sections will know. Many layers are discontinuous, appearing in one side of the section only or changing in composition across the cutting to re-appear in a different form on the opposite face.

Clearly it is not sufficient to dig a section either by hand or with a machine and attempt an interpretation on the basis of the observed vertical surfaces. The old archaeological maxim 'it will all come out in the section' is simply not true. Extensive excavations on sites previously trenched (eg. Dorestad, *van* Es, 1969, 183 ff.) have so often shown that the earlier conclusions have been completely misleading, that it is now clear that only total, or near-total, excavation will yield results which are not deceptive. One possible exception is the more formalised, stereotyped Roman building which may be dug in small areas, the plan then being extrapolated from them with some confidence, but this presupposes that there are no anomalous or unexpected buildings above or below the stereotype. Even Roman forts are now seen to contain so many unconventional, even eccentric features, that argument from the part to the whole is becoming increasingly hazardous in an area of investigation once thought to be comparatively simple (e.g. The Lunt Roman Fort, Hobley, 1973).

Too often a trench cut across the defences of a site has been held to reveal, in concise form, the whole sequence of events on the site. Subsequent area excavation usually shows that the facts are much more complex. One section of the ditch of the outer bailey at Hen Domen, Montgomery showed the ditch there to have been dry, V-shaped, and once recut; another section, 15 metres away, showed that there the ditch was of at least three periods, flat-bottomed and wet. It might have been assumed from these cuttings that there were three phases in the life of the castle, but five sections of the motte ditch, all different in their evidence, showed a minimum of seven phases. In some of these sections, drawn within a few metres of each other, varying depths of recutting had removed almost all traces of two or three of the earlier ditches; and careful collation of all the sections was needed to produce a solution which total excavation of the whole ditch system might yet modify (figs. 8 -11).

It is astonishing how close a trench can be dug to a stone or brick structure without revealing its existence. Take, for example, two short emergency excavations on moated sites in Shropshire (Barker, 1958 and 1964). In both, trenches passed within a metre or two of the foundations of brick or stone buildings, in one case the foundations of the Manor House at Shifnal, without encountering any evidence such as fragments of tile, brick, stone or mortar which would have suggested the imminent presence of a major building. At Shifnal, a subsequent trench cut at right angles to the first, encountered the massive sandstone foundations of the house. In both these cases, geophysical prospecting would probably have discovered the structures in advance, in which case the trenches would not have been needed, or could have been sited more usefully.

The problem for the prehistorian interested in the earliest periods of man's activities is a very difficult one, since structures are unlikely to be discovered, partly because they were flimsy and partly because they will have suffered far more from weathering than later structures (see Atkinson, 1957, 219-33). Localising scatters of palaeoliths or mesolithic flints depends more often than not on recent ploughing or other disturbance, and the element of chance introduced here may be compounded by test holes sited in the wrong places, where perhaps the flints were nearer the surface and were therefore more disturbed by the plough, giving a false emphasis to the scatter. There is no easy solution to this problem.

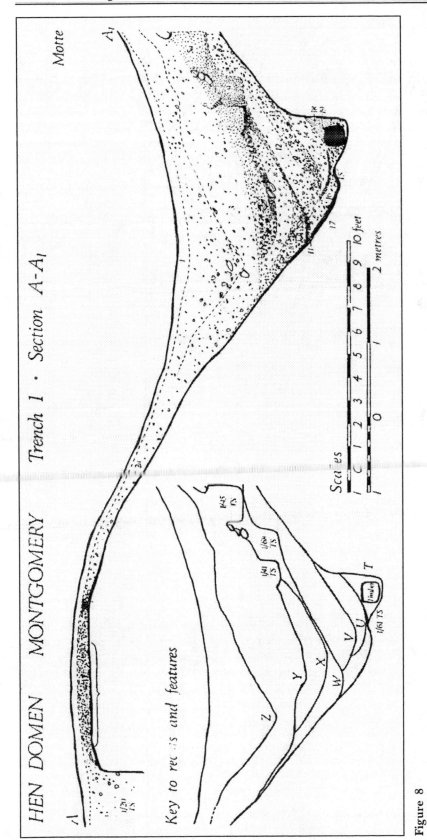

Figure 8

Figure 8.11 Four sections of the motte ditch at Hen Domen cut within a length of 20 metres. As will be seen, each section is different so that only correlation of all the sections produces a reliable picture.

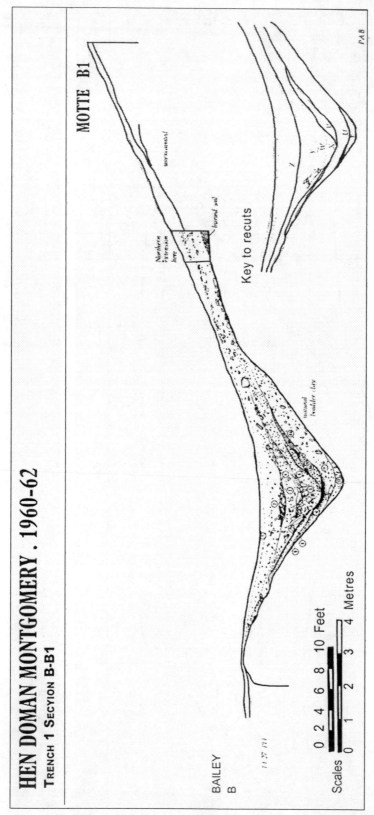

HEN DOMAN MONTGOMERY . 1960–62
TRENCH 1 SECTION B-B1

BAILEY
B

MOTTE B1

Key to recuts

Scales

0 2 4 6 8 10 Feet

0   1   2   3   4 Metres

Figure 9

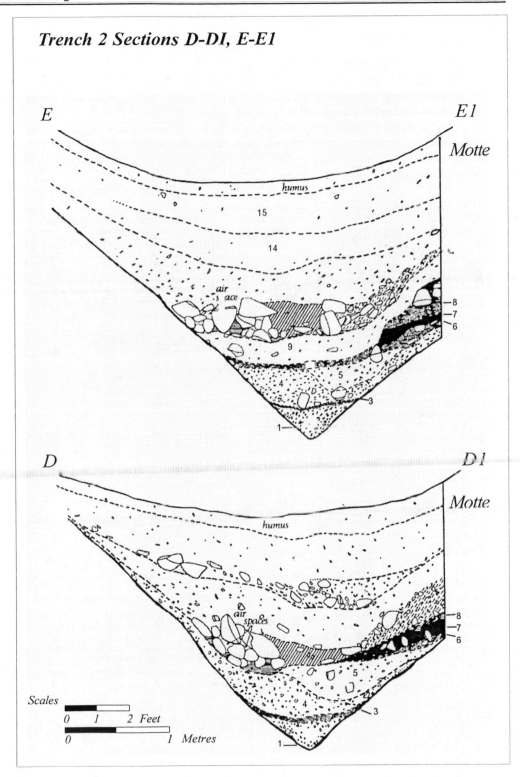

Trench 2 Sections D-DI, E-E1

Figure 10

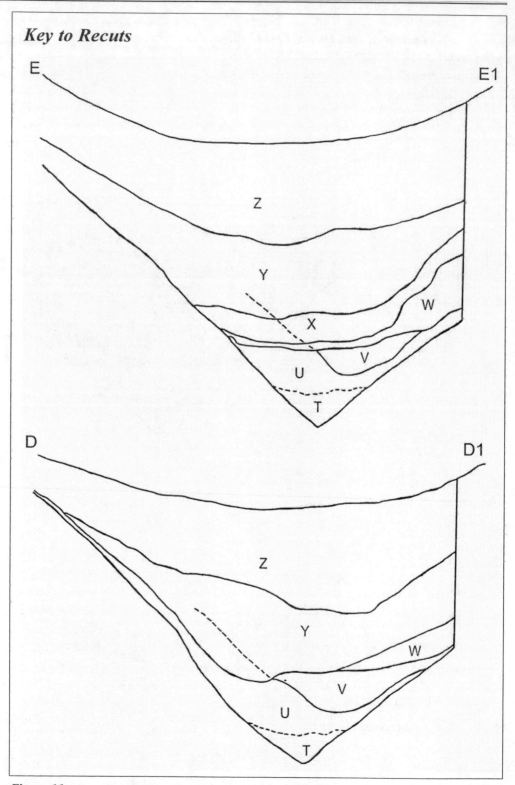

Key to Recuts

Figure 11

A further form of sampling excavation may seek to obtain environmental evidence from a sequence of waterlogged ditches or drainage channels. I have in mind the investigation of, for instance, a system of medieval fish ponds. Total excavation would be impossible, even ludicrous, but a series of trenches across the ditches, leats and pools might produce very valuable and valid environmental samples. Even here however any structures on the islands surrounded by these pools and ditches will have to be given the full treatment. (See reports on excavations on a fishpond site at Washford, Worcestershire, M. Gray, forthcoming and at Bordesley Abbey, S. Hirst and P.A. Rahtz, 1976.)

Nevertheless, trenches often give immediate and apparently satisfactory results. The broad dates of the site, the nature of its occupation; whether it had timber or stone buildings; the richness of its deposits and the wealth of its preserved finds may quickly become apparent. Thereafter the law of diminishing returns rapidly begins to operate. Six trenches will not give three times as much information as two, and the second, third and fourth weeks' work will not quadruple the information of the first.

What, then, is the value of the trench? It can test the site's potential for future exploration and it can check the results of geophysical surveys, or establish the depths of deposits and the nature of the subsoil. Although this information may be of considerable value, and although trial trenching may be unavoidable in the planning of some emergency excavations, I believe that if possible trenches should not be dug below the surface of the first archaeological layer encountered, that is the latest occupation layer. Only an excavator who has dug on a site already riddled with trial trenches from previous excavations will know how almost inevitably these trenches destroy areas of vital evidence; sometimes in the only places where relationships between structures can be tested. On other occasions they will have removed parts of timber buildings, unrecognised because the trench was too small in area.

It may be useful here to use an analogy. Imagine a room the floor of which is covered to some depth by an assortment of carpets, rugs, blankets, newspapers, magazines and sheets of cardboard, the whole covered with a wall-to-wall carpet. A person wishing to understand fully the layers covering the floor will naturally begin by rolling back the uppermost carpet and then recording the surface revealed beneath. He will then remove one by one each overlying rug, newspaper or blanket, recording its removal and the layers revealed beneath, until he reaches the floor. Surely no one faced with this problem would take a knife and cut a rectangular hole in the carpet and then continue this hole downwards to the floor removing the partial layers of paper and cloth as he went. How could he in this way know that, though he has recovered a portion of yesterday's *Times*, a whole Persian rug may lie a little to his right?

This seems a fair parallel to the archaeological situation, even down to the fact that, on most sites with timber buildings, the layers will be as difficult to see and interpret in section as the layers in my analogy.

There are some occasions, of course, when for sheer practical reasons a trench is all that is possible. This is particularly likely to be the case in towns, where the work has to be confined to the space between two buildings, or along a sewer trench, or to the hole dug for a manhole or so forth. Classic examples of such trenches on the grand scale are those dug by Dame Kathleen Kenyon in Jericho and Jerusalem where, short of a nuclear holocaust, it will never be possible to dig very large areas. The restrictions here are extra-archaeological, so to speak, and they are not trial trenches dug into sites which could, and might in the future, be dug more extensively.

It is argued also that there is some value in knowing the depth of the deposits before work starts. If this is really felt to be necessary then an auger hole or a mechanically bored test-hole will do much less damage than a 2-metre square trench. Such exploration only gives very limited information, perhaps determining the eventual size of the spoil heaps, or the number of lorries required to remove the spoil. Nor can it give a clear idea of the time needed to excavate the site, because it cannot give any indication of the site's complications, which will only be revealed when an area is stripped. In the course of an excavation, it sometimes happens that a deep pit of one of the latest periods is cleared of its infill revealing the stratification of the underlying and hitherto unseen layers in its side. This is of interest but must not be allowed to alter the strategy of the excavation, which should continue to concentrate on the uppermost layers.

Still less should holes be dug into the site to determine the nature of the subsoil. If the subsoil is homogeneous over the whole area it can be examined at a point away from the site; but if this is not the case, in drift deposits, for instance, there is no point in taking a sample at one or two points within the site; it will have to be recognised afresh everywhere it is eventually encountered. In many areas of Britain the subsoil changes so rapidly that is is pointless to examine it except within the area of the excavation.

In a recent excavation, directed by the writer, on the floor of an occupied thirteenth-century timber-framed hall, there was some doubt as to the nature of the subsoil on which the yellow clay floor was based. The subsoil under the garden immediately outside the house, and no more than 20 m. from the excavation, was dark red marl. This marl was therefore expected under the floor. The excavation showed, however, that the house was built on an outcrop of grey-green lower lias, a fact which caused some confusion at first. In this case examination of the surrounding subsoil had not been helpful but the reverse.

A way of examining the depth and nature of deposits on town sites, particularly large ones, without damaging intact archaeological layers, is to remove modern recognisable surfaces, such as concrete platforms, rubble foundations, floors and so forth, and then identify recent wells, pits and other intrusions into the underlying layers. If these are emptied it will be possible to observe the stratification in section at a number of places around the site. Cellar walls can be selectively removed and the stratification behind them examined. In this way assessments of the depth and nature of deposits can be made, and costings estimated without damage to the site. Since, in towns particularly, vital evidence often survives only in small 'islands' or 'peaks' left between pits and other disturbances, it is vital that these should not be lost in blind trial trenching, or their understanding jeopardised by digging them in trial holes, where their context cannot be appreciated. Only if such methods of prior examination fail should one resort to trial trenching, and especially to trial trenching by machine.

The problem is more difficult in the countryside, where recent holes are likely to be fewer, or non-existent. It may be possible to trace field drains (by magnetometer, resistivity meter, or even dowsing) and empty them as a first stage. Where stratified sites survive they are so precious that we should exhaust all non-destructive methods of examination before we begin to destroy them.

However, all these methods will only give a broad picture of the depth and nature of the thicker deposits at the places examined—they will not reveal the existence of the thin or discontinuous layers which are often of crucial importance and may even represent whole periods of occupation. It is, perhaps, safe to say that any site is likely to be at least three times more complex in plan than it appears in section, so that when estimates of time and money are being calculated a multiplier of at least three should be used.

A stronger case can be made out for trenching linear features, such as ramparts, dykes, and roads. Obviously it would be impossible to excavate Offa's Dyke or the Fosse Way completely, so a series of carefully selected sections across such monuments will give a great deal of information about their construction; and, if circumstances are fortunate, about their date. However, the same limitations which apply to all excavations do still apply here. A trench cut across an undated dyke may recover Iron Age pottery from the old ground surface beneath it, and if no other sections are cut a post-Iron Age date can correctly be assumed for the dyke. But for how much of it? It may not all be of one build; centuries may separate two periods of its construction, or two short portions of pre-Roman dyke may have been joined together in Saxon times. The evidence from the section only relates to the sectioned part of the dyke, and cannot be projected to a point two or three miles away unless very careful fieldwork makes it virtually certain that the dyke is all of one build (for a good example which illustrates this point see Hill, 1974).

However, a section cut only a few metres away from our original section may recover a medieval sherd from the lower layers of the dyke's make-up. Are we then justified in putting the whole earthwork into the medieval period? Is it perhaps a park boundary? Or is this section a late infill? Only more extensive work can hope to provide a satisfactory conclusion. Furthermore, sections cut across ramparts and dykes will not provide answers to important questions such as the existence, or not, of a palisade. Even Sir Cyril Fox, in his great work, did not advocate the stripping of a length of Offa's Dyke to see if it was palisaded although this would be the only way to find out.

In the case of Roman (or any other) roads the limitations of sectioning can be reduced by cutting wide trenches which enable each road surface to be seen in plan before it is removed. In this way a great deal more will be learned about the road than from a narrow vertical trench. The existence of buildings on its latest surface, or the traces of cart ruts, will be much easier to discover in a wide section, dug layer by layer.

The choice of site to be dug and methods used

With limited time and resources, all excavations cannot be total, so that partial investigation of many of our sites must be planned to give optimum results, and, to that end, must be problem-orientated, and the limitations of such excavations realised and accepted.

The factors which govern the choice of sites to be dug vary enormously. They will include purely practical considerations, such as the availability of money, and, more important, of competent directors and site supervisors, the length of time the site is available (which will determine the strategy of the digging) and its size and probable complexity. If the dig is to be financed by public funds then the site's relative national importance *vis-a-vis* sites not only of the same type and period, but of a totally different kind must be assessed. To make a decision on the importance of a small but complex and apparently unique crop- mark site in rural Shropshire relative to a development in the centre of a well-known Roman town in Warwickshire is difficult almost to impossibility, but is the kind of choice which is being constantly forced upon us. If neither can be dug completely, the amount of information likely to be achieved by a partial excavation of one or both must be estimated (perhaps incorrectly), and a strategy for each devised. This strategy will itself depend on a number of factors. It may be agreed, however reluctantly, that some aspects of the site must be abandoned if we are to shed light on those aspects which we consider the most important. In the case of the crop-mark site these may be its dates, and its length of occupation rather than the details of its structures. In the case of the town site it may be suspected that an earlier defensive line runs through the available site and therefore that this, rather than any overlying or underlying buildings, should deserve the highest priority. Note that in both these cases, and in many others which one could postulate, it is the *buildings* that take the most time to elucidate, and thus tend to be abandoned first. Broad dating ranges and defensive works (together with massive stone buildings) can be more rapidly dealt with.

Other factors which may affect the decision to dig entirely, or to sample, or abandon, perhaps with a watching brief, are the uniqueness, or conversely the ubiquity of the type of site in the region—whether it is an anomaly or representative of a common, generally recognized type; the paucity in the region of previous studies of the period thought to be represented by the site; its degree of preservation or its apparent relationship with structures of other periods which seem to overlie or underlie it, promising a relative stratigraphy. These are the considerations which will affect problem-orientated *strategy*. Problem-orientated *tactics* will depend on the practicalities outlined above, such as time, and the availability of finance and skilled labour. If these are not sufficient for a full-scale excavation, yet the site is irrevocably to be destroyed, painful decisions will have to be made as to what will be sacrificed and what, if possible, recovered. All such decisions, made before the start of the excavation, are liable to drastic modification within hours of the commencement of the dig, since the immediate results may be quite unexpected. It is, therefore, necessary to maintain a flexible approach and not to plough on, determined to solve only the problems discussed round the committee table. New, more important, problems may be revealed by the emerging evidence, or it may transpire that the evidence for the solution of the original problems is not there.

Sometimes we are faced with the situation, such as the construction of a motorway, where many sites will be destroyed or damaged, and only one or two can be dug. Here the decision may well be based on gaps in our knowledge of a particular kind of earthwork or crop-mark site, rather than on other more practical considerations such as the longer availability of another site or its clearer indications on the ground, or its state of preservation. The decision to dig one site rather than another having been made, the question of techniques will then depend on the time, money and other resources available. If there is only time for a short excavation it will be necessary to decide whether to dig a number of trenches across the site in the hope of establishing a chronological sequence, to strip off the top-soil over a large area in order to recover a broad plan of the structures; or whether to use geophysical methods, basing one's decision as to the method of excavation on magnetic anomalies or other similar evidence. If, in the latter case, magnetic or resistivity anomalies indicate the existence of a building in one area of a complex of earthworks, the decision to recover the plan of this building rather than attempt, in the time available, to sample the whole site for other equally interesting information will be a conscious decision based on what is currently needed in the archaeology of the region, or of that class of earthwork. If the opposite decision is taken, to strip the site summarily in order to recover the broad picture, losses of detail and perhaps some confusion of chronology must be expected.

To summarize: it seems to me that where ten sites are to be destroyed it is far better to dig two of them totally and salvage-excavate the others than trench or partially excavate all ten. Of course, the choice will be a difficult one and mistakes are inevitable; but the principle should stand in spite of this.

Total excavation of a non-threatened site, which inevitably means its destruction, must not be undertaken lightly. Trenching will mutilate it, and extensive trenching will make it virtually impossible to excavate the site properly in the future. Total excavation of half a site, leaving the other half for future more refined excavation is a solution that has been suggested, although the two halves of even a small site may be very different from one another in the length, intensity and nature of their occupation.

This my colleagues and I have found to our cost at Hen Domen (Barker, 1969a) where the quarter of the bailey now under excavation has presented quite different problems and a different sequence of events from the immediately adjacent area, excavated earlier. Another team of excavators, digging the new area independently some years after the end of the first stage of the excavation, would have been baffled (as we were) by the results, and would probably have concluded that our earlier conclusions were totally mistaken. It is only because we have much the same personnel digging the site in exactly the same way as in the first stage that we know that it is the site which is changing across the width of the bailey (a mere 30 or 40 metres) and not the result of a different technique.

The problem of sampling resolves itself ultimately into the question of the *size* of the sample. Ideally the smallest valid sample is a complete site, or better still a whole area of ancient landscape, but since we do not live in an ideal world, we have to compromise and accept all the external constraints which leave us with far smaller samples than we would wish for; and we must be wary of projecting those aspects of the excavated evidence which cannot justifiably be extended into the surrounding undug areas on whatever scale we may be digging.

Only full, highly-detailed excavation will yield all the available evidence, itself only a fraction of what was originally there. Anything less than total excavation must be problem-orientated if it is to give the maximum results, and, in my view, is only justified if the site or part of it is to be destroyed, or if it is too vast to be dug completely, when the excavation must be planned on the assumption that the rest of the site may one day be dug.

If a site is inevitably going to be destroyed, and time, finances or other considerations forbid excavation on a large scale, then it may be decided to sample for particular aspects of the total evidence which is assumed to be present. For example, it might be considered that the most important aspects of a large multi- period prehistoric site are not the structural sequences, but the environmental changes which have occurred since before the site's occupation up to the present day. A sampling strategy, based on extensive bore-holes and test pits may answer these questions in a very economical way, though other questions which may be asked will evade such a strategy.

Other strategies may be devised to sample pottery scatters over a large site, to determine the lengths of phases of occupation or shifts in their nuclei. A difficulty here is that aceramic phases will escape this net, and the picture thus become distorted.

Patterns of sampling pits and trenches are described by Champion in Cherry, Gamble and Shennan, 1978, pp. 207-226. To the present writer, who still remembers vividly the impossibility of understanding the evidence produced by the not dissimilar trenches and pits of the 1950s, such techniques must be used with great caution and their limitations fully appreciated.

So far it has been implied that all sites should be excavated in the same way, regardless of date or type of structure or function, that is, whether they are military, religious, secular, domestic or palatial.

To take first the question of period. It has often been maintained that excavations should only be carried out by specialists in the particular period of the site concerned, and there is some force in this argument. It is reasonable to expect specialists to concentrate on their chosen periods, and to dig those sites of particular interest to them. Only thus, it is argued, will the peculiar features of barrow or iron-smelting furnace be discovered, since the specialist will know what to look for. Here we have, however, the teleological argument, that people may find what they wish, albeit subconsciously, to find.

The opposite point of view sees the excavator as a technician producing evidence from the ground regardless of its date or function. In an ideal archaeological situation in which excavation was a scientific discipline with the excavator able to choose precisely the material on which to conduct his experiments, specialisation would perhaps be automatic. But this is not the case. With few exceptions our sites consist of a multiplicity of periods, and, more often than not, prove to be entirely different from what we expect. What is the barrow digger to do if he finds he is digging a motte based on a barrow? Or the medievalist if an Iron Age settlement underlies his deserted village? The situation is even more complex in towns. The urban archaeologist must be prepared to find evidence of any date from the palaeolithic onwards immediately under the pavement. It would obviously be ludicrous for a medieval archaeologist to abandon the site and call in a Romanist because he had encountered a Roman building, the Romanist in turn passing on the excavation to a prehistorian when an Iron Age hut circle appears. Under these circumstances, which we cannot avoid, the excavator must be an all-period technician, recording in meticulous detail evidence which he does not necessarily fully understand at the time, but which he can discuss, hopefully while the excavation is open, with his specialist colleagues. If this is not possible, the discussion will have to be based on the recorded evidence, which must therefore be of the highest quality if it is to be properly understood.

I do not believe that sites or monuments of different periods require differing excavation techniques. A Bronze Age hut should be dug with precisely the same techniques as a medieval long-house, a Roman villa with the same methods as a medieval manor house.

Nor do I think that the function of a building or site determines the way in which it is dug. A temple should not be dug differently from a palace; a castle should not be dug differently from a lead mine. It is only when the site is very large that it might have to be sampled. In that case the choice of area or areas to be dug may depend on previous knowledge of similar sites so that the maximum information can be obtained with the resources available. However, when the areas are dug I believe they should be dug in the same way regardless of the type of site.

The excavation of timber and stone buildings – are different methods required?

The fundamental principle of all excavations should be to remove and record each layer or feature in the reverse order from which it was deposited, over as extensive an area as possible. There will be some occasions on which this ideal must be modified. One of them is the presence of standing walls which may introduce complicating factors into the day-to-day planning and direction of the excavation.

To take a typical example: a large and complicated stone building may lie under continuous or intermittent layers of plough soil, rubble and debris, including the deposits of later timber buildings. These layers should be dug horizontally in the way described in Chapter 5. When the tops of the walls of the underlying building are reached the layers on each side become separated by the walls and the site divides itself into smaller areas which can (in fact, must) be dug separately, in some cases room by room. This introduces a complication, since the site grid is unlikely to coincide with the shape and size of the building's divisions or rooms. If the walls are standing to an appreciable height measuring over them from an external grid point may become tedious and inaccurate. In this case a subsidiary datum point can be established within the walls, or when the walls themselves are accurately plotted they themselves, or points on them, may be used. Excavation within the walls can then proceed like any small-scale area excavation, with cumulative sections taken wherever desired. This excavation of the levels associated with the building should ideally continue downwards until the pre-building layers are reached. However, the situation is unlikely to be as simple as that. If the walls have been built in construction trenches (fig. 12) these trenches should, in theory, be emptied before the layers into which they cut. But the walls themselves are by definition later than the construction trenches and therefore should be removed first. Usually, at this point, non-excavational factors enter. Walls, unlike post-holes, are tangible, emotive fragments of the past, capable of being preserved and displayed to the public. Unless the site is irrevocably to be destroyed, it may well be desirable to keep the walls intact. Under these circumstances it will not be possible to excavate those layers which run under the walls, and the site will have to be dug in smaller areas. This may make interpretation of underlying timber structures exceedingly difficult, if not impossible.

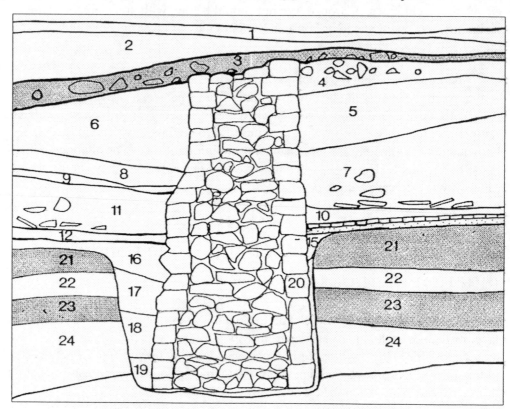

Figure 12   **Diagrammatic section of wall built in construction trench layers 15-19, cut through earlier layers, 21-24.**

At this point also safety factors must be considered. Foundation trenches, emptied along the lines of the walls, may seriously weaken their stability, and any attempt to dig pre-building layers may leave the walls standing on highly unstable balks. If the walls are to be preserved for eventual display, they must be shored professionally. This further reduces the area archaeologically available.

The situation is even more complicated if the stone walls have been robbed out in antiquity, so that robber trenches as well as foundation trenches have to be dealt with (fig. 13 shows a typical situation in section). Ideally the robber trenches should be emptied in sequence before any earlier layers are removed, but this is not always practicable. If the robber and foundation trenches have been cut through soft or friable layers the risk of collapse will be considerable. In this case it may be necessary to lower the filling of the robber/ foundation trenches a little ahead of the main excavation. This requires strict control of the digging and recording but guards against the loss of evidence which collapse would make inevitable. If resources are available the robber trenches may be emptied completely and then backfilled with sand or sifted earth in order to preserve them intact while the excavation proceeds from the upper levels.

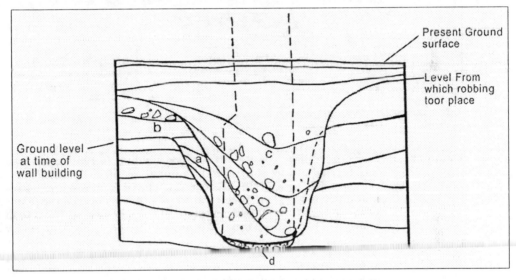

Figure 13   This figure shows diagrammatically a section the through a robber trench in which it is possible to distinguish: the ground level at the time of building; the construction trench for the wall, a: the accumulations of material with debris during the life of the wall, b: and the robber trench with unwanted debris thrown back into the trench, c; d represents the mortar raft on which the wall originally stood.

One temptation, which all excavators of stone buildings must have felt, is that when a stone wall or floor is encountered it is very easy to become careless of the fine details of stratification and to follow the wall or expose the floor in a sudden flush of enthusiasm. A subtle form of this aberration shows itself in the outlining of stones or walls by slight over-digging. Establishing the presence of the tops of walls or foundations is almost irresistible, but may destroy important stratigraphical relationships and therefore must be resisted.

The recording and interpretation of standing buildings is beyond the scope of this book. Nevertheless underground archaeology cannot be separated from that which is visible. There have been some notable investigations of standing or ruined buildings together with their uriderlying archaeology, particularly on the Continent where the opportunities for excavation presented by the bombing of churches were grasped and their interiors excavated before rebuilding took place. Recent examples in England have been the excavation of the interior of All Saints' Church, Oxford, by the Oxford Archaeological

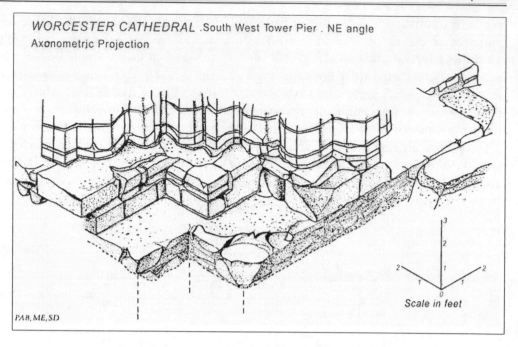

WORCESTER CATHEDRAL .South West Tower Pier . NE angle
Axonometric Projection

Scale in feet

PAB, ME, SD

Figure 14 a, b   An example of the excavation of a stone building. In 1981 a small excavation
was carried out to examine the foundations of one of the piers of the
central tower of Worcester Cathedral. The present tower dates from the
mid-fourteenth century but it was known that it stood on the foundations
of the tower of the Norman cathedral begun by Bishop Wulstan in 1084.
However, there is a record in the annals of Worcester that the new tower
of Worcester collapsed in 1175 (*nova turris Wignorniae* curruit). Victorian
writers were sure that this was the central tower but more recent opinion
asserted that it was one of the western towers. The excavation at the base
of the pier showed conclusively that there were *three* phases of
construction: first, a massive base of uncoursed rubble, clearly, for reasons
which there is not space to detail here, the Norman foundations of c.1084.
On this stood a foundation which, at first sight, appeared to have a
chamfered plinth of Norman date and to be contemporary with the base
below. However, closer examination showed that the stones of which it
was constructed (*d*) were, in fact, reused *abaci* from capitals or string
courses paralleled exactly in the nearby crypt of 1084, but here reused
upsidedown. Mortar samples were taken from joints at *a* and *b*, examined
and compared and shown to be different from one another. Mortar samples
from joints in the fourteenth century pier at *c* were also examined and
proved to be different again. Clearly there were three phases of
construction. However, it was also seen that the fourteenth-century pier,
which was a different shape from the underlying bases, had itself been
packed with reused Norman architectural fragments, including a column
drum, *f,* and a double capital, *e. g* is a floor, probably of the first period,
which has sunk and tilted, while *h* is a posthole, perhaps for a scaffold pole,
set in a pit, *i.* The probable sequence of events is thus: the building of the
first Norman tower, *I,* after 1084 and perhaps as late as 1150; the collapse of
this tower and the building, after 1175, of a second tower, *11,* on foundations
derived from the collapsed masonry;the building of the third tower, *111,*
in the late fourteenth century, again reusing Norman masonry, but this
time probably from the destruction of the ambulatory of the crypt when
the east end of the cathedral was rebuilt in the thirteenth century.

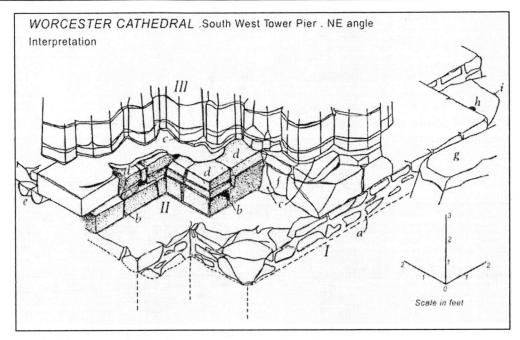

WORCESTER CATHEDRAL .South West Tower Pier . NE angle
Interpretation

Scale in feet

Figure 14b

Unit (Hassall, 1971), and the excavations of Rivenhall and Hadstock Churches, Essex
(Rodwell, 1973 and Rodwell, 1976). Axel Steensberg carried out a classic excavation of a
farmstead at Pebringe in Zealand on the occasion of the removal of the standing buildings
to the Open Air Museum at Sorgenfri near Copenhagen (Steensberg, 1952) and at
Wharram Percy the buried internal and external remains of the church are being fully
examined in conjunction with the standing fabric (Hurst, 1969). The Clarendon Hotel in
Oxford was an early example, being fully recorded and its underlying deposits excavated
before redevelopment (Panton et al, 1958) while a highly detailed study of the fabric of
Deerhurst Church coupled with sampling excavations has completely revised the long
history of this important building (Taylor, Butler and Rahtz, forthcoming). In general
though, the opportunities presented by the extensive demolition of buildings with long
histories in our towns and cities have only recently been grasped, notably by the units now
being established in increasing numbers. A recent example is that of Pride Hill Chambers,
Shrewsbury (Carver, Jenks and Toms, in preparation).

The excavation and interpretation of buried walls and foundations appear at first sight
to be easier than that of timber buildings. If anything they are more difficult. This is perhaps
because the excavated masonry presents more evidence in tangible form than the elusive
post-hole or fragment of pebble floor. Post-holes or stake holes which are not understood or
which do not fit a pattern can be (and are) conveniently overlooked in the final
interpretation. (If this statement is not believed compare almost any field drawing of the
excavation of a complex of timber buildings with the final publication.) They can after all be
dismissed as the remains of ephemeral structures such as scaffolding, or peat stacks,
temporary enclosures or whatever the fertile imagination can create. It is not so easy to
ignore fragments of masonry, brickwork or concrete foundation, which must represent
something large and solid, even if short-lived.

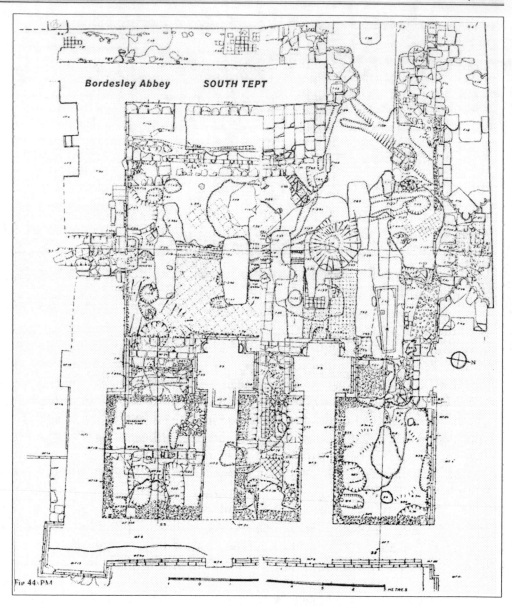

Figure 15   Bordesley Abbey: plan of south transept. This illustrates some of the complexities of digging a series of superimposed floors, and overlying builders' levels, all cut by a series of graves. The palimpsest shown illustrates the history of one part of the church over a period of four centuries. The complex evidence represented is not normally recovered on abbey sites, where digging has in the main been done merely to uncover masonry foundations (Rahtz and Hirst, 1975).

One of the best ways to learn about or to teach the complications and unravelling of the development of a masonry structure is to study a church with a long history, or simply to examine one wall of such a church. Even without a detailed knowledge of ecclesiastical architecture it is usually possible by a logical dissection of the evidence to determine the sequence of building periods, alterations and repairs. Add to this an acquaintance with the styles of church architecture and the relative periods of building

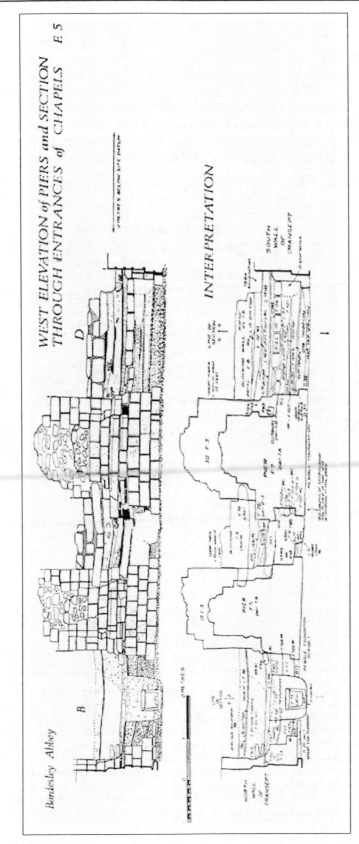

Figure 16   Bordesley Abbey: west elevation of piers and section through entrances of Chapels (E5). This illustrates the recording, stone by stone, of the elevations of a complex masonry structure, together with sections of layers and features accumulating between masonry piers on the plane of the elevations. It also illustrates how the 'objective' upper drawing of what is actually seen is supplemented by the 'subjective' naming and interpretation in the lower drawing. Neither part of this drawing would be adequate by itself. Together they supply the information needed; combined in one drawing, however, they would be very confusing (Rahtz and Hirst, 1915).

can be given dating brackets. As in excavated buildings and foundations, the interpretation of standing buildings is very often complicated by repairs, late renovations in earlier styles or reused fragments of earlier stonework or sculpture.

Differences in types of masonry, of stone, of mortars, of stone dressing, and the existence of butt or bonded joints must all be looked for and recorded with the same meticulous detail that is given by the excavator to the recording of a series of thinly stratified floors or groups of stakeholes. The only satisfactory way to record and study masonry is by a stone-by-stone drawing annotated with the types of stone, mortar samples and other relevant detail. In the case of large expanses of standing masonry or brickwork photogrammetry is a fast and accurate method of recording the elevations.

If all that is left of a complex of masonry buildings is a series of robber trenches, these must be excavated with the same attention to detail which is given to the rest of the site. It is not enough merely to empty them along their length in order to obtain the outlines of the former buildings.

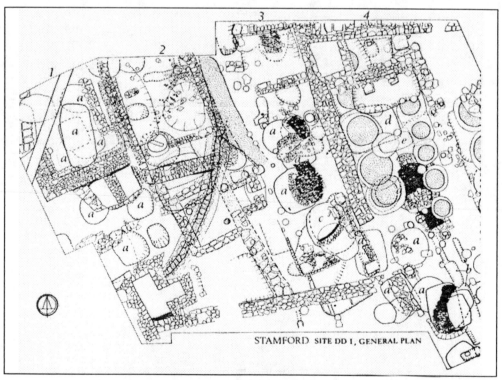

STAMFORD SITE DD I, GENERAL PLAN

Figure 17   St Martin's, Stamford, 1968. The drawing shows a typical urban situation in which five rectangular buildings dating from the thirteenth-fourteenth centuries with later cross walls inserted overly Saxo-Norman pits ('a' on plan) and timber slots ('b' on plan). The tilefloored ovens are thirteenth- fourteenth century and the tannery pits ('e') are fifteenth- sixteenth century and are associated with the re-use of Building 4. Other superimposed walls and features are nineteenth-twentieth century. Although this is not an example of the very complex situations sometimes found on urban sites, which often span two millennia, it illustrates graphically the contrast with rural sites such as Moel y Gaer, fig. 30 and Belle Tout, figs. 58-9, or the sort of timber buildings encountered at York, figs. 80-1 or Wroxeter, figs. 82-5.

Close study of the back-filled material and its stratification will give information about the mortar used in the robbed wall, about the direction from which the back-filling was made, about the level and therefore perhaps the date from which the robbing was carried out, and whether the robbing was carried out in two or more stages. It may also yield dating evidence in the form of coins or pottery. Careful trowelling of the bottom of the robber trench may reveal the imprints of the stones, bricks or tiles which formed the structure.

The excavation of the Old and New Minsters at Winchester was a brilliant example of the way in which robber trenches can be made to yield the maximum information (see Biddle and Kølbye-Biddle, 1969, and interim reports in *The Antiquaries Journal*, 1964-75).

CHAPTER

7

The Processes of Excavation

Introduction

Here Barker provides a practical guide to excavation, starting with necessary tools and extending to the manner in which surfaces are removed, identified and understood, with special attention to features within them and cut through them, reading the dressed sections, and the recording of layers forming a cumulative section. Other issues discussed are the special treatment of waterlogged material, and graves/cemeteries. Finally, he gives suggestions as to the way in which a working site may be organized efficiently.

T his chapter describes the methods and processes of a long-term, highly-detailed excavation. Under present circumstances, when a great proportion of all excavations are carried out under rescue conditions, few of us are fortunate enough to have at our disposal the time and resources to dig at the pace dictated by the nature and complexity of the site, but unless we keep the ideal situation firmly in mind during even the most rushed salvage dig we will lose more information than is necessary. Just as 'all art constantly aspires towards the condition of music', all excavation should aspire towards the condition of total excavation. The excavator's aim should be to explain the origin of every layer and feature he encounters whether it be structural or natural; made by man, animal or insect, accidental or purposeful. It is not enough merely to excavate and explain the structural remains without attempting to understand the processes of accumulation, change and destruction to which they have been continuously subjected. There will always be many aspects of the site which are not fully understood, and others which will be ambiguous in interpretation; but the effort to explain the smallest observed phenomenon will help considerably towards a fuller understanding of the site and its history.

The principle of all excavation, large or small, is to remove the superimposed layers one by one in the reverse order from that in which they were deposited, recording each in as much detail as is necessary to reconstruct, in theory at least, the site layer by layer, complete with its features and finds, long after the actual process of excavation has destroyed it. Only by doing this can we obtain sufficient evidence to begin to understand the evolution of the stratification of the site, let alone interpret its periods and structures.

In any excavation it is a good general rule to regard all observable features as equally significant until they are proved not to be. Only in this way may rubble spreads prove to be building platforms, lines of stones to mark the edges of structures, gaps in the finds plots the sites of buildings, and so on. The alternative is to go for the immediately obvious structures, with the considerable risk of missing equally vital, though more tenuous, evidence (e.g. fig. 18).

The key to all good excavation is the scrupulous cleanliness of the excavated surface. Soil is, regrettably, opaque. A layer of dust or mud only a few millimetres thick will obscure all but the grossest differences in colour and texture. This is why most surfaces are at their best when newly trowelled and why it is useless to use a brush in wet weather. The cleanliness of the surface is so important that site supervisors should require trowellers to go over the surface time and again if necessary until, colloquially, they could eat off it. Sometimes though, stony or rubble layers 'improve with keeping', as they are washed by rain. The improvement in the cleanliness of the extensive rubble layers on the baths basilica site at Wroxeter, currently being excavated (1982), is very marked after a winter's rain, though the individual stones were cleaned as thoroughly as possible during the excavation. Trial hosing of stony surfaces will show if they may be cleaned in this way without damage.

As little spoil as possible should accumulate on the site. It should be the rule, followed wherever possible, that each troweller only accumulates as much spoil as will fill a hand-shovel before it is removed to the bucket, sieve or barrow. In this way the site is kept clean, and the spoil does not get trodden or knelt into the surface. It is sensible to use kneeling mats when trowelling, as they save the knees from becoming sore after long periods of work and, more important, protect them from damp. Rheumatism and arthritis are the occupational diseases of the long-term digger and every precaution should be taken to avoid them.

Tools

The trowel is the fundamental excavation tool. Whatever supplementary tools, such as knives, teaspoons, ladles and the like may be used, the small (3"- 4" long) trowel is the most versatile implement in the hands of the competent digger. The art of trowelling can only be taught in the field, so that if newcomers to archaeology are employed it is a very good idea to use the monitorial system whereby inexperienced trowellers are set to work next to or between experienced ones who will be specifically told to teach them by example. This process considerably lightens the teaching burden of the site supervisors who, nevertheless, keep overall control. The beginner should be taught to use the trowel delicately or strongly, as circumstances dictate, to use the point, either with a scraping motion, or a chopping, digging one, or to clean a horizontal surface with the straight edge with millimetre accuracy.

The basic advantage of the small trowel is that it allows much greater pressure to be put on its point than on that of the 5" or 6" trowel, when, for instance the layer to be removed is clayey, or pebbly. It is also capable of much greater delicacy if a new, more vulnerable surface or a fragile find is encountered. On sandy sites, however, the flat edge of a large trowel may be the most useful hand tool.

The hand-brush is an essential adjunct to the trowel. When it should be used is a matter of constant judgement, controlled by the site supervisor. In dry it is easy to brush a soft or dusty surface and produce something that looks like a new layer, or even a floor, especially if the brush removes fine soil stones from between other stones which are in fact an integral part of the layer. Equally a stiff brush used on a dry clayey surface will often polish it, producing a surface resembling a floor. On the other hand, the brush, whether hard or soft, used at the right time can be a most delicate and subtle instrument. Churn brushes with very stiff bristles which project forward from a wooden handle, softer-bristle and plastic brushes of varying degrees of stiffness, and paint brushes, varying in width from 1/2" to 2", all have their uses.

Figure 18

Tenuous evidence. The photograph shows the north portico of the baths basilica at Wroxeter after the removal of an overlying rubble platform which had supported a timer-framed building. From the angle at which the photograph is taken four equidistant parallel lines defined by pebbles, tiles, mortar, slight hollows and ridges are visible. The most likely interpretation of these traces is that they mark the lines of parallel joists supporting a board-walk which had replaced an earlier portico floor of tiles or pebbles. This view is reinforced by the fact that a number of uncrushed OX skulls were found between the putative joists, suggesting that they lay in the spaces under the floorboards. It will be obvious that only area stripping would have revealed this phase in the site's development. (Photo: Sidney Renow.)

Like many apparently simple operations, brushing is not so easy as it looks and usually has to be taught. The stiff brushes should be used with a motion which rotates them about their long axis, so that the springiness of the bristles flicks the spoil from the surface rather than spreading it across it. It is remarkable how effective this technique is. The brush should be kept clean and once the surface becomes damp enough to clog the bristles with dirt, brushing should be abandoned and the surface cleaned by scraping alone.

In addition to trowels and brushes any implement which will do a job properly may be employed. Teaspoons, dental probes, scalpels and spatulas, all have their uses. Ladles of all sizes and a variety of spoons with the bowls bent at an angle are very efficient post and stake-hole emptiers. A blunt penknife will excavate delicately without damage and for really fragile objects a wooden toothpick might be the most suitable tool.

'The testimony of the spade' is a phrase which has come to be synonymous with archaeology, but in reality the spade is little used on most excavations except perhaps for taking off the turf or trimming baulks. A turf-cutter used in conjunction with a sharp spade will lift turf cleanly and in squares or rectangles of a manageable size. On sites where the turf cover is thin and the underlying layers stony the initial turfing may reveal the latest occupation layer almost immediately. In such cases the turf must be taken off very carefully in order that the archaeological deposits are not disturbed.

Beckford

Figure 19   **This drawing shows part of the excavation of a long stretch of intensively occupied river gravels at Beckford on the Avon in Worcestershire. The area illustrated was dug under the direction of William Britnell in 1972-73. The features shown include a Bronze Age linear ditch, early Iron Age settlement sites, Roman field boundaries, enclosures and a scattered inhumation cemetery. A later, medieval, field system has been omitted for clarity. The bulk of the topsoil was machined off and the underlying features were then dissected by hand, but a small area, that outlined at the northern end of the site, was dug entirely by hand. The drawing shows clearly the increase in the quality and detail of the evidence recovered by hand methods. These methods are inevitably much slower and are there-fore not often practicable on the scale demanded by most rescue excavations on sand and gravel sites. If machine methods are chosen for reasons of speed the resulting loss of evidence, demonstrated here, must be accepted**

Spades and shovels with D-shaped, rather than T-shaped, handles are more comfortable to use for long periods but this is perhaps a matter of individual choice. Shovels with metal shafts and handles can be obtained and will last a long time, but are cold to use in winter and vibrate uncomfortably when they strike buried stone. Some directors favour the use of a fork for digging in clayey ground, but it has to be used with extreme caution if it is not to do a good deal of damage, not only to the stratification but also to any objects it may encounter. Most people will need to be taught how to use spades and shovels efficiently. An experienced navvy is the best instructor as he will be able to achieve the maximum effect with the minimum of effort, and will work with a rhythm that can be maintained for long periods. It must be one of the responsibilities of site supelvisors to learn to use tools properly, and to teach their workers to do so too. Both spades and shovels should be kept clean the whole time they are being used, since if they are dirty or rusty the soil will not slide off them, and they will then become very heavy. Needless to say all tools should be cleaned at the end of the day.

Picks of various sizes are sometimes necessary, but heavy picks can only dig 'blind', simply removing soil or clay or shale or whatever in bulk, whereas small hand picks, either of the types used by miners, or those adapted by a blacksmith from coal hammers or other small hand tools, are a necessity when it comes to dissecting a rampart of boulder clay or a mound of chalk. Such small picks are ideally made with one end pointed and one end flattened, for chopping, and used properly, they can be delicate tools. The choice of tool for each job is ultimately the responsibility of the director or his assistants, for while there are undoubtedly great excavators who could dig anything with a 6-inch trowel, the majority of us only achieve the optimum results with the right tools. Coles, 1972, 166-75, contains many useful hints on tools and their uses.

Earth-moving machinery

A great deal of time can be saved by the use of earth-moving machinery, principally in the removal of the over-burden of topsoil or other non-stratified material, but also to speed up an excavation which is being conducted against the clock. Two most useful pamphlets on the use of machinery in archaeology have been published —D.F. Petch, 'Earthmoving Machines and their Employment on Archaeological Excavations', Journal of the Chester Archaeological Society, (1965) and Francis Pryor, 'Earthmoving on Open Archaeological sites', Nene Valley Archaeological Handbook, I, 1974. In addition, useful accounts of methods used on the Continent will be found in van Es, 1969, and Farrugia, Kuper, Luning, and Stehli, 1973. It is unnecessary to repeat here the information and advice given in these publications.

In addition to the more conventional bulldozers and front-loaders, mini-bulldozers and dumper trucks are now increasingly used to considerable advantage in the small areas left for manoeuvre on many archaeological sites.

The two chief concerns of directors using mechanical equipment on a site must be the safety of the workers and the possible loss of evidence due to the bulk removal of earth. Safety precautions are discussed on p. 105 below. The losses of evidence are not so easily dealt with. Only on those excavations where both mechanical and hand excavation have been used and compared can an assessment of loss of evidence be made. At Beckford in Worcestershire, the Rescue Archaeology Group, led by William Britnell, stripped a large area of prehistoric occupation before gravel working. The bulk of the area had been stripped mechanically, but one area 40m. by 50m. was dug by hand. The results are shown in fig. 19. The losses will be proportionately greater if the mechanical stripping is taken below the immediate topsoil into the junction between the topsoil and the subsoil (the B - C horizon).

In large rescue excavations it is common practice to strip large areas down to the subsoil and to record only those features which have been preserved because they have been cut into the subsoil at its present level. While this undoubtedly gives a swift and broad picture of the occupied landscape the losses here will be at their maximum (see p. 129, below).

Trowelling

It is often difficult to know how best to instruct trowellers in the removal of the uppermost layer. One cannot say 'take this layer down to the clay/pebbles/sand below', since there is no way of knowing in advance what underlies the uppermost layer at any point even if a visibly underlying layer runs under its edge. This layer may peter out, or an intervening layer may start a little way further on. To give an example: A director instructed an experienced troweller to remove a layer of earth 'down to the boulder clay beneath'. The troweller did precisely as he was told, and in doing so removed part of a pebble floor which began some inches from the edge of the earthen layer. The director, not 'the troweller, was at fault for giving the wrong instructions. It must be impressed on the beginner that one layer only is to be removed at a time. The only general and golden rule which one can give trowellers is to remove the uppermost layer until a change of any kind is encountered, or in other words, 'until you find something different, even if this is only millimetres below'.

It is probably unnecessary to stress that the troweller should move backwards across the site, so that he does not kneel on the freshly trowelled surface and so that he can look at the newly-revealed surface at the optimum time for the distinguishing of soil colour and texture changes. It should be the rule, in fact, that no one may walk on an excavated surface unless they have imperative reasons for so doing. Few archaeological surfaces will stand repeated treading and many will not survive the pressure of even one pair of feet. The necessary encroachments of draughtsmen, finds plotters and photographers should be kept to the minimum, and in some cases paths on to the site can be indicated, by, for instance, using large stones as stepping stones and avoiding fragile pebble surfaces. Backfilled robber trenches (or earlier excavations) are often useful means of traversing the site. If planks or Summerfield tracking are available, pathways supported on sandbags (or fertilizer bags filled with earth) will keep traffic off the site. Control of movement around and over the site is part of the essential site discipline which must be instilled from the beginning.

The direction in which the surfaces are excavated is of fundamental importance. Nothing causes so much confusion among diggers and loss of intellectual grasp of the site by the supervisors as people trowelling in all directions. The ideal situation is that where a line of diggers, stretching the whole width of the site, can trowel downhill. In most cases of course one has to compromise but I am quite certain that a change in the direction of trowelling has to be strictly controlled if layers are not to be destroyed, even if only in part.

Ideally, again, one would choose, if one could, to trowel from a more complicated stratified area into one less complicated, viz:

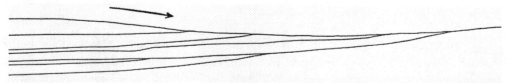

Figure 20

In this way the layers 'run out' and there is less danger of digging two layers at once, which may happen if one is trowelling in the opposite direction where layer A is found to run under layer B and so on.

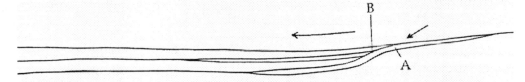

Figure 21

Unfortunately the situation illustrated is more likely to happen if one is trowelling downhill since there will have been a tendency for layers to accumulate downhill or in hollows. A typically awkward situation is often met with on a defensive site where layers tend to be eroded from the tops of the successive ramparts, to build up in their lee and in the accompanying ditches. If the centre of the site is slightly raised then the following situation may well be found:

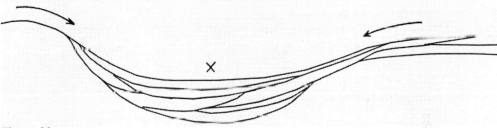

Figure 22

If we accept the fundamental principle that one layer only at a time should be removed it becomes hard to reconcile this with the sheer practical difficulties of trowelling. If one trowels in the two directions shown in fig. 22 there is likely to be trouble when point X is reached since this means trowelling uphill perhaps steeply. We have so far talked as if layers are neat, homogeneous slices that can be peeled off the surface of the site, but even on more or less level surfaces the situation usually becomes much more complicated and one is often confronted with discontinuous layers interleaved in bewildering variety and, worse, merging imperceptibly into one another so that their edges are impossible to define. In this situation one can only do one's best to determine which layers overlie others, and to do this one may have to explore the junctions of the layers in question, without damaging the site, by miniature trenching. If mistakes are made, and a layer thought to be uppermost is trowelled away and proves to run under one or more adjacent layers, the best action to take is to record the situation by means of a drawing and a detailed note and then proceed to remove the uppermost layers.

Trowelling on a steep slope, such as the sides of a rampart or a motte can be not only arduous but very difficult since the rampart or motte material will almost certainly have slumped or crept down the slope. Under these circumstances, post-holes, timber-slots and other such features will become distorted, so that it is necessary to excavate under an overhang.

The situation is further complicated if the post-hole has been cut into underlying structural layers of similar composition as the filling of the post-hole. viz:

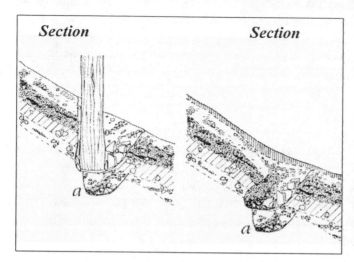

Figure 23

Shows a post set vertically in a sloping surface such as that of a mound or rampart. a is an earlier post hole. On the right is such a feature when the post has rotted and the upper wall of the hole has slumped. It illustrates also the possibility of confusing the fill of the post hole with the layers into which it has been cut.

Here it is almost impossible to avoid overdigging in order to establish the slope of the post-hole.

A somewhat similar problem occurs with the excavation of slanting post-holes in level ground, where a typical section might be:

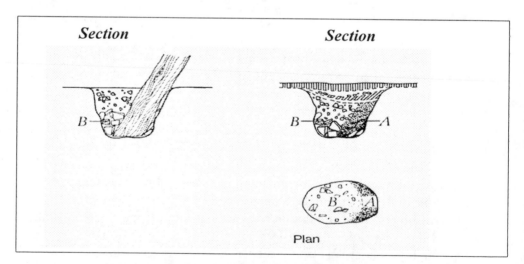

Figure 24   Diagrammatic sections and plan of a raking post showing the tendency of the packing to collapse into the post-void, distorting it. Such a post-hole is difficult to dig sequentially because of the distortion.

It is very difficult to excavate the post-hole, A, as distinct from the post-pit, B, especially if the material is sand or gravel or loose earth. The emptying of A will almost certainly cause the collapse of the backfilled pit into the empty post-hole. In loose soils, moreover, it is probable that the post-pit material will have slumped into the post-hole when the post is withdrawn or has rotted *in situ*. It may then be hard to establish the fact that the post-hole was originally slanting. A classic instance of such a misunderstanding was made in the excavation of the Viking fortresses at Trelleborg (Nølund, 1948) and Fyrkat where the outer posts of the large bow-sided houses were believed to be vertical, until they were re-excavated between 1961 and 1967 (Olsen, 1968).

Methods of soil colour enhancement, photography with coloured filters and an instrument known as a 'penetrometer' were all used to establish the fact that the outer rows of posts of these buildings were not vertical but sloping inwards.

However, this re-excavation depended on seeing the post-holes in section by cutting a trench across the site of the post-hole and its surrounding post-pit, viz:

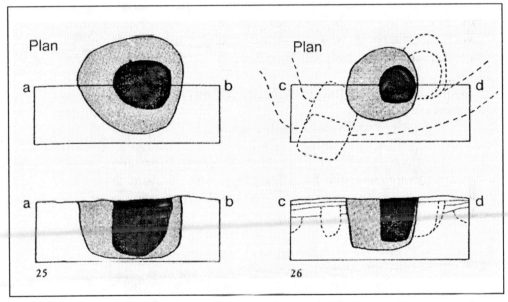

Figure 25   shows a simple the post-hole in a post-pit in plan and section. The situation is, however, much more likely to resemble 26 where post-pit is cut through a number of earlier features. In such a case, cutting a trench to section the feature will destroy the earlier features unrecorded, and although they will be seen in the section they are not likely to be understood.

It should be a golden rule that every excavational problem should be tackled horizontally, from above. In other words, do not dig in from the side of a feature to determine its limits, but lower the whole surface, if necessary a few millimetres at a time, until the soil differences can be seen. In this way much less damage will be done and far fewer mistakes made.

Natural processes of weathering and leaching, of soil formation and worm action, coupled with the effect of, say, the original occupants of the site treading on the newly cleared surface around buildings under erection, all tend to make the junction between the lowest layers and some subsoils, such as clay and sand, difficult to determine. As a result we probably all over-dig quite considerably in our determination to 'establish the natural'.

On some subsoils, particularly on sands and gravels, and permeable rocks such as chalk and sandstone, confusion is often caused by natural formations which simulate archaeological features. Solution holes look like post-holes, fissures resemble ditches, palisade trenches, or timber slots and ponded hollows can be deceptively like man-made pits (Limbrey, 1975, 281, ff.). On sites where the archaeological features themselves are filled with clean material, and where there are few finds, the help of a geologist or soil scientist is invaluable. Ultimately, experience may be the only guide, and it will almost certainly be necessary to grade the features into all degrees of archaeological validity from positively manmade to positively natural. When the report comes to be written care must be taken not to use too many 'uncertain' features in the interpretation, unless this fact is clearly stated so that the report can be treated with caution.

Care must also be taken in the use of the word 'natural' as a synonym for the undisturbed subsoil, since many layers on archaeological sites are natural in origin. Some may be so thick and free from artefacts that they may be deceptively like the subsoil. Gravel redeposited by flood water, for example, may seal occupation layers under many metres of entirely clean material. Even down-wash from a nearby hill-side can cover archaeological features with 'natural' silt. And, of course, the earlier the periods in which one is interested the more likely it is that the remains of human occupation will be embedded in natural strata, so that most palaeolithic archaeology is carried out in what specialists in later periods would call 'the natural'.

On difficult sites, where the layers are varied in composition and thickness, where, for instance, a very thin floor may lie on a layer of make-up 5-10cm. thick, composed of rubble in earth, it may be necessary to excavate the underlying layer a centimetre or so at a time, to explore it by means of a miniature *planum* excavation in order not to miss interleaved layers which may be structural. The strictest control must be exercised over this operation as it is only too easy to invent new surfaces (and even new buildings!) halfway down a thick layer.

If timber buildings are founded on rafts of rubble or other material, or their post-holes and slots are packed with stones or tiles and other debris, this sub-structure must be dissected and not merely stripped off until the next putative building layer is reached. It goes without saying that this is a slow process but it is often within these sub-structures that evidence of changes in plan or repairs are to be found.

When a stratified site is being dug it should, whenever possible, be kept 'in phase', that is, all recognizable features of one phase should be exposed at once. This will lead to greater understanding of structures and complexes of structures, since they can be seen and discussed as a whole, rather than as discrete parts reconstructed on paper afterwards. Naturally, there will be many occasions when features of more than one period are visible, or when features, thought at first to be contemporary, will prove, on closer examination, to be of different periods. Nevertheless, the effort to maintain the 'wholeness' of the site is valuable in that it counteracts a tendency to concentrate on the parts, and not to see the wood for the trees. Keeping the excavation, as far as possible, 'in phase' follows naturally from horizontal digging techniques, and is in sharp contrast to the vertical approach, in which the excavator tries to establish the sequence of events from the bottom of the stratification upwards as soon as he can. The temptation to have a look at earlier layers is almost irresistible to some excavators but it is a temptation which should be strongly resisted. We have seen that holes dug into extensive layers can be disastrous for their subsequent interpretation, and anyway the information gained by a 'sondage', however small, relates only to the area of the sondage. One may show that there are ten floor levels at one end of a building, but it does not follow that there will be ten at the other end—there may only be two, and it would clearly be nonsense to dig holes all over the floor to find out where the change in floor makeup occurred. 'Be patient; take it from the top, and all will be revealed' should be the motto.

Needless to say, if later pits, graves, gullies, post-holes or other features have been cut into the earlier layers, examination of their sides once they are emptied, often provides a helpful preview of the layers to come, without further damage to the site. Similarly, backfilled trenches from previous excavations may be emptied for a similar preview. If there is any danger of these emptied features or trenches collapsing they should be backfilled again with sand or sifted earth and lowered progressively as the excavation proceeds.

Sieving

However competent the trowelling on an excavation some small objects such as tiny coins, gems, intaglios, fragments of metal objects and other potentially important finds may be missed. In addition there is no doubt that some excavators, however reliable in other ways, are less sharp-eyed than others. It has been found that dry-sieving with ordinary garden sieves with a mesh of c. 10 mm. recovers a sufficiently large number of otherwise lost finds to make the extra work and time worthwhile. At the excavation directed by the writer at Wroxeter, in spite of very carefull trowelling, some ten percent of all small finds come from sieving. The sieved earth should be kept in a separate spoil heap for winter backfilling or other similar purposes, or even for sale as topsoil, for which there is a considerable demand in some districts.

Finds from the sieve will not be closely stratified, though, if each bucketful of soil is sieved individually, its general context will be known. As far as possible the spoil should be sieved from each layer or feature independently.

Finds from sieving should be marked as such so that the degree of their reliability of stratification is made quite clear. A coin or other datable object found during sieving of a layer from above which a number of layers have been removed can be rightly held to provide a *terminus post quem* for the layers above since it must derive from the underlying layer, even though its precise horizontal position may not be known. Such as assumption depends of course, on the careful and complete excavation of the upper layers.

Sections

Vertical sections

Vertical sections, just as much as horizontal surfaces, must be meticulously clean if they are to yield the maximum information. They should be cleaned from the top downwards (an apparently obvious rule not always observed), with the tip of the trowel and/or with the tip of a stiff brush. With a very loose section a paint brush may be sufficient. It is important to reveal the textures of the various layers by cleaning round stones, tiles and other fragments protruding from the surface. It is not sufficient simply to cut the section vertically with a spade or trowel, when protruding stones will be knocked out of the surface leaving holes, and perhaps causing miniature landslides, or, by being dragged across the surface, produce false patterns or textures. As Limbrey (1975, 271) has pointed out, the nature of the soils which make up a vertical section will best be revealed by using the tip of a sharp trowel in a chopping motion, rather than by scraping, which always tends to smear the junctions of layers. Under some special circumstances, in hard packed gravel, or where there are concrete floors, roads, layers of tile and other rubble in the section, it can be cleaned with a thin high-pressure jet of water, which washes out small particles and leaves a clean section with its textures enhanced. This method should only be used after careful tests on a small area. A soft brush and an air line, if available, can also be used on some loose and dusty surfaces.

Too much insistence has been made in the past on the vertical cutting of sections. If there' is any doubt about the stability of the soil there is no reason why the section should not slope at an angle sufficient to reduce the risk of collapse and the resulting loss of evidence. Needless to say, if the cutting is more than 1.5m. (5ft.) deep it should be shored and the Health and Safety at Work Act, 1974 observed (see also Fowler, 1972). A side effect of sloping sections is that in narrow trenches more light is reflected from the surfaces, making them easier to draw and photograph. Equally there is no reason why, under some circumstances, sections should not be stepped. Whether they are sloped or stepped it is important to record them in exactly the way they are cut, and not to make them appear more vertical than they really are, as if in shame at a transgression of one of the cardinal laws of archaeology.

As will be clear from the earlier parts of this chapter, it is my opinion that the cutting of vertical sections should be kept to the minimum. Nevertheless, all sites, however large, have edges, which may ultimately reach considerable depths and provide long sections encircling the excavated area, and on other occasions trenches and sections may be archaeologically unavoidable. A flexible approach is needed, in which no appropriate technique is outlawed on doctrinaire grounds.

The cumulative section

One of the greatest difficulties with horizontal excavation is to reconcile the need for a constant overall view of the excavated surfaces with the need for sections. One of the principal values of drawn sections is for publication, for the visual demonstration of relationships which are otherwise difficult to describe though they may be fully appreciated while the excavation is in progress. (It will be noticed, for instance, that most of the diagrams in this book are sections, though illustrating situations which are often encountered horizontally.) My belief is that if sections are cut, and they reveal relationships not detectable in horizontal excavation, then the excavation is a bad one. The assertion that many layers, easily observed in plan, cannot be seen in section has become a commonplace. It follows therefore that horizontal excavation, so long as it is sensitive enough, is always likely to recover more information than can be seen in a section. The reservation which must be added to this statement is that the section demonstrates the vertical relationships of soils and their development in a way which is not possible by horizontal excavation.

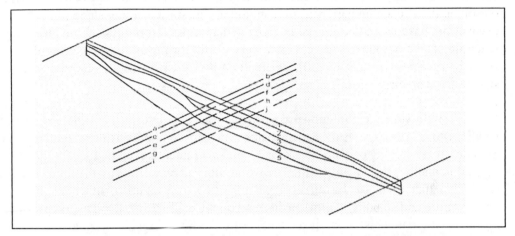

Figure 27   The Cumulative Section. Fig. 27 above shows diagrammatically a simple situation, in which a cumulative section is drawn by removing Layer 1 up to the proposed line of the section (operation a). The section is then measured and drawn visually and the remainder of it removed (operation b). This process is repeated, pausing each time after operations c, e, g, and i, to draw the section before proceeding.

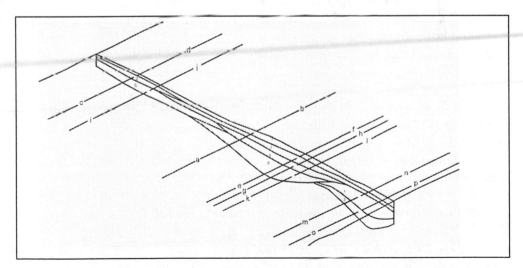

Figure 28   below shows a slightly more complex situation where, again, the operations are carried out in alphabetical order. Since the upper layers will have been removed before the section of each exposed layer is drawn it is easier to use a level and staff than a horizontal string to determine the upper surface of the new layer. Needless to say, the plan of each layer is drawn before it is removed.

How therefore to reconcile these two requirements: to see the site in plan and in section? The best solution, I believe, is a compromise, using the cumulative section. In this method, the excavation is carried up to a predetermined line and the section drawn. The excavation then proceeds beyond this line. Each time the excavation reaches that line in the future-the section will be drawn (figs. 27 -28). Needless to say, with this method, accuracy of levelling and surveying are necessary if mistakes are to be avoided; but it has one very considerable advantage over the section cut on a notional line, say along a grid line or at 45° to the grid, in that it can be sited to section particular large-scale features, such as a building, or a rampart, invisible at an earlier stage of the excavation. There is no reason at all why a cumulative section should not be started at any stage of the excavation, based on a line chosen to give the maximum information about an emerging structure. The cumulative section is also very useful for the excavation of large pits or similar structures (figs. 29 and 30), especially if they themselves contain floors or other subsidiary structures.

A slightly different solution used at Winchester and described in Biddle and Kølbye Biddle, 1969, 212-3, is to leave narrow balks which are continuously drawn and removed. This involves working on both sides of a 20cm. balk rather than up to a section line and beyond it, and has the advantage that the whole site can be worked all the time. The height to which a 20cm. balk can be left, i.e. the depth of the excavation on either side, will depend on the nature and stability of the deposits, and on the complexity of the features. For instance, where there is a complicated mass of stake-holes in each layer, the balks will have to be removed at each level if the stake-holes within the balks are to be seen and understood in relation to those around them. On the other hand, in heavy rubble it may be necessary to leave a wider balk. One must adopt a flexible approach which takes into consideration all the special problems posed by the site.

In most cases the edges of the excavation will ultimately form a section round the whole site, and one moreover that can be seen at once and drawn from the vertical face. It should be noted how many layers drawn in plan and cut by the edge of the excavation are not visible in the section seen at the edge of the site. Of course, it may be that some are visible in the section and have not been seen in plan! Here an inquest should be held.

In Scandinavian countries a method of very precise and detailed levelling of all excavated surfaces together with each of their associated finds enables theoretical sections to be drawn at any point and in any direction across the site. Good examples of this technique can be seen in Hatt, 1957. This method is a further step removed from drawing the section visually and I feel that the cumulative section is preferable. However since the site should be close contour surveyed at every stage, profiles and theoretical sections can be reconstructed along any transect if required.

The life history of a post-hole

Posts can be inserted into the ground in a number of ways. The most usual is to dig a hole larger than the diameter of the post, which is then inserted, sometimes against the side wall of a round post-pit, or in the corner of a square one, and sometimes in the centre of the hole. If the subsoil or underlying layers are soft the bottom of the pit may be packed with stones. The post-pit is then backfilled round the standing post either with the spoil taken from it, or with stones or rubble brought from elsewhere to hold it more firmly (fig. 31). The possibility that the post-pit may have been packed with billets of wood must not be excluded. Rarely, the post-pit may be dug the exact size of the post, which is then fitted into it. Occasionally, even quite large posts may be sharpened and driven into the ground like stakes, especially in soft, stone-free soils.

Where timbers are incorporated in ramparts or mounds and are designed to be part of the structure from the first, the rampart material may be piled around the standing timbers which would be either framed or temporarily supported during the operation. There will therefore be no construction pits. Subsequent posts erected on the rampart or mound will have to be set in pits, and by this are distinguishable from the original post holes.

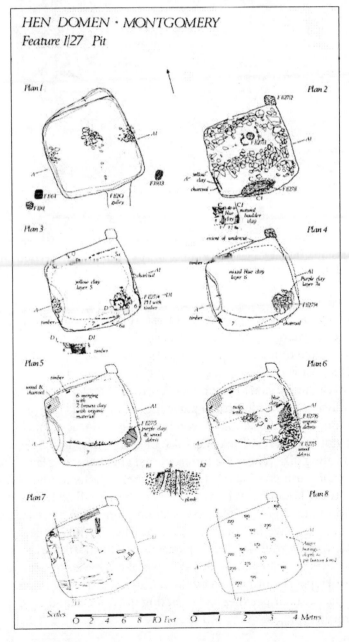

Figure 29

Hen Domen, Montgomery, Feature 1/27; Pit Plans at successive levels (see fig.30)

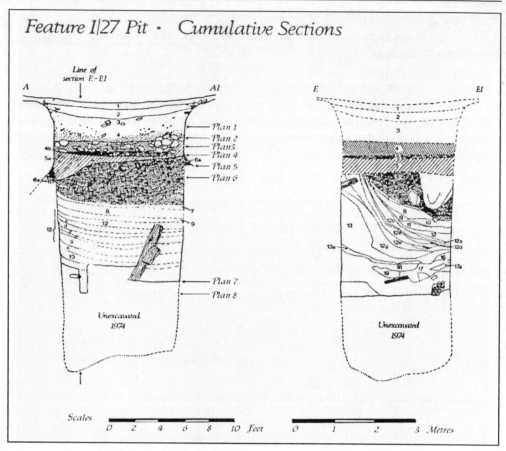

Figure 30   **Hen Domen, Montgomery, feature 1/27, pit. Cumulative sections on two axes A-AI, E-EI (see fig. 29).**

A number of things may happen to a ground-fast post. It may gradually rot *in situ*, principally at the point where it enters the ground. Waterlogged posts, preserved to the present day, may be found to have rotted away at the level at which waterlogging was not permanent. Alternatively if a post is no longer needed it may be extracted or sawn off at ground level. It may be replaced in the same hole, on a slightly different alignment, or replaced in a different spot. If it is allowed to rot in place the rotting wood may be gradually replaced by fine soil, due to the action of wood-consuming insects, and of earthworms passing in and out of the area. Dust and silt will accumulate in the upper parts of the post-hole making its filling different at the top from that at the bottom. Here the action of worms in 'sorting' the earth is debatable (see p. 117 below). Sometimes silt will be prevented from entering to replace the rotting wood, when a void will be left, which may outline precisely the form of the post. If the post is an important one a plaster cast can then be taken. Should the post have been extracted, it may be possible to detect the 'rocking' of the post to loosen it, by observing the displacement of the post-pit filling; or one or more sides of the post-pit may have been dug out to make it easier to get at the post. At Yeavering Dr Brian Hope-Taylor postulated the use of sheer-legs to remove very large posts vertically, after part of their packing had been dug out (Doctoral thesis, Cambridge University Library).

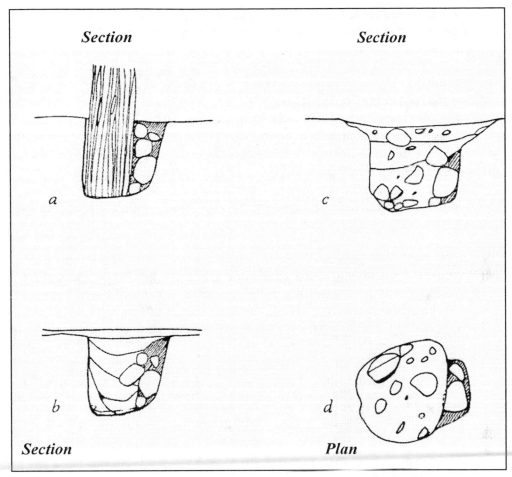

Figure 31   (a) shows a post standing in its post pit supported on one side by the wall of
               the pit and on the other by boulders, stones and earth packed into the pit. (b)
               shows a typical section of such a post-hole and pit if the post has been allowed
               to rot. (c) and (d) show the section and plan of such a post-hole if the post has
               been dug out, when it is possible that the original post-pit will have been
               enlarged by the robbing. The material thrown back forms a mixed fill.

When a post has been extracted the post-hole is very often backfilled in order not to
leave an open hole in occupied ground. This backfilling should be readily distinguishable from
the slow silting described above. However, if posts are being removed from an abandoned
site, ragged holes may well be left to fill with water, silt, leaves and other debris.

Alternatively, the post may have been burnt *in situ*. In this case it is probable that
the ground immediately surrounding the post will be charred or reddened. If the heat
developed was great, the burning may extend to the bottom of the post- hole when, since
combustion would have taken place with little oxygen, the post will have turned to
charcoal instead of ash. This, if found, must be distinguished from the deliberate charring
of the post, before it was inserted, in the hope that its life would be prolonged, in which
case the charring will be a thin layer between the post and the side walls of the post-hole,
rather than a thicker charcoal layer in the bottom of the hole, usually associated with the
charred edges or sides mentioned above.

All the events here described as happening to posts may happen, with modifications, to other features such as timbers lying horizontally in trenches, wattle fences, lined pits, and so on.

Some long-term experiments on the rate of decay of posts set in the ground have been carried out at the Princes Risborough Laboratory of the Building Research Establishment and their results published in Morgan, 1975. The rate at which wood decays depends upon a number of environmental factors, though decay is completely arrested if the organism is deprived of either water or air. If wood is kept dry (i.e. at a moisture content below 20 per cent) there is no danger of fungal attack. Equally, if timber is kept saturated with water, as it may be if submerged or deeply buried, fungal attack will be inhibited through lack of air, though slower bacterial attack may develop under these conditions.

Posts with their bases set in the ground invariably undergo conditions which fall between these two extremes and are therefore subject to differing degrees of rot. Woods vary considerably in their natural durability. The table reproduced below (Morgan, op. cit. table 1) is based on the average life of heartwood stakes, 50mm. x 50mm. in cross-section, buried to half their length in the ground. Timber of larger cross-section has a longer life and it is found that the life of buried stakes is roughly proportional to their

Table 1: Natural durability of some home-grown timber species (based on the time taken for 50mn x 50 mm, stakes to decay in the ground)

Perishable	Non-durable	Moderately Durable	Durable	Very Durable
Less than 5 years	5 - 10 years	10 - 15 years	15 - 20 years	More than 25 years
	Douglas fir	Larch	Yew	
	Grand fir	Lawson		
	Silver fir	Cypress		
	Lodgepole pine	Sequoia		
	Scots pine	Western		
	Norway Spruce	red cedar		
	Sitka Spruce			
Alder	Elm	Turkey Oak	Spanish	
Ash			Chestnut	
Beech			Oak	
Brich				
Horse				
Chestnut				
Lime				
Poplar				
Sycamore				
Willow				

narrowest dimension. Thus timber with a life of 10 years in 50mm. x 50mm. stakes would be expected to last 15 years in 75mm. x 150mm. size. A massive post 350mm. x 350mm. should, on this reckoning, be expected to last 70 years.*

It should be born in mind that this classification refers only to the heart of wood, and that the sapwood of all species (even the durable ones) has no resistance to decay.

In a further series of experiements at Princes Risborough untreated posts 100mm x 55 mm were tested under similar conditions against posts treated with various kinds of preservative. The results for untreated posts are tabulated blow

Table 2: Percentage failure				
	18 years	20 years	34 years	36 years
Oak	15	25	45	60
Scots pine	80	95	100	100
Douglas fir	85	100	100	100
Beech	100	100	100	100

It will be seen that the figures for oak are rather better in this experiment than Table 1 would suggest. However the life of a timber building is dependent on all its major timbers, so that if even 15 per cent of its posts have decayed after 18 years (Table 2) drastic repairs or complete rebuilding will be necessary.

Sometimes post holes are found with charcoal around their sides and it has been suggested that attempts have been made to prolong the life of the posts by charring them before they were buried. Experiments with charred posts' give the following results (Morgan, Table 3, 24):

This table shows that charring increases the life of posts made of softwood, but not of two of the hardwoods tested, including oak, the most commonly used medieval building timber. Although insufficient evidence for the species of timber used in ancient buildings is available, clearly the figures quoted in the tables above should be considered when estimates of the probable life of wooden buildings are being made.

Table 3: Average life of fence posts given in years								
	Oak1	Beech	Birch	Corsican Pine	Scots Pine	Douglas Fir	Spruce	Jap Larch
End charred	8	4	3	4	5	8	7	10
Untreated Controls	8	4	2	3	5	3	5	6

* These approximations will, of course be affected by the position of the post in the building. Aisle posts, completely enclosed under a roof, and buried in a dry floor, can be expected to last much longer than wall posts exposed, at least on one side, to the elements. Evidence of such differences has been observed, for instance in the West Hall at Cheddar (Rahtz, 1964) where the north wall posts were renewed while the aisle posts were retained.

Special problems

The excavation of structural features

Post-holes and pits normally appear as shapes differentiated from the surrounding area by colour or texture or both. However, not every dark patch is a post-hole, and the features must be dissected in order to establish their character. There are a number of ways of doing this. One is to section them either on one or two axes thus: removing either half or two quadrants of the fill to the bottom of the hole when it is possible to draw sections A-B and/or C-D.

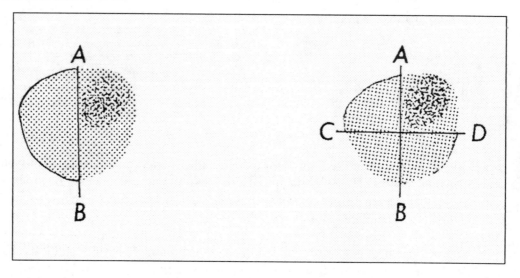

Unfortunately it may be that the feature is a post-pit (as the drawings indicate) and that the post-hole may lie completely in either the excavated or the unexcavated portion. In either case no vertical section of the post-hole is seen, which is a disadvantage in rescue excavation, since although removing only half the fill may halve the work, it might recover less than half of the evidence.

If the post-hole can be seen in the post-pit at the surface it may then be sectioned across an axis which cuts both (fig. 000).

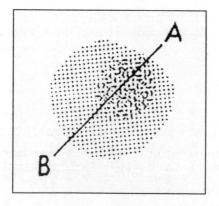

Another method, much used in some rescue excavations because it can be applied more mechanically, is to reduce the filling of the feature 5 cm. or so at a time, drawing the series of resultant plans (fig. 34 below).

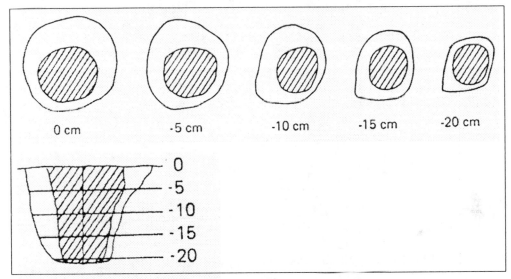

| 0 cm | -5 cm | -10 cm | -15 cm | -20 cm |

0
-5
-10
-15
-20

Figure 35   The cumulative sections showing a stylized gulley with post-holes. It is decided to excavate it so that one longitudinal and two transverse sections can be drawn. Segments 1, 2 and 3 are removed first and the exposed faces of layer 1 are drawn. Segments 4, 5 and 6, are then removed, and the plan is drawn (this stage is not illustrated). Segments 7, 8 and 9 are removed and the process is repeated. When 10, 11, and 12 are removed dark patches, possibly indicative of post-holes, are seen and drawn in plan. The post-holes are themselves quadranted, and drawn in section and plan before 13, 14, 15, 16, and 17 are removed. The process is repeated until the feature is cleared either down to the undisturbed subsoil or until the layers into which it was originally cut have been fully exposed.

The advantage of this method is that the feature can be reconstructed three-dimensionally with some accuracy, especially if the excavated levels are close together. But it requires considerable skill and vigilance on the part of the troweller to ensure that finds from the post-bole are not confused with finds from the post-pit since they may be crucial in dating, and there may be as much as half a century between the digging of the post-pit and the eventual filling of the post-hole. If the post-hole or pit is large enough the methods can be combined and cumulative sections drawn along any required axes. This method has the added advantage that the line of the section can be changed if circumstances require it; for example, if the post-pit proves to contain two post-holes of different periods. The same principles may be used to excavate the other features cut into the sub-soil or into earlier levels. Gullies may be sectioned lengthwise as well as transversely, and cumulative sections drawn at all stages thus:

Large pits should certainly be excavated in great detail if the maximum evidence is to be extracted from them; and here, presuming that the filling is in detectable layers it is better to excavate them separately, using cumulative sections rather than the planum method (figs. 29-30).

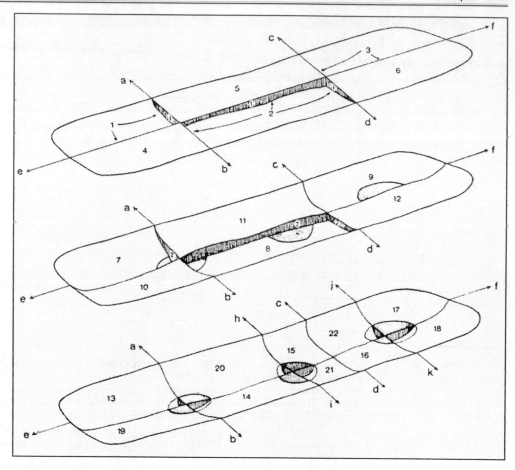

Methods of enhancing the soil colour differences

Every excavator of timber structures is aware of the considerable changes in soil colours brought about by the dampening or soaking of the soil with water when colours which are only faintly differentiated in a dry state become much stronger, making features such as post-holes or pits easier to distinguish. This is a different effect from that of the drying-out of the surface after rain or artificial soaking, when pits, post holes and the like may retain the moisture longer and thus appear as damp marks in the drying ground. This is an ephemeral effect which can sometimes, though not always, be repeated by a new shower of rain or a second spraying, followed by a period of drying.

Methods of enhancing the soil differences which are the only means of detecting post-holes and other structural anomalies have been tried with varying success. Olsen (1968) describes some of the methods used in the re-excavation of the Viking fortress at Trelleborg, first excavated between 1934 and 1943 (Nørland, 1948). Doubt had been cast on the validity of the evidence obtained from the earlier excavation and the site was therefore in part re-excavated using a number of methods to enhance differences in the colour of the soil. Use of a blue filter brought one of the post holes up as a darker stain (Olsen, op. cit., plate F) and another post-hole was treated after sectioning with hydrochloric acid and potassium sulphocyanate, which take on a strong red colour when in contact with traces of iron in the soil.

Olsen found that the use of coloured spectacles was not very satisfactory, nor did infra-red photography give very decisive results.Clearly there is still scope for considerable experiment in the detection of decayed timber structures and related soil disturbances. One of the values of long-term research excavation is that such experiments can be mounted there under something approaching laboratory conditions, usually impossible on an emergency dig. Moreover, the results of such experiments might ultimately speed up the excavation of threatened sites.

The excavation of small finds

The generic term 'small find' tends to be given to almost anything that can be lifted out of the ground, from a Roman *minimissimus*, 2mm. in diameter, to an architectural fragment, so that it is difficult to lay down rules to cover all eventualities. It has been well said by Coles (1972, 185) that every find is important and 'never more so than at the moment of its recognition when its precise relationship with other finds and with its containing deposit can be seen'. Ideally finds should not be removed from their surrounding material by levering or pulling, but should be taken out with the layer itself. Unfortunately this is often impracticable. As a feature or layer is removed finds may be seen protruding from the layer beneath. If these finds are not in any way fragile or vulnerable to exposure they can be left until the layer in which they are embedded is removed; but this might be days, months or even a year or more later, according to the size and nature of the excavation, so that a decision will have to be made on the basis of the lesser of two evils. If the exposed features/layers are given identifying numbers as soon as they are exposed (as they should be) then the finds can be removed from them and labelled as coming from these underlying features. If a find should be deeply embedded and yet vulnerable it may be best to cover it with sand, or polythene and sand, or re-bury it in its own soil until the excavation again reaches that point and the object can be removed with the feature/layer. Only in the last resort should a miniature trench be cut round the find in order to release it from the ground. Doing this destroys its relationship with unseen layers and may well obscure its real function, origin or derivation.

Often a find will first be seen in the loose earth just trowelled from the surface. If the excavation is being kept scrupulously clean, and one layer only removed at a time there should be little doubt from which layer, and, within a few centimetres, from which spot the find came. If, however, finds appear during the demolition of a rampart or the shovelling up of a hastily removed deposit, their provenance should be regarded with considerable suspicion. Sometimes characteristic soils such as clay or sand still clinging to the find may make its provenance more certain, but it would still be unwise to use the discovery of such finds as important interpretative evidence.

Again, finds often appear at the junction between two layers. While it is usual, under these circumstances, to assign such finds to the upper, later layer rather than the one below, a more subtle approach may be necessary. Imagine a pebble surface in use for a century. When it was laid, pottery and small finds contemporary with it and earlier than it become incorporated in it by accident. During its lifetime pottery and small objects and perhaps coins were dropped on it, some of them becoming embedded in its upper surface. When it was abandoned, another layer accumulated or was laid over it. This layer incorporated slightly later material (together, no doubt, with some residual material from earlier deposits). It is useful therefore to distinguish the finds (both pottery and objects) from layer A and layer B and from the junction of the two layers A/B. In practice, it has proved possible in this way to separate out pottery of the medieval period, spanning only a century or so, more critically than if the material from A/B had been labelled simply A. Nevertheless, it must also be borne in mind that potsherds and objects tend to sink through the soil, due to worm action, until they reach a more solid layer (see pp. 118 below), so that some of the material labelled A/B may have moved downwards. Thus the activity of earthworms on the site should be taken into account.

All finds, however indestructible they may seem, should be treated with the greatest respect, and their removal undertaken, as far as possible, without touching them with any tool likely to mark or damage them. Finds which may look most unprepossessing in the ground may prove to be of major importance when they have been cleaned and conserved. Every find, then, should be given equal care in its removal, recording, immediate treatment and storage.

Finds that have been lying in the earth for centuries will have reached a more or less stable chemical and physical state until they are disturbed by the excavator. Immediately they are exposed to the air, to drying, or moisture or any other change of environment, processes which have been halted or slowed to an imperceptible rate will begin to affect them, sometimes so rapidly and irreversibly that within minutes irreparable damage may be done to them. In the case of any find which is considered to be vulnerable the golden rule is to keep it in the environment in which it was found. This may mean leaving it embedded in its matrix of earth and lifting it as a block to be dissected under laboratory conditions. If this is impracticable, the find should be kept in conditions approximating in moisture or dryness to its recent environment. For this purpose sealed polythene boxes or bags used in conjunction with dessicators or wet wrappings are invaluable. For some exceptionally fragile or vulnerable finds immediate field treatment will be necessary.

An essential handbook, *First Aid for Finds*, has been published by RESCUE (Leigh and others, 1972). This gives short but explicit instructions on the immediate treatment and packing of objects made of all the materials likely to be found during an excavation, emphasising that 'with the majority of metal and organic remains deterioration of some kind is inevitable unless positive steps are taken in the field to arrest it'.

The materials and methods of first-aid treatment described in *First Aid for Finds* should be within the budget and competence of even the smallest excavation. (If they are not, the excavation should not be taking place.) It must be emphasised, however, that only immediate and essential procedures for arresting deterioration in finds are described. Ideally a trained conservator should be attached to every excavation, but since there are comparatively few conservators in Britain (and probably in the world), and since the annual output of trained conservators does not begin to meet the need, directors have to fall back on their own resources and stabilize their finds at least until they can be drawn, photographed, studied and handed to a museum.

The exacavation of fragile finds

An excellent maxim is to treat all finds as fragile until they are proved not to be, although proving that a find is not fragile may damage it irrevocably! This is a problem to which there is no straightforward answer. One can only urge trowellers to be vigilant and to ask for help if there is any doubt about the robustness of a find, preferably at the moment at which it is first seen.

The excavation of finds of potential importance (which will vary according to the site and the circumstances) should be photographed at every stage, and they should be carefully drawn before lifting. Such a record may be crucial to the eventual understanding of their significance, or their relationship with adjacent finds.

If a find is almost completely rotted away and is little more than a stain in the ground the only way to lift it is to cut out the whole block of soil in which it lies. There are difficulties, however. It is seldom easy to see how large the object is, or was; the stain may simply be the tip of the iceberg. Investigation round the object will destroy its relationship with its environment and isolate it from its contiguous layers. Above all one must not become so excited by the presence of an unusual find that the fundamental principles of excavation are temporarily forgotten. Later, when the object comes to be interpreted and its relationship to the site assessed every scrap of evidence will be needed.

Whenever a block of soil has to be taken from the site every effort should be made to record its stratification as it is cut out, and every stage of the operation should be photographed. Here the polaroid camera is most useful. The block may be firm enough to be lifted out on its own, though more often it will need to be supported on all sides with sheets of plywood or hardboard until a sheet of ply, hardboard or metal can be slid underneath it. In extreme cases the block may have to be encased in plaster of paris or polyurethane foam and then in a wooden box in order to get it out intact.

If, to all intents and purposes, the object has disappeared, leaving only an impression of its shape in the ground, a plaster cast can be made of this impression. A recent large-scale example of the use of plaster was in the re-excavation of the Sutton Hoo Ship burial mound (Bruce-Mitford, 1974, 170 ff.).

On other occasions the object may be consolidated in the ground before its removal. Ideally, this should be done by a conservator, who will choose the materials to be used with due regard to the nature of the object, since the consolidating agents may have to be removed in the laboratory before the object can be studied. In general, a 5% polyvinyl acetate solution in toluene for dry objects, and a polyvinyl acetate emulsion for damp or wet objects is recommended. The emulsion can be thinned with water, when it penetrates the object more easily and can be painted on in a number of operations rather than one thick layer. This enables the excavator to judge the effect of the treatment and to use the minimum amount of emulsion necessary to consolidate the object sufficiently to hold it together while it is lifted. It is useful to note that the emulsion hardens without drying so that the object can be kept damp during the operation. If a fairly large find, such as a shattered pot or a mass of metal work, it to be held together, a crepe bandage may be useful as it has strength combined with gentle elasticity. Needless to say, any fragile object should be taken to the conservation laboratory as soon as possible after lifting so that it can be given skilled treatment. Comprehensive packing instructions for all kinds of objects are given in Leigh and others, 1972.

The excavation of waterlogged finds

In waterlogged deposits organic materials such as wood, leather and fabrics are preserved to a greater or lesser degree due to the fact that their environment is anaerobic, and so does not provide sufficient oxygen for the support of fungi and the bacteria of decay, or for the oxidation of metals. Immediately preserved organic materials (or metallic objects) are exposed to the air they begin to deteriorate, partly due to oxidation but, more quickly, due to drying. This deterioration begins even while they are being uncovered and removed from their layer of deposition; while, for instance, they are being photographed or drawn *in situ*.

Excavation and the subsequent packing of waterlogged finds should therefore be swift and delicate. Sometimes objects such as preserved shoes, or fragments of wood can easily be detached from their matrix, but very often, in cesspit fillings or the bottoms of moats, the layers may consist almost entirely of preserved organic material: reeds, bracken, twigs, branches, leaves and seeds, together with the remnants of human occupation. If the amount of this solid organic fill is only small it can be saved complete, but in the case of large deposits the logistic problems of lifting and storage and the impossibility of working on tons of preserved material make sampling of the matrix essential. The preserved artefacts then have to be removed from the matrix, an operation which may be quite distinct from environmental sampling. As it is often impossible or highly undesirable to walk on the surface of the deposit, a system of planked cat-walks should be arranged so that they do as little damage as possible to the deposit. The excavators can then lie on the cat-walks in order to dissect and remove the layers. If the deposit is in a deep cutting, such as a ditch section, or in a cesspit or well, it should not be difficult to erect scaffolding from which a cradle can be suspended. The excavator or excavators can then lie on this cradle (preferably on an air bed if they are to work for long periods).

Where the waterlogged deposit includes extremely fragile objects preserved in quantity the problem of excavating them on the spot becomes almost insuperable, but equally the removal of blocks of the matrix involves the grave risk of damaging unseen objects while the block is being cut out. Obviously under these circumstances the larger the mass of matrix that can be lifted the less damage will be done, and if the deposit is of major importance a civil engineering contractor should be brought in to deal with the problem on a large scale. If sufficient funds are not available, the deposit should be left where it is until it can be dealt with properly. Only under salvage conditions should the matrix be dug out wholesale.

When waterlogged finds have been lifted they should immediately be packed in an environment as close as possible to that from which they came. Polythene bags and polystyrene boxes are the most convenient and efficient means of doing this , and both can be obtained in forms which are self-sealing and watertight. Self-sealing bags are made with white panels on which details of the find can be written in Pentel or similar pens, but they cannot be opened and resealed more than once or twice without losing their water-tight property. Polythene boxes with air-tight lids can be obtained in many sizes and are useful for more bulky finds.

Large objects can be made into parcels with heavy duty polythene sheet. A waterlogged bridge timber from Hen Domen, Montgomery, a foot square and 14 feet long, was fed into a large-diameter polythene tube and the ends firmly tied, so that it looked rather like an oversize Christmas cracker. It has remained in this tube since 1962 and, when last examined, was still in excellent condition, since the lack of air had inhibited fungal growth and the timber had dried out very slowly.

The lifting and preservation of large timber structures such as dug-out canoes, or complete bridge foundations is not easy but does not always require elaborate museum facilities if one is prepared to be patient. Timber will begin to deteriorate immediately it is exposed. Although the core may be extremely hard, the surface, to a depth of a centimetre or so, is likely to be very soft, and to be bruised even by the pressure of the fingers. While the timber must obviously be handled if it is to be removed from the ground and studied, this handling should be kept to the minimum, and the exposed surfaces kept wet by constant spraying, and covered with saturated sacking or similar materials at night. In the case of especially important remains 24-hour spraying should be maintained if possible. A good account of the large-scale excavation of preserved timber is contained in the Skuldelev Ship report (Olsen and Crumlin-Pedersen, 1968). Except in the most unexpected emergencies, the excavation of large waterlogged finds should be made with the active cooperation of the museum in which they are ultimately to be housed or, in the case of DOE sponsored excavations, with the aid of the Inspectorate's Laboratory. Only thus will the finds be guaranteed professional treatment.

The storage and safe-keeping of portable finds

This is one of the most difficult problems facing the excavator. The rescue excavation explosion of the last five years has added a vast quantity of archaeological material to the crowded and sometimes neglected store-rooms of our museums. As a result a high proportion of all excavated objects is rotting away, most of it unpublished. The training of conservators, the provision of museum or other suitable storage space, and the availability of laboratories are all woefully inadequate. A contributory factor in this crisis in conservation is the apparent reluctance of excavation directors to take an interest in their finds once the more important among them have been drawn and photographed. There is a largely unspoken feeling that from then on they are someone else's responsibility, probably that of a museum, although which one is not often specified. The days are over when excavations could be lightly undertaken, without a great deal of thought about the publication of results or where the finds were to be stabilized and stored. Excavation must be seen as a long and complex process ending only with the publication and storage of the data, and its interpretation and proper treatment, and the storage and display of the finds. It follows that arrangements of all of these should be made before the excavation begins. If a total lack of facilities in the area prevents this it is the *director's* responsibility to make adequate temporary arrangements. If necessary he must train a conservator in the immediate treatment of the material, and obtain access to a store-room for the finds so that they can be kept under the optimum conditions until disposal arrangements can be made.

Museum directors in general are acutely aware of this hiatus in archaeological provision but lack of funds, space and trained staff make the prospect of an early solution improbable. In the interim, excavators and museums must work closely together to make temporary arrangements, and to agree on their areas of responsibility. One sympathizes with the hard-pressed museum director who blanches at the thought of storing hundredweights of undisplayable pottery, bone, and formless lumps of iron. But it is no solution to keep only selected objects, rim sherds and the like and get rid of the rest, since we do not know what questions we shall be asking of our material in the future. For example, tons of Roman pottery, particularly body sherds, have been dumped from earlier excavations on major sites in the belief that they had told us all we needed to know. However, the study of Roman pottery is constantly changing our views on its dates and places of manufacture. Here quantitative analysis may be as important as qualitative. In addition it is only comparatively recently that it has been realized that a very considerable quantity of pottery was imported into Britain from Gaul, North Africa and the eastern Mediterranean in the late and post-Roman periods. Very probably a great many sherds from these pots have been dumped unrecognized and as of little interest. Storage of all the finds from very prolific Roman, medieval and post-medieval sites is a daunting task, but inescapable if we are ultimately to extract the maximum information from the material.

Excavating graves and cemeteries

Brothwell (1963) has written the standard text-book on the excavation of human remains and the reader is referred to this. However, he does not pay much attention to the recording of skeletons (and their possible accompanying grave goods) beyond advocating photography *in situ* before lifting. Vertical photography is preferable to oblique if there is only time for one photograph of each grave in a cemetery and ideally a stereoscopic colour pair should be taken of each burial. Very tall tripods with a reversible head enabling the camera to be attached pointing vertically downwards can be obtained and are more convenient to use than the larger structures described in Chapter 8. Since the orientation of graves is crucial in the interpretation of cemeteries it is most important that a north point should be included. Scales should be laid with the skeleton, not on the side of the grave. If grave goods are present the whole complex should be photographed in black and white, and in colour (to show, for example, verdigris staining on bones where bronze ornaments have been). Here oblique and detail photographs of the positions of ornaments, weapons, dress attachments, and so on will be necessary, if the full implications of the grave-goods are to be understood, or if it is intended to reconstruct the burial for museum display.

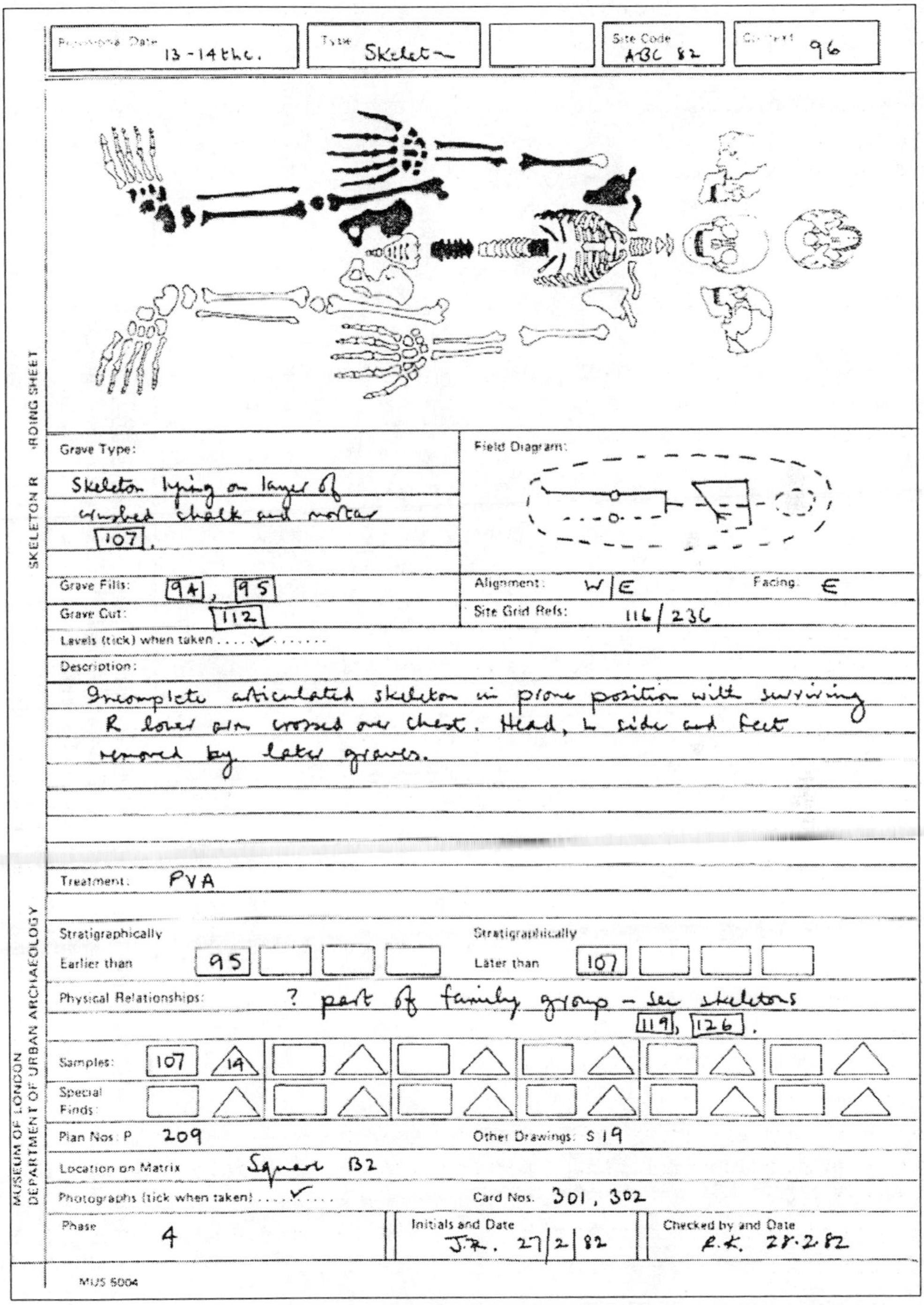

SKELETON RECORDING SHEET

MUSEUM OF LONDON DEPARTMENT OF URBAN ARCHAEOLOGY

Provisional Date: 13-14thc. | Type: Skeleton | | Site Code: ABC 82 | Context: 96

Grave Type: Skeleton lying on layer of crushed chalk and mortar [107].

Field Diagram:

Grave Fills: [94], [95]

Alignment: W/E — Facing: E

Grave Cut: [112]

Site Grid Refs: 116/236

Levels (tick) when taken ..... ✓ ......

Description: Incomplete articulated skeleton in prone position with surviving R lower arm crossed over chest. Head, L side and feet removed by later graves.

Treatment: PVA

Stratigraphically Earlier than: [95]

Stratigraphically Later than: [107]

Physical Relationships: ? part of family group – see skeletons [119], [126].

Samples: [107] △14

Special Finds:

Plan Nos: P 209

Other Drawings: S 19

Location on Matrix: Square B2

Photographs (tick when taken) ..... ✓ ....

Card Nos: 301, 302

Phase: 4

Initials and Date: J.R. 27/2/82

Checked by and Date: R.K. 28.2.82

MUS 5004

Figure 36 **The *pro-forma* for the recording of cemeteries used by the Department of Urban Archaeology of the Museum of London. The surviving bones of the excavated skeleton are filled in with coloured pencil on the outline provided and the position of grave goods can be indicated in relation to the bones.**

Detailed drawing of all the skeletons in a large cemetery may be an impossible log task, especially if the work is being done under rescue conditions. A most useful form, including a diagrammatic skeleton, has been designed (by S. Hirst, fig. 36), and this is

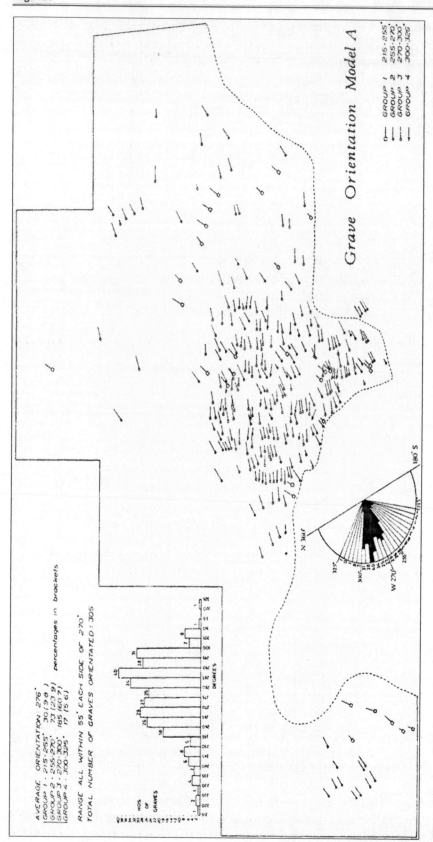

Figure 37   Cannington Cemetery: Grave Orientation Model A. This is an attempt to illustrate groups of differently orientated skeletons in a cemetery of the late and post-Roman centuries. The pie-diagram and (more effectively) the histogram show the numbers which fall within objective diagrams. They show clearly that the cemetery has a 'norm' of orientation between 255^0-300^0 (direction of head) with 'abnormal' groups beyond each end of this range, though they all lie within a range exactly 55^0 either side of due west. goes beyond this in interpretation. While illustrating the location of 'abnormal' groups 1 and 4 by distinctive symbols, the 'norm' is split on either side of 270^0. This is a purely arbitrary and in this form meaningless division, but is the first stage in an attempt to explore the hypothesis (= Model A) that graves on either side of 270^0 might have different locations in the cemetery. (It now appears that the changing orientation is connected with the azimuthal direction of sunrise throughout the year. P.A. Rahtz, personal communication)

intended to be used in conjunction with photographs, the intended bones being indicated on the diagram by means of coloured pencils. Needless to say, is this method is used it is absolutely necessary to be sure that the photography is satisfactory before lifting the bones. If a dark-room is not available on the site, a polaroid camera will ensure that a photographic record is obtained, though at present polaroid prints are no substitute for large, detailed photographic.

A carefully surveyed plan of the whole cemetery is vital if its grow, use and abandonment are to be fully understood. Changes of orientation (fig. 37) or the size and shape of the graves, or their grouping, can only be studied from a full and accurate plan. This plan will also be the basis for overlays, demonstrating in coloured diagrammatic form, the types and distribution of grave goods, on which much of the interpretation of the ceremony may depend. Further overlays containing details of the skeletal material, such as age, sex, height and other characteristics an eventually by constructed from the anatomist's reports.

In some cases, where the soil is unsuitable for the preservation of bone, the skeleton may only be revealed as a soil-mark, a series of discolouration in the bottom of the grave (see Jones 1968, plate Lb.) Here filters of various colours may be needed to give the clearest black and white photographs, or methods of soil colour enhancement may be tried.

If possible, an environmentalist or soil scientist should be present during the excavation in order to sample the soils around and within the skeletons for organic remains, such as clothing or food. If this is impossible, samples, whose origin in relation to the skeletons are carefully noted, should be taken for laboratory examination.

More information will be obtained from inhumations if an anatomist can be present on the excavation since he will be able to examine the disposition of the bones *in situ* and will also be to draw attention to the possibility of finding galls-stones, or the remains of food, etc. Chemical analysis of the soils which have replaced the various organs may, under some circumstances, also yield vital information. The evidence to be obtained from human burials will include not only demographic statistics, details, of ritual and in some cases a corpus of grave and other relationships and evidence of disease or skeletal distortions resulting from patterns of work (Wells, 1964).

Berthe Køolbye-Biddle has published a frank and illuminating account of the excavation of the deeply-stratified cemetery north of the Cathedral at Winchester (1975). Because this cemetery overlay the foundations of the Old Minster, its excavation was accelerated by more summary digging than would be normal on a research excavation. Nevertheless the carefully considered compromise strategy employed recovered a mass of detailed information regarding the medieval population, medieval grave types and graveyard topography 'probably at present unequalled in Britain' (*ibid.* p. 92). The whole article is required reading for excavators of cemeteries, whether under research or rescue conditions.

Vertical stereoscopic colour photography combined with recording on preprinted forms would speed up the mechanics of planning very considerably and thus leave more time for detailed excavation. The outline plans of the graves must, of course, be plotted on to a master plan as the work proceeds, with the double check of carefully recorded co-ordinates. This is Købye-Biddle's 'approach 2' (*ibid*. p. 97) with the addition of stereoscopic photography to offset the disadvantage of drawing skeletons at the rather small scale of 1:20.

Site oranisation

Providing an optimum micro-climate

For most of its existence British archaeology has shared a serious drawback with other major sports in that rain stops play, sometimes for days on end. Even when the rain clears the pitch is seldom fit for hours or even days, and then, in excavation as in cricket, a day's rain can produce a drastically different result from that predicted when the sun was shining.

Apart from the loss of time and temper, relying on the vagaries of the weather is extremely inefficient. We must, especially in these days of increasing emergencies and decreasing resources, use our time and skilled manpower as intensively as possible. I do not believe that the best way to do this is simply to press on regardless through all weathers. Saturated ground is rarely fit for efficient trowelling and often becomes so sticky that it is impossible to work properly. I no longer believe either that 'any information is better than none'. If the information produced under bad weather conditions is only partial, with great loss of detail and possible loss of whole periods of occupation, the evidence is so distorted that it might have been better not to have dug the site at all.

As far as resources permit we must attempt to create over our excavation a micro-climate which will enable us to extract the maximum information from the soil. Anyone who has dug in a temperate, variable climate will know that the changes of humidity in the soil, rain followed by a drying wind, for instance, will reveal soil differences quite invisible when the ground is either dry or soaking wet. What we have to do therefore is not simply to keep the site dry so that we can work in comfort, but vary the humidity (and, if possible, the temperature), thus giving the optimum soil conditions for the area being excavated.

The first necessity is shelter. Ideally a shelter should be waterproof, stable (that is, not so light that it will be blown away by strong winds), and large enough to cover not only the area immediately being excavated, but also to leave room for the removal of spoil behind the excavators. For a comparatively small site, such as a barrow, an inflatable tent of the kind used for temporary exhibitions would be perfectly adequate since these shelters are kept up by a small difference in the interior air pressure. Since this is maintained by a pump (either electric or petrol-driven) it has the advantage that either cold or warm air can be circulated. Air conditioning would be necessary here, as shelters of all kinds become very hot in sunshine, and the type under discussion is, in fact, completely enclosed.

A much less expensive form of shelter is provided by large horticultural tunnels which can be obtained in bays up to 10m. wide and 5m. long. Each bay can be joined to the next forming a tunnel of any required length. Heavy duty polythene sheeting is attached to the supports by means of spring clips. The polythene must be drawn very tightly over the framework so that rain water does not collect in pockets in the roof, and to prevent the wind from turning the whole thing into a highly inefficient sail-plane. In practice it has been found advisable to anchor the shelter along the sides with sand bags, or fertilizer bags filled with spoil. The 'skirt' of polythene on which the sandbags rest also stops water running off the roof from cutting channels in the excavation. The metal framework has proved to be sufficiently flexible to adapt itself to the undulations of the site, as long as these are not too violent.

The surface of the site can be protected from damage by sandbags placed under the edges of the shelter and sandbags can also be used to pack hollows crossed by the edges of the shelter. These shelters, though heavy, can be carried by about six people per unit. They do have a number of disadvantages, however. They produce a feeling of claustrophobia in some workers, they are noisy in rain and in wind, and because they reduce the visible area of the site it may become difficult for trowellers and supervisors alike to see the context of the part being excavated, so that a sense of perspective is lost, and the site cannot be viewed as a whole.

These disadvantages can to some extent be overcome by rolling back the polythene sheeting when the weather clears rather than leaving it on permanently. It is an advantage too if the shelter can be erected so that its back is to the prevailing wind, when the front can be rolled up, lessening the claustrophobic feeling and giving the trowellers a view of the area that has been completed. Shelters, of whatever kind, will keep the site dry, but it is also necessary in almost all cases, to keep it damp. For this purpose hoses with variable jets or lawn-sprinkling attachments are most convenient. The rotating sprinkler should make the droplets as fine as possible so that an evenly soaking 'Scotch mist' falls on the area. On very large sites agricultural sprays of the sort used to water market gardens and race courses would be more appropriate. If mains water or water carriers are not available, hand pumps, such as stirrup pumps or those used for portable showers or for spraying insecticide, are ideal for giving a spray varing from a fine mist to a downpour. For small sites these are preferable to the more indiscriminate lawn sprinkler.

It is important to spray finely and evenly, soaking the site gradually and thoroughly so that false damp marks are not created by the sprayer. Merely dampening the surface is of little use. Great care should also be taken not to flood the site so that hollows become filled with a fine layer of silt, and do not dry out for several days. Spraying is useful, if not essential, on a very dusty site where working conditions can become highly unpleasant, and thus counter-productive. Now that the cost-effectiveness of excavations in both time and money is being more and more studied, it is an economy to spend money on hoses, sprays, pumps and, if necessary, water tanks, in order to provide optimum conditions, where the site can be kept working at maximum capacity. A pleasant aspect of spraying on very hot days is the cooling not only of the surface but of the surrounding air, so that working conditions are improved. The days when it was a test of stamina to dig under the most atrocious conditions are surely on the way out. Efficiency, both in digging and recording, falls off markedly in extreme weather conditions: in rain, ancillary services, such as drawing and photography become difficult, if not impossible, and on a sun-baked surface both the draughtsman and the camera will see less.

If an excavation has to be left open for long periods it is important to protect it from damage by weathering. The surface should, of course, first be recorded as thoroughly as possible. Any vertical face which is left open will be liable to erosion or collapse, taking with it unrecorded evidence. Once useful by-product of area excavation is that, with few balks, there is less risk of this kind of loss. Nevertheless every excavation has edges, and excavated pits, post-holes, gullies and the like will need protection. One way that has proved successful is to fill, or better, over-fill, the pits, post-holes etc. with clean sand, and in the case of especially important or vulnerable features, cover them with polythene sheet, preferably black to exclude the light and inhibit plant growth. The features can then be emptied accurately and swiftly on the resumption of the excavation of that part of the site. If they cut through a number of surrounding layers, these layers can be removed progressively, while lowering the backfilling of the features in parallel. If sand is not readily available sifted earth (derived from the sifted spoil of the site) may be used. If there is any reason to suspect that it might be difficult subsequently to distinguish the backfill the features can be lined with polythene sheet before they are filled. This is in some ways less satisfactory as the free movement of water is impeded and, in the more extensive features, worms are liable to die under the sheet in considerable numbers leaving an unpleasant layer to be cleaned off. The edges of shallow excavations can be protected by packing sand or sifted earth along them; and horizontal features, such as floors or hearths, can be protected in the same way. Additional protection from frost may also be required, and here straw bales packed on top of the polythene sheet will give adequate insulation. If a ready source is available, expanded polystyrene chips give excellent insulation, are easily removed, and can be re-used. Polythene sheets will need to be anchored against strong winds, by means of large stones, bricks, planks or straw bales.

So long as holes and other features with vertical surfaces are protected in the ways outlined above, extensive areas of varied soils, from soft sands to boulder clays, can be left open for long periods. An area of sandy clay at Wroxeter had to be left open for two years. At the end of this time it was trowelled, and an average depth of some 1-3cm. was removed. The underlying surface was in good condition and the features of the immediately preceding period of the site's occupation were intact. The same encouraging results have been experienced on boulder clay, and on rubble surfaces. Naturally, some soils weather less well, and all will erode if the site has an appreciable degree of slope.

A site that has to be left for more than a few months will need to be sprayed with weed killer to prevent weed growth, particularly of deep-rooted weeds, as their removal is not only tedious but, more important, will damage the stratification. It is unlikely that a weed killer such as paraquat will alter the chemical balance of the soil for any subsequent soil analysis.

Site logistics

The siting of spoil heaps and the removal of spoil should be given a good deal of thought before the excavation starts. Only too often, spoil heaps prove to lie over crucial areas of the site and have to be moved before excavation can expand, and if this has to be done by hand it can be very dispiriting.

If the site has eventually to be backfilled and the spoil kept for this purpose, the heaps should be as neat as possible with a clear 2 metres between the spoil and the excavation, and if necessary they should be revetted along their bottom edges with sandbags or stones or with planks held upright with pegs. If the excavation is expected to achieve any depth, it must be remembered that spoil is very heavy, especially if it becomes waterlogged, and should therefore be kept as far away from deep excavations as possible; this also considerably reduces the risk of collapse.

If the excavation has to be backfilled and returfed, the turf should be cut carefully and stacked, grass-face to grass-face, well away from the rest of the spoil, and should be kept damp. Topsoil should also be reserved in a separate heap so that it can be replaced on the surface before re-turfing.

If the excavation does not have to be backfilled, skips can be used to remove spoil, and if necessary a number of them can be stood end to end in a line and joined across the top by a plank runway, the furthest away being filled first. Lorries standing waiting are pointlessly expensive, so that if skips are not available it is more economical to employ an earth-moving machine to fill lorries from a spoil heap in one operation, as required.

For barrowing, either on the level or up on to spoil heaps, Summerfield tracking, developed during the war for emergency runways, is preferable to planks, which become slippery and potentially dangerous on steep slopes. This tracking, supported on sandbags, also makes excellent barrow-runs across the site, especially as the separate sections can be wired together to form continuous runs.

Anything that can be done to shorten barrow-runs will save time and labour. It may be more economical of skilled labour to make spoil heaps near the excavated face and employ mechanical or unskilled hand labour to move them rather than to have trowellers barrowing hundreds of yards to a major dump.

Any way of reducing unnecessary work should be used. For instance, it takes less energy to turn an empty barrow to face the way it will be pushed when full, than to turn it after it is full, a simple precept not always observed. Mechanical means of removing spoil include conveyor belts and small cranes driven by electric motors or petrol/diesel engines. Even if such aids are not available it is a simple matter to rig up a system of pulleys over a deep excavation rather than to haul up buckets at their dead weight.

The removal of spoil from the surface of the excavation has always been a tedious and time-consuming task and one has often wished for a series of large vacuum cleaners to do the job quickly and easily. Industrial vacuum cleaners capable of sucking up dirt and stones up to 2in. diameter are available and may be hired. Though it is obviously impracticable to equip each troweller with a vacuum cleaner there are occasions when it might be invaluable, such as in the emptying of a large group of stake holes or the cleaning of a pebble surface. Obviously this would only be feasible in dry weather. On the other hand, excavation inside standing buildings is often a very dry and dusty process which can be made much more efficient with the aid of a vacuum cleaner.

Site logistics are ultimately a matter of practical commonsense, of constantly seeing ways in which work can be made easier and more efficient. However, efficiency in the mechanical sense can be taken too far. On one excavation I suggested that, as it was a very large site divided into its separate areas, each individual area should have its own detached, subsidiary finds-recording box to obviate the necessity for trowellers to leave their area in order to take individual finds to the central finds hut, but the site supervisors pointed out that the average number of objects found per troweller per day was about two, and that the trowellers not only welcomed the break from what was, in effect, a production line, but that they thereby became familiar with the workings of the finds hut and saw finds from other parts of the site. From the other end, the finds assistants welcomed the arrival of trowellers with their finds. The centralised system, though involving more walking and a bit less trowelling, was more efficient psychologically, creating something of a rapport between the trowellers and the finds staff, and giving everyone a brief change of scene and viewpoint.

From another point of view there is an optimum length of day. If an excavation is to work at maximum efficiency it should not go on each day after the point at which enthusiasm and interest wanes. On an emergency or salvage dig this might be at one in the morning, but on a large long-term excavation it is probably counter-productive to work more than eight or nine hours a day as the losses of evidence in the last hour may well be considerable. Loss of efficiency at the end of a long day or after two or three weeks' continuous digging might be monitored by the number of tiny finds missed in the ground but recovered afterwards by sieving. On any large excavation one can almost plot a graph of increasing tiredness as time goes on. It is here that careful consideration of site logistics will save time and energy, and keep morale and enthusiasm high. On permanent or semi-permanent excavations it is clearly necessary for workers to have breaks at weekends or other agreed times if they are not to become stale and work merely mechanically.

Safety precautions

The Council for British Archaeology has recently produced an essential pamphlet, *Responsibility and Safeguards in Archaeological Excavation*, 1972, edited by P.J. Fowler. This outlines the law regarding excavation current at the time, and describes the C.B.A. insurance scheme for third party and personal accident cover for archaeological societies and groups affiliated to the C.B.A. It has a section on precautions against soil collapse and another on working with machinery. One of its most cogent sections is that on personal safety and medical precautions. The pamphlet as a whole is required reading for all field archaeologists, and as it is cheap and readily available there is no need to reproduce it here.

A facility not mentioned in the pamphlet is the Post Office telephone number Freefone 111 which can be reached via the operator. Through this, information on the position of Post Office telephone cables can be obtained before excavation begins, and expensive accidents avoided. The positions of all other services such as sewers, electricity cables, gas and water pipes should also be accurately ascertained before work begins.

This is obviously important in towns and cities, but it must also be remembered that many stretches of open countryside are now crisscrossed with gas or water pipes, electricity cables and drains, the lines of which may only be vaguely known. If in doubt, a geophysical survey should pick them up. In the absence of geophysical equipment dowsing might be tried. Though this technique is regarded by many as suspect, it has been proved to work, in the right hands and given the right conditions.

In 1974 Parliament passed the *Health and Safety at Work etc. Act 1974*. This Act considerably tightens up regulations concerned with duties of employers to their employees in regard to health and safety, and to the general public who may be affected by activities of which they are not a part, such as falling masonry from a demolition close to a public highway, or subsidence of a footpath due to excavation. The Act also includes the self-employed and other persons (not employed by them) who may be affected by their activities. The Act defines an 'employee' as 'an individual who works under a contract of employment' (Chapter 37 Part I, 53, (1)). There is no doubt, therefore, that archaeologists working under contract to units or other excavating bodies are employees within the meaning of the Act, as are self-employed archaeologists, such as some conservators or other specialists, who will be liable, for example, for the effect of any toxic chemicals or effluents they may use.

The position of volunteers of all grades is less clear. An Inspector of Factories consulted on this point thought that the Act was meant to cover anyone at work and at risk, and that it would be reckless to assume that persons called volunteers and paid subsistence would not be covered by the Act if an accident occurred. He felt that it would need a test case to prove the point. Since the maximum penalties for those convicted under the Act are a fine not exceeding £400 and a term of imprisonment not exceeding two years, it would seem advisable to avoid such a test case!

The parts of the Act particularly relevant to archaeology appear to be Chapter 37, Part I, Sections 1, 2, 3, 4, 7, 8, 9, 33, 36, 37, 40, 52, and 53. Other important regulations include the Construction (General Provisions) Regulations, 1961, (Statutory Instruments 1961 No. 1580); The Construction (Working Places) Regulations, 1966 (Statutory Instrument, 1966 No. 94) and the Construction (Health and Welfare) Regulations 1966 (Statutory Instrument 1966 No. 95). These are all obtainable very cheaply from H.M. Stationery Office and should be used as guidelines even by those directors who do not believe that their fieldwork and excavations are covered by the Act, since it should always be borne in mind that a volunteer, even a totally unpaid one, might bring a civil action for damages against a director in the case of serious accident. Under these circumstances, it would be a powerful defence if the director could show that all the relevant aspects of the excavation conformed with the standards laid down in these regulations, and that every other reasonable precaution had been taken. In spite of a few serious incidents within the last few years, British archaeology has been very fortunate in its accident rate, although safety precautions on some sites are frighteningly non-existent. Now that excavations are larger, and archaeology in general more public, it would not only be potentially tragic for individuals but damaging for the discipline as a whole if it were seen to be amateurish and negligent in its safety precautions.

Site discipline

The best site discipline is a careful balance of that which is self-imposed and that imposed from above; where all the members of the excavation do what they are told or what is required because they understand what they are doing, and the way it fits into the overall development of work rather than through unthinking obedience. This closely parallels the best war-time air-crew discipline where groups of men (most of them the age of the present-day archaeological volunteer) had to learn very quickly to work together under an acknowledged leader, without resentment, and with an understanding of the problems and difficulties under which the other crew members worked, so that unreasonable demands were not made, but above all without bickering or quarrelling, which could, and quite often did, prove fatal. The results of poor site discipline on an excavation are not so drastic, but can be very disruptive, leading to inefficiency, needless mistakes and a resulting loss of evidence.

It is important, if volunteers, site assistants and specialist assistants, such as draughtsmen, surveyors and photographers, are to give of their best, that they should be told the background to the excavation, its aims and progress to date and just where they fit into the team. Sometimes this is best done by means of introductory talks; sometimes, if people are turning up at intervals during the dig, by means of interim reports and other hand-outs. It should be made clear to everyone that they are free to ask why they are doing what they are set to do, to question the need for doing it, or the way in which it is done. If these questions cannot be convincingly answered by the director or site supervisors, they are in the wrong job. The volunteer who works without understanding will work badly.

There should be a clear hierarchy in the organisation, a chain of command known to all, so that each individual knows of whom he should ask questions or to whom make complaints and suggestions. Above all contradictory orders must be avoided. Nothing causes more confusion than an instruction given by a site supervisor reversed by an assistant director minutes later, to be reinstated by the director who turns up demanding to know what is going on in his absence. Situations such as this can be avoided by a meeting of the directing staff before the dig begins so that a broad policy can be agreed upon. Daily site conferences and adequate discussion between all concerned should ensure that this policy is implemented or modified in consultation with the supervisors. Everybody should be aware that the buck stops with the director and that he is available to all for complaints and suggestions. On large excavations and archaeological units he will naturally be sheltered from trivial interruptions by his senior assistants, but the remoter and more inaccessible the director becomes the less sense of unity and cooperation there will be among the body of workers.

No excavation is without its awkward characters, eccentrics or misfits. These must be dealt with sympathetically or firmly as required, and here the patience and skill of the director and his assistants in man-management will sometimes be stretched. A volunteer who disrupts the workers around him by compulsive chattering can be tactfully moved to work on his own; a desperately keen but ham-fisted volunteer who is ineducable as a troweller can be invited to help with something more suited to his talents, or, at worst, placed where he can do least harm.

If paid non-archaeological labourers, prisoners or Borstal boys are used, they too should be given the background and purpose of the excavation if they are to work well and become members of the team. The initial resentment and cynicism of prisoners can be dispersed by careful handling; and if they become interested in the site they will often work with unexpected skill. One of the best trowellers I have known was a 60-year-old window-cleaner serving a prison sentence for petty theft.

This book is not intended to cover the organisation of the domestic side of a large excavation in detail. The welfare of all workers on the site is the director's overall responsibility, though aspects such as catering, first aid, organisation of accommodation and so on should be delegated. There is no doubt that an excavation trowels on its stomach: if the domestic and catering arrangements are not efficient the dig will suffer very considerably. Domestic bursars and cooks should therefore be chosen with great care—they are key personnel.

Cost effectiveness

In these times of economic stress, galloping inflation and the wholesale destruction of sites, cost effectiveness, that is, 'getting', as Philip Rahtz has put it, 'as much history as possible per £', is crucially important. At first sight it seems obvious that the bigger the area you cover and the faster you dig the more you are likely to get for your money, but I believe that this is a fallacy, like driving faster to get to the filling station before your petrol runs out. These thoughts arose from discussions with friends who maintained that very slow, detailed excavations while admittedly producing interesting, even unexpected results were not appropriate to rescue archaeology, where time was of the essence, and the maximum results had to be obtained for the money spent.

It is difficult, if not impossible to quantify the results from excavations on any agreed scale of values, but it is self-evident that some excavations are very fruitful, while others are a waste of time and money, and that many fall somewhere between these two extremes.

It may be argued that on some deeply ploughed sites there is little to find beyond the features dug into the undisturbed subsoil and that therefore the fastest methods of recovering these features will be appropriate and that there will be little chance of recovering a great deal more evidence even if the work is carried out much more slowly and carefully. On stratified sites I do not believe this to be the case. Experience has shown that highly detailed (and therefore necessarily slow) digging can produce a markedly greater quantity of evidence, in the form of buildings and other structures, many of them unsuspected, than fast digging could possibly have recovered.

It is apparent, for example, that the bailey of the timber castle at Hen Domen was packed with timber buildings of which the plans or partial plans of almost 50, spanning some 250 years, have been discovered in one quarter of the bailey's interior. This has taken about 50 weeks' work (spread over 10 years, though under other circumstances the work could have been carried out continuously over one year). However, faster digging would have recovered only the plans of the more obvious structures, of which there are

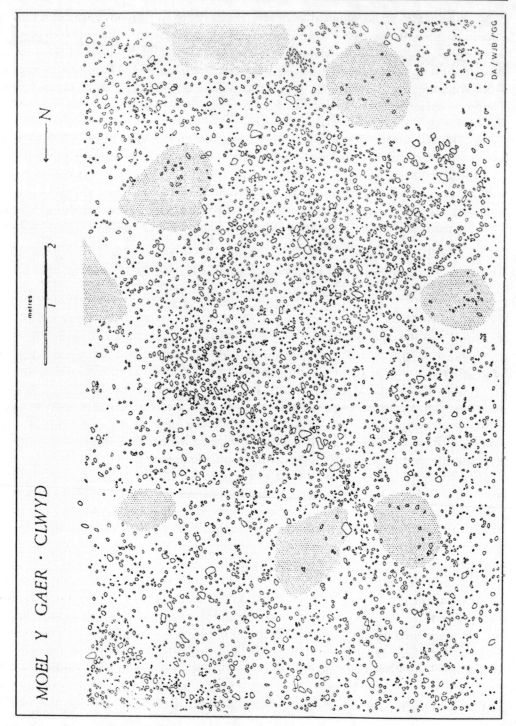

Figure 38   This is a plan of part of the latest layers within the hill fort of Moel Y Gaer, Clwyd, showing the distribution of stones within rectangular patterns, together with roughly circular heaps of topsoil. These rectangular patterns are the only evidence for a series of timber buildings of the last phase or prehistoric occupation at this point

only about a dozen. The recovery rate would have fallen off very sharply as the work was accelerated beyond the point where every thin layer and every pebble surface was cleaned and dissected. It need hardly be added that the recovery rate for finds of all kinds is likely to be higher if the digging is more careful and that the finds will be more securely stratified in closer contexts so that the results adduced from them will be correspondingly more reliable.

Equally at Wroxeter, on a site which had been dug in more summary fashion by a number of previous excavators, the recovery of many periods of unsuspected buildings has only been made possible by slow excavation over a large area. At the same time, the recovery rate of finds of all kinds, including pottery and bones, has been high and should provide information at a level unprecedented for the site. I maintain that more information, and more reliable information, is obtained pound for pound by slow, detailed digging than by digging which is faster than the site demands and which produces a 'broad picture' but one that may be grossly distorted.

This, therefore, is another argument for planning a long-term rescue strategy which permits excavation at the optimum speed and not at speeds dictated by the quarryman or developer.

An example of highly detailed excavation under rescue conditions is appended below.

Appendix A. The identification of rectangular timber buildings in the rescue excavation at the hillfort of Moel Y Gaer (Rhosesmor)

Immediately after the turf and thin topsoil are removed the uneroded contours of the final phase occupation deposits are exposed. These consist of a variable layer of stone rubble, nowhere more than 10cm. in thickness, whose continuity is broken by a spread of low humps of pale brown, sandy, stone-free soil. The distribution of these humps is apparently random; equally, their contours and plan would seem to be meaningless. The stone-covered areas are fairly level and it is here that detailed cleaning and recording (i.e. planning stone by stone) has revealed a pattern of stone densities amongst which the former positions of timber buildings can be postulated. Approximately rectangular areas of uniform stone density are recognisable, as in the plan (fig. 38) where a relatively small area, measuring 11.5 x 7.0m. has been selected and all the recorded stones are shown with the humps stippled. A number of these rectangles have been recognised within the 3000 sq. m. of the excavated area. They range from c.10-18 sq. m. in area. The rectangle shown in the drawing is the best example for illustrative purposes, it being rare for all four sides to be this clearly defined. Since these units recur across the site in a relatively standardised size and shape it seems reasonable to interpret them as the floor areas of rectangular timber buildings. There are no associated patterns of post-holes or timber slots and the stones remain the only evidence of the buildings which must have been timber-framed structures founded on sleeper-beams sitting on the ground surface. The stones themselves seem to have been spread over the occupied areas after the buildings had been constructed, probably for no more reason than to produce a hard-wearing surface upon which matting of, say, straw could be laid, or even as a preparation for timber floor boards. The humps probably represent dumps of turf and humus cleared from the building plots when the occupation was implemented.

It is clear that such evidence as this would only be archaeologically detectable under exceptional circumstances and, in this respect, three factors hold sway at Moel y Gaer.

Firstly, the undamaged condition of the site is an important precursor to the preservation of such tenuous remains. One ploughing, however light, would undoubtedly have totally destroyed all the evidence for this phase of occupation at Moel y Gaer.

Secondly, it will be evident that this must represent the final phase of occupation on the site, for had there been a later one the patterns of stone densities must have been disturbed and thus rendered impossible to record adequately, let alone interpret. This must always be the case on this type of site where successive deposits are not cumulative but where later activity tends to erode the evidence of its forerunners; namely, on hilltops and sloping ground where there is nothing to arrest the downhill movement of soil and stones.

Last, but most certainly not least, it should be stressed that the method of excavation effectively controlled the destiny of the evidence. Since the identification of the rectangles depended upon relative stone densities it was essential that large areas should be examined at any one time. The truth of this statement was brought home to the excavators by the difficulties of interpretation near the limits of the excavation which covers less than a sixth of the interior of the hillfort. It was undoubtedly the large scale of open area excavation which allowed the recognition of the rectangles and provided the repeating pattern which prompted their interpretation as buildings. Whilst it should be pointed out that this identification is merely an interpretation of an observed phenomenon (indeed, an interpretation which other archaeologists may choose to challenge), the important thing is that the phenomenon has been systematically recorded in the most objective way that seemed possible under the circumstances of the excavation.

G. C. Guilbert, February 1974

The Soil

Introduction

An all-important skill on most archaeological sites is the interpretation of soil. Understanding its deposit and disturbance is key, especially on sites of timber structures, as traces left in the soil are fundamental to their identification as such and the chief indicators of their form in plan, which with an understanding of architecture, can lead to a reconstruction of their original appearance. But a much broader knowledge of soil is needed, with ways of distinguishing discrete layers in terms of color, texture, and, often, chemical analysis, required to understand its deposit and modification over time. Barker stresses how natural agencies act upon it: leeching of chemicals, the growth of tree roots, animal burrowing, worms and microorganisms, all modifying the composition of the soil. Recognition of past use of an area of a site as well as its earlier and later environment need be considered. Experience in the field is fundamental to ability to distinguish the subtleties of interpreting the soil and examples of methods of removing it are suggested. Throughout, Barker uses the illustrations of cases of misinterpretation as cautionary advice.

T imber buildings are by far the most common structures to be found on the majority of our archaeological sites. These sites now consist almost entirely of superimposed layers of soil, or soil and stones, containing the ghosts of structures which themselves have undergone an earth-change into soil. Those of us who excavate these sites often have to interpret soil layers with little more than our intuition and experience to guide us. We say that this feature is a hearth (might it not be a small dump of burnt clay?); this layer was washed down (could it have been wind-blown?); this post-hole filling looks and feels the same as that one (are they therefore contemporary?); does this micropodsol, itself a natural event, reflect a man-made disturbance? – what is the source of this vivianite and what archaeological significance has it? – and so on. An archaeologist who uncovers the substantial remains of stone buildings must have a reasonable knowledge of architecture in order to be able to interpret them. Equally an excavator digging timber structures will need at least a basic understanding of the soils he will encounter if he is to understand fully the medium into which his buildings have been transformed (see Cornwall, 1958, L. Biek and I.W. Cornwall in Brothwell and Higgs, 1963, 108-22, and Limbrey, 1975).

In the process of understanding our excavated structures and their surroundings we must not only be able to recognise and explain structural features such as floors, post-holes, hearths, drains, fences and the rest, but we must also attempt to understand the derivation of every layer that we encounter.

From geological times to the present day the surface of the earth, this very thin series of layers which so preoccupies us, has been subjected to continuous change. Some of these alterations have occurred slowly; the development of the soil, the establishment of vegetation, and centuries of cultivation; some have been much faster. From the moment the site is occupied by man its surface undergoes rapid and drastic changes; and it is principally these changes which we have to excavate and attempt to understand. But the process of change does not stop when the last occupants leave the site and it reverts to pasture or is ploughed or adopted as a car-park. Natural agencies continue to transform it, frost and ice break up exposed surfaces, rain and wind fill its hollows with mud, dust, soil and stones. Water seeps through the underlying layers, leaching out chemicals and redepositing them in new forms. The roots of bushes and trees grow along and into organically rich layers, post-holes and pits, or create their own root-holes. Animals and insects traverse the site with burrows; micro-organisms feed on debris and the remains of timbers, and worms move up and down through the soil, passing, if we are to believe Darwin, millions of tons of our sites through their bodies in the course of a century or so (Darwin, 1881). It is a wonder that we have any understandable archaeology left!

Clearly, we must learn to recognise all the changes that have occurred on the sites we are digging and not merely those which are structural and man-made, attempting, as we do so, to explain or account for every piece of detectable evidence. We shall make mistakes, but these can be minimized by the intensive study of natural, as well as human, factors. We should like to know the subtle but real differences between a number of what we glibly call 'occupation layers' for example, whether a floor has been used by cattle or for corn storage. Experiments in determining comparative amounts of phosphates, lignite and other residual traces have not been uniformly successful; but a comprehensive analysis of soil composition, presented visually and laid over plans of the excavated areas, may prove to be more valuable.

Ultimately, it should be possible to sort apparently un-differentiated post-holes into groups by comparative analysis of their filling. However, observation of the contents of post-holes known to belong to one building often shows that they contain different materials; and it may be that dating techniques such as thermo-luminescence will eventually prove to be of more use than physical or chemical analysis. Again, the bottoms of post-holes may contain pollen spectra that will differentiate them into widely separated periods eg. neolithic and Saxon, when superficially they are similar.

At the moment the sampling methods used by soil scientists are often at odds with the excavation techniques advocated here. Soil scientists quite reasonably require to see the whole soil profile, from the surface to the subsoil, in vertical section. Not only is this patently impossible all over the site, unless one dug it by means of a series of thin vertical slices, a sort of *planum* technique (see p. 130-4) tilted through 90° (a method which might be tried on a selected site just to see what happened), but the excavator often does not know that he will require crucial soil information until he has uncovered a layer or feature; by which time, of course, the superimposed layers will have gone; and the very last thing he wants is a column dug through a floor or a buried soil into the underlying layers (about which he knows nothing). It is sometimes possible to reserve columns of soil, leaving them standing until the soil scientist can sample them *in situ*. Again, one would have to know in advance, or predict, what layers lay below the point where the column was to be left.

The only possible solution to this problem is for a soil scientist to work continually on the site, alongside the excavators, taking samples where necessary, and observing the vertical relationships as they are revealed by horizontal methods. This may not be entirely satisfactory for the soil scientist, but test holes or trenches, except on the smallest scale, are unacceptable on an area excavation, especially as they will inevitably be dug into *terra incognita*, and therefore of little value to the excavator who cannot have any idea what the underlying layers may represent when the samples are taken. More important, a dialogue between an excavator and a soil scientist is likely to raise questions that would not have occurred to either individually.

On an excavation where a soil scientist cannot be present, samples may be taken from layers and features. They must be labelled in sufficient detail for a person who has not seen the site to identify them, with the aid of plans, sections and photographs, preferably in colour; and they must be accompanied by specific questions, of a kind which might reasonably be solved by soil analysis. No soil scientist will thank an excavator who sends him 200 polythene bags full of samples divorced from their context and without comment, and the excavator must not expect miraculous solutions to his problems simply because he has collected spoonsful of each layer he has removed.

Soil analysis falls into two main categories: the physical and the chemical examination of the profile or sample. The physical examination will give information about the parent geology of the sample (which may not be that of the underlying subsoil), the particle size, the proportion of humus, the presence of mortar or other building materials, whether the material is wind blown or water-sorted, and so on. Hopefully, this will not only throw light on the derivation of the material, but may also give information about aspects of the site which would be obtainable in no other way. For example, post-holes filled with earth containing flecks of painted plaster may be the only evidence for the former existence of a timber building with rendered or painted walls. Analysis of the back-filling of robber trenches which appear to be the same superficially, may show that the robbed walls were of different materials and therefore perhaps of different dates; or it may be possible to show that a gulley has been filled in its early stages with wind-sorted rather than water-borne silt.

Layers or fillings of features which seem at first to resemble each other may prove, on detailed examination, to be very different. Quite often layers occurring on different parts of a site have been said to be identical simply because they look alike. This in turn has led to generalizations about 'destruction levels' and 'building levels' which may well not be justified.

The chemical analysis of soil provides information of another kind. Sometimes it will go hand in hand with the physical examination to prove the existence or composition of mortars and plasters, or it may be a purely chemical examination which attempts to show, for example, that floors have been occupied by animals; or determine the existence of industrial processes otherwise undetectable.

At the long-term and very meticulous excavation of the deserted medieval village at Wharram Percy, Yorkshire, it has usually been possible from the house plans to determine their internal sub-divisions and to distinguish the living end from that used for cattle or storage. However, in one area, 6, a house was excavated without any trace of sub-division. The site was left open until the following year, when it was noticed that the vegetation growing within the house was sharply differentiated between the 'upper end', the 'living room area' and the 'cross-passage area' (fig. 39). This clearly indicated that soil differences, hitherto undetected, had operated to provide a different environment in each of the three areas. A highly detailed analysis of the soil would presumably have detected the unseen elements responsible for these differences. While it is not feasible to undertake a total analysis of each layer of our sites it is obvious from this example that much significant information might be obtained from overall examinations, even from one in which specific questions were not asked. Mr. Norman Bridgwater has been working on the theory that oak beams lying on the ground will leave a deposit of tannin that will show where they have been. While the value of this technique has yet to be verified, it is a good example of the type of experimental approach that may reveal hitherto unsuspected buildings.

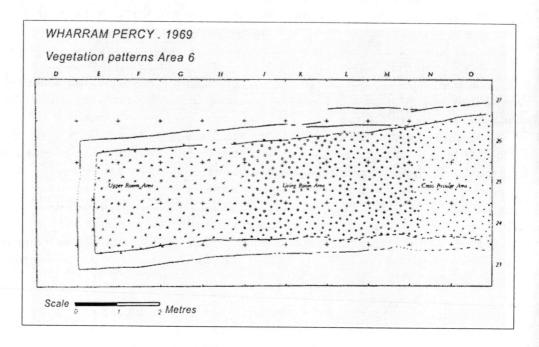

Figure 39   This illustration shows the excavation of a house at Wharram Percy, Yorkshire
                 under the direction of J.G. Hurst and Professor Maurice Beresford. Elsewhere
                 in the village such houses were divided into two sections, one the living end,
                 the other the byre end, separated by a cross passage. Here there was no
                 indication of different use for the two halves of the building, but after the
                 excavation had been left open for the winter the plants which began to grow
                 on the house site were different in each half indicating soil differences which
                 were not visible but which were positive enough to affect plant colonisation.
                 Analysis of this phenomenon is not yet completed and I am grateful to Mr.
                 Hurst for permission to mention it in advance of publication.

It is no longer enough to bag up samples of soil from post-holes, pits and the silting of ditches and despatch them to a soil-scientist, with a list of questions in the hope of solving the outstanding questions of interpretation that are not immediately obvious to inexperienced eyes. On all but the shortest excavations, therefore, a soil-scientist should be a permanent member of the team, available for consultation at every stage about problems of soil interpretation *in situ*. However, this is only part of the solution. For obvious reasons it is vitally important that the soil-scientist and the archaeologist should speak the same language.

We must learn to use each other's terms not only in the field, but in publication. At the moment archaeological colloquialisms like 'the natural' (meaning the undisturbed rock or subsoil) have no meaning for soil scientists who rightly point out that a lot of archaeological layers are 'natural'; while the word 'silt' used loosely by archaeologists to describe the soil that has filled a hollow has a much more precise meaning for the soil scientist. A textbook by one of the country's leading authorities on soil-science in archaeology has recently been published (Limbrey, 1975), and it is very much to be hoped that the stimulus this book gives to the archaeological study of soils will convince all directors and would-be directors of excavations to train themselves in soil science; and that this study will be given a greater prominence in all future archaeological training.

There is little point in attempting to summarize Dr Limbrey's book here. It is required reading for all excavators, but it may be useful to reemphasize some of the points she makes. Soil descriptions should be a normal entry on feature/layer record cards, and the terminology used should be that standardized by soil scientists. Limbrey makes the good point that it is the trowellers themselves, closest to the soils in an excavation, who should be responsible for the soil descriptions, since they will be most sensitive to soil variations, as they are the first to encounter and identify them.

The two chief characteristics of soils are colour and texture. Colours are described using a Munsell Soil Colour Chart, or its cheaper Japanese equivalent. Colour determinations should ideally be made on the soils in both moist and dry conditions. However, the labour, in a damp season, involved in drying a sample of each layer or feature filling encountered on a large site would be enormous and it is probably more reasonable under these circumstances to record all the soil colours when they are damp, since it is obviously much easier to moisten a sample than to dry it. In practice, on very large and complex sites where the colour changes run into thousands it may be necessary to record only those which seem to be significant or anomalous, or different in some way from the general matrix of soil which often covers large areas of a site. These alone may run into many hundreds.

Soil texture, structure and consistence can best be taught in the field, though Limbrey, *op. cit.*, 259-70, is a concise introduction. She makes the point also that the traditional method of using the trowel, by scraping, is not the best way of revealing the nature of the soil since it tends to smear clay soils and obscures the structure of all other soils except sands. Rather the soil should be 'made to part along its structural planes'. This is best achieved by 'a levering or flicking action' with a sharp trowel. In this way also the nature of the boundaries between the layers, often a most difficult problem of identification, is made clearer.

Limbrey's chapter on 'Soils associated with archaeological features' is an essential discussion of the development and composition of soils in pits, post- holes, tree-holes, ditches, mounds and other man-made features. There is little to add to it except to point out that the filling of ditches particularly, but also of pits and post-holes, may be partly deliberate and partly natural. The sleighting of defences on a rampart may lead to a tumble of stones into the adjacent ditch. This may be followed over the next few days or weeks by washed-down soil and small pebbles, which may partly fill the spaces between the stones. If the defences are refurbished, the builders may re-dig the ditch though not deeply enough to remove all the recent tumble and wash-down. The new ditch will immediately begin to silt naturally in the manner described by Limbrey (290 ff), but may again be recut or filled with debris. This process may be repeated a number of times (figs. 8-1 1).

Worms and weathering

This is the title of a crucial paper by Professor R.J.C. Atkinson (Atkinson, 1957) in which he discusses the role played by earthworms in the modification of archaeological sites, and the weathering of the natural subsoils which lie below the archaeological layers, and which are often considered by archaeologists to have remained sealed and unchanged from time immemorial. It is not my intention to repeat Atkinson's paper here but simply to stress one or two of his most important conclusions.

In favourable soils, the worm population is commonly as much as half a million per acre, and may even be as much as six times this number. Worms passing up and down through the soil and the subsoil below it, transport fine soil, in the form of worm casts, from lower levels to the surface.

Amounts from 2 to 24 tons per acre per annum have been recorded from Britain and amounts up to 36 tons on the Continent. This represents the formation of a surface-layer of fine mould varying in thickness (in Britain) from 1/50 to 1/4 in. per annum, or from 1/5 to 2 1/2in. in ten years.

However, this process clearly cannot go on without modification since at 2 1/2 in. every ten years, there would theoretically be a mould layer 25 in. thick in a century, or 20ft. 10in. in a thousand years. Even at the lowest figure of 1/5in. in ten years the mould layer would be 20in. thick in a thousand years. Observation of worm-rich sites that have remained untouched by the plough since they were abandoned shows that they frequently have only a thin soil cover above the uppermost archaeological levels. At Hen Domen, Montgomery, which is built on boulder clay, and has lain untouched for 750 years, worms have burrowed to a considerable depth, and the layer of fine stone-free humic soil lying on the uppermost archaeological layer is only an average of 3in. (7cm.) in depth. It is possible that the chief activity of the worms was confined to this thin layer of topsoil, except in winter when they burrowed deeper to escape the colder weather and when casting on the surface would be at its minimum. On deeply stratified sites where movement up and down through the layers is easier the movement of fine earth to the surface is likely to be greater. A very important side-effect of this movement of fine soil by earthworms is stressed by Atkinson. This is the burial of small objects, which are continually undermined by the worms' burrows and the deposition of casts on the surface. Small objects left on the surface of a lawn will gradually disappear, moving downwards until they reach a more solid layer. It is a matter of common observation on many archaeological sites that modern objects such as coins, bottle tops, fragments of Victorian teapot and so on lie on the uppermost archaeological surfaces *together with* the objects deposited on those surfaces by the last occupants. This can lead to considerable confusion if the cause, earthworm activity, is not appreciated. As Atkinson summarises:

in many cases significant archaeological finds have been displaced downwards from the position in which they were originally deposited; and in some cases at least the amount of displacement may have been sufficient materially to alter the apparent stratigraphic relationships of the objects concerned (*op. cit.* 222).

He goes on to cite two examples of the way in which the burying activities of worms may affect the interpretation of stratified finds. They are so important that it is worth repeating them here (in slightly shortened form):

In many Romano-British and medieval excavations, for instance, floors are uncovered consisting of *opus signinum* (cement), *tesserae* or tiles. The surface of these floors is often sealed by a layer of fine soil containing sherds, coins and other debris of occupation, which is itself covered by a thicker layer of rubble derived from the decay and collapse of the surrounding walls. Such 'occupation layers' are usually referred to a reoccupation of the building by squatters, after it has been abandoned by the original inhabitants and has perhaps already become partially ruined.

The exact processes by which such 'occupation layers' have been formed is seldom if ever discussed in excavation reports. In fact, such 'occupation earth' is almost certainly the product of earthworms, which penetrate cracks in apparently solid floors and gradually build up a layer of castings on their surface. Meanwhile this layer will itself have been colonized by worms, whose activity will bury coins and other objects dropped on it, and some of these will be displaced downwards so that they eventually come to rest immediately on the surface of the original floor.

Now finds discovered in this latter position will usually be interpreted as belonging either to the very latest stage of the original occupation, or to the initial stages of 'squatting'; in either case they will be held to date approximately the period at which the building was initially abandoned. But in fact, as a result of the processes outlined above, the objects found *on* the floor may be of widely differing dates, and will include not only those dropped just after the abandonment of the building, but also those of much later date which have been displaced from above. Consequently, if the normal practice is adopted of dating a horizon by the *latest* objects contained in it, the date assigned to the initial abandonment of the building may be significantly later than it should be.

Another common case in which the activity of worms may lead to serious misinterpretation of the evidence occurs in the silting of pits and ditches. Such silting usually exhibits four basic divisions. On the bottom, and up to half the depth of the ditch, there is coarse or rapid silting, formed chiefly from the weathering of the sides. Above this is a thin deposit of earthy streaks, due to the undermining and collapse of the surface soil on the lips of the ditch. Both these stages are normally completed within a few years at the most. Thereafter, silt forms much more slowly, and usually contains a far higher proportion of earth, particularly in structures of the second millennium BC, such as barrow-ditches, which collect considerable quantities of wind-blown surface-soil. Finally, at the top, there is the 'turf' layer of virtually stone-free soil which supports the surface vegetation.

Since the first two stages of silting take place rapidly, the formation of the lowest levels of the third stage may be regarded as virtually contemporary with the original excavation; and in the absence of finds from the primary silt (those in the secondary silt, being derived possible from the adjacent surface-soil, are unreliable), objects occurring at the base of the tertiary silt may often be used to date the original excavation. But it is clear that such finds *may* have been displaced vertically through considerable depths of silt particularly where a high proportion of windblown or other soil encourages the activity of worms. Since such vertical displacements may take centuries to achieve, the date ascribed to the structure on such evidence may be grossly in error.

The classic case of the probability of an error of this kind of afforded by the Y and Z Holes at Stonehenge, in which the main part of the silt consists of earth, apparently wind-blown and almost free from stones and rubble. This silt contained Iron Age and Romano-British sherds at quite low depths, which have in the past been held to date the holes to not earlier than the last few centuries BC. But once the possibility of vertical displacement is recognised, it becomes clear that this pottery must have bene deposited *on the surface of the silting* many centuries after the digging of the holes; and in fact other evidence suggests a date for the holes as much as a thousand years *earlier* than that of the pottery they contain.

These examples, and particularly the last, may perhaps be regarded as extreme cases; and certainly it would be foolish to deny that in many instances the vertical movement of objects, though it has undoubtedly taken place, has no significant effect on their interpretation. Nonetheless, one may justly say that the excavator who ignores the capacity of worms to displace small objects downwards does so at his peril.

Although there is no doubt that objects can travel downwards through considerable depths of comparatively friable soil* they tend to stop when they reach a harder layer, one that is either resistant to penetration by worms, or at least does not collapse internally if there are worm burrows in it.

Two things should be noted. First of all it is most unlikely that the vertical stratifigraphic relationship of objects will be *reversed* by eathworm action; that is, objects will rarely overtake one another so that a later object finishes up below an earlier one in the same series of layers. Secondly, objects will never travel *upwards* due to the action of earthworms. Though it may seem ludicrous to point this out, it should be stressed that the worm cannot be held responsible for every anomalous find in the recorded stratigraphy.

---

* At Wroxeter a considerable accumulation of eighteenth- and nineteenth-century sherds was found on the surface of a Roman street on the Baths Basilica site (excavated from 1966 onwards). These sherds had probably been brought onto the site from the mid-eighteenth century when the field was first ploughed. They had travelled between 60cm. and 1m. (2-3ft) downwards through deep layers of top soil before they reached the gravelly surface of the street where they remained. Since the excavation has proved by horizontal stratigraphy that the street is unquestionably late Roman, the eighteenth/nineteenth-century sherds have no dating significance for the street or the layers immediately above it.

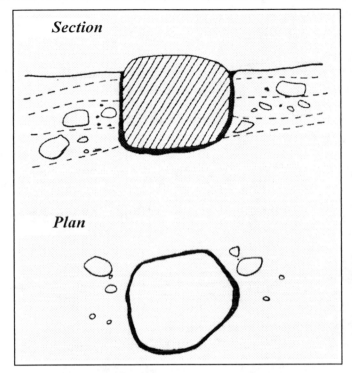

Figure 40

Diagrammatic plan and section of a large stone showing enveloping layer of fine soil (in black) deposited Plan by worms travelling round stone.

Another effect, not noted by Atkinson, is that one often finds a layer of dark humic soil surrounding buried stones or large architectural fragments. It is easy to assume this to be a pit into which the stone has been set, though it is more likely to be caused by worms coming up underneath the stone and being forced round its sides (fig. 40).

As Atkinson explains, the familiar thin and irregular deposits of pea-sized pebbles, free from admixed soil, found at the bottom of pits, etc., and on the buried surfaces of floors, arise from the long accumulation of the small stones used by worms to line the terminal chambers of their burrows. These layers of tiny pebbles tend to be concentrated at the lowest levels to which worms can penetrate locally (*op. cit.*, 225).

The second part of Atkinson's article concerns weathering and its misleading effects, particularly on permeable and partially soluble subsoils. The section is too long to summarize satisfactorily here, but, together with the section on worms, is required reading for excavation directors.

Rescue and Salvage Excavation

Introduction

In this chapter, Barker discusses the ongoing threat to archaeological sites, mainly by building within and outside towns and cities, new roads, some kinds of quarrying, as well as deep plowing of fields that contain archaeological deposits. Much of this destruction cannot be halted or avoided, so there is the question of what sorts of archaeological intervention might be taken before the disappearance of sites and whether the priorities of archaeology should be tied to the threat of such sites. Can a space of time be mandated for investigation before destruction; can resources be allocated for such "priority sites," how are the "priority" sites chosen, and who pays for the work? In addition, there is consideration of the kind of recording that can be made in short periods of time, and Barker illustrates a variety of strategies that have been employed. His authority in this area is not only based on his experience as an archaeologist, but on his place in the establishment of Rescue Archaeology and the Institute for Field Archaeologists.

At the time of writing (1982) British archaeology has faced a crisis situation for some years. The implantation of new towns and the enlargement of existing conurbations, with the proliferation of motorways; the extraction of sands and gravels for aggregates; the exploitation of peat bogs containing preserved timber structures and the afforestation of hitherto untouched marginal land, all represent threats to archaeological sites on an unprecedented scale. But the most extensive and insidious threat of all is that of ploughing, particularly deep ploughing, which, though justified on the grounds of increased agricultural yield, levels earthworks and cuts into the underlying structural evidence.

The statistics of damage and destruction have been collated and are published elsewhere (Rahtz, ed., 1974) and they have forced a fundamental debate on archaeological policy. Is there any excuse, in the face of this widespread and inevitable devastation, for the archaeological destruction, in the name of research, of otherwise unthreatened sites; or should field archaeologists devote all their time and energy to rescue and salvage excavation? The crux of the debate is whether sites which are in no danger should be left untouched for future examination and the whole of our archaeological resources, both amateur and professional, used to rescue whatever information can be extracted from those sites which are imminently threatened.

It is often argued that any information rescued from a site about to be destroyed is better than none. But if the documentary analogy, begun in Chapter I, is allowed to continue, one must imagine a newly-discovered manuscript available only for a minute or two before destruction. Under good conditions a few sentences or even whole paragraphs might be rescued before the document vanishes for ever. Some of these sentences might contain information which could revolutionise ideas; other phrases or sentences, perhaps the majority, may be highly ambiguous or positively misleading. A single paragraph, torn from its context, could lead to misconceptions on which a whole series of false assumptions might be based. This is certainly the case with some rescue excavation, which at its worst is done hurriedly and incompletely, often under tremendous pressure, against a background of thunderous machinery or collapsing masonry, when all discussion must be shouted, and when there is no time for the deliberate thought, amounting to contemplation, which is necessary if fundamental errors of interpretation are to be avoided.

Too often we have been led to believe that a sample of a site provides us with a microcosm of its development; but further work, perhaps undertaken many years later, all too often reveals that the earlier interpretation was entirely wrong. If the site had been destroyed during the initial excavation these revisions could never have been made, and the earlier evidence would have been accepted as part of the corpus of archaeological data which we use to build up our picture of the past. If sampling excavations, carefully planned to answer specific questions can be so misleading, how much more so will be those whose course is dictated by the progress of a building schedule or the availability of a bulldozer?

There is also a tendency to believe that a hurriedly carried out total excavation will give a précis or abstract of the site, recovering all its essential information and merely leaving the details to be filled in by further work, if this were possible. Nothing could be more mistaken. Swift excavation by machine or coarse hand-digging is not so much like a photographic negative, which, as it develops, progressively reveals the broad outlines and important masses of light and shade of the subject, but is more like an X-ray, which shows many important elements of the structure but fails to reveal others which are of equal importance in its function.

Here we have the core of the dilemma. If total excavation of most of our sites is patently impossible and partial excavation is known to be potentially misleading, what are we to do? We must, I think, be acutely and continually aware of the situation and its limitations, and attempt as far as possible to reduce these limitations to a minimum. Those sites which are to be completely destroyed by other agencies must claim priority for total excavation, if only we can get at them in time. This will require planning, perhaps years in advance of their destruction, if we are to be able to conduct rescue work in the manner of a research excavation, with the tactics and pace dictated by the archaeologist rather than the developer or gravel extractor.

This desirable situation has already been achieved on a number of sites, and is a policy which is gradually being implemented by the Inspectorate of Ancient Monuments as the limitations of hurried and partial excavation become more generally recognized.

One of the greatest difficulties in assessing the viability and strategy of a rescue excavation is the impossibility of knowing beforehand how complex the site may be and therefore how much time should be spent on each phase of the occupation. This is particularly the case with urban sites. A machine-cut trench may show that there is a complex of Roman and sub-Roman banks and ditches 3m. below the surface, with prehistoric occupation beneath, and many undatable layers above, heavily mutilated by post-medieval pits. It would be easy to strip off the first metre or so by machine and then to deal with the comparatively undisturbed major features below. But by doing so a whole sequence of medieval and post-medieval tenements might be lost.

Alternatively, there is strong argument for the detailed area stripping of the upper layers on the grounds that we should never know what we were losing if they were bulldozed away.

Such slow and detailed stripping might produce plans of ten successive backyards and leave us oblivious of the Roman and Dark Age defences below. If there is not time to do everything (and we must work strenuously towards making sure that there is time for everything) then painful decisions must be made. These decisions should be based on an assessment of the nationally considered academic priorities, and not on personal research interests or the ease with which the more obvious features might be excavated. The strategy of any large-scale excavation, whether urban or rural, should be a matter for discussion so that a balanced view can be considered and a consensus of opinion achieved. It is true that a great number of our most spectacular excavations of the past have been the result of individual flair, but the centres of our historic cities and our major rural sites are too precious to be left to arbitrary decisions or personal whims.

Before decisions are taken to sacrifice the uppermost structures, late and comparatively unimportant though they may be, it must be remembered that the attitudes of developers, sand and gravel extractors, farmers, and the Inspectorate of Ancient Monuments itself can be changed in the light of what is discovered. The meticulous demonstration of a group of post-medieval buildings combined with suitable propaganda may convince all those concerned, not only that the excavators are competent, but that they are capable of revealing the whole history of the town in a way quite unexpected by the laymen on the Council who are impatient to add to the town's car parking space, and that they should therefore be given time to do so. Nothing succeeds like success, and it is correspondingly much easier to convince the various interests concerned that they should delay development and even contribute funds to the excavation if the results can be seen and explained, rather than postulated on the grounds of probability.

In an ideal archaeological world all sites would be examined before they were lost or deeply damaged, but the rate of present destruction is far beyond our existing resources. We are forced to choose a course lying between two extremes: to concentrate on a few of the threatened sites, digging them slowly and entirely, and letting the rest go; or trying to salvage something from every site before it vanishes. There is something to be said for both points of view. The total excavation of very large settlement sites such as Warendorf (Wincklemann, 1958) and Dorestad (van Es, 1969) is enormously impressive, and they yield information far in excess of that given by a hundred smaller excavations. On the other hand, it can be argued that if concentration on a few sites means the abandonment of the rest, the overall picture is bound to suffer; there being no guarantee, for instance, that the sites chosen for full excavation are typical of their kind, or that those left unexcavated were not of even greater importance. Devotees of the distribution map will point out that enough small excavations should eventually provide coverage for the whole country; and that from these maps the broad pattern of invasion, settlement, trade, and social and religious groupings should emerge.

The answer lies somewhere between the two extremes. The selective preservation or long-term digging of carefully chosen sites where optimum conditions for excavation can be arranged, together with the rescue and salvage excavation of as many other sites as can be adequately dealt with, is a policy already being implemented in Britain, and may be thought to achieve the best of both worlds.

What is the relevance of this dilemma for the future of archaeological techniques and attitudes? Clearly, we must keep in mind the limitations and dangers of misinterpretation inherent in the hurried and partial excavation. Beyond the difficulties outlined above there is the much more insidious hazard, unadmitted by most excavators, that, when a site is being totally destroyed, there is an unconscious slackening in the precision with which observations are made; an attitude brought about partly by the necessity for speed, but also by the knowledge that the results can never subsequently be checked, or disputed. For this very reason rescue excavations ought, if anything, to be more rigorously directed than research excavations. They certainly do not require less skill.

Rescue excavations also suffer from the fact that, since layers and features are often only visible for a matter of hours, it is rarely possible for them to be the subject of consultation or second opinion. Thus they represent a particular danger in that the excavator may find, unconsciously, what he wants to find; and, once the evidence has gone, there is no basis for argument. These excavations, therefore, demand the strictest intellectual honesty from the director. This is not to suggest that anyone deliberately falsifies the evidence, since this would be about as satisfying as cheating at Patience, but it is particularly important when digging under pressure, perhaps with the press, the landowner or even one's colleagues expecting instant expositions of work in progress, not to allow sub- conscious patterns of thought to colour the immediate interpretation of the evidence as it appears in the ground. Attractive hypotheses suggested by the emerging evidence tend to crystallize, especially if apparently supporting evidence goes on accumulating. If at some point a crucial, contradictory piece of evidence emerges it can then become very painful to perform the volte face necessary to accept that one's previous theories are wrong and that everything has to be rethought.

In the face of all this destruction is there any justification at all for research excavation? So far as technique is concerned, the calmer pace and controlled strategy of research fieldwork and excavation enable us to evolve and test new techniques and, at the same time, to assess the validity of our rescue work. One discipline illuminates the other. In particular, research excavations warn us how much is likely to be missed under the conditions in which rescue and salvage excavation has to be carried out. To use again the example of Hen Domen, Montgomery, the excavation of a length of 20 metres of the bailey rampart has taken ten seasons' work. The rampart, of boulder clay, has been taken apart entirely by trowel or small hand-pick. A machine-cut section or one dug with pick and shovel would have shown the existence of a number of post-holes but would not have detected the thirteen or so buildings on the rampart's crest and rear slope, nor would it have revealed the sequence of the earliest defences. Beyond this, many features of timber buildings can only be seen under optimum weather conditions, so that one has to be patient and wait for just these conditions if one cannot create them artificially. But during a rescue excavation there may be no chance whatever of obtaining such conditions, and we have to be grateful for what we can salvage.

The recent increases in the scale of rescue excavations, brought about by the need to excavate whole sites and even whole landscapes, have required the development of new techniques of area stripping, principally to speed up the clearance of large areas of topsoil from sand, gravel, chalk, clay and loess sites. There are however no obvious short cuts in the excavation of deeply stratified sites containing stony layers and/or stone buildings.

Under rescue conditions much time may be saved by first examining the site using all the known non-destructive methods. On the collated results of such surveys a reasoned plan of campaign can be based. But it should be remembered that the most important structures on the site might very well escape the various forms of geophysical examination; either because their remains are not anomalously magnetic, or because they are not founded in deep post-holes or on walls which can be detected by the resistivity meter. In such cases, a limited excavation based solely on geophysical anomalies may be seriously misguided; and there are no certain safeguards against such an eventuality.

Under present circumstances a planned sequence of quasi-research excavations may be impossible; but the situation can nevertheless be exploited in two ways. Firstly, even if sites are fully examined in the random sequence in which they are threatened, the accumulating sum of information thus gained can eventually be synthesised. Secondly, if we accept that we cannot dig or even satisfactorily observe all the sites that are being destroyed, we can with sufficient notice select well in advance those sites which we would choose to excavate under ideal conditions; and, if these sites cannot be preserved untouched, try to arrange the most favourable circumstances for their excavation. This will involve the provision not only of much more money for longer and more complex excavations, but of more highly trained personnel, so that an intensive field training scheme will have to go hand in hand with any expanded rescue scheme.

The comparatively recent formation of a number of regional and urban units is an encouraging step towards rationalizing the otherwise *ad hoc* situation which has existed for too long in British archaeology. The even more recent formation of ministerially-appointed regional advisory committees and a national advisory committee may mean that sites will be selected for preservation or excavation on a sounder academic basis than has often been the case, and with a long-term strategy for ensuring that adequate techniques of exploration are readily available for the most important sites.

The rescue excavation of crop-mark sites[*]

By definition, most crop-mark sites will have been ploughed, and in many cases all, or most, of the vertical stratigraphy of the occupation layers will have been removed, leaving a palimpsest of ditches, pits, post-holes and other features which were dug deep enough to have penetrated the subsoil. The situation may be complicated by non-archaeological features caused by erosion, ice action, solifluction, the filling of hollows with naturally silted material, and the solution of calciferous rocks by leaching water. It is imperative that these natural features should be recognized and separated in the record from the archaeological evidence, since otherwise far-reaching mistakes may be made (Limbrey, 1975, 283).

In sites without vertical stratification, separation of contemporary and related structural features depends very largely on pattern making (what van Es has called the sport of 'granary building', van Es, 1967, 87) and on the intersection of ditches, pits and post-holes where a sequence can be demonstrated. Both problems are illustrated and discussed in a concise article

---

[*] For a concise description of the discovery of sites by aerial photography and of methods of locating sites on the ground see Coles, 1972, 21-45.

by M.U. Jones (1974) which includes an excellent plan of the excavation of an area of gravel terrace, part of a whole ancient landscape currently being destroyed by quarrying. It is a most useful exercise, for those wishing to understand the principles of interpreting sites of this kind, to take such a plan and attempt to sort it into periods, based on the intersection of features, and into coherent structures, based on pattern making. It is particularly instructive to see how many alternative 'building plans' can be made using the same features kaleidoscoped into different (but mutually exclusive) patterns. The extensive plans included in the Wijster report (van Es, 1967) are ideal for the purpose (see back endpapers). The student's interpretation can then be compared with that of the excavator and discrepancies discussed.

One of the chief difficulties in excavating a crop-mark site lies in locating the crop-marks precisely in the field in which they occur. Very often the photograph shows a field or fields without readily distinguishable landmarks and often, too, the bearing of the aircraft is not precisely recorded. The problem is increased if the photographs are oblique, though it is often only oblique photographs which reveal crop-marks clearly, since in many cases they result from the reflection or absorption of light from the leaves of growing crops, so that a vertical photograph, looking, as it were, straight down the leaf, is least effective.

Two simple methods of transferring oblique aerial photographs on to maps are described by Irwin Scollar in Wilson (ed. 1975, 52). One is the paper-strip method and the other the Mobius network method. Neither requires any apparatus beyond a pencil and a ruler. The degree of accuracy depends on the size and clarity of the photograph, and the corresponding size and detail of the map. Errors are also introduced if the ground is undulating, or, worse, hilly since the method assumes the ground to be flat. If a number of oblique photographs of the site taken from different directions are available they can be plotted together on the map and the mean of the errors taken. Once they are plotted on to the relevant map at the largest feasible scale the best way of locating them on the ground is by geophysical survey, either by magnetometer or resistivity meter. The use of divining rods should not be despised; on some sites remarkably consistent results have been obtained where other, more conventional methods have failed. If there are ditches of clearly defined shapes the identification of these should be aimed at. The problem is greater if the crop-marks consist of a complex of pits and post-holes, or parallel ditches where features may well be confused one with another. If geophysical methods do not locate the features sufficiently accurately, it may be necessary to cut one or more trial trenches across the site in the hope that the features can be related unambiguously to the crop-marks, though it must be borne in mind that all sites prove, on excavation, to contain many features which do not appear on the photographs, so that one must beware of being misled. Such trial trenches also recover significant amounts of pottery, building material and so on which all help in the assessment of the character of the site.

The least damage to the site will be done if the trial trenches are cut down only as far as the uppermost surfaces of the features. In this way their pattern can be recovered without their relationship with surrounding features being destroyed unobserved.

If there is any doubt about the location of the crop-marks on the ground the trial trench or trenches should be wide and sited so that they will certainly cross the crop-marks at some point, preferably where they are densest and have readily identifiable shapes. Trenches narrow enough to pass between pits or post-holes are obviously not satisfactory.

Such wide but shallow trial trenches should pick up recognizable features without damage to the site. The whole area can then be plotted from these as datum points, and the excavation strategy planned on a proper basis.

Where formerly stratified sites have been ploughed it is possible that the latest occupation layers have been destroyed, especially if they were only of timber with pebble or clay floors. In such cases the pottery used by the last occupants will still be there, churned up in the plough soil. If the field has been allowed to revert to pasture, a common occurrence, the latest pottery will drift downward due to worm action until it rests on the undestroyed archaeological layers. It may then be mistakenly considered to relate to these earlier levels instead of the later levels from which it derived.

Inevitably, all fast methods of stripping large areas of topsoil involve the risk of losing not only structural detail and associated finds but also whole periods of occupation. Most, but not all, of the excavators who use these or similar methods are aware of their limitations (eg. Jones, 1968, 229) but are prepared to accept them. The excavator of the Carolingian city of Dorestad has quantified the loss of coin evidence. In the earlier excavations of 1842 Janssen found 11 Carolingian coins in an area of about 400 m.[2] In the excavations of 1967-8 only ten coins were found in an area of about 55,000 m.[2] (van Es, 1969). These losses must be weighed against the eventual recovery of the plan of an entire early medieval city.

Where the site has been under the plough (and the fertile nature of the soils mentioned above has usually resulted in a long history of cultivation after the abandonment of settlements), it is usual to strip off the ploughsoil by machine on the assumption that the uppermost structural evidence will be found at the junction of the ploughsoil or humus and the undisturbed subsoil, into which features are cut, or, exceptionally, at some stratified levels below the ploughsoil. However, this assumption has been jolted by the discovery that on some crop-mark sites features seen on aerial photographs have not been discovered when the site has been excavated. Peter Reynolds has suggested that the soil differences which caused the crop-marks were contained within the ploughsoil. A possible explanation of this phenomenon is that ploughing disturbs the soil, but, especially on flat ground, does not move it very far from its original position. The chemical differences that cause crop differentiation, visible in the photographs, may therefore persist in the ploughsoil, which, if the site is to be fully excavated, should be examined archaeologically. This situation is paralleled by soil marks which may be seen on newly-ploughed land. Usually these soil-marks are reflections of features and other changes in the subsoil, but it is quite possible that some of them do not reach the subsoil. Work needs to be done on this problem before we can assess the losses of this sort of evidence due to topsoil stripping.

It is normal to machine-strip topsoil down to within a few centimetres of the subsoil, or, if they exist, of the occupation layers. The subsoil is then cleaned by hand, either with trowels, or dutch hoes (fig. 41) or with spades used horizonrally (fig. 42). The latter method is the fastest but the crudest. On stonefree sands, clay, or loess, machine stripping can be refined to produce a surface almost as clean as necessary. The Dutch State archaeological service has developed a dragline cradle with a knife-edge that can strip layers from 5 to 10cm. thick, leaving a relatively clean surface (fig. 43). This sort of machine is ideal for fast excavation of the *planum* kind.

An outstanding example of large-scale rescue excavation both in technique and speed of publication is provided by J. G. Wainwright's work on Durrington Walls (Wainwright, 1971). The reader is urged to study it.

The planum method and the horizontal section

In this method, which can only reasonably be used on sites on stone-free soil and without stone buildings, layers of arbitrary thickness are removed over a whole area. These layers have no relation to vertical stratigraphy, and the method should therefore not be used where there are any preserved occupation layers. Where all the features are cut into the subsoil it can be used more successfully and with considerable speed. As each successive thin layer of the site is removed, the plan of the area with its exposed features is drawn to an appropriate scale. Slowly the pattern of the various features builds up. Some disappear with depth, others emerge, or become clearer. At no stage are the features of one period exposed and dealt with at one time, enabling a view of one building or structure to be seen in its entirety. As small features are not emptied separately and in the order in which they are stratified there is a danger that finds from discrete features will become mixed together, confusing the chronology and perhaps the constituent parts of structures. It is necessary, therefore to plot the finds three-dimensionally, in order that they may be related precisely to the features from which they derive. The method, together with its interpretation can be seen clearly in van Es 1969, figs 7-11. In contrast to the usual methods, in which the subsoil is left unexcavated, this technique involves the removal of enormous quantities of spoil, since slices of the subsoil are removed together with those of the features. It can nevertheless be useful on a smaller scale, for example where the junction of a series of ditches or a complex of post-holes cannot be emptied in sequence, because the soil differentiation is not sufficiently clear. In this case, the attempt to distinguish intercutting features may easily result in overdigging and the loss of evidence, and the planum method used discreetly may be more successful.

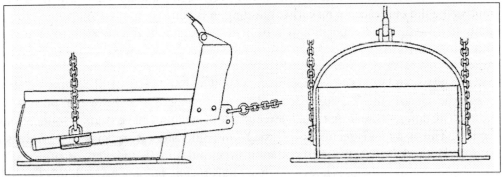

Figure 41   Dutch hoes in use in London

Figure 42   Shaving the surface with long-handled spades after removal of top-soil by drag-line Dorestad, Holland.

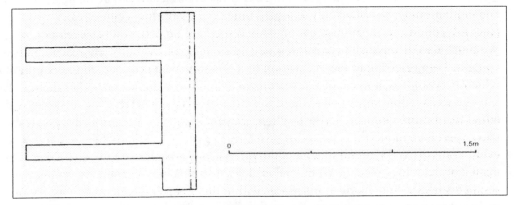

Figure 43   Drag-line bucket as modified by the Dutch State Archaeological Service for large-scale excavation of flat, stone-free sites.

It may also be necessary, and valuable, to use arbitrary layers, where, for example, the soil or rubble make-up of a timber building is being removed. It may not be at all clear how thick the layer is, or whether it is uniform in thickness and composition. Under these circumstances, rather than taking the risk of overdigging and perhaps destroying or mutilating the evidence for an earlier building, it is better to remove the layer a little at a time. In this way, its composition will be better understood; and interleaved layers less likely to be missed.

Gravel and sand sites are often excavated by bulldozing off the upper layers to the top of the subsoil, the B/C horizon, leaving only the bottoms of the deeper pits and post-holes. The danger here is that much larger buildings, if they have slighter foundations, will be lost. The problem is seen in its classic form on the sites of pagan Saxon villages where sunken-floored huts are the most common structural find. If evidence for larger buildings with shallower post-holes is lost through natural erosion, bulldozing or simply through an inability to recognize the evidence, a completely false concept of these villages may gradually crystallize and become history. Our remoter English ancestors may have lived underground. But we must be acutely aware of the limitations of the excavated evidence and examine it hypercritically before we assert that they did.

In the report of his classic excavation of the Anglo-British complex at Yeavering in Northumberland, Brian Hope-Taylor describes (Hope-Taylor, 1977, pp. 32 and n. 49) what he calls primary and secondary horizontal sections, the first being the surfaces of all the archaeological strata lying immediately under the plough-soil, which had been carefully cleaned off with trowel and brush. His secondary horizontal sections consist of the horizontal dissection of the structures revealed by the first process. He admits, on p. 35 *ibid.*, that if he were to investigate further buildings on the same site he would 'dispense with most of the longitudinal sections and work more directly in terms of successive horizontal sections'.

Salvage excavation and recording

In the ideal long-term excavation every aspect of a site can be dealt with slowly and meticulously; but when only a limited time is available the techniques evolved under research conditions must be streamlined and speeded up and, where necessary, adapted. We must also distinguish between rescue and salvage excavations. By rescue, in this context, I am referring to the excavation of a threatened site conducted under conditions which may approach those of a research excavation to a greater or lesser degree. By a salvage excavation I mean one where the excavator salvages what he can from a site either just before or during its destruction. Salvage excavation requires the greatest skill and experience of all if the questions posed by the site are to be recognized and solved, even if only partially, and if fundamentally disastrous mistakes are to be avoided. This is instant archaeology indeed. When one is cleaning a machine-cut section or a newly scraped surface, both likely to disappear within the hour, a considerable mastery of archaeological technique is essential together with a flexible approach and the ability to interpret the evidence as it appears and to record it quickly and accurately.

Ultimately the value of the evidence from a salvage excavation will depend on the quality of the observations made on the site.

For example, in almost all cases, only positive evidence should be used. Under the sort of circumstances which give rise to salvage work the argument from negative evidence is highly suspect.

A salvage excavation may prove conclusively from a mass of stratified pottery that a site was occupied in medieval times, but it is unlikely to be able to prove that it was just as intensively occupied in the preceding aceramic period, though total detailed excavation may have done so. It may be argued that information at this level is not worth having, but if the pottery comes from an earthwork or crop-mark previously assumed to have been prehistoric or Roman, the evidence may be considered to be worth the day or two spent retrieving it.

As I write, a salvage excavation is being carried out on one of the medieval gates of the city of Worcester, and it provides a good example of the kind of information which can be gained from such smash-and-grab tactics.

A stretch of City ditch and a wide trench behind the wall were being cleared by machine. As the clearance progressed it was realized that it was approaching the site of the Friar's Gate, believed to be a postern in the wall close to the site of the Grey Friars. The machine was digging into the face of the cuttings in the usual way, a method which would have destroyed any remains of the postern without it being seen. Accordingly, the driver was asked to dig the area horizontally in layers. As a result stonework both on and behind the wall and in the ditch was revealed. Rapid cleaning by one person with a trowel and spade, working with the machine, showed that the remains were sufficiently well preserved to justify a salvage excavation. The optimum work force would have been two skilled excavators/recorders plus five or six volunteers/ labourers working with the machinery. The results, though much less than total retrieval of all the available evidence, fully justified the time spent. They showed that, far from being a postern gate, the Friars Gate led to a wide bridge with abutments of many periods, the latest of which appeared to be the foundations of a building spanning the whole width of the city ditch. This additional knowledge of Worcester's history certainly justified the comparatively small outlay of time, skilled labour and money spent. A subsequent salvage excavation further along the city wall of Worcester is illustrated in figs. 44 and 45.

The loss of information due to the rushed and partial nature of the work is not so easy to assess, simply because we have not seen it. The excavator himself should qualify all his recorded observations with estimates of their reliability on a scale which ranges from certain to only possible. The dating of structures by means of stratified pottery, coins and other artefacts is particularly difficult under these circumstances, and the excavator must be certain that the datable material really was derived from the significant layer or structure and not introduced by machinery or the soles of boots. The bucket of a drag-line, cutting a section of a ditch, can embed material from the upper layers deep into the primary silting, and cover it with a smear of the same material. When the ditch section is

cleaned back it is disconcerting to find a half-brick stratified in the bottom of what is quite
certainly a Roman ditch of the first century. The half brick can be discarded as
contamination and the section cleaned back further until uncontaminated layers are
reached, but if instead of a brick a sherd of late Roman pottery or a fourth-century coin
had found its way similarly into the early ditch, it would not have been discarded so
promptly, thus causing real confusion. For the same reasons, the provenance of finds
handed in by workmen or unskilled volunteers must be treated with the greatest reserve
unless they can be checked on the spot.

Figure 44   **Talbot Street, Worcester, 1975; an example of opportunist salvage archaeology,
                    where a long trench dug by bulldozer behind the City Wall of Worcester (fig.
                    44) was seen to be densely stratified. An emergency cleaning and recording
                    operation was mounted, and part of the result is shown in fig. 45.**

The minimum equipment for a salvage recorder should be two good cameras,
$2^{1/4}'$-square for colour negative film, and 35mm. for transparencies, with two high-level
tripods; a quick-set level and staff, if necessary with tripod attachment for single-handed
use; a large clipboard mounted with squared polyester film overlaid with drawing film to a
predetermined standard size, such as A4, A3 or a square format if this is preferred;
coloured pencils to an agreed area (or preferably regional) colour code; record cards, as
fully printed as possible, for sites, features, finds and photographs. Thus armed, a salvage
recorder or a team of two or three working together can clean features and sections,
draw them in outline and photograph them in colour negative and reversal film. The key
drawings of both sections and plans must have spot heights inserted, so that they can be
related to previous or further work in the area. If the work is in a town or city it should be
possible to get the colour negatives processed and printed within 24 hours. If prints (of a
section for example) are made to a predetermined scale, they can be pasted together and
annotated on the site. This obviates all but the most skeletal drawing. It is also cost-
effective. A section 45m. long and 3m. high would take a week to draw and colour in
detail. Photographically it can be recorded, printed and fully annotated in 2-3 days, the
cost of the prints being offset by the saving of time.

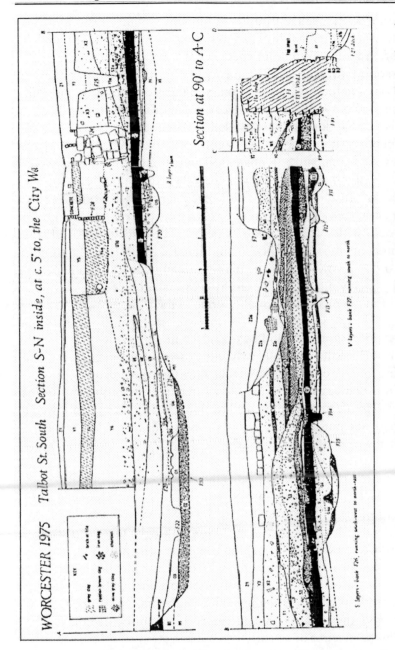

Figure 45

Among a good deal of other detail, evidence of Roman iron-smelting (already attested elsewhere in the city) is shown by layers prefixed with Q; these are overlain by R layer, which represents the immediate post-Roman period; the S layers are a bank of unknown date preceding the medieval wall and running at an acute angle to it; the V layers are a longitudinal section of a pre-wall bank perhaps of the twelfth century; the W layers are the construction trench for the City Wall, while the U layers are the upper fill of an early (perhaps Roman) scoop or gulley (0 layers). This short salvage recording has added much to the evidence for Worcester's defences, though it has also raised a number of problems which only further excavation will solve.

Such recording should be carried out by an archaeologist with considerable experience in research and long-term rescue excavation, experience against which he can assess the significance of features that may only be visible for an hour or two, or even a few minutes. It is not a job for an inexperienced enthusiast. Nevertheless, it is here that local volunteers can be trained and used effectively. A group of eight or ten unskilled but energetic volunteers can enormously increase the amount of information retrieved, by cleaning surfaces, sections and walls, assisting with measuring, surveying and photography, and dealing with pottery and finds on a simple basis. Usually among such a group one or two will rapidly develop skills enabling them to draw plans and sections under supervision, and to adapt previously acquired photographic techniques and so forth.

In the post-excavation work, such a group is of immense value, washing, marking and sorting pottery and other stable finds, assisting with the redrawing of plans and sections, and often going on to more specialised work. In Worcester, between 1965 and 1970, some extremely skilled drawing of finds and pottery, the stabilization of leather shoes and their reconstruction, and the reconstruction of highly decorated pottery were carried out by local volunteers, none of whom had had previous experience. This can, no doubt, be paralleled in rescue and salvage excavations all over the country. It has the added benefit of drawing local people into the archaeology of the town or area, and is a powerful educational stimulus as well as an intensely satisfying recreation for those who take part. Not only that, it also extends and enhances the limited funds available for rescue archaeology since most part-time local volunteers are happy to work on their own town, or on a local site for nothing, except perhaps help with expenses such as petrol. The director of a salvage excavation, however competent and experienced, can increase his potential output tenfold by the recruiting of local volunteers. The maximum number which one person can direct is probably 10-15. Beyond this, a hierarchy of assistant directors or site supervisors will be needed in the proportion of about one to ten.

Needless to say, such local groups should be organised in such a way that they are insured in a scheme such as that of the CBA and, while they may come and go on site at odd times or days according to their other commitments, they must be prepared to accept all the normal site disciplines, and be subject to the same safety precautions as a full-time team. For this reason it is advisable to enrol members by name before they are allowed to take part. The director cannot and must not accept responsibility for casual visitors and small boys who may join in the work uninvited.

Another constraint on excavation techniques is the sheer size of some sites, either in area or in depth. We have seen that unstratified sites of many acres can be stripped progressively by machine and then hand-dug, and in theory, if the money and skilled manpower were available, a site of almost any extent could be dug simply by multiplying the numbers of workers at all levels. This is not the case, however, on sites with very deep deposits where the number of people who can be deployed on the ground is limited by the surface area. If there is a multiplicity of thin but significant layers there will be a maximum speed at which they can be individually stripped and recorded. If, on the other hand, the situation is made more awkward by deep layers of sticky clay or heavy rubble the niceties of sensitive area excavation may be hard to achieve. Here one simply has to excavate with as much precision as is possible. Remembering that our canals and railways were all dug by hand, it should be possible to recruit a gang of navvies who could deal with such a situation, and there is no doubt that hand labour has great flexibility and is less potentially destructive than machinery, although it is far more expensive.

The aim of the director of either a rescue or a salvage excavation must be maximum time and cost-effectiveness; in other words the maximum amount of reliable evidence for the time and money available. Any method of digging and recording that accelerates the excavation process with minimal loss of evidence or accuracy must be tried and exploited.

Assuming ample money, equipment and skilled personnel to be available, the speeding-up of a rescue excavation might be achieved without appreciable loss of detail and accuracy by making the excavation as mechanically-assisted and labour intensive as possible –a piece of high-priority archaeological civil engineering. As many people (assuming them to be skilled) as could work on the site at once should be employed. It would be necessary, of course, to have a carefully balanced hierarchy of supervisors, recorders, photographers etc., and a very clearly understood chain of command. Adequate shelters, where necessary, and floodlights, using mains electricity or generators, would allow work to continue in two or three shifts of eight or ten hours (with breaks) so that work could go on for 20 or 24 hours a day. Floodlit football is a commonplace. There is no reason why floodlit excavation should not be also.

Shift working would need a considerable degree of organisation and close cooperation between the teams working jointly on the site. Its success would depend on the site supervisors being highly competent, thoroughly briefed, capable of working together, and overlapping with each other in their shifts to ensure continuity. It would be an advantage if some of the excavators and recorders overlapped also to avoid a sharp break in personnel. The director, who clearly cannot be on site continuously, would need to have complete faith in his principal supervisors in such a cooperative scheme and there would be less scope for the brilliant, intuitive individualist. The director would, in fact, chiefly play the role of adviser, organiser and coordinator.

The deployment of a large number of people on a site requires clear thinking and careful coordination if there is not to be chaos. If the work could proceed across the site from one end to another it would be easier for the excavators to be followed by finds-recorders, draughtsmen, surveyors, photographers and so on. In such an excavation the bulk of the recording would be photographic, using polaroid film in large format, and vertical and oblique stereoscopy in colour (see Chapter 8). Nevertheless a minimum of surveying and drawing would still be needed. If it were intended to draw the site photogrammetrically by machine, an accurate prior survey of each run or area would be needed. If the photographs were intended to supplement the plans, outline drawings to the necessary degree of detail rendering the photographs intelligible when related to the skeletal plan would be needed.

The removal of spoil is often a slow and laborious process. Conveyor belts, either with or without buckets, considerably speed up the process, and experiments should be made with vacuum removal of the finer spoil. In either case, it would be possible, with care, to remove the spoil from discrete features or layers separately, so that sieving, either wet or dry, flotation or other sampling could take place outside the excavation area.

Hand in hand with the swift recording of the visual evidence must go streamlined methods of finds recording. Here index cards, bags, boxes, labels and so forth should be printed beforehand, so far as possible, so that the minimum amount of writing is needed. Automatic consecutive numbering and lettering stamps and other such devices would all save valuable time.

The thought of such a high-pressure excavation, with its non-stop activity and continuous noise, will seem a nightmare to many, especially to those of us who enjoy excavation in sylvan surroundings where the silence is broken only by the music of a dozen trowels. And it may be that, however urgent the destruction, noisy work at night would be unacceptable in residential areas. In that case, it may be necessary to do without machinery during the night, and concentrate on those tasks which can be done quietly.

It must be remembered that, whatever accelerating techniques are invented, there is a point beyond which it is impossible, for sheer logistic reasons, to speed up excavation. No technical aids, no amount of money or number of people can strip an acre of thinly stratified deposits in a day. Furthermore, high-speed excavation loses that most essential quality of the slower excavation, the opportunity to think quietly, to contemplate the evidence, to go back to it *on the ground*, and, if necessary, to reassess it drastically. It is useless to achieve speed without understanding.

The sort of intensive excavation outlined here would, it is hoped, only be used as a last resort. We must, therefore, work towards making such extreme measures unnecessary, by means of forward planning coupled with legislation which will permit sufficient time for thorough, less hurried, investigation.

Analysis: Recognising and Recording the Evidence

Introduction

Recording is, of course, a fundamental activity in excavation, but what is seen and what is recorded are related to the mental set of the investigator; careful observation is not sufficient. This does not mean, however, that the archaeologist is guided by what is expected or dictated by the needs of the problem-oriented approach discussed earlier. So a background of experience is needed, but, equally, there should be openness to the unexpected. Analysis and interpretation must happen as a continuous activity as excavation proceeds, and a wide range of questions should always be at hand. But, with the kind of detailed recording recommended by Barker, we realize that a total record is not possible. Thus guidelines should be set up concerning the retrieval of data for the record of excavation. Barker then outlines the criteria for recording and the method of recording, including record cards, daily accounts and reflections, the manner of recording vertical and horizontal of finds and features. He makes detailed suggestions concerning the creation of a master grid for the site, triangulation and leveling, drawing and photography

Only what is observed can be recorded; and observation is not an automatic process. It depends entirely on the particular knowledge of the observer. Hanson (1967) deals with just this point:

There is more to seeing than meets the eyeball, and there is more to scientific observation than merely standing alert with sense organs at the ready . . . . . The visitor (to the laboratory) must learn physics before he can see what the physicist observes. Only then will the context throw into relief those features in the phenomena which the physicist observes as indicating (e.g.) resistance. This obtains in all cases of observation. It is all *interest-directed and context-dependent*. Attention is rarely directed to the space between the leaves of a tree. Still, consider what was involved in Robinson Crusoe's seeing a vacant space in the sand as a footprint. Our attention rests on objects and events which because of our selective interests dominate the visual field. What a blooming, buzzing, undifferentiated confusion visual life would be if we all arose tomorrow morning with our attention capable of dwelling only on what has heretofore been completely overlooked. Indeed our mental institutions are full of poor souls who, despite having normal vision, can observe nothing. Theirs is a rhapsodic, kaleidoscopic, senseless barrage of sense signals-answering to nothing and signifying naught.

However, in scientific investigation there remains a basic and necessary duality of approach. On the one hand the selection of criteria of significance is crucial to the outcome of any investigation. As Alan Gregg, Director of Medical Sciences for the Rockefeller Foundation has said (Medawar, 1969);

Most of the knowledge and much of the genius of the research worker lie behind his selection of what is worth observing. It is a crucial choice, often determining the success or failure of months of work, often differentiating the brilliant discoverer from the plodder.

On the other hand it is often the unsuspected fact that turns out to be crucial to understanding. Beveridge (1950) warns:

If when we are experimenting, we confine our attention to only those things which we expect to see, we shall probably miss the unexpected occurrences and these, even though they may at first be disturbing and troublesome, are the most likely to lead to the explanation of the usual. When an irregularity is noticed, look for something with which it might be associated. In order to make original observations the best attitude is not to concentrate exclusively on the main point but to try and keep a lookout for the unexpected, remembering that observation is not passively watching but is an active mental process.

He also adds this corollary:

Effective scientific observation also requires a good background for only by being familiar with the usual can we notice something as being unusual or unexplained.

As Binford (1972) says:

Excavation must be conducted in terms of a running analysis and against a backdrop of the widest possible set of questions to which the data are potentially relevant. This is no technician's job. This is the job of an anthropologist specialized in the collection and analysis (and, I would add, synthesis) of data concerning extinct cultural systems.

All writers of excavation reports will know how difficult it is to keep the excavated evidence separate from its interpretation and this dilemma starts during the excavation itself. It is very easy to slip into the habit of calling dark circular soil marks 'post-holes' before they have been excavated. This not only prejudges the evidence, but can become that habit of mind which is capable of finding what it wants to find. Once a dark area has been presumed to be a post-hole it requires considerable mental discipline to accept, when it is emptied, that it is a root-hole or some other non-structural disturbance, especially if it is in just the place where a post-hole is expected (or even needed!) to complete a structure. On the sites of timber buildings the opportunities for the creative imagination are immense. In the same way, 'timber slots' may turn out to be drainage gullies, or grooves worn by eaves' drip, or intermittent plough furrows, and what at first sight seems to be a dump of broken tile may turn out to be a floor, or vice versa.

One must add the subtle but real pressure from one's colleagues to provide instant interpretations of phenomena as they appear. One has to steer a course between a neutral, non-interpretive approach which will quickly deflate the enthusiasm that buoys an excavation along, and flights of fancy which the evidence finally cannot support. One can occasionally see the fossilized remains of fancies of this kind embedded in excavation reports.

In order to minimize the interpretive element in the record a neutral term such as 'feature' or 'context' is perhaps best used to describe each separately recognizable anomaly, whether it is a layer, a post-hole, a floor, a hearth or whatever. Each anomaly can then be given a serial number either by grids viz: 1/1, 1/2, 1/3, 2/1, 2/2, 2/3, or throughout the whole site. This system has proved to be easier to use than that in which the term 'feature' is used only for anomalies within or cutting through layers. The difficulty arises in marginal cases, for example where a layer may be a hearth, or a hearth may be made up of many layers. 'Context' is an appropriate word to describe a layer or feature from which finds or other specific information are derived; but, being an abstract noun, it lacks reality when used in speech. You cannot section a context, or lower its surface by half a centimeter. There is no reason why the word 'layer' should not be retained for continuous deposits of material. In other words all 'layers' are 'features' (and should be called so in the record) but not all 'features' are 'layers'.

It is difficult to separate in our minds the excavated evidence from its interpretation, which inevitably begins as features are seen, dissected and removed. There are some aspects of the interpretation of features (the word is used in its widest sense) that are at their optimum when they are first revealed, since the site can never again be in that pristine, freshly-cleaned state. Time and weather will immediately begin to alter it. Sometimes weathering produces new information, and sometimes it destroys the uppermost surface entirely; and although subsequent cleaning may reveal new detail, much of the original detail will have disappeared. In addition, however meticulous and accurate the recording, it is impossible to draw every texture of the exposed soil, and record all the nuances of colour in layers which may merge imperceptibly with one another. In addition aspects of the site which cannot be seen or felt are likely to go unnoticed. Differences of chemical composition, for example, may not be visible but may exist and be of considerable significance in the understanding of the site. Some soil colour changes may only be made visible by ultra-violet or infra-red light or when enhanced by chemical treatment (p. 94 above); some important differences of level may only show up under conditions of glancing light; other features may only appear as dry or wet areas, invisible on ordinary days and disappearing when dissected.

To take a wider view there is the necessary contemplation of the excavated area (preferably when work on the site has temporarily stopped, so that there are no distractions), when relationships, unseen before, will become apparent, and when the overall pattern of the evidence will begin to emerge. This, seen three-dimensionally as one walks round or over the site, may be very difficult to record adequately, and virtually impossible to demonstrate in the eventual publication.

Thus at present the adequate and total recording of the evidence is beyond us. It follows that our responsibility for the immediate interpretation, made soon after the structures are uncovered, together with subsequent modifications, made in the light of all the observed evidence, is very great since the interpretive element in the recording can never be completely isolated, nor can drawings, photographs and written records ever be a substitute for the observations which are possible when one is present on the site. In other words, no mechanical process of recording even the nuances of the excavated surfaces will ever replace acute and sensitive observation by minds alive to all the possibilities presented by the evidence.

'Only connect' said E.M. Forster, and I believe that the most important need in archaeological excavation is to establish relationships, to interconnect structural layers and features, to relate them to the finds of all kinds, from sculpture to pollen, embedded in them and to relate the excavated site to its surroundings and to other comparable sites. Contiguous areas of excavation are almost always more illuminating than those separated from one another even by a meter or so, and inter-relationships established across and through large sites by a feature matrix are essential if the site is to be fully understood.

On most sites, except for those in towns, Layer 1 will be humus, topsoil or ploughsoil (though see p. 33). The removal of Layer 1 usually reveals a surface made up of a series of features adjoining, overlapping and running into one another. Even on a small site the number of separately distinguishable features making up the exposed surface may run into hundreds. Each of these has to be identified and recorded. Each distinguishable feature should be labelled as it appears, with a plastic label marked with a waterproof, light-proof 'dry-marker' type pen of Pentel type. It is a good idea to reserve one colour of plastic label for features, keeping other colours for finds or the positions of samples taken and so on. Labels are conveniently pinned to the ground with spring-headed galvanized nails.

Data retrieval

The object of all excavation recording is data retrieval. At the end of the excavation all that remains are the site records, the drawings and photographs, and the finds. Any information which is not contained in one of these is lost for good. If it is there somewhere, but is difficult to find, its retrieval may be as laborious as the excavation itself. All aspects of the site recording system – visual, in the form of drawings, sections, contour surveys, together with photographs, vertical and oblique, in color and black and white; or written, in the form of record cards, notebooks, punched cards, or tape – should be devised so that they make interpretation, publication and storage as easy as possible. It is not simply a question of data retrieval, but of producing from the data interpretive drawings of the site's phases and periods, buildings and structures; of wresting meaning from thousands of features, hundredweights of pottery and bone, and hundreds of finds, photographs and drawings. All this has ultimately to be distilled into readable prose, museum displays, popular books and reconstructions. Anything, therefore, that shortens this daunting process ought to be considered. What this means in practice is that the end product of the excavation should be borne in mind before the work begins.

There can be no hard and fast rules for excavation recording systems suitable for all types of excavation since sites vary so much in the nature of their structural evidence, and the types and quantities of finds. However, any system must satisfy the following criteria:

1.   It must be simple and logical to use and understand.

2.   It must be capable of indefinite extension, since the excavation itself may be extended beyond the original intentions or the quantities of finds may be very much greater than anticipated.

3.   It must be flexible. For this reason index cards are better than books since they can be sorted into any order, and later interpolations can be inserted in place quickly and comprehensively.

4.   The information must be retrievable. To this end, any large excavation should devise its recording system with one eye on computer storage, which, if not immediately available, may become so within the near future.

5.   The information should be presented in a form that makes the writing of the final report as easy as possible.

It is maintained by some that none of the data from an excavation is objective; that an excavation produces no *facts*. Nevertheless, a block of sandstone is a fact; mortar is a fact (demonstrable if necessary by chemical and physical analysis); and it is only a slight shift towards subjectivity to call a hundred blocks of sandstone, coursed and mortared together in a line, a wall. Beyond this, however, we become increasingly subjective. The wall's possible or probable function and date, and its relation to other structures must be considered; and ultimately the discussion may, properly, enter the realms of speculation. What is important is that all these stages should be distinguishable one from another.

For this reason, immediate on-site recording, the first stage in the process, should be as objective as it can be. It helps towards objectivity if the written recording is formalized, on cards or sheets, with spaces for answering specific questions and the provision of required categories of information. This is preferable to notebooks which contain paragraphs (sometimes essays) of descriptive prose whose loose format invites the writer to confuse the stages of recording, deduction, interpretation and speculation. The minimum information required on the index card is:

1.   The abbreviated name of the site.

2.   The area and grid numbers.

3.   The feature number.

4.   The position of the feature (as a grid reference).

5.   Its relation to features above, around and, eventually, below it.

6.   A description of the feature, including its composition or filling.

7.   Finds directly associated with the feature.

8.   A sketch, if this would be helpful, and/or a Polaroid photograph.

9.   Cross-reference to the measured drawings, sections and photographs.

10.   Subsequent interpretive notes, e.g. post-hole, part of structure XIII, kitchen, Phase 2.

11.   The considered reliability if this interpretation.

SITE RECORDING SHEET

MUSEUM OF LONDON
DEPARTMENT OF URBAN ARCHAEOLOGY
MUS 3477

Provisional Date	Type		Site Code	Context
Medival :?14thc.	Wall	110/215	ABC|82	1023

Description of Context

Random uncoursed ragstone (? Kentish) predominantly rough-hewn in large fragments and occasional blocks (eg. 0·23 x 0·38m in elevation) with occasional flint and medium frags of chalk (E side only); also 2 horizontally-laid medium frags of Roman tile. Patches of plaster for 2·6m from S end on E face, with horizontal bottom edge in two parts (see S67) 0·1m above 1067. Included in fabric, when excavated, was a sculptured stone 39 and 2 large frags PTO →

Site Grid Refs.   112·35 / 216·80

Levels *(tick)* a. when taken ....✓....   b. when transferred to plan(s) ....✓....

Stratigraphically Earlier than

1018								

Stratigraphically Later than

1067								

Method of Excavation   Trowel and gentle picking

Risk of Intrusive Finds *(tick one)*   Low ✓   High ....   Unknown ....

Finds

	Pot	Glass	T.Pipe	Metal	Brick/Tile	Other B.M.	Leather	Bone	Molluscs	Seeds	Wood/Charcoal
(tick if present)					✓	✓ Plaster					
(collection keyword)					A	S					

Other Finds *(specify & give keyword)* _____

Special Finds   △39 △ △ △ △ △ △ △ △ △ △

Samples

	Bulk Sample	Wood/Charcoal	C14	Dendro.	Pollen	Arch.Mag				
(tick if taken)	Type									
(number of bags)	Multi-context YES/NO									

Plan Nos: P 292	Initials & Date
Other Drawings: S 63, 67	Y.W. 25·6·82
Site Book Refs. N/A	
Location on Matrix Square A3	Checked by & Date
Photographs *(tick when taken)* ✓ Card Nos. 135, 140, 169, 232	R.K. 26·6·82

Interpretative Notes

N-S wall on foundation 1067. West wall of Building A. Plaster level at 11·06m OD (see elevation, S67) indicates interior floor level - presumably a wooden floor, see ? joist impressions 1092, 1165, 1166.

Phase	Group	Initials & Date
IV·7	68	RK 31·10·82

Figure 46   The context (or feature) record sheet used by the Department of Urban Archaeology of the Museum of London.

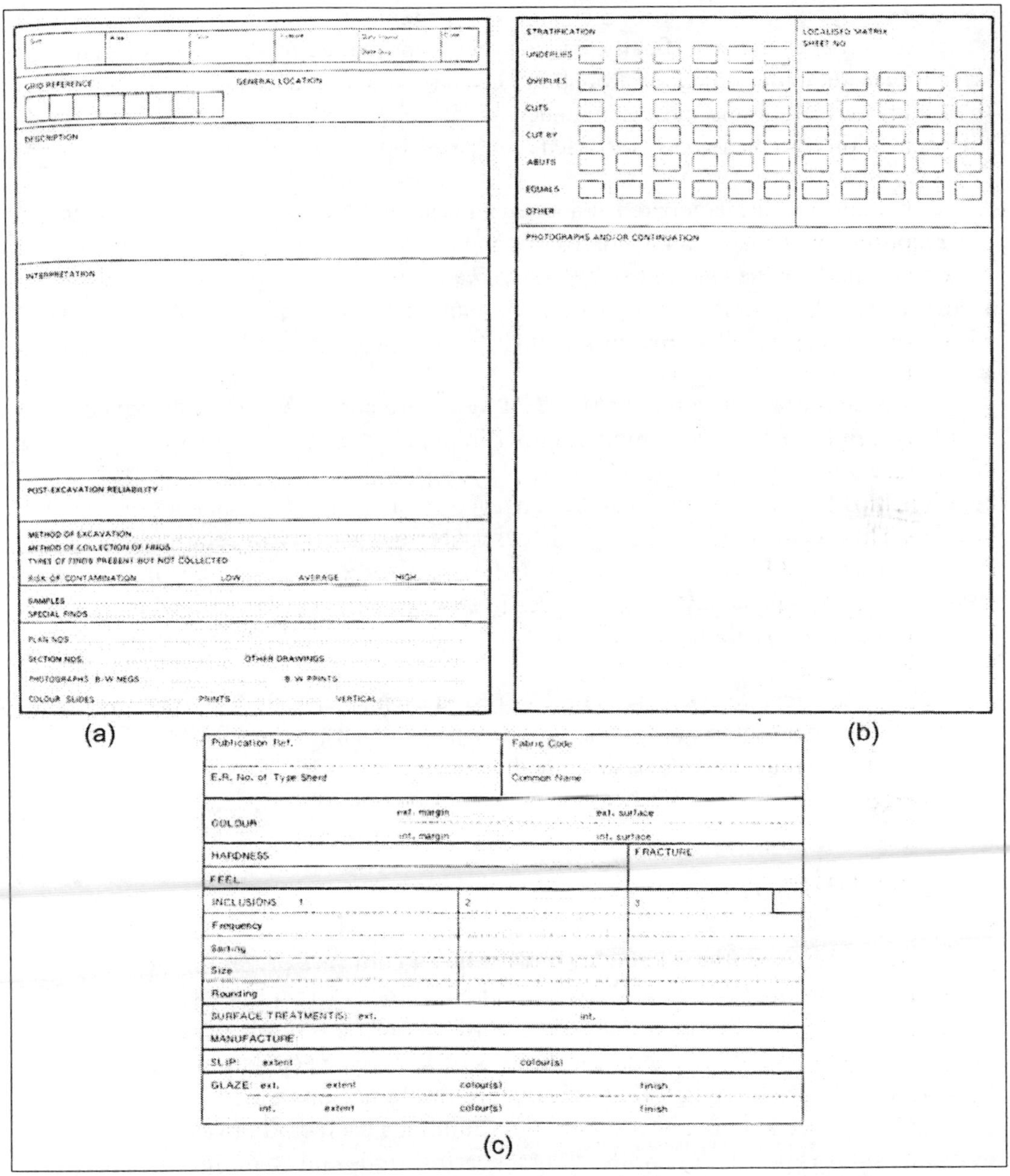

Figure 47   **Examples of record cards. (a) and (b) The feature card used at Wroxeter and Hen Domen. (c) The pottery record card used by the Department of Urban Archaeology, Museum of London.**

Suggested layouts of cards for recording features and layers are illustrated in figs. 46-7. These written records are complementary to the visual records which consist of the site plans and sections and the drawings of individual features, pottery and other finds together with both vertical and oblique photographs. The written records and the drawings and photographs must be cross-indexed so that the complete information about a feature or layer can be readily found. The information relating to an individual feature, for instance, should consist of: a completed feature card; a set of drawings, including plans and sections; photographs; cards for small finds and pottery found within the filling or structure of the feature; and, finally, the drawing of the feature on the main site plan, which relates it to the structures around it. On a site which produces hundreds, perhaps thousands, of features this may seem unnecessarily laborious, but there is no short cut if the excavation is to be properly recorded.

A number of the larger archaeological units are producing their own handbooks on site recording, which lay out the procedures and conventions to be adopted on their sites. A good example is the *Site Manual, Part 1, The Written Record*, published by the Department of Urban Archaeology of the Museum of London and obtainable from them. Figs 46 and 47(c) are taken from this booklet.

It is suggested by some that the feature record cards should be designed so that they can be fed into a computer, either in punched card or tape form. In this way if the necessary three-dimensional measurements are included on the cards the relationships between features can be retrieved in the form of a print-out or visual display. This seems to me to be an unnecessarily abstract way of recording and interpreting the site, except in conditions of extreme urgency where it is impossible to draw or photograph the layers or features in stratigraphical order, and where the only, or principal, records are the cards.

In excavations where there is time to record each layer/feature as it is revealed it is much more economical to use superimposed plans or a matrix or graph of the features, which is built up progressively as they are discovered.

Site notebooks

For reasons mentioned above (p. 147) index cards are preferable to site notebooks for recording of features. However site notebooks should be kept for recording information not to be found on the record cards; a brief day-to-day account of work in progress, observations on areas or clusters of features, speculations and hypotheses. Where a site is full of evidence for buildings and other structures if may be helpful to have a separate card index for buildings each card drawing together the evidence such as post-holes, walls, floors, hearths, finds and so on for the existence, from and function of the building. Such a card index will be of great help when the report comes to be written.

The site grid

The skeleton of any recording system must be the site grid. Under all but emergency conditions this should be laid out before the excavation begins; and it is essential to relate the excavation and its grid to permanent features in the landscape. With the advent of ever larger areas of development in towns, and the wholesale removal of hedgerows and other landmarks in the country, this is becoming increasingly difficult, and the excavator, in these circumstances, may become disorientated and literally may not know where his excavation is. In urban areas it is necessary to obtain the cooperation of the engineers and surveyors concerned with the development in order to locate precisely the excavation areas in the old and new townscapes. In the country, in the middle of a large gravel pit or an area of 'prairie' farming, the situation may not be so easy; rather like fixing one's position in the desert, it may be necessary to do some very accurate surveying. Anticipating the chapter on publication below, it is necessary, where an excavation is taking place in a radically altered landscape, to publish its relationship to the old landscape as well as to locate it in the new.

On any but the briefest excavation a base or datum line should be chosen and its terminal pegs concreted into place at each end. A hooked metal rod is perhaps the most convenient type of peg, so that the ring of a tape will not slip off it when under tension. Needless to say this base line must be measured with great accuracy and in the horizontal plane. A third peg, on an axis at right angles to the base, should be concreted in at a convenient point outside the proposed area of the excavation. From these two lines a coordinate or grid system in the horizontal plane can be established. Other subsidiary pegs should then be fixed on or outside the excavation to form an accurate basis for the rest of the grid. Wherever possible, the intersections of the grid lines should be marked by thin steel rods driven into the ground, thus reducing the inconvenience often caused when nails are used to mark the grid intersections, since they are easily displaced and have to be re-aligned – a tedious and time-wasting job.

Metric units, once adopted, are easier to use than feet and inches. Whether the coordinate system or a system of numbered or lettered grids is used, the corners of the squares should be pegged with accurately placed metal pegs, and it is an advantage to paint these corner pegs a bright colour so that they can be easily seen. The grid can then be sub-divided into as many smaller squares as the site demands, and the corners of these smaller squares pegged.

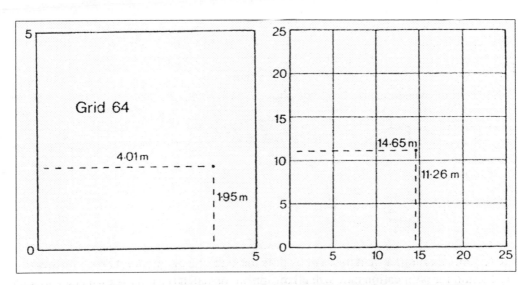

Figure 48   The position would be recorded as G64. 401 195; *right:* as 1465.1126.

The problems of planning excavated areas have been dealt with by Atkinson, 1953, 229, Fryer, 1971 , Biddle and Biddle, 1969, and Coles, 1972. The Biddles' paper, which the reader is urged to study, advocates the use of a coordinate system based on a metric grid, rather like the National Grid Reference system. This has the advantage that any point on the site can be referred to by a single unique reference given by two coordinates (fig. 48). It is usually convenient to lay out the whole site in a grid of ten meter squares marked out with string (coloured plastic coated varieties are not only easily seen but have the necessary elasticity) so that the excavators can easily orientate themselves on the site. Plastic letters or numbers in the centre or at one corner of each major grid will enable one to see at a glance in which square one is working.

Site planning

The most usual way of recording features visually is to draw the plan of the surface at a scale large enough for the smallest feature to be accommodated: 24:1 when feet are used, or 20:1 in metric scale are usually sufficient. Since features and layers will often merge almost imperceptibly into one another, or are distinguishable only by changes of texture rather than of colour, it is sometimes impossible to draw hard lines round the limits of each feature in which case the drawing should depict the character of the feature as closely as possible, even though it may be necessary in the interpretation to distinguish the junction more clearly. In fact the principle of separating the evidence from the interpretation should be adhered to as far as it can be, though, inevitably, the field drawing will include many elements of interpretation, at least in part due to the limited flexibility of drawing techniques. The range of colours and symbols used cannot be as infinite as the variations in composition of the features and layers, and the completely pictorial representation of plans (and sections), especially if in colour, is apt to be overloaded with detail, and 'unreadable'. Some of Professor Bersu's 'impressionist' drawings, attempting to include everything, err in this direction. Simplification involves selection and is therefore subjective, and this is the strongest argument for photographic recording.

If more than one draughtsman is used on a site the work should be co-ordinated. For instance three different draughtsmen drawing the same stony surface will in all probability produce different results because they will include stones of different minimum sizes. Many surfaces consist of stones of all sizes down to lmm. across, and therefore a minimum drawn stone size has to be chosen. At 1:20 a 2cm. stone will appear like this:

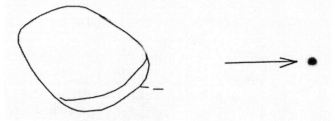

Stones smaller than this will be dots the size of a pencil point. With further reduction for publication they will all disappear, or will have to be drawn at an artificially enlarged scale. In cases of doubt the director should make a ruling, but usually stones of lcm. are the smallest that can reasonably be drawn at 1:20 scale. As far as possible all the draughtsmen on the site should draw in the same style; and they must certainly all use the same conventions and methods otherwise the resulting mosaic of drawings will be incoherent.

A considerable problem is posed by hollows and scarps on the excavated surface. Ideally each small hollow, each scarp, each post-hole should be contour surveyed, but lack of time usually prevents this. A compromise which may be used is to contour survey the whole site separately on a transparent overlay on a 20cm. grid for small sites or a 50cm. or lm. grid for large sites, dependent on the degree of detail required. Minor undulations, small scarps, etc. are then put on the site drawings as form lines with an arrow indicating the downward slope. Other conventions such as hachures or 'tadpoles' can be used; but on complex sites they tend to be more confusing than form lines and tend to obscure detail.

In special cases, where it is required to demonstrate the existence of slight but significant undulations, the contour survey can be made tighter and the contour lines drawn at very close intervals. A fine 'gravel' street was discovered at Wroxeter. On this street differential wear had left only slight humps and platforms like miniature earthworks. Since these were considered to be the sole evidence for a second phase of use of the street, with facades or booths of some sort encroaching on it, the survey was made at 20cm. horizontal intervals, and the resultant contours plotted at 2cm. vertical intervals in order to bring out the subleties of shape of these undulations, which would have been missed in a survey on a coarser grid plotted at a greater vertical interval. For detailed levelling of very uneven surfaces, or rows of post- or stake-holes, structures of rock or rubble and so on a thin staff may be made by attaching a 3m. tape to a metal or wooden rod. If necessary, the rod can be fitted with a long spike for precise positioning in holes or crevices. A more easily read staff of this kind could be made by accurately painting the divisions and lettering them with Letraset or similar stencils which should then be varnished.

Any method of drawing that shortens the steps between the original field drawings made on the site and those eventually published should be tried and developed. If the field drawings are clear and accurate, and are directly and precisely relatable to the site grid it should be possible to trace the final drawings straight from them so that there are only two drawings of the evidence, one made in the field, the other the published figures. To these may be added separate interpretive plans, sections and so on if the amount of detail in the published evidence is considerable.

If plans on translucent plastic film are made of each stage of the excavation, together with subsidiary plans of intermediate stages they can be superimposed on one another so that their relationship can be understood visually. At the same time the inter-relationship between all the features on the site can be recorded and demonstrated schematically by means of a matrix such as that developed by Edward Harris (Harris, 1975); see Chapter 10.

There are four or five principal ways in which the site plan may be drawn:

The drawing frame

One method is to use a frame the size of the grid unit, say a meter square, divided into smaller units such as 20cm., and laid on the excavated surface. Through this the features and details of the surface can be directly related to sectional drawing film on the drawing board, and drawn to the desired scale. The bulk of the drawing can then be made by eye without further measuring. A frame of slotted metal or braced wooden slats is divided either by plastic or nylon string which has sufficient elasticity to stay taut, by wire, or by expanding plastic-covered curtain wires. Frames 2m. square may be found rather large and unwieldy and a 1m. square is often preferable. Snags with the use of a frame arise when the ground is not reasonably level, or more particularly when large stones or other obstructions prevent the frame from being laid horizontally. It is of course important that the frame should be levelled, and not simply laid on the ground if there is a slope. This can be done by propping the corners with stones or wooden blocks and levelling with a builder's level, but more efficiently by making some form of adjustable leg. A simple method of levelling drawing frames is to use long malleable wire pins, like surveyors' arrows, which can easily be bent to any desired shape. They are inserted into the ground and bent to hold the corner of the frame at the height required. If the angle of the pin is placed inside the frame, it will hold it more firmly in place, e.g.:

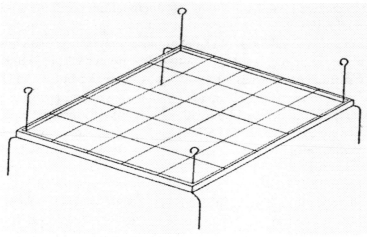

Another method, more suitable for stony ground is to make a clamp for each corner of the frame thus:

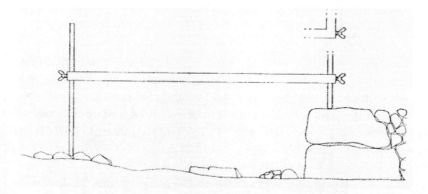

with a butterfly nut for quick release. The legs can terminate in small flat plates or rubber balls so that the site is not damaged.

If the frame is divided into 20cm. squares, the draughtsman can usually draw most of the detail (at the suggested scale of 1:20) by eye, taking care to look vertically down on to that part of the surface which he is drawing. If the frame is on sloping ground and has had to be levelled up it will of course be necessary to use a plumb bob on the areas where the frame is more than a few centimeters above the ground.

On steeply sloping ground it may be more convenient to lay out a string grid, using tapes horizontally in conjunction with a plumb-bob, and then draw the detail between the strings by eye, checking by triangulation (fig. 53).

In practice it may be found that the most convenient size for field plan units drawn with a grid is the 5m. square, at a scale of 1:20, which gives units of drawing material 0.25m. square. These are convenient for handling and can be joined together in an infinitely expanding mosaic covering the whole site. If, as the units are drawn, they are taped into place, for instance on a hut wall, the whole site plan can be seen to develop. Interpretation, instruction, and discussion of excavation problems become much easier, and any unit can be removed for completion or emendation. Hard-board is at present sold in units of 8 by 4 ft., and if these are cut into 1ft. squares they make convenient lightweight bases for the 0.25m. drawings, leaving enough overlap for taping the drawing to the board. Larger drawing boards tend to become heavy after some hours of use and are more affected by the wind.

It has been found most convenient to tape sectional paper or plastic film on to the drawing boards, using this as a gridded underlay for the transparent plastic film on which the drawing is made. If the edges of the plastic film are completely taped, the sectional paper is protected from damp. However, if it is felt that this does not eliminate possible inaccuracy due to the stretching and contraction of the sectional paper, plastic film with a printed grid may be used under the drawing film. One important advantage of this method of drawing is that, once the string grid has been laid out on the ground, the draughtsman does not require an assistant to help with measuring.

Offsets

An alternative method of plotting when a grid is not available is by means of co-ordinates set off from a tape stretched across the area to be drawn. In this method a 3m. metal tape or measuring rod is used to measure the distances of features at right angles from the datum tape (fig. 53b). The accuracy of this method depends on the ability of the draughtsman's assistant to judge a right angle. One of the easiest ways of doing this is to swing the tape with the centre at the point to be plotted until the shortest distance is read off against the datum tape (fig. 53b).

Figure 52 The illustration shows a method of drawing on a steep undulating surface. The string grid joins nails located accurately in the horizontal plane by means of a level and plumb-bob. The draughtsman then draws each square as a mosaic to scale (in this case 1:20).

However, since the angle of cut between the arc of the swing tape and the datum tape is minimal at the correct point on the datum tape, it may be thought that this involves an unacceptable degree of inaccuracy and a more accurate method of measuring a right angle such as a wooden or metal frame is to be preferred.

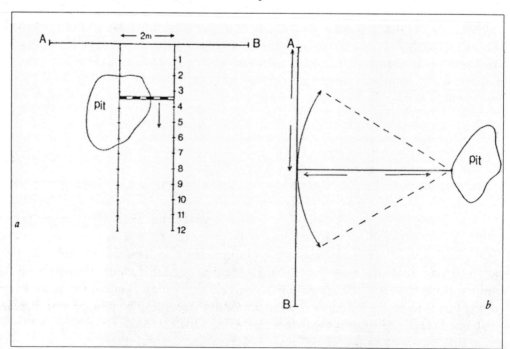

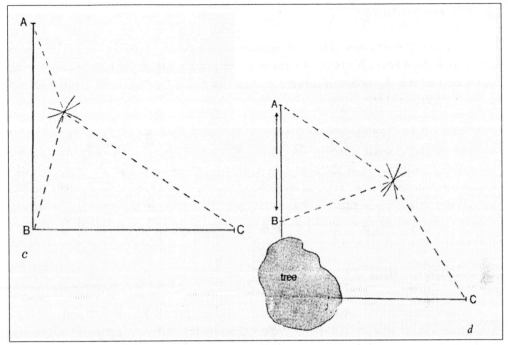

Figure 53   **Plotting: four methods**

(a)   **Traverse method of plotting an area.**
(b)   **Determining a right angle by swinging the tape until the minimum reading is obtained.**
(c)   **Triangulation.**
(d)   **Triangulation where an obstruction necessitates the use of a false datum.**

Two parallel tapes

A somewhat similar but more accurate method is to lay two parallel tapes across the site a short distance apart. A 3m. metal tape or a measuring rod is then laid across the point to be plotted so that the lengths along the datum tapes are equal, and therefore the cross tape is at right angles, and the distance from the datum 'AB' is read off (fig. 53a).

A variant of this method was used with some success on a training school at Wroxeter when the evidence for the timber buildings on Site 68 was recorded by a team of students none of whom had drawn before, each working across the site in strips 2ft. wide, using the offset method. The site looked rather like a running-track divided into lanes, each student producing a drawing two feet wide and the length of the site. This method was used on this occasion to ensure maximum objectivity, since there was some doubt about the interpretation (or even whether buildings were present at all), and, in a sense, the draughtsmen were working 'blind'. The drawings were finally pasted together and the plan redrawn by tracing (fig. 82). As can be imagined, the quality of draughtsmanship in the strips varied considerably and this method is not one to be highly recommended, though it is swift if time is short, as it can absorb all available manpower.

Co-ordinates

A fourth method is to plot co-ordinates from two axes of the grid. This method using as it does two offsets is, of course, more accurate than the single offset method described above. A variant of this method is triangulation, preferably from two or three corners of the grid (fig. 53c, d).

In order to plot the distances on the site plan, if it is large, it will be necessary to use a trammel and it must be remembered that three measurements will be more accurate than two. If only two are taken a good angle of cut between the arcs must be assured by choosing suitable points of origin on the grid. It is possible to plan single-handed in this way if the tapes are secured to the datum pegs, though able to rotate. The planner can then hold the two tapes in one hand at their junction, using a plumb-bob if necessary with the other hand.

Plastic film

In spite of its cost, plastic film should be used for all drawing. Tracing paper, linen and other similar materials expand and contract under varying conditions of moisture sufficiently to move features as much as half a meter (to scale) according to the weather; and this is clearly unacceptable. In addition, with the use of plastic film, drawing in pencil can continue in wet weather, which may be a crucial factor at the end of an excavation when recording in any other medium may be impossible.

Coated plastic films should be avoided as they are likely to crack with time or the coating may detach itself from the base material. Films based on uncoated Melanex (ICI) are the only suitable materials.

It is suggested that a comparatively soft pencil, HB or F, should be used; partly because these softer varieties give a more flexible line, but also because it is much easier to trace the drawing through the overlay if the field drawings are black in line rather than pale grey. Softer pencils must, of course, be sharpened more often if the line is not to become diffuse, though clutch pencils using very thin leads do not require sharpening. The problem of smudging can be overcome by working from the top of the drawing downwards, by masking the completed part of the drawing, and by the use of aerosol fixatives such as those used for pastel drawings (though these render the surface unsuitable for subsequent colouring with crayon). Better still, the drawing may be made directly in ink using Rapidograph or similar pens, though this precludes drawing in wet weather.

Although costs prohibit the publication of archaeological plans and sections in colour except in the most lavish productions, colour should nevertheless be used on the field drawings, since it considerably extends the range of variety of the recording.

The range of colours to be used throughout the excavation must be decided on at the beginning and a sufficient stock of pencils obtained to avoid unnecessary variations in tint, especially during the course of a long excavation. A number of paler colours, particularly pink, fade within a few days of exposure to light – even during the time taken in drawing the plan! It is therefore advisable to test crayons and colored pencils for fastness before the excavation begins. Mars-Lumochrom pencils have been tested on site for permanence and can be recommended. Almost all other pinks fade within a week. Colour codes for the varieties of stone, tile, clay, mortar and other building materials anticipated must be decided upon, and adhered to. Other colours may then be used for the plotting of nails, coins, small finds of different sorts and the many other categories of information which may be desired on the plan. In the case of complex sites it is better to avoid confusion by plotting finds and other non-structural information on separate transparent overlays.

Inevitably an element of interpretation will enter the drawing. It is therefore essential that not only the interpretation of the site, but also the drawing (which incorporates, however subtly, some of this interpretation) should be subject to constant discussion and criticism, and not merely left to a lone draughtsman. There is a tendency for some draughtsmen to simplify, and worse, to stylize, the features seen on the ground. Post-holes become more circular on the drawing than they really are; pebble surfaces become more uniform in the size and shape of their pebbles, and courses of stones become stereotyped. Checks on the accuracy and fidelity of the drawing must therefore be frequent, especially towards the end of the day. As an aid to accuracy of the draughtsmanship, it is very useful to have vertical stereoscopic photographs of each sector of the site printed at the same scale as the field drawings and made available to the draughtsmen while they are drawing in the field. This is not very difficult to achieve if a hut can be made into a dark-room, or if a local professional photographer can produce results quickly on demand, and the benefits are considerable. Drawings can then be checked immediately against the photograph and the two used to form an amalgam which is perhaps as near to an accurate record, combining objectivity with a degree of interpretation, as we can hope to achieve at present.

For reasons discussed below (p. 164) there will inevitably be radial distortions in the scale of features recorded by the vertical camera, so that features and detail cannot be traced directly onto the plan from the photographs, except close to the centre of each photograph. However, for practical purposes, and taking into account the eventual scale at which the drawings will be published, errors even towards the edges of photographs carefully enlarged are not totally unacceptable. They can be eliminated by a radial-line plotter if such a machine is available.

Even when a grid, a frame and photographs are being used it is advisable to cross-check the accuracy of the whole plan by triangulating the main features such as walls, major post-holes or timber-slots from the principal fixed datum points, since it is possible for gross errors to occur unnoticed in a mass of detail.

The drawing of sections has been dealt with exhaustively in a number of text books, notably in Wheeler, 1954, Webster, 1963, and 1970, Kenyon, 1964, Alexander, 1970 and Atkinson, 1948. Essentially, section drawing is drawing the plan of a vertical surface: indeed, in Britain such mystique became attached to the importance of the section during the period between the wars and for some years after, that one could have wished that the opposite truth had been realized – that drawing the plan of a site is merely drawing a horizontal section – and that the plan had been given the same precise attention to detail as the highly complicated section drawings which have filled excavation reports for the last 40 years.

The drawing of a straightforward ditch section need not be described here, as the references given above are more than adequate.

However, as Limbrey, 1975, 273-5, points out, sections are often drawn in a stylized way, by joining the dots made on the paper by someone receiving vertical and horizontal co-ordinates and not observing the layers closely while drawing them. Such a section will be meaningless to the soil scientist asked to discuss it later. It is important therefore that generally understood symbols should be used to describe the layers in pedological terms, rather than, or at least as well as, archaeological terms, such as 'destruction layer', 'build-up of foundations' and so on.

Photography

A number of good text-books on archaeological photography is available dealing with the techniques of both site photography and the photography of portable finds. Among the best are, Cookson, 1954, Matthews, 1968, Simmons, 1969, Bracegirdle, 1970 and Conlon, 1973.

In addition there is a multiplicity of books on photography in general, both in black and white and in colour, together with text-books on individual cameras with their related accessories. There is no need therefore to go into the technicalities of photography here, but merely to outline and comment on those aspects which are particularly relevant to the recording of excavations.

Without doubt the larger the negative used the sharper the detail on the photograph. For this reason a 5"x 4"camera is best for photographs which are to be used for publication, or for museum displays; but such a camera is very expensive. The 2¼" x 2¼" or 3¼" x 2¼" format is suitable for most archaeological photography, with 35mm, used for colour transparencies. However, some 35mm. enthusiasts maintain that, properly handled, the miniature camera is capable of producing results that are more than adequate for any archaeological photograph. In these days of relatively cheap 35mm. camera systems with built-in exposure meters and interchangeable lenses there is no excuse for poor pictures. Superb ones are a little more difficult.

The three chief categories of photograph that are required on most excavations are the record photographs, vertical and oblique, both in black and white and in color, which are specifically taken to supplement the plan and section drawings; color transparencies designed for lectures and talks; and photographs, both of the site and of finds, which are taken to illustrate the eventual publication of the excavation.

Figure 54   G.P.O., Newgate Street, London, 1976. This photograph, of more than 500 post-holes driven into Roman destruction levels, shows the importance of diffused lighting, especially in urban excavations where surrounding buildings cast dark shadows in sunshine. Nevertheless, even with diffused lighting the modelling of the surfaces is clear. This sense of the contours in enhanced by the angle of the shot. A higher viewpoint would have tended to flatten them. (*Photo -Trevor Hurst*)

Vertical photographs

Many methods, from ladders to balloons, have been used to suspend a camera vertically over a desired point on the excavation. A number of ordinary folding tripods have a reversible vertical section to which the camera can be attached pointing vertically downward. This method is most useful for photographs of small features, or finds *in situ*, but some large tripods have legs long enough to enable whole graves to be included on one negative. A ladder firmly lashed to two scaffold poles is a cheap and easy way of achieving a tripod up to 4-5m. above the ground. Above this height a scaffolding tower is recommended, though mobility then becomes a problem and the weight of such a tower may damage the excavated surface. Mobile towers such as the Tallescope (made by Access Equipment Ltd., Hemel Hempstead) which extend up to some 10m., can be moved easily about the site but are not very rigid at full height. When the extending ladder is used double, a fairly stable platform is achieved. Any apparatus that lifts the photographer safely above the site may be used, ranging from the bucket of a bulldozer to a fire escape. Such aids are of course equally valuable for high-level oblique photographs.

Figure 55   New Fresh Wharf, London, 1975: view along the Roman waterfront structure, dated AD 155±5 years. This photograph is a model of descriptive clarity. The carefully selected viewpoint gives maximum information about and three-dimensionality to the structure, and the use of an exceptional lens combined with a very small stop gives great depth of focus. (*Photo – Trevor Hurst*)

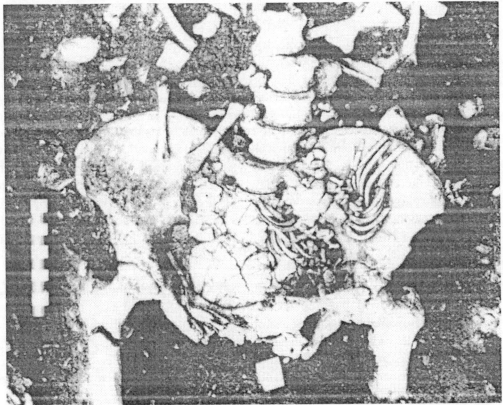

Figure 56   **Medieval female skeleton with unborn foetus, from G.P.O., Newgate Street, London 1975. The recording of this long-forgotten tragic incident required very skilful cleaning (in the wind and rain of a winter excavation) which demonstrated the existence of the foetus yet left each bone in place for photography.** (*Photo – Trevor Hurst*)

Kites and tethered meteorological balloons fitted with a cradle from which the camera hangs have been tried, and experiments have also been made with radio-controlled model aircraft. The chief difficulty with all these methods is that of sway due to turbulence of the air which, even if slight, will give considerable angular movement of the lens. But on a perfectly calm day, a kite or a captive balloon carrying a camera triggered by radio has much to recommend it.

It is more difficult to devise a method for making an overlapping mosaic of vertical photographs. Whatever apparatus is used must be easily transportable across the site, and not so heavy that it destroys the excavated surface. Ideally, it ought not to cast shadows over the area being photographed, and it must be as quick and simple as possible to operate if large numbers of photographs are to be taken during the comparatively short time during which the site is at its best, and when the weather, in a country like Britain, is co-operative; and it must support the camera as rigidly as possible. The critical factors are the height to which the camera can conveniently be raised coupled with the focal length of the lens. The greater the height of the apparatus, the heavier it will be, the more unwieldy to move and the more affected by the wind. The longer the focal length of the lens the less radial distortion there will be on the photograph, but the smaller the area covered by each photograph. A compromise between these two factors has to be devised.

The apparatus evolved (principally by Terry Holland and Sidney Renow), for use on the writer's excavations, consists of a quadrupod of square-section aluminium, braced by wooden slats, with an aluminium cradle holding a 2¼" x 2¼" format twin-lens reflex camera. The square-format is preferable to the 35mm. rectangular format because the negative is larger, and the derail therefore clearer, and because the square shape is directly related to the shape of the quadrupod.

Appendix B describes the simple cradle which holds the camera in place. The quadrupod is designed so that the area photographed is bounded by the four feet of the apparatus, so that, once it is set up, the feet show the corners of the photograph on the ground and there is no need to use a viewer. The quadrupod can be put precisely into place by the photographer's assistants, and it is levelled by means of two spirit levels taped to two adjacent horizontal members, and by means of extendable feet inserted into the tubular framework. The feet are fitted with sorbo-rubber balls to stop them from damaging the site. This method has proved to be better than plates mounted on ball-joints.

Various ways of winding-on the film and cocking the shutter without lowering the camera have been tried, but they have been discarded for one reason or another, and now the camera is lowered by means of a simple pulley on nylon cord, and the film wound on by hand. This takes very little time, and eliminates most of the causes of failure in the apparatus. It was found in practice that even with mechanical or electrical cocking of the shutter it was necessary, due to constantly changing English light, to lower the camera quite often in order to change the aperture setting. However, now that automatically metering cameras are becoming increasingly available (though still extremely expensive in the 2¼" x 2¼" format) it is obviously an advantage to have such a camera, and if this is fitted with a motor-drive (or electrically-driven wind-on mechanism, which in some cases is cheaper) the camera can be left aloft and the apparatus moved across the site very much more quickly. In this way a large area can be photographed in a few hours.

The whole apparatus has the virtue of simplicity and cheapness, and is easily transportable by car. Its one major drawback is that in sunshine it is impossible to avoid the shadow of one or more of the legs falling across the area being photographed. In the ordinary way this is no handicap since the photographs would not be taken in sunlight, but there are occasions when, if photography is urgent, it becomes a nuisance. Various methods of screening the ground with semi-opaque polythene sheet have been tried, without success.

One method which may overcome both the problems of cast shadows in sunlight and that of changing light on the surface to be photographed is to mount four electronic flashes (of the type which automatically adjust the length of the flash according to the distance from the subject and its tone) on the legs of the quadrupod. The flashes would have to be mounted at different heights to provide varied light which would model the subject. This method has not yet been tested so far as I know, but, if successful, it would give complete independence of all weather conditions but rain. Among other advantages it would extend the time available for photography into the dusk and even the hours of darkness, given a floodlight by which to work. If mains electricity is available three or four floodlights could be mounted on the legs of the quadrupod for use at dusk or during the night.

An apparatus which does eliminate the problem of shadows is the tripod with a boom extension which projects out over the area to be photographed (Nylen, 1964). This method is satisfactory, but the boom is more susceptible to wind vibration and the apparatus, which has to be built of heavier section tubing, is less easy to transport across the site and its weight may damage delicate surfaces. On the whole, we have preferred a lighter and more stable support than the facility of taking pictures in sunlight.

Vertical photographs are taken with a 60 per cent overlap along the length of the run and a 15 per cent overlap between the runs. This gives adequate stereoscopy, although for accurate contoured photogrammetry of the site the camera would have to be at a constant height above datum, not a constant height above the ground. There is no reason why a line overlap or mosaic of a large excavation should not be taken from an aircraft, though this is an entirely different matter from the highly detailed mosaic required by the site record, in which the smallest stones can be seen in detail. Obviously it is most important that the photographer keeps an accurate plan of the photographs that make up the vertical grid, and that they are labelled so that their precise position on the grid can be quickly found. On many excavations it is unlikely that single photographs will be recognizable from the features in them, so that if the cross indexing fails a great deal of time will be wasted in indentification.

Bipod for vertical and oblique photography

Another method of raising the camera above the ground is a bipod made of wood or tubular metal, which carries a cradle at its apex. The bipod is raised and held in position with the aid of two ropes attached to the cradle, one on each side. In this way heights of up to 10m. have been achieved. The method has considerable advantages on rough or sloping ground or where there are walls or deep rooms. The additional height not only gives greater coverage but also greater depth of focus, necessary if the surface is undulating or if it contains deep holes. Another advantage claimed for this method is that the camera can be tilted, relative to the legs, to take oblique high-level views.

Oblique photography

Oblique photographs of the whole site or large parts of it are very valuable for record as well as publication. In addition oblique photographs should be taken of all but minor features. In many cases groups of small features can be photographed together. All evidence for buildings should be photographed from a variety of angles and with a variety of lighting as sometimes the details of a building will show best in a photograph taken against the light or in sunshine. Normally the best light is strong but diffused, up to pale sunshine. Structures and features can be given more solidity and detail by arranging a large white board or sheet to reflect light into the shadows, or by using flash to fill them in.

A clear but unobtrusive scale should always be used, together with a readable label in the case of features. The scale should be placed in a position which does not distract the eye from the features to be illustrated, and it should not cover or cut across them. Often one or more ranging rods can be placed so that they define the edges of a surface, though they should not be placed on the edge but rather parallel to it so that its character is not obscured. Interchangable plastic figures and letters that fit into slotted wood covered with black baize are a useful form of label, and a small but clear north point should always be included.

Oblique photographs will be needed not only for the site record but also for the eventual publication. In many cases one photograph will serve both purposes but if possible some extensive photographs should be taken, from a neighboring building or a fire escape or an aircraft, showing the site as a whole as well as its surroundings. Some features or structural details of buildings can be better illustrated by oblique 'three-quarter' views than by plans and sections. It is very helpful to imagine the caption to an illustration while the subject is in the view-finder. In this way the' most comprehensive view will be taken. Without this sort of planning it may be found that two views of a vital part of the site have to be published where one would have been adequate.

On most sites a wide-angle lens (35mm. or 28mm. focal length) will be the most generally useful, though it must be remembered that the wider the angle the greater the distortion, since a larger field of view has to be compressed into the same size of negative. With very wide-angle lenses, straight lines become curves, verticals slope and relative sizes are wildly distorted. When taking close-up photographs of features stretching back into the middle distance remember the snaps of father feet-first on the beach at Blackpool, and use a long focal length lens so that distortion is minimized. Rising-and cross-fronts on 3¼" x 2¼" or 5" x 4" cameras will eliminate distortion due to perspective and are especially useful where architecture is involved, or where a section has to be photographed from within the trench.

A cable release and the most solid and stable tripod obtainable should always be used. These, in addition to eliminating camera shake, will enable the lens to be stopped down to give greater depth of field when photographing features or structures which stretch from the foreground into the middle distance.

Experiments should be made with filters to find out which give the best results on the type of soil or other material being excavated. A green filter, for instance, will give more contrast to a hearth of reddened clay surrounded by yellow clay, a yellow filter will enhance dark features in sand, and so on.

When the excavation is within range of electrical power floodlights can be used to give ideal lighting, glancing across textured surfaces or modelling features such as hearths. Three floodlights will give great flexibility so that reflected lights can be used in the shadows to give the maximum detail.

Floodlights or car headlights can be used to photograph faint ridge and furrow or other slight earthworks, or subtle undulations of the excavated surface that would otherwise be difficult to see. Since archaeological photography is rarely concerned with movement, a slow, fine-grain panchromatic film such as Ilford Pan F (50 ASA, 18 DIN) will give maximum definition. Under poor lighting conditions, or if a tripod is not available, Ilford FP4 (125 ASA, 22DIN) or the very much faster HP4 (400-600 ASA,

27-29 DIN) will give satisfactory results if properly developed and printed. However, two new films, Ilford XP1 and Agfa Varia, combine high speed (400 ASA, 27 DIN) with very fine grain and have great exposure latitude (from 200 ASA to 1600 ASA) and this may eventually prove the ideal material for black and white photographs taken under difficult conditions but still producing prints suitable for publication or exhibitions. Meanwhile, nevertheless, under normal lighting conditions, orthodox films, such as those recommended, remain preferable. Perhaps the ideal solution is a true-colour stereoscopic mosaic of photographs of the whole site at each stage of the excavation backed up by interpretive overlay drawings. Trials with the new Kodak Vericolor I1 film have been most encouraging. Vertical over-lapping colour prints enlarged from 2¼" x 2¼" negatives to a scale of 1:20 and printed on glossy paper have proved to show a high degree of detail; for example, pea-grits or 'dried peas' at the bottom of stakeholes are clearly visible as are the divisions and numbers on the 30m. tape included in the print. The colour rendering is exceptional, though dependent, of course, on the colour temperature of the light, which changes according to the altitude of the sun, the amount of blue sky or cloud and the reflection of surrounding trees or buildings. The effect of this is to alter subtle colours continually. Reds become redder towards sunset and purpler or bluer at midday without cloud and the colour of the ground itself changes with the changing light. Moreover this effect is enhanced and exaggerated by colour film. In crucial cases Munsell colour chart numbers should be used. It may be that it will be possible to build an apparatus which will take all photographs by flash, when the colour rendering will be constant and relatively comparable.

There is no reason why sections should not similarly be photographed stereoscopically in colour (if necessary obliquely) when their textures could be viewed in detail.

There is no doubt that such a series of stereoscopic colour photographs is a very adequate, sometimes startlingly naturalistic, record of the site. Further prints from the same negatives can be pasted together to form a mosaic photograph of all or part of the site at any desired scale. If it were not for the necessity of publication the two sets of photographic prints with interpretive overlays might be considered all that was required for site planning. The publication of such photographs with their overlays would, at present, be prohibitively expensive, though not perhaps very much more expensive than a series of highly detailed colour drawings. The distillation of publishable plans and sections from field drawings is discussed in Chapter 13 below. Meanwhile, so far as the primary record of the site is concerned, colour stereoscopic cover is highly desirable since it is comparatively inexpensive. In the trials carried out at Wroxeter in 1975 complete coverage of an area some 200 sq. metres cost less than a group of draughtsmen drawing the same area in comparable detail, over a period of about a week, whereas the photography took only a few hours. The application of colour photographic recording to rescue and salvage excavations therefore is obvious.

It may be argued that vertical stereoscopic photography is only practicable on more or less level sites, but I believe that its value is, if anything, greater on sites where, for archaeological reasons, a number of surfaces at different depths need to be recorded, or the layers slope steeply, or where, under waterlogged conditions, timbers project in all directions from the layer in which they are embedded. Under all these circumstances, drawing itself it difficult, sometimes near impossible. What is needed is an accurate record of the excavated surfaces, features and structures. If photography can provide this record, in colour and three dimensions, it is arguable that detailed site drawing, in the accepted sense, is superfluous, and that the drawing can be confined to outline overlays, which include all the feature/layer numbers. In addition, overlays could incorporate a greater or less degree of interpretation. Such a system would enormously speed up the recording of all kinds of site, but in particular those where the layers consist of stones, tile, tesserae, rubble, pebbles, boulders and so on, where it has become customary to draw the surface in great detail and then to colour each element. Such drawings are often very beautiful, but they cannot, as a rule, ever be published. They simply form part of an archive from which the published drawings are distilled. It may be that we are no longer justified in the expense, in skilled time particularly, of such elaborate drawing but should rely, for the primary record, on photography – which can be equally beautiful. In practice, however, we have found that the attempt to reduce site drawing to a minimum has a number of snags. Permatrace, Ozaflex and other drawing films are translucent, not transparent, and the details of the colour photographs, which have about the same tonal contrast as the site itself, cannot readily be traced through the drawing film, even if a light box is used. There is the added difficulty that, even if the print is enlarged to 1:20 linear, strictly speaking only the centre of the photograph is at the right scale and the distortion increases radially towards the edges. We have, therefore, for the time being, continued to draw in detail and to use the photographs as a check for the post-excavation draughtsman and as an invaluable archive.

There is a danger, however that the excavator will unconsciously let photography take the place of intensive observation. The very act of drawing a plan or section on the ground necessitates close contemplation of the evidence and dependence on photography could weaken this concentrated observation. This is a problem not confined to rescue or salvage work since on any large-scale excavation it is impossible for the director or site-supervisors to do all the drawing. It is important therefore that where detailed drawing is being done by others they should check the drawings carefully with the ground and discuss them and their meaning with the draughtsman.

Photogrammetry

If stereoscopic photographs, either vertical or oblique, are taken of the site the plans or sections can be drawn at a later date. While not ideal, this does provide insurance for loss of drawings or checks on disputed planning. A number of textbooks on photogrammetry are available, eg. Williams (1969), so that there is no need to enlarge on the subject here. Radial line plotters such as the Watts SB 100 or Stereosketch are within the reach of the larger archaeological units and arrangements can be made for the hire of time on the bigger machines.

Oblique photogrammetry using two cameras on a sub-tense bar is used by German traffic police for the rapid recording of plans of traffic accidents. Stereoscopic photographs are taken from a number of points of view round the accident and the plan plotted later. This is very quick and obviates the need for policemen to walk about in the road with tape measures (see *Instruments of Photogrammetry and Photo Interpretation*, Zeiss, 1967, U7, and references on U4). Both the speed of the method and the fact that it enables planners to work outside the required area make it ideal for rescue and salvage excavation, as well as in situations where the excavated surface is too vulnerable to be walked on. An example of this use is in the planning of the Skuldelev Ships, five Viking ships sunk in Roskilde Fjord. The wood of the ships and the soft matrix in which they lay was planned by photogrammetry without risk of damaging or losing the evidence (Olsen and Crumlin-Pedersen, 1967). A small bar with a sliding camera mounting equipped with a tripod bush is a simple piece of apparatus which enables oblique stereoscopic photographs to be taken with any available camera. Needless to say the same methods can be used for the recording of architecture. Infra-red film can be used for the recording of hearths, kilns and other areas of burning or significant colour differences on sites which are notoriously difficult to photograph in black-and-white for publication.

Polaroid film

Polaroid photographs, which have the advantage of instant development, have proved to be invaluable as a supplement to the feature record cards. The photographs can be fixed (with drafting tape rather than paste) to the back of the card and annotated, or may have an explanatory sketch added. Partially excavated features can be recorded in

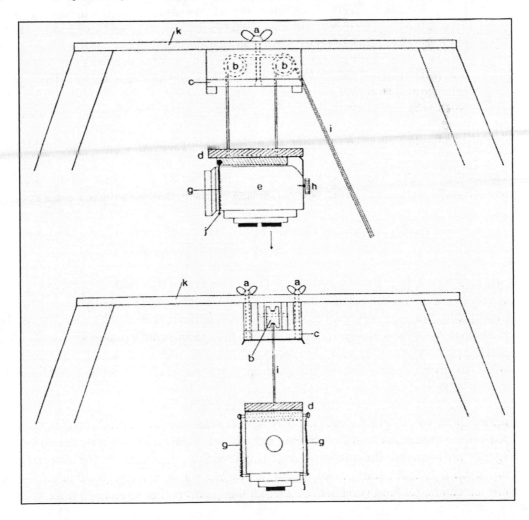

this way without delaying the work and the excavation of a fragile or fragmentary find can be recorded in a rapid series of photographs which may be of great help in the eventual reconstruction. The method has the advantage of comparative cheapness, since it has been found that the simpler, less expensive polaroid cameras are perfectly adequate for the purpose. The rectangular, 110mm. x 85mm., format is preferable to the slightly smaller square format since it gives greater detail and is a more convenient shape for oblique photographs.

Appendix B

Sidney Renow, who was responsible for the development of the quadrupod head writes:

> After a good deal of experimenting it has been found that the most practicable means of suspension of the camera is by attaching it to a cradle which is raised and lowered by a double cord running over pulleys in a head box bolted securely to the top plate of the quadrupod in such a position that the lens of the camera is centrally positioned (fig. 57). Various ways of winding on the film whilst the camera is in the raised position have been tried but have had to be abandoned because of insurmountable difficulties. In practice, lowering and raising the camera cradle after each exposure has not proved to be a nuisance, and following the principle that the simplest mechanisms are usually the most reliable and trouble-free, the arrangement to be described has been found to work very satisfactorily.

The base of the camera cradle is a plate of aluminium or brass bent at right angles and drilled to take an ever-ready case retaining screw which secures the bottom of the camera to one face. The back of the camera is held against a block of ½" chipboard by a padded rod across the top front which is spring or elastic loaded from screws on either side of the chipboard. Another block of chipboard is secured to the baseplate by bolts passing right through both blocks and the plate. The second block is drilled and suitably recessed to take the doubled nylon or terylene suspension cord.

The head box is made from four similar pieces of chipboard screwed to a chipboard face block the same size as the second block of the camera cradle. The two inner pieces are drilled to take the spindles of two pulleys over which the cord runs. The face block has holes corresponding to those in the camera cradle and it will be obvious that the pulleys have to be suitably positioned to match. The face block is also provided with two strips of aluminium or brass appropriately bent and screwed to it to form mating guides so that when the camera cradle is hauled up it is precisely located against the head box. Long bolts pass through the two outer pieces of the head box to secure it firmly to the top plate of the quadrupod. Butterfly nuts can be used for ease of attachment and removal. It is essential that the camera cradle when in the raised position should be held against the head box under tension, and to achieve this use is made of the natural elasticity of the cord. The free ends of this are knotted together in such a position that the loop so formed can be passed over a bolt on a leg of the quadrupod or to an anchorage specially provided. When the camera is lowered the knot will of course ascend to the head box and it should be arranged that it comes to rest against a stop so that the cradle, which in any case cannot slip to the ground, is suspended at a convenient point for manipulation. The doubled length of cord below the knot can be knotted at intervals to provide grips when hauling on the cord. The most convenient way of operating the shutter is by using a pneumatic remote control release such as the Kagra.

The Recording of Pottery and Small Finds

Introduction

Recording is, of course, a fundamental activity in excavation, but what is seen and what is recorded are related to the mental set of the investigator; careful observation is not sufficient. This does not mean, however, that the archaeologist is guided by what is expected or dictated by the needs of the problem-oriented approach discussed earlier. So a background of experience is needed, but, equally, there should be openness to the unexpected. Analysis and interpretation must happen as a continuous activity as excavation proceeds, and a wide range of questions should always be at hand. But, with the kind of detailed recording recommended by Barker, we realize that a total record is not possible. Thus guidelines should be set up concerning the retrieval of data for the record of excavation. Barker then outlines the criteria for recording and the method of recording, including record cards, daily accounts and reflections, the manner of recording vertical and horizontal of finds and features. He makes detailed suggestions concerning the creation of a master grid for the site, triangulation and leveling, drawing and photography

R are and exotic finds from excavations inevitably attract most attention in the press, and on radio and television, and more significantly in archaeological exhibitions. This high-lighting gives such pieces an exaggerated importance compared with the mass of dull body sherds, animal bones or fragments of wall plaster. Yet, as Pitt Rivers pointed out almost a century ago: ' . . . the value of relics, viewed as evidence, may . . . be said to be in an inverse ratio to their intrinsic value' (Cranborne Chase, Vol 111, 1892, ix.). The collection, recording, cleaning, marking and storage of every sherd of pottery, every fragment of bone, every nail, every scrap of painted plaster is tedious, and time and labor-consuming. But only by the study of large quantities of everyday evidence can we approach an understanding of the site and its occupants as a whole and not simply the more immediately attractive aspects, such as those which lie on the fringes of art or architectural history. An understanding of English medieval life cannot be gained wholly from the study of church architecture, painted missals and *objects d'art* —it is necessary to dig complete villages, including the barns and pigstyes, and collect the whole mass of unaesthetic evidence if we are going to penetrate deeper than the aristocratic crust of medieval society. If this is true of medieval times, where we have considerable documentation to add to the rest of the evidence, how much more true it is of earlier, less literate societies.

The horizontal distribution of pottery and finds is as important as their vertical distribution. It is for this reason that all finds, of whatever material, must be recorded in plan with sufficient precision to make analysis possible. Plots of the distribution of various classes of finds on transparent overlays make it easy to relate the finds to buildings, fences, enclosures and other structures. This distribution may be the only evidence for the use of a building or area. Lines of building nails may give the only clue to the former presence of a building and the quality of the finds from different buildings or areas may be a pointer to the wealth or social position of the occupants. At Wroxeter, sherds of a type of calcite gritted pottery are distributed mainly outside and around the major buildings of the last period, which must, from the evidence, have had wooden floors. This pottery was, therefore, perhaps in use in the last period, being swept off the floors and out on to the grass or trodden areas round the buildings.

Another, more subtle use of the horizontal distribution of finds is demonstrated by the analysis of flints of the beaker period at Belle Tout, East Sussex, by Richard Bradley (Bradley, 1970). This assumes that 'the outline of a building would probably be marked by a break in the horizontal density of finds simply because the material could not pass through a solid barrier. In addition such a barrier might be marked by a build-up of material at its foot' (*ibid*. 317). These effects can be enhanced by using trend mapping, as described by Haggett (1965, 270). In this method the general trend of finds across the site is mapped as a series of contours and the positive and negative residuals where the local density of finds differs from the general trend are mapped separately as contours and compared with the other evidence, of post-holes, lines of stones and etc. (Bradley, 1970, figs 3 and 5, reproduced here as figs 58 and 59). Orton, 1980, 140-155, describes, principally for those of us who are less numerate, the various methods which may be used to study the distribution patterns of artifacts from a site.

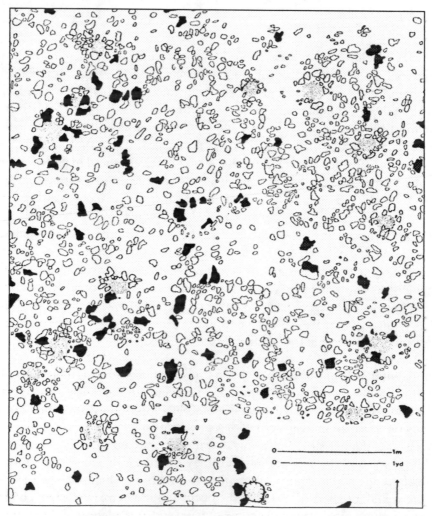

Figure 58   Belle Tout, Sussex: Structure I as excavated. Possible post-holes are stippled and intrusive flints lying upon the surface of the natural flint rubble are represented in solid black. The enclosure ditch forms the northern limit of the plan. For interpretation see fig. 59 below.

The study of pottery as archaeological material deserves a book to itself. Because it has a high survival rate, pottery has often been given more evidential weight than it can justifiably carry. The origins, dating and distribution of any pottery are still uncertain. New discoveries change the stat of knowledge annually, making it unwise to date sites or phases of sites on the evidence of pottery alone.

The study of prehistoric pottery has had to be drastically revised in the light of recent C14 and dendrochronological dates (Renfrew, ed., 1974) and the dating of Roman and medieval pottery is undergoing similar, though less radical, revision, as more groups, dated by evidence external to the pottery itself, are excavated. In view of these considerations alone, all earlier excavation reports should be revised, where possible, in line with current theories on pottery dating, more than this, they should be kept up to date as present theories themselves are modified. This is a daunting task, especially when the incomplete and ambiguous nature of most pottery report is considered.

The uses and limitations of pottery as archaeological evidence

Sherds of pottery are by far the most common finds on the majority of excavated Roman and medieval sites. The reason is obvious. Pottery was quickly made and often as quickly broken. The expectation of life of a pot is difficult to assess but it seems likely that jugs, bowls, jars, etc. would have lasted longer than cooking pots, which, by their nature, had to undergo the stresses set up by differential heating, especially if, as is probable, they were embedded in the embers of a hot fire. A pot was virtually useless once it was broken or even cracked since it was very difficult to mend satisfactorily, though riveted repairs and holes plugged with lead are occasionally found on particularly valuable vessels. Its scrap value, unlike that of a metal object, was small unless it was crushed and used as grog. Since the sherds which remain were virtually indestructible there was little to do with them except bury them in a convenient pit. Here the majority of large sherds and nearly complete pots are found, fragments small enough to be ignored becoming scattered over the site, embedded, and eventually stratified. Complete pots are rarely found except in graves, wells and in abandoned kilns, or occasionally as the containers for hoards or other material. The discontinuance of grave goods with the coming of Christianity, though doubtless a spiritual advance, robbed the archaeologist of his chief source of supply of whole pots, and for each complete or nearly complete vessel the majority of sites yield many hundreds of sherds.

Pottery has the archaeological advantage over most other materials that it is affected comparatively little by most soil conditions. Only if it is grossly under fired will it be soft enough to be weathered away; many prehistoric and most Roman and medieval wares are hard enough to remain unaltered indefinitely under most conditions. Metal objects, on the other hand, with the exception of those of gold, are subject to corrosion in varying degrees, this corrosion tending to obliterate just those decorative features which are likely to be datable.

Factors other than that of mere survival must, however, be taken into account. The objects most susceptible to the close dating so desirable archaeologically are those whose characteristics, whether of form or decoration or both, change most rapidly, and such developments are most likely when details of form and ornament are not dictated by function but by fashion. The design of knives, shears, nails and other common objects, having reached their optimum shape, changed slowly, if at all. Some objects, sheep-shears, cleavers and hand-axes for example, have scarcely altered from medieval times up to the present day (see the *London Museum Medieval Catalogue*, 1954 ed., 153-7). The writer has recovered from the castle site at Hen Domen two figure-of-eight hasps from the thirteenth-century levels which are virtually identical with a hasp at present in use on one of the farm gates leading to the site, and with a hasp found during excavation of the Roman fort at Segontium and now in the site museum there. All these, though interesting from the social and economic points of view, are useless for dating purposes. More personal objects such as brooches, daggers and spurs were not only more highly decorated but changed their forms with changes of fashion and can thus often be grouped typologically and given a relative chronology on the basis of form alone. Coins, on the other hand, whose basic disc shape remains constant, had inscriptions and decorations which were changed frequently, and it is from these that we can date them precisely.

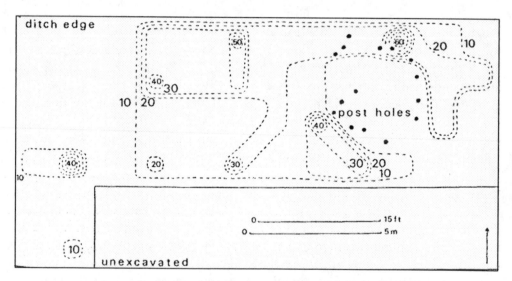

Figure 59   Belle Tout, Sussex: the suggested outline of Structure I in relation to the density of all finds of Beaker date. Possible post-holes are represented in solid black and the inner lip of the enclosure ditch forms the top of the plan. Contours are at intervals of 10 finds to the 5 foot grid square.

A discussion of the complexities of typological developments in pottery would be out of place here, but it is important for the excavator to be highly sceptical of simplistic schemes which place sherds of pottery in plausible sequences based on appearance alone.

As J.G Hurst has pointed out, in Eastern England Anglo-Saxon pottery is finer and more accomplished than that of the twelfth century, though the reverse is true elsewhere, and 'rim forms in some areas become more developed and complicated, while in others they become more simple' (*Med. Arch.,* vi-viii, 148). In some regions (the West Midlands for example) there seems to have been a tendency for cooking pots to have been made increasingly large during the course of the twelfth century, but in other regions this is not apparent. Coarseness of fabric is by itself no criterion of date, nor is the presence or absence of glaze. Some forms of simple decoration persisted throughout the medieval period, while others reappeared after a temporary eclipse. The thumb-pressed base, for example, so common on thirteenth century jugs, reappears on otherwise quite different jugs of the fifteenth century. It is clear, therefore, in a way which was not fully realized a few years ago, that medieval pottery will only be closely datable on the basis of intensive regional study, and on the study of the composition of fabrics, the shapes of rims, the details of decoration and character of glazes rather than on the general development of types.

The same is true of Roman coarse pottery, which is as regional in character as its medieval counterpart. However, other forms of Roman pottery, in particular samian wares and stamped mortaria, are more closely datable, and, if found stratified in quantity, probably provide the most reliable *termini* post and *ante quem* given by any pottery before the industrial revolution. The absolute dates of prehistoric pottery have been dependent in recent years on the revised radiocarbon dates for the main periods in British prehistory, but there is a very strong regional element also which means that local typologies must be established for most areas.

Any establishment of a typology, even for a restricted area, will have to be based on the study of the more rapidly evolving details of pottery forms rather than of their basic shapes and fabrics, though these may in some cases also show a steady development. Ultimately every characteristic – fabric, shape, size, the treatment of rims, handles, lips and spouts as well as decoration itself – will have to be considered before a pot or sherd can be placed correctly in its local typological sequence. (See Gardin, 1966, for an attempt to categorize all the characteristics of French medieval pottery.) It does not follow that sherds of obviously similar style and superficial characteristics are not by the same potter merely because the composition of fabric or glaze proves to be different. The difference may be due to circumstances: clay from a different bed, or a deliberate change of glaze; but even if the sherds or pots prove to be from different hands, the similarity of style carries its own significance of co-operation or influence between potters. Every scientific aid available should be enlisted to provide as much information as possible on which to base judgements. The composition of fabrics and thus their probable source, the composition of glazes and the temperature to which they have been fired and, with the development of thermo-luminescent and remanent magnetic methods, the possibility of accurate dating independent of both stratification and typology, are all clearly of major importance for determining the relationships of groups of pottery.

It is already apparent that ideally developing typological sequences, in which shapes and decoration proceed logically one from another in the manner relied on by historians of art and architecture may never be established. At Adderley, in Shropshire, for instance, a number of associated thumb-pressed bases seem to exhibit every stage in the development of this form of decoration, yet there is every reason to believe that they are close together in date, and it may well be that all these variations were made at the same time (cf. *Med. Arch.*, vi-viii, 148). Their value as a dating series would therefore be nil. In the face of such difficulties any attempt to establish a precise chronology might seem doomed to failure, but the attempt must be made if we are to date more accurately the sites in which we are interested.

It seems most unlikely that it will ever be possible to date a pottery group more closely than within a bracket of 25 years. Even if we were able to date our pottery closely by archaeometric methods it would still have limitations as dating material. It must be stressed that pottery, like all other dating material, provides only a *terminus post quem* for the layer in which it was found (see below p. 80). Even a coin, whose date of manufacture may be precisely known, gives no more information about its find-layer than this. Too often coins are said to 'date' a layer or building, and a superstructure of dated periods is erected on this basis without regard to the strict logic of the evidence. An example, so extreme that the wrong conclusions could not possibly have been drawn, is provided by the finding in 1774, in the Roman villa at Acton Scott, Shropshire, of Greek coins of the fourth century BC (V.C.H., Shrops., i, 1908, 260-1). These must have been collector's pieces or souvenirs (or were, perhaps, 'planted'), but if they had been Roman souvenirs only 50 years old, might this not have been used, even today, to give a closer date to the structures than would be justified? The danger is as great or greater in the case of pottery. P.A. Rahtz has shown at Cheddar that 2000sq. ft. of levels, dated firmly to the ninth century or later by coins, contained no pottery but Roman (personal communication, publication forthcoming). If a smaller area had been excavated and no coins found, these layers might have been considered to be Roman, whereas within the strict logic of the evidence they should have been dated to the Roman period *or later*. One may wonder how many small excavations producing only Roman pottery have in fact been on post-Roman sites.

These are extreme cases; the danger is more subtle and therefore more likely to mislead when the time-lag is shorter, or when conclusions are drawn from too small a sample, either of the site or of the finds. There is no need to reiterate the misconceptions which may arise from one or two cuttings made into a complex site – examples of the pitfalls which may be encountered are mentioned in Chapter 4. A small sample of pottery may be equally misleading. One or two sherds found in a critical position may be given a significance out of porportion to their real value, unless it can be shown that they were positively sealed and could not have arrived in their position by the action of burrowing animals, rainwash, or other misleading effects. The opposite also holds. A single sherd, positively stratified, which gives an inconveniently late *terminus post quem* for its layer or structure, must not be discarded by the excavator because he cannot bring himself to face the fact that his preconceived theories were wrong. Similarly, among a number of sherds from a sealed layer, it is the latest which gives the *terminus post quem* to the layer, so that a single late sherd among a mass of earlier material must not be discarded – it is the rest of the sherds that must be treated as residual.

By the same reasoning, pottery cannot be dated simply by association, however close, with other datable objects in the same layer. A friend of the writer recently found, on a Roman site, a coin of Edward I of c.1300 positively sealed with a sherd of hard green glazed pot. It is tempting, under these circumstances, to date the pottery, with the layer, to a period after 1300 but, had it not been possible to date the sherd independently, on the evidence of its appearance, it could have been prehistoric, Roman, Saxon, medieval or modern. In other words, the association of coin and sherd tells us *nothing whatever about the date of the sherd,* only that it arrived in the layer after c.1300.

This simple but inexorable logic has so often been ignored or not applied rigorously enough in the past that it is necessary to re-examine critically many excavation reports in which far-reaching conclusions regarding the dating of pottery have been based. Too often, also, the tentative conclusions of the original report have hardened into accepted fact in subsequent references.

Considerations of this kind demand the most careful excavation in layers and the most accurate recording. Without these pottery can be made to prove anything. In addition, the larger the quantity of pottery discovered from each period of a site's occupation, the more valid will be the conclusions which can be drawn. Similarly there is no doubt that the greater the number of sites from which pottery is obtained and the more representative their distribution, the more accurate will be our deductions regarding the pottery's development and economic distribution.

In order to assess the significance of the pottery we find (or do not find) on our sites we must be aware of the general distribution of pottery types in the region and in the country as a whole.

Two examples from the Welsh border will illustrate the point. There is a thin but positive scatter of prehistoric pottery in the region. Neolithic sherds have been found on a number of sites, beaker pottery is very rare but present, Bronze Age pottery is found in some variety, while Iron Age pottery, though not plentiful, has been found on excavated hill-forts and lowland sites dated to the Iron Age by other means. With the Roman occupation comes a flood of pots. All the specifically Roman sites in the area, with the exception of marching camps, produce large quantities of sherds. However, between AD 400+ and 1100 ± 50 there is virtually no pottery in use in the whole region. (See Barker, 1970 for discussion of the problem.) After the beginning of the twelfth century pottery is again in common use and all excavated medieval sites have produced quantities of material.

The first example is taken from the excavations at Hen Domen, Montgomery. Here, sealed under the boulder clay rampart of the eleventh-century castle and under a ploughsoil beneath dated by radio carbon and, more tentatively, historical means to the late Saxon period (Barker and Lawson, 1971) were the post-holes of a rectangular, slightly bow-sided, building with centre posts and with a drainage gulley at the upper end. No pottery or other finds were associated with this building though from the ploughsoil above it came an amulet carved from a sherd of ordinary red Roman pot. The date of the building is uncertain; its form is not easily parallelled in the Bronze or Iron Ages, though rectilinear Iron Age buildings are increasingly being discovered. If it were Roman, it would certainly, in this area, have produced an appreciable number of sherds. The complete absence of pottery suggests a date within the aceramic period outlined above. The Roman sherd, carved into an amulet, speaks of the rarity of pottery at this time, and it is significant that it and the handful of Roman sherds from the overlying castle are all red and abraded. Some have suggested that Hen Domen castle is built on the site of a Roman signal station and have cited the Roman pottery in support of this argument. But there is a massive fort less than a mile away and a more reasonable explanation for the presence of the Roman sherds is that, being red (including samian ware), they were attractive – in an aceramic period, unique – and in the castle period quite unlike the Norman pottery which is mostly black or brown, never bright red. These sherds were probably therefore brought on to the site as curiosities, which would also explain the fragment of Roman tile impressed with a baby's footprint, and more exotically still a late Bronze Age socketed axe-head found lying on a twelfth-century pebble path. We should not underrate the antiquarian interests of the people we dig up.

The second example comes from Wroxeter where excavation revealed the remains of a building whose plan, bow-sided and tripartite with a cross-passage, was that which one would expect from a medieval peasant village, the typical 'long-house'.

The building contained nothing but Roman material, though there was no pottery (smashed round the hearth, for example) which could be shown to have been in use during the occupation of the house. All the pottery which was picked up could have been residual (some of it was samian) used to pack stake-holes. Our building, therefore, could be late Roman (a fourth-century sherd embedded in the clay floor gave a positive *terminus post quem*) or could fall into the aceramic period discussed above. It could not, in spite of all appearances, be medieval since it is inconceivable that there would not be a single sherd of medieval pottery in it at a date when pottery is plentiful. Other methods of dating and the general stratigraphy of the building reinforce the late Roman or 'dark age' date suggested by the lack of medieval pot.

Residual pottery

Mention of the bow-sided 'peasant' building at Wroxeter raises the whole question of residual pottery. The problem is seen in an acute form on deeply stratified Roman, medieval or post-medieval sites where pits, wells and foundations have brought earlier pottery up to later surfaces. The last period layers of such sites may contain a very high proportion of residual pot. Indeed, it is possible that in some Roman towns, whose occupation enters an aceramic period, the latest 'Roman' layers will contain nothing but residual pottery. As one removes the layers of occupation, one by one, the problem will tend to resolve itself.

The situation can be shown diagrammatically thus:

Structural Periods	Layers	Pottery Types
Z	1	g + f + e + d + c + b + a
	2	g + f + e + d + c + b + a
	3	g + f + e + d + c + b + a
Y (ACERAMIC)	4	f + e + d + c + b + a
X	5	f + e + d + c + b + a
	6	e + d + c + b + a
W	7	e + d + c + b + a
	8	d + c + b + a
	9	d + c + b + a
V	10	c + b + a
	11	b + a
U	12	b + a
T	13	a
	14	a

When the pottery eventually comes to be studied as a whole, the points of entry of types b, c, d, e, etc., can be seen. Other types are then shown to be either residual or to go on being used and/or manufactured in parallel with the later types. Resolution of this problem will depend on the relative quantities of the earlier pottery surviving and on its condition, e.g. whether the sherds are large and unabraded, or small and weather-worn.

Some highly regarded pottery, such as samian wares in Roman times and fine jugs in medieval times, may have had a longer life because they were more carefully looked after, and it is common to find examples of the finer Roman wares mended with rivets in order to prolong their life. The date of deposition in an archaeological layer of sherds of one of these more highly prized pots could therefore be a century or two later than its manufacture. It is much less likely that ordinary cooking pots or dishes would have a long life. Once again, the greater the quantity of data, in this case the amounts of pottery, the more reliable will be the conclusions that can be drawn from it.

Because pottery looms so large in the archaeological record of many excavated sites it is easy to overestimate its importance in the lives of the people in whom we are interested.

It is always salutary to keep in mind that there have been long aceramic periods in our history, particularly in the highland zones, or periods during which pottery was scarce and could not have been regarded as an everyday necessity. As far as one can tell the whole Welsh nation managed without pottery from the fifth century until the twelfth, except for small quantities of exotica imported from Gaul and the Mediterranean. But no one would dare suggest that this represents cultural poverty in pre-Norman Wales. And on the other side of Britain, it is illuminating to look at the ugly, badly made flask that is the only pot included in the Sutton-Hoo ship burial. If the splendid objects buried with, or in honour of, this Anglian king had been perishable whatever conclusions should we have drawn about him simply from this pot? Care must be taken not to give too much weight to any surviving evidence as against the evidence which has not survived, but which can reasonably be assumed to have existed.

The recording of pottery and animal bones

Where little pottery is found, its importance is likely to be very great and each sherd should be treated as a small find. Where pottery (and animal bones) are recovered in quantity they must be treated in bulk, to some extent, or the system will be overwhelmed. It is perhaps most convenient to divide the major grids into quarters or sixteenths dependent on the degree of precision required for the subsequent analysis. Each site's pottery and bones recording will have to be assessed on its merits and it may be necessary to modify the system if the quantities recovered are much greater or much less than expected.

Pottery should be stored in polythene bags or boxes, or cardboard boxes. Paper bags are unsuitable as most types disintegrate after a few years. The life of some kinds of polythene bags is uncertain and the storage of pottery, bones and other finds should be checked annually, and the material repacked if the containers are deteriorating. In a number of important cases the re-assessment of excavations carried out only 20-30 years ago has been made impossible because of the complete disintegration of the paper bags in which the pottery was stored. For this reason, also, each sherd of pot should be marked individually with Indian ink. If the fabric of the pottery is friable the marking should be protected with a coating of varnish. The marking of each individual sherd, however tedious on a large site, means that the sherds can be re-sorted into fabrics or shapes without losing a record of the context from which they were derived.

Just as with portable finds, there are three entirely different questions asked of the pottery assemblage. The first is related to the groups of pottery from within a layer, a building or a phase of the site. The second is concerned with the development of the pottery itself, its earliest and latest occurrence, its group or fabric or glaze or form, or its relationships with the pottery of the region or the country as a whole. The third is the function of the various types of pottery found – cooking pots, jugs, dishes, lamps and so forth. It is important therefore to label and store the pottery in a way which makes retrieval as simple as possible; otherwise its subsequent study could become exceedingly laborious, if not impossible.

The quantitative analysis of large groups of potsherds presents a number of difficulties. Counting the numbers of sherds of each recognizable type is not very satisfactory since its validity depends on the sizes of both the original pots and the fragments into which they have been smashed – any number of sherds can be doubled simply by breaking them in half. Similarly, weighing the sherds of each type has its limitations since the results will vary according to the sizes of the original pots and the thickness and density of the fabrics used. A more valid method is to attempt to estimate the number of pots represented by reconstructing each type on paper and estimating the minimum numbers of each type in the assemblage. Orton, 1980, 15ff. describes very lucidly the problems of the analysis of a mass of potsherds and concludes that the idea of estimated vessel equivalents (*ibid.* pp. 164-166), though it has practical difficulties, is at present the most fruitful line of study. The validity of an analysis of pottery (or any other finds including, in particular, animal bones) depends upon the percentage of the total original deposit on the site which is recovered. Clarke, Clarke ed., 1972, 26ff., has demonstrated graphically the considerable distortions in a 60 per cent sample of a series of assemblages (*ibid.,* fig. 1:8). As in every other sphere of excavation, therefore, the nearer we approach the total recovery of any category of evidence the more closely our analysis will approach the truth. Our sample must be as large as possible and from all parts of a multi-purpose site, where there may be kitchens, stables, great halls, workshops and many other buildings and areas from which sherds may come not only in varying quantities but in types related to the function of the buildings – glazed jugs from a medieval hall, cooking pots from the kitchen area and so on. Add to this the cleanliness of many communities who swept their floors and disposed of large sherds in rubbish pits often well outside the settlement site, and it will be seen that typological analysis is liable to a series of vagaries not all of which can be quantified or even predicted. It may simply not be worth analysing small groups of pottery (or anything else). However the cumulative assemblages from large long-term excavations or from a series of related excavations, for example, within towns, will provide enough material to set up a flexible analytical framework which will produce increasingly refined and well-founded results.

The division of an assemblage of pottery into types will depend on a qualitative analysis of its fabrics, glazes, and forms. Usually this has been macroscopic and intuitive, depending on a more or less subjective assessment of the colour and texture of the fabrics– 'buff', 'orange', 'red with grey core', 'coarse', 'fine' or 'sandy'– without any clear definition of what these terms mean, together with similar descriptions of glazes as 'apple-green', 'yellowish-brown', or perhaps 'brownish-yellow'. In an attempt to standardize the description of colours, a Pottery Colour Chart has been published by RESCUE (Webster, 1970). This is a simplified version of the sort of charts used for the descriptions of soils, and should remove some of the subjectivity from pottery publication. The standardization of fabric descriptions is a great deal more difficult as anyone who has thought that he has found published parallels for pottery he has excavated will know, when he holds the comparative material in his hand and finds that it bears only a superficial resemblence to his own material.

The Medieval Pottery Research Group has produced a suggested *Key to Identification of Inclusions in Pottery,* which is 'designed to facilitate visual identification of the principal inclusions found in pottery in Britain'. This has not yet been accepted, but something of the kind is urgently needed.

The only really adequate description of fabrics would be based on thin sectioning, when the geology of the fabric can be identified and the origins of inclusions examined by heavy mineral analysis. This would be a formidable, if not impossible, task for all the pottery excavated in Britain every year but anything less must be recognized as being inadequate and potentially misleading.

The comparative study of forms, both of whole pots and of their parts, such as rims and bases, and of their decorative treatment is immensely complicated since the total repertory of forms and decoration is so wide.

Any system must include every form from the smaller globular cooking pot to the most elaborately decorated jug, and since almost all the pottery from excavations is hand-made (as distinct from moulded or machine-turned) the forms will tend to vary slightly from pot to pot. Thus, although broad divisions can and must be made, there will always be a number of examples which shade off into one or another type.

The study of glazes also needs to be more systematized, with analysis of their composition and added colouring agents. By determining the nature and quantities of trace elements in the glazes, it may be possible to sort an assemblage of potsherds into groups distinct from those determined by form and fabric. Since behind the pottery sits the potter, a man making more or less aesthetically pleasing objects for a market, whether local or continental, in the study of pottery we enter the realm of art-history and aesthetics, and must assess the degree of influence which one potter or group of potters has had on another, and whether a potter has moved about the country making his characteristic wares from the available local clays. An example of potters moving across the country is postulated by P. Webster (1975) where the production of Iron Age and Roman tankards is shown to move from the Durotrigian region on the south coast up into the Severn valley. This is a more or less clear-cut example spanning two centuries. Other movements were undoubtedly more complex, and on much shorter time-scales. It will obviously not be sufficient to sort pottery simply by fabric, or by decoration or by form but by a combination of all these characteristics. Pots of a similar form but differing fabrics may well be found to overlap in their distribution with pots of one fabric but differing forms according to whether the potters were influenced by style or by the availability or desirability of local clays and tempering materials. A well-known example of an apparently alien style being imposed on an already well-established technique is the so-called Romano-Saxon pottery found chiefly in Eastern England. This combines the hard, usually grey fabrics of wheel-turned Roman pottery with the forms and decorative slashes and dimples of pagan Saxon pots – a combination which was perhaps an attempt by Roman potters to capture the Saxon market, to make their wares attractive to recent immigrants with different tastes in pottery shapes and decoration.

Very large quantities of pottery must be studied before any generalized observations can be made with confidence about places or origin, distribution and stylistic affinities. The discovery of kilns with their accompanying mass of wasters is of great help, but much pottery was fired above ground in clamps or kilns which have now been destroyed without trace, so that the study of such wares is correspondingly more difficult.

The recording of small finds

Recording systems for small finds must aim primarily to record the find positions sufficiently accurately in three dimensions that they can be 'put back' into the excavation long after it is over. For this purpose two-dimensional grid coordinates for each find are essential. However, it is not necessarily helpful to record the absolute height of the find above Ordnance Datum or its depth below the ground surface or some other site datum except in special cases. What is needed for the reconstruction of the site is to know from which layer (however thin, or discontinuous) the find came; its absolute depth may be misleading unless at the same time the find is tied into the layer from which it derives. A clear example of this is seen in the practice, advocated particularly in the digging of ditch and rampart sections, of projecting find-spots horizontally on to the section. If all layers within the ditch and rampart were themselves horizontal the method might be valid, but they seldom are. More often the situation will be that shown in fig. 60, where a ditch cutting is shown in transverse section, the removed layers being indicated by dotted lines.

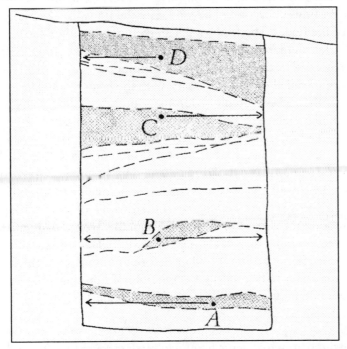

Figure 60

If the positions of the four finds are projected on to either of the drawn sections A or B, they will be transferred to a layer above or below the one to which they really belong, with consequent distortion of the interpretation. This is a simple example, but it is not difficult to visualize its extension into more complicated situations. Only if the find comes from a thick layer will a vertical measurement be necessary. This should be taken as a spot height which can be plotted on the site plan so that it is directly related to the contour survey of the layers. Since the upper surfaces of all layers should be levelled (and ideally contour surveyed), the absolute depth of the find spot can, if necessary, be recovered. However, the really important information is the position of the find relative not only to its own layer or feature but to those above and below it. If the procedures advocated in Chapter 9 are followed, the position and dimension of each feature/layer are recorded on its layer record card and visually on the series of site plans. All that is necessary therefore is to refer the find to its feature/layer without further elaboration on its vertical position.

The essence of a finds recording system should be simplicity. The position of the find must be marked in the ground, so that it can be recorded three-dimensionally, and the point plotted on the site plan or overlay, to ensure that, subsequently, the find can be married to its find-spot, long after the site has gone. Each find should be given a serial number, which is attached both to the find and the recorded spot on the plan and it should have its own record card on which the grid reference, feature (or layer) number and, if necessary, depth or spot height, are recorded. On large sites, when finds are pouring out, the system should be streamlined as far as possible to avoid time wasting in recording. A system of double numbering is useful, in which cards, each with a serial number printed twice, or ordinary raffle or cloakroom tickets, are used. One of the pair is pinned to the ground in the find spot while the other is put in the bag with the find to identify it with its find spot. As a double check a finds book should be kept with the finds listed serially by date and by the signature of the finder. The find spots can then be plotted by the triangulation or the use of grids on to the plans or overlays at a convenient time, such as the end of each day. If both horseshoe and building nails are plotted, each ancient nail can be replaced by a modern large-headed nail, if necessary with the head painted to distinguish one type from another. These are plotted in the same way on the plans and overlays and each find should be given a record card, conveniently printed as a pro forma.

A description of the find when it was first discovered is required and this description will be expanded when further details are revealed by cleaning, X-rays, or other scientific examination. Details of cleaning and conservation treatment should be added to the card as work proceeds so that the history of the find as it passes through the excavation and post-excavation processes is recorded. Only in this way can either specialists in the type of object, or laboratory technicians, properly assess degrees of wear, corrosion and loss due to chemical action (either before or after discovery!). Preliminary identifications may have to be modified in the light of subsequent treatment. In cases of doubt the first attribution may be pencilled in or given a question mark so that second thoughts are not inhibited.

Ultimately, there are three principal ways in which the data regarding the finds will need to be retrieved. One is the relationship of the finds to structures and to important structural, occupation or dating layers. The second is the classification of finds into types or into groups according to their function and the third is according to the material from which they are made.

The first category will throw light on the evolving occupation of the site; the uses to which buildings or areas have been put; the changing economy of occupants; the extent and nature of imports and so forth. The second will be used to demonstrate the development of particular categories of object, both in relation to the site and in relation to comparable objects from other excavations and museum collections. The third will demonstrate the ways in which particular materials such as bronze, or shale, or ivory have been worked and the types of object which have been made from them.

On excavations producing large quantities of finds, computer storage is the most efficient means of handling them, since the computer is not only able to produce lists of required categories of information but can also provide distribution plots either printed or on visual display. Where the quantities of finds do not justify the use of a computer, edge-punched or light-hole cards are perfectly adequate.

Sophisticated techniques of statistical analysis are being developed to deal with artefacts of all kinds recovered from excavations. These techniques and their origins are described in Binford and Binford (1968), Binford (1972), Clarke (1968) and Orton (1980). No statistical analysis, however, can be better than the quality of its raw data, the true reflection of the nature and distribution of the samples used in the analysis. This is not the place to discuss analyses based on such disparate data as the location of Roman towns or the chance finds of a distinctive type of medieval pottery. But so far as evidence from excavations is concerned it will be obvious that only securely stratified, correctly identified and closely recorded evidence; whether of portable artefacts or of bones or other environmental material, will give a basis secure enough to justify conclusions based on an analysis which otherwise may be far more sophisticated than the digging on which it is based. Statistical analysis of material derived from partial and inadequately recorded excavations will inevitably be misleading though unprovably so. It is, therefore, incumbent on those of us who dig to provide the most reliable data possible and this can only be done, on the one hand, by large and strictly controlled excavations, and, on the other, by the adoption of agreed scales of reliability for those excavations, such as salvage digs, which by their nature, cannot provide the necessary degree of precision.

The value of coins as archaeological evidence

Coins, together with seals, tokens and specifically datable inscriptions, are probably the most closely datable of all archaeological finds. As a result, they are welcomed in excavations as providing positive dating evidence. But it must never be forgotten that they provide only a *terminus post quem* for the deposit in which they are found (see p. 193 below). Nevertheless, it is helpful to try to estimate the date at which the coin was lost as distinct from the date at which it was minted, by considering its condition, that is how much wear it seems to have suffered during circulation, and to translate this into years. Before the introduction of decimal currency in Britain it was highly instructive to look at a handful of coins taken from a pocket at random and to see how different the amounts of wear were on coins of similar date. Pennies dating from the beginning of this century would range in wear from crisply readable to almost smooth discs. The writer was with P.A. Rahtz one day when he took from his pocket four old pennies in order to make a telephone call from a pre-STD phone box. This was in the early 1960s. None of these pennies was later than 1914. If Rahtz had been buried at that time in the clothes he stood up in, his interment would almost certainly have been dated half a century too early. One could only hope that his excavator would apply the *terminus post quem* rule as rigorously as he does himself.

Another factor affecting the estimates of wear on coins is the nature of the soil in which they have lain, so that it is important to attempt to distinguish between wear and corrosion, and to record the nature of the surrounding soil. For this reason, it is especially important not to overclean coins, and in fact they should, ideally, be cleaned by a trained conservator. However, sometimes it is desirable to know the date of a coin immediately (though whatever the date the coin proves to be, the *strategy* of the excavation should not be altered, since the relative chronologies will remain unchanged, the coin merely providing a *terminus post quem* —see p. 193). If light cleaning with a stiff brush or glass bristle brush (not a metal bristle brush) does not render the inscription legible under a magnifying glass or binocular microscope, a scalpel can be used for careful mechanical cleaning. Harder corrosion products can be removed by vibratool. Careful mechanical cleaning is to be preferred to chemical stripping but is comparatively time-consuming. If mechanical methods fail, the following chemical methods may be used:

Acids

30-40% formic acid or 5% citric acid made up in fresh distilled water. Action is rapid, and the solution should be changed when it becomes deeply coloured (either dark green or blue). The coins should be kept under observation and removed before the metal becomes etched. Formic acid is to be preferred as it is less likely to do harm.

Alkaline Glycerol

120g NaOH

40ml glycerine

1 litre distilled water

Coins should be soaked in the solution in glass or polythene containers. This method is rapid and the coin should be removed for observation periodically. The solution should be changed when it becomes deeply coloured.

Calgon

15% solution

This method takes longer than the methods described above but it is less likely to cause damage. This method can be used for the removal of calcium and magnesium salts. It may etch the coin if it is left in for too long.

Sodium Sesquicarbonate

5% solution

Not a very good method. The solution should be changed every week or when it gets too blue. After stripping, coins should be brushed with a glass bristle brush to remove any powdery deposits.

All treatments should be followed by impregnation in a 3% solution of Benzotriazole preferably under vacuum. The coins should then be dipped in alcohol to remove any Benzotriazole from the surface. When dry, they should be lacquered using Incralac or other chloride-free cellulose nitrate lacquer. This treatment prevents further deterioration.

It should be stressed that chemical stripping should only be used when absolutely necessary.

The assessment of the archaeological and historical significance of coins depends on factors other than mere dating, especially where whole coin series are discovered. An understanding of the economic conditions in which the coins were issued is of vital importance if gross errors in interpretation are not to be made, since the recovery rate of coins from sites will have to be measured against the known profusion or paucity of the issues. The subject has been concisely dealt with by Casey (1974). His paper deals with Romano-British coins but the principles apply to all coin finds.

It is tempting to equate richness of coin finds with periods of economic prosperity or growth, but histograms of coin recovery plotted against known economic conditions show considerable anomalies. For example, far more Anglo-Saxon than medieval coins have been recovered from Worcester, a city which was of great importance in the twelfth and thirteenth centuries, especially as a place of pilgrimage, where one would expect coin loss to be high and varied in content (Barker *et al*, 1970). There is no ready explanation for this, but obviously an assessment of Worcester's prosperity based simply on the coins discovered there over the last century would be wildly misleading. In Russia, the long sequence of coins from Novgorod exhibits a similar hiatus (Thompson, 1967, XVI, 7 and fig. 18). The excavations at Novgorod, which were almost entirely carried out on the preserved wooden levels of streets and house foundations, are also instructive on the relationship between the presumed dates of coin losses and the dates of the streets and buildings provided by dendrochronology (Thompson, *op. cit.* 30-4). In general, dating from the coin and seal evidence tended to be too early; in other words, it was assumed that the coins had a shorter life than they had in fact.

Over and above their value as dating evidence, coins often tell us, obliquely or directly, a good deal about the aspirations and intentions of the rulers who issued them. The propaganda uses of Roman coinage are well known, and the inscriptions on these coins are documentary sources of considerable importance. The size of coins together with the progressive debasement of the metal from which they are struck reflects inflation, while the restoration of the currency will be reflected in improvement in the composition of the metals and usually in the quality of the dies from which the coins are struck. Similarly the study of forgeries and spurious issues can throw considerable light on economic conditions in the regions where they circulate.

No less important than the study of coinage is the appreciation of the significance of lack of coins. At Hen Domen, a castle of some importance from the Norman Conquest to the late thirteenth century, only one half silver penny has been found in sixteen years of excavation. Clearly the soldiery were either not being paid in coin, or they were exceptionally careful. It seems probable, in this case, that payment was almost entirely in kind, castle guard being an imposed service for which payment would not be made, though one wonders how many mercenaries, if any, were employed on the Welsh border in these violent centuries.

Any assessment of the significance of coins, or lack of them, from excavations should be made with the help of an historian who is familiar with the economy of the periods being examined.

CHAPTER

12

The Interpretation of the Evidence

Introduction

This chapter deals with the assemblage of evidence from the site and how it is put together in order to interpret features and to create a sequence of phases. Such phases are the basis for a relative chronology, which relies on being able to identify and understand the relation of layers. As an aid to plotting the sequence, Barker recommends and describes the use of the diagrammatic chart design by Harris (the Harris matrix). Dateable items in the sequence help suggest an absolute chronology for the site.

T he detailed dissection of a site and the elaborate recording of all its observable phenomena are simply the preludes to an attempt to give meaning to the evidence: to decide how layers were formed; to recognize and interpret patterns in the excavated surfaces which show the former presence of buildings, fences, ditches, ramparts, fields and all the other traces which human occupation leaves in the ground; to explain, as far as possible, the complete sequence of events on the site.

This mass of evidence must then be set into a pair of chronological frames, one relative, one absolute.

The relative framework is based on the study of the superimposition of layers and features, or the intersection of walls, post-holes, slots, ditches, gullies and other similar features. Such a framework gives only a 'floating chronology' which can be moved up and down, or extended or contracted according to datable finds securely stratified within the sequence. Such finds may be coins, seals or tokens, datable pottery or other artefacts, or architectural or sculptural fragments; or they may be samples taken from the layers and dated by scientific methods.

The relative chronology of a site is likely to be more certain than the absolutely dated chronology, since there is usually little doubt about the broad sequence of events, even if the details are not unequivocal, or the horizontal relationships cannot be demonstrated. However, the absolute, or calendar, dating may be subject to considerable fluctuations, as the evidence of coins is supplemented by that, say, of dendrochronology (eg. Novgorod, Thompson, 1967) or radio-carbon dating; or if the dating of a pottery group is reassessed in the light of research elsewhere; or the excavation, as it proceeds, uncovers further dating evidence which modifies that already used.

The establishment of structural patterns and chronological frameworks is itself only the first stage towards the economic, cultural and, in the widest sense, historical interpretation which should follow. Obviously, if the earlier stages of the interpretation are mistaken, the subsequent stages will be further removed from the truth about the site as it was in the period under investigation. If we add to this Coles's reminder of the law of diminishing returns: that the evidence which we understand from an excavation is less than we record, which, even in the best excavations, is less than has survived, which in turn is less than the total evidence once existing on the site, we shall see that our understanding of an ancient site or settlement or landscape will, at best, be severely limited. We must strive, therefore, to minimize these limitations. For example, there is little doubt that the larger and more complete the excavation, the more valid will be the interpretations which we can draw from it. Though this is particularly the case with the excavation of timber buildings, even stone structures are more certainly and completely understood in large areas.

It is not possible to give detailed advice on all the problems of the interpretation of evidence that will occur in a complex excavation. The best general advice that can be given is to keep an open mind, expect the unexpected, and then, when a provisional interpretation has been made, stop, and take the opposite view or views of its meaning. By thus initiating a dialectic, false assumptions are not so likely to be perpetuated and built upon by the addition of subsequent plausible, though mistaken, evidence. For example, if a pebble surface, bordered by stake-holes, is assumed to be an internal floor, it is likely that further emerging evidence will be adduced to support this theory. But if someone then says 'Let us assume it is an outside yard', the matter can be debated in detail, and either resolved on the balance of the evidence, or, if no positive conclusion can be reached, alternative explanations published. This is a simple, perhaps simplistic, example, but it should be extended to cover everything found on the excavation.

It follows that it is a great advantage to have supervisors or assistants on the site who are capable of taking and expressing a constructively critical view of every stage of the work. Conversely the interpretation of an excavation by a forceful individual with inexperienced volunteers or labourers can easily go awry simply because he is not obliged to consider all the alternatives. Under these circumstances, he should, if he is wise, dispute with himself over the meaning of each piece of evidence.

It is often valuable to think 'laterally' when considering the meaning of what we have dug up. In 'lateral' thinking we discard our preconceptions of the solution to a problem and look at it from a new viewpoint, perhaps one that at first sight appears ludicrous or at least highly improbable, but which may be ultimately seen to fit the evidence better than any other of the postulated solutions. Lateral thinking has been described in a number of books by E. de Bono (e.g. 1970).

A valuable aid in the interpretation of excavated evidence (and a check on flights of fancy) is to attempt to explain the origin, derivation and purpose of every recognizable feature in the light of commonsense and practicability. This involves imagining the process by which a structure might have been built, the actual work of barrowing, shovelling, and

Figure 61   This photograph shows the very worn threshold stone of one of the west doorways of the baths basilica at Wroxeter. Earlier excavations have destroyed the stratification above and beside the threshold and a considerable area in the background of the photograph has also been dug in earlier times. However, the rubble beyond the threshold in the centre of the picture can be seen to be of two sorts –a light coloured area of worn stone, bounded by an area of darker, unworn stone. The area of light, worn stone leads diagonally towards the site of the door of the basilica, and is clearly a path leading into the interior of the former basilican area long after the threshold was buried by rubble (removed by the earlier excavators). It follows that the west wall of the building was still standing to an effective height at this time, otherwise there would have been no need to have entered at this point. It can be further deduced, therefore, that robbing of the end wall took place after this. Since the worn rubble surface is of the last period occupation, the robbing is likely to have taken place after the site was deserted. This contrasts with the robbing of many of the other walls of the building which can be shown to have been robbed as early as perhaps the third century. *(Photo-Sidney Renow)*

spreading rubble, digging post-holes, laying foundations and so on. For instance, in determining whether a bank has been piled against a wall, or whether the wall has been built against a vertical face cut into the bank, an examination of the character of wall where it met the bank will usually show whether the joints of the wall were pointed, or whether mortar had been merely poured down behind the stones as the wall-building proceeded up the face of the cut-back bank, since it would be impossible to point the joints if the bank was there first, unless there was a construction trench wide enough to take a man. Often explanations of excavated phenomena can be tested by trial and error, or by observation of similar situations on present-day demolition and construction sites. A simple example of the information which may reasonably be deducted from the observed evidence is shown in fig. 61.

The understanding of a series of robber trenches, for example, is helped by taking the practical view and imagining a group of labourers faced with the job of digging out the walls, or perhaps only the facing stones, of a ruined building. Were the walls visible? If not, how did they find them? Trial trenching? Stone robbers will work as economically as possible, digging the narrowest possible trenches, and usually backfilling them afterwards. If the walls have been completely robbed out, the unwanted stone and mortar debris thrown back will give a great deal of information about the walls as they were when they stood. Biddle and Biddle (1969) have discussed the interpretation of robber trench excavations in some detail. To their suggestions can be added the analysis of the mortars thrown back into the trench, which may differentiate walls of more than one period.

However, the commonsense, practical approach to interpretation does not always work, partly because our habits, modes of thought, and our view of what is practical may be very different from that of the people we are digging up. Robson Bonnichsen (1972) describes an illuminating exercise in the interpretation of a recently deserted Indian camp site, Millie's Camp, where the debris, litter and other evidence of occupation were recorded as carefully as in an area excavation, and their interpretation subsequently checked by reference to the recent occupants. The mistakes made showed the fallibility of some 'commonsense' reasoning. The behaviour patterns which produced the anomalous, misunderstood evidence were unfamiliar to the archaeologists and the reasons behind these behaviour patterns could not have been deduced from the available evidence, so that we must be careful not to project back into the past our own habits and ways of thinking except into situations where they can reasonably be assumed to be valid, either because we have lived and worked in comparable situations, or because we know of living communities who do so now.

Another limitation of the 'practical' approach is that we may be reluctant to accept the evidence in the ground for what it is, if it seems impractical or unlikely. An example is the discovery on a number of sites of very shallow post-holes and circles of small stones which in many cases form definite structural patterns, thus implying a style of building in which posts are set on, not in, the ground. At first sight, this seems a highly impractical, if not impossible, manner of construction, but as the evidence has accumulated from a number of excavations, the former presence of such buildings has become undeniable. Accordingly instead of working from our preconceptions of what the evidence for a timber building ought to look like, we should explore methods of construction that would fit the evidence. This has resulted, among other things, in the full-scale simulation of such a structure, Building I from the Baths Basilica excavation at Wroxeter which, though not yet complete, has already proved that post-built structures will stand even if their posts are not embedded in the ground.

Dating

The understanding and strict application of the concepts of the *terminus post quem* and *terminus ante quem* are of fundamental importance in the relative dating of layers and features. Unless these concepts are applied in all cases with the most rigorous logic far-reaching mistakes in dating and interpretation will be made. The rules can be set out simply as follows:

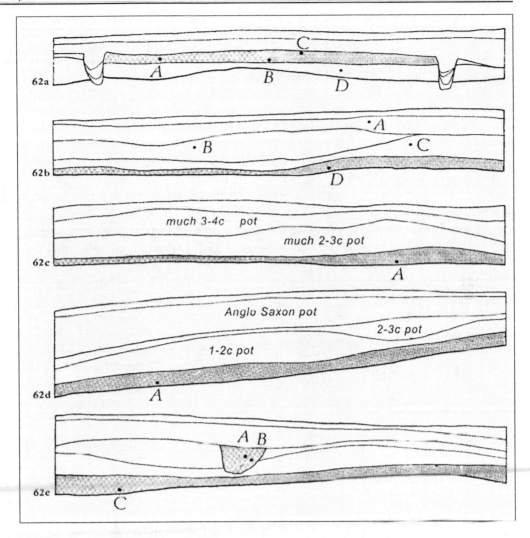

Figure 62a   A clay floor is bounded by post-holes. The floor contains three coins of the
               second century AD. Coin D is of the first century. The floor was therefore laid
               during or after the second century AD. On the basis of this evidence alone, the
               floor could be twentieth century. It certainly might be fifth century or Anglo-
               Saxon. However, if coin D was third century, coins A, B, and C are all negated
               as dating evidence, and the floor which seals coin D must be third century or
               later.

Figure 62b   Coin D is first century AD, Coin C second century; coin B third century and
               coin A fourth century. Here is a fairly common situation, somewhat simplified,
               in which we have a superficially plausible sequence of dating evidence which
               suggests that the four layers span whole Roman period in sequence. However,
               if we apply the *terminus post quem* rule strictly, as we must, the whole lot could be
               post Roman, even modern. Other dating factors would have to be discovered
               and assessed before Roman sequence could be maintained.

Figure 62c   In this figure there is increased probability that the layers above A were laid
               down in the second-third century and the third-fourth century *but no certainty*.
               Again A is crucial. If it is a ninth century coin or thirteenth century pot, all of
               the material above it must be considered residual.

Figure 62d   In this similarly plausible sequence, if A is an otherwise undatable sherd or object
               one must be careful not to use a false *terminus ante quem* reasoning and maintain
               that A must be earlier than first-second century. It may ultimately prove to be, say,
               fourth century, when the two layers above take their *terminus post quem* from it.

Figure 62e   The two objects A and B, though found together in a pit, tell us *nothing* about each other except that they were buried in the pit together at some time *at or later than* the date of the later of the two objects. However, if object C can be shown to be of later date than either A or B then the whole sequence takes its *terminus post quem* from C.

The terminus post quem

A datable object, such as a coin, or other datable find, such as a radio-carbon sample from a layer or feature, only gives the date *on or after which the layer or feature was deposited,* that is, the so-called *terminus post quem.* It follows that in any continuous sealed layer in which there is a number of finds of varying date, the find of latest date is the one which provided the *terminus post quem.* It must be established that the object is not intrusive, that it has not been taken down an animal hole, or slipped down the interstices between the stones of a wall. If there is any doubt about this the object should be rejected for dating purposes. The argument is most easily demonstrated graphically (figs. 62-3).

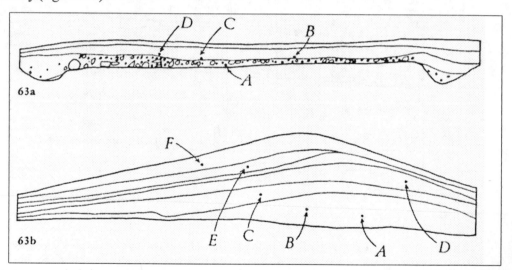

Figure 63 a   A is a Roman coin or sherd, B is a medieval spur. It is tempting to see this as a Roman road still in use in medieval times. However, the road could be of any date, from the Roman period onward. (It cannot be pre-historic if the sherd is thoroughly sealed). It is even possible that the spur was an antique dropped recently.

Figure 63 b   This illustration is based on an actual example (at Quatford in Shropshire, Mason and Barker, 1961).
F -19th-century sherd
E -medieval sherd
D -medieval bronze object
C -Roman sherd
B -neolithic flint
A -1881 halfpenny
The presumed medieval rampart was shown to be dated to 1881 or later by the presence of the Victorian halfpenny. The danger here is that the halfpenny might not have been dropped, or that it would not have been found if the cutting had been made elsewhere along the 'rampart'. In fact, the bank was formed by ploughing during the 1939-45 war, so that the 1881 coin gives a *terminus post quem* some *60* years too early.

The terminus ante quem

The *terminus ante quem* argument arises when features or layers are sealed by or are cut through by later, datable features. The later features give a *terminus ante quem* (that is a date *before* which the earlier features must have been deposited) to all those features which can be demonstrated to be earlier. For example, if a series of layers is sealed by a mosaic floor of unquestioned fourth-century date then all the layers below will be fourth century *or earlier.* Similarly, if a wall itself can be dated, say by architectural features, then the layers which are cut by its foundation are given a *terminus ante quem* by the wall. Thus, if the wall can be shown to be Norman, the cut layers are Norman or earlier. They may be Saxon –or palaeolithic.

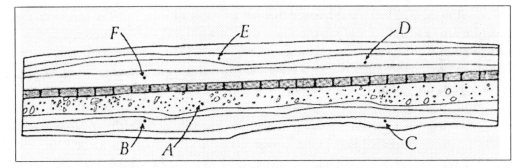

Figure 64   All the layers under the tiled floor including finds A, B and C in the illustration are given a *terminus ante quem* by the floor. If the floor is made of, say, fourteenth century tiles then all the layers beneath must be fourteenth century or earlier. They might be prehistoric. Be sure that the floor has not been taken up and relaid in later times, perhaps in a nineteenth century restoration.

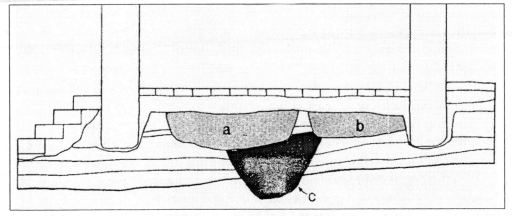

Figure 65   This again is a diagrammatic representation of an actual situation. The walls are those of an early Norman passage leading to the cloisters in Worcester Cathedral. The steps lead down into a Norman under croft.

Both these buildings are firmly datable by their styles of architecture. The two graves *a* and *b* are therefore clearly given a *terminus ante quem* by the early Norman passage since they must have been dug from the contemporary floor level. They are therefore late Saxon or earlier. Similarly the underlying pit *c* is given a *terminus ante quem* by the graves. The pit produced a large sherd of pottery of a type not readily paralleled in the region. However, it must be late Saxon or earlier. It is very possibly Iron Age.

However, we must be careful not to be led into a circular argument. *A terminus ante quem* cannot be given by a layer which is dated by an object embedded in it which merely gives it a *terminus post quem*. For example, if a floor in a house contains a coin of AD 267 firmly stratified in it, the floor must have been laid in 267 *or after*. It does not follow that the layers below the floor were deposited in 267 *or earlier*. Subsequent excavation of another floor many layers below the first might produce a stratified coin of, say, AD 370. In that case all the layers above take a new *terminus post quem* of 370 *or later*. The whole complex might ultimately turn out to be tenth century. Unless the limitations of stratified datable objects are fully appreciated there is a danger that serious dating errors will occur in interpretation, to be perpetuated in the literature.

It must also be re-emphasised that a number of objects retrieved from one layer or feature are 'associated' only in the sense that they have a common context in the excavation. Their 'association' implies nothing about their relative or absolute dates, or ultimate provenance. In the past, a great deal of weight, has been placed on the argument that objects are 'associated', and quite unjustifiable conclusions drawn from this. (See the example cited on p. 175 above.) Pottery cannot be dated by 'association' with a coin. It is only too easy for a stray Roman coin to get into a medieval rubbish pit. No one would redate a group of glazed jugs to the Roman period on that evidence alone. But how many times have we seen objects and pottery dated by association with coins when the dates look more plausible?

Nevertheless, under some circumstances the association of objects can be accepted as of considerable importance. Objects found together in a grave, for instance, though they may not all be of one date or even of one style or culture, are associated in the sense that they were deposited either on or with the body for specific reasons—as heirlooms, trophies, equipment for the after-life or perhaps even as sentimental keepsakes. Similarly, objects found strewn on the floor of a house, particularly one that has been burnt down, when it can be supposed that the occupants fled without stopping to collect all their belongings, may be assumed to have been in use by, or at least in the possession of, the occupants when the house was abandoned. The greater the quantities of material in association the more reliance can be placed on conclusions drawn from them. The objects in a single grave may be a unique assemblage. If similar objects are found in a majority of graves in a large cemetery, it can reasonably be assumed that the finds were a normal part of the belongings or equipment of the people interred. Similarly, if great quantities of pottery and coins are found in a stratified sequence, as they are on many Roman sites, it strengthens the argument for assigning in broad terms the assemblages of pottery in the layers to the dates of the coins in those layers. For example, if there is a military presence on the site which is followed by a civil development, clearly marked off in the stratification, and the earliest civil phase is followed by a period of demolition and rebuilding, the associated groups of sealed pottery, coins and finds can reasonably be assumed to be broadly contemporary, though increasingly contaminated by residual material.

Relative chronology

The principle of stratification is fundamental to archaeological excavation. This principle states that if one layer can be shown to lie upon another, the lower layer must have been deposited before the upper. The interval between the deposition of the two layers may be a millennium, or the time it takes to tip two separate barrow-loads of rubble, but the relative chronology remains the same. On a simply stratified site, the layers may be stripped off one at a time, in the reverse order to that in which they were deposited, and the result shown as a straightforward table—which amounts to a diagrammatic section of the site:

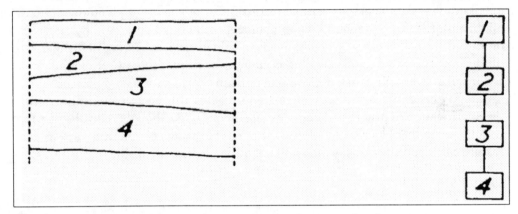

However, things are not usually so simple. Much more often layers are discontinuous so that a theoretical section across the site might look like this

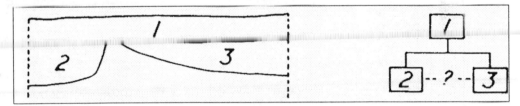

It will be apparent that the relationship between layers 2 and 3 cannot be demonstrated directly—but that they have a common relationship with I—they are both earlier.

In more complicated cases the stratification can be shown diagrammatically thus:

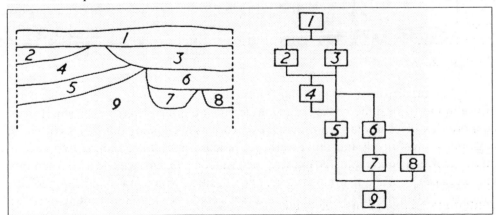

The problem of stratigraphic relationships and their demonstration has been discussed at length by Harris (1975) with illustrations of a number of theoretical situations. His figures 26 and 27 (reproduced here figs. 67 and 68) deserve close study, since they show a typical, though very small, excavation analysed by means of a matrix or graph of layer numbers. Most excavations are far more extensive than this example and are thus likely to produce many more discrete layers and features. One advantage of stripping the largest possible area of a site is that in this way the layers are removed progressively over the whole area and recorded on the plans and photographs in the order in which they were removed. If the plans are drawn on plastic film the whole relative sequence can be seen and understood as a series of transparent overlays. These are supplemented by detail drawings, photographs and the record cards for each layer, feature or context. From all this information a graph of feature numbers such as that described by Harris can be produced. The chief use of such a graph is to help to clarify thinking in the understanding of the site. The exercise of including each layer or feature somewhere in the graph ensures that every piece of evidence is taken into consideration, and that inconvenient or apparently insignificant features are not ignored. It is also a convenient way of displaying the stratification of a large and complex site on one page, though in an abstract form which must either be taken by the reader at its face value, or referred back to the mass of feature cards and site plans, which will not normally be publishable in the necessary detail.

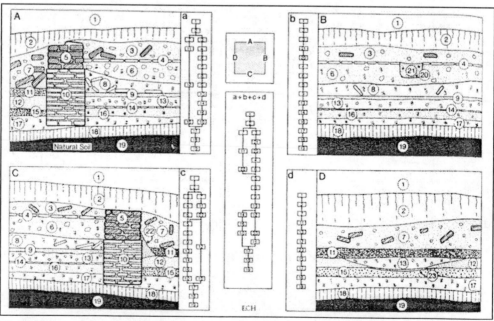

Figure 67

Two modifications of the matrix form as printed by Harris are suggested as a result of use in the field. If the boxes for feature/context numbers were square the forms would be more flexible, since large horizontal excavations need many numbers written across the page but comparatively few downwards. In practice also, it is common to construct the matrix in rough before transferring it to the printed form, a process which often involves much crossing out and rearrangement. A board, fitted with rows of slots, made either of bands of cloth or metal, so that numbered cards could be slotted into them, or, alternatively, a peg-board with a series of movable numbers, would save time and aid clear thinking. Needless to say, the numbers could be used repeatedly.

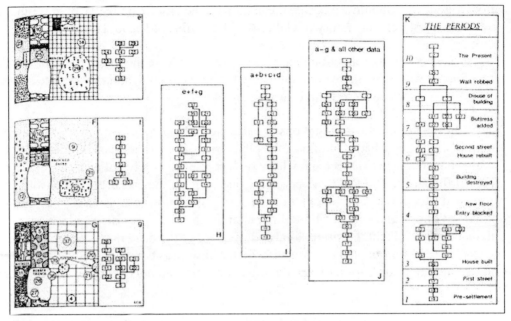

Figure 68

Such a graph can be made more informative by inserting in the appropriate places the structures represented by the features listed, and the principal dating evidence relating both to these structures and to the whole sequence.

Where, in my experience, such a graph of feature numbers has been used it has not altered the interpretation arrived at from the study of the ground and the plans and sections. It is more an instrument for aiding clear thinking and coherent publication than for primary interpretation.

The limitations of archaeological evidence

In every excavation we must expect aspects which are beyond interpretation from the material evidence alone. A reed pipe will tell us its range of notes but not the tunes played on it.

If we can temporarily forget all that we know of the last two thousand years, we can play a salutary archaeological game. What would we make of the archaeological remains of Christianity if we knew nothing of it except what evidence could be recovered by excavation? Recurring fragments both sculptured and painted of a crucified man, of a gentle mother and her child, of other figures, male and female, some of them being tortured and killed, others surrounded by singing winged figures; flagons and dishes included with selected male burials; temples varying in size from tiny to gigantic, many of them cruciform, perhaps significantly, perhaps not; palatial buildings set round courtyards, often in remote and beautiful settings. What reconstruction of this religion would we attempt from such remains? A cult of human sacrifice connected with worship of a mother goddess? Should we equate the child with the crucified man? Could we make the connexion between the oratory of Gallerus and the ruins of Rievaulx?

It is a sobering reflection that we can never excavate the upper room in which the Last Supper was held, and would not recognize it if we could, and that the site of the Crucifixion would be merely three large post-holes.

In spite of the clear limitations of excavated evidence, some deductions can be made about the spiritual aspirations, the pretensions, hopes and fears of the people whose house foundations we dissect and whose rubbish we reverently collect. Two examples must suffice here. The fact that very many burials from the earliest times onwards are furnished with grave goods or other evidence of posthumous provision suggest that man has always hoped for continuation of life after death. If the provisions which are made include the equipment, furniture, food and weapons of the dead man's everyday life, it is a reasonable assumption that the after-life, in that case, was considered to be a continuation or resumption in some form of the life he had just left, and not a spiritual Nirvana, or a Dantean paradise.

Another example is furnished by the petty king (if that is what he was) who rebuilt the centre of Viroconium sometime in the late fourth or fifth century (Barker, 1975). He had pretensions to former grandeur; his buildings, though all in timber, are symmetrically planned on classical lines, with colonnaded porticoes and a private alley or arcade (*ibid*).They are quite unlike the aisled halls of the immediately following Arthurian period or the Saxon palaces of Yeavering. We can see in his mind a conscious attempt to revive (or keep alive) the rapidly fading past, the last flicker of the classical tradition in Britain until Inigo Jones and Wren.

The importance of negative evidence

Negative evidence should be 'that which can be shown to have been absent from the site in antiquity'. It may, however (for instance in the case of organic materials), be 'that which is absent from the site now'. Unfortunately it may also be 'that which was not found' or alternatively 'not recognized'. In order to use negative evidence, one has to be aware of what is missing, which implies being aware of its presence in a similar context elsewhere. A gap in the distribution of a type of pottery or a class of bronze object only becomes apparent when the positive evidence is plotted. Similarly a gap in the distribution of a type of pottery over an excavated area only becomes apparent if the rest of the pottery is recorded and plotted accurately enough to reveal the gap. The recognition of the absence of structural evidence will depend on similar evidence having been found on another similar site, or on a comparable part of the same site, for example, in a stretch of defensive rampart in another part of the circuit. Clearly the distinction must be made between negative evidence which is adduced from the absence, *at present*, of the class of information concerned, and that which can positively be said not to be there. If one is certain that, had the evidence been there, it would have been found, then one can reasonably, if paradoxically, speak of positively negative evidence. If arguing from the mere absence of evidence, it may be safer to enclose the term 'negative' in inverted commas. An example from Wroxeter will illustrate the point. A number of fragments of human skull were found in the upper rubble layers of the site. If the excavation had been partial, confined to trenches or boxes, like those on the same site in the 1850s and the 1930s, the skull fragments would have been construed as the remains of disturbed burials (especially since Professor Donald Atkinson had found complete burials in the gutters and elsewhere in his excavations of the Forum nearby in 1923-27). When the vast collection of animal bones from the same layers was searched for human long-bones, none was found. Since our excavation was total, we were able to say with confidence that there were only skull fragments present, and that they were therefore not from disturbed burials of the sort found by Atkinson. Further examination of the skulls showed that they had been soaked in or anointed with a yellowish oil containing linoleic acid, perhaps sunflower or linseed oil. Some of the skulls also had post-mortem knife or sword cuts on them. The inescapable conclusion is that we have here evidence of a cult involving skulls either as trophies or relics. Without the negative evidence of the lack of long bones, vertebrae, and etc, it would not have been possible to make this assertion. It is also extremely probable that the earlier excavators found skull fragments in their excavations, but discarded them, since under the circumstances, they could not have recognized or proved their significance.

Alternative explanations of excavated phenomena

Whether interpreting single features, or whole structures, or periods of occupation, it is satisfying to be able to offer clear-cut explanations. As a result, doubts expressed in the field about whether a post-hole might not be a root-hole; a hearth, a dump of burnt clay; or a floor, a mere random scatter of pebbles, tend to dissipate themselves as the field drawings are converted into final definitive plans, and when the interim report, necessarily concise, comes to be written. The process may be accelerated by radio or television interviews (who wants to sound doubtful about almost every aspect of his site in front of six million viewers?), or by lectures even to learned societies. When the final report comes to be written all the doubts and uncertainties should be retained in it, but even here this makes for such dull reading and gives such an impression of vagueness and lack of conviction that it is tempting to opt for positive, even dramatic, assertions rather than pedantic fumblings after the truth. When we also bear in mind that the reservations and alternative explanations we express in our reports will very probably be removed before the results of our work reach the specialist text-books and history books, we must take the greatest care to record them from the start and find some way of preserving them throughout the distorting processes our work will subsequently undergo.

It is helpful to adopt in the field a series of grades of probability, from certain, through probable and possible, to very uncertain. (But see cautionary notes by Rahtz,

'How Likely is Likely?' 1975.) These, which should be incorporated in the record card, can either be expressed in words, or in a series of numbers, say 1 to 5, with 1 the most certain and 5 very dubious. If this system is also reflected in the field and published drawings by a colour code (which may be complicated if colour is being used already for other purposes, such as identification of materials) or by the number code written next to the feature, or by means of dotted outlines or hatching, the written record is reinforced. If the drawings appear to give all features equal status, reference will continually have to be made to the record cards. Not only is this time-consuming but the picture given by the drawings will be unnecessarily misleading.

It is only reasonable, however, to offer the reader our carefully argued opinion as to which of the alternative interpretations we favour, and why. If two or more interpretations carry equal weight we must say so, even if [his does mean an inconclusive final chapter in the report. What we must not do is to favour one interpretation before another because it furthers our research interests, or tends to prove a theory we expounded a year or two before.

An excellent example of the way in which evidence, unequivocal in itself, may be interpreted in a series of alternatives is provided by C.R. Musson's study of building forms at Durrington Walls, Woodhenge and the Sanctuary, in Wiltshire (Musson, 1971). He analyses, from the point of view of an architect, the possible structures which could be represented by the excavated circles of post-settings, and while reaching no firm conclusion, frees the reader from stereotyped interpretations not only of these but of other similar monuments.

Scientific Aids

Introduction

The methods and techniques of science have played a major role in modern excavation and interpretation of sites. The techniques of dating have multiplied and been refined during the last one hundred years from tree-ring dating in the early twentieth century to radio carbon in the 1940s and thermoluminescence later, to name the most prominent. Each technique has its limitations in terms of useable time period, size of sample, etc., and there can be difficulties in the employment of techniques without proper understanding of the process. Time and cost limitations may also influence the results.

C ompared with the situation as it was only fifteen years ago, the amount of information which can be added to and deduced from excavated evidence by scientific means is enormous and increases annually. It is instructive to compare the descriptions of techniques in Brothwell and Higgs, 1969, and in Sherratt. ed., 1980,416-432.

One of the most important advances is in the development of dating techniques. These include radio-carbon dating, which is based on the assumption that upon the death of a living organism, whether animal or vegetable, carbon 14 atoms present in the organism decay at a measurable rate (Brothwell and Higgs, 1969, 46 ff.). While the early theories postulated by Libby in the years immediately following the second world war have undergone modification, particularly in methods of calibration, and while tree-ring analysis of the same samples has achieved greater precision, the method remains of supreme importance for the dating of organic material (Sherratt, ed., 1980,417). Another important though less widely applicable technique is that of thermo-remanent magnetism, in which the directions of the magnetic fields induced in hearths, ovens, kilns and the like while they are being fired, are compared with the earth's magnetic field at the present day (Brothwell and Higgs, 1969, 76 ff.). Though the method is still being developed it provides dating evidence from material not susceptible to other forms of analysis. Thermo-luminescence, in which pottery is heated until visible, measurable light is emitted by released electrons, is a method of dating the pottery, since for reasons explained in Brothwell and Higgs, 1969, 106 ff., the greater the age of the pot, the greater the thermo-luminescence. Though at present the method is liable to errors up to ± 10%-15% it is a most important technique, offering, for the first time, a method of pottery dating independent of stylistic or typological criteria. Other scientific dating methods include the dating of obsidian artefacts based on the fact that the surface of obsidian absorbs water from its surroundings at a known rate from the moment it is chipped or flaked until the present day (Brothwell and Higgs, 1969, 62 ff.) and the determination of relative dating by means of the fluorine, nitrogen and uranium contents of ancient bones (Brothwell and Higgs, 1969, 35 ff.). These techniques are independent of the usual stylistic or typological criteria, the studies of which were tending to become bogged down due, very often, to lack of independent dating criteria, so that there had been a tendency for circular arguments to develop between excavators and finds specialists.

In the environmental field, examination of the contents of pits, ditches, wells, cess-pits and other deposits in which organic materials are preserved has revolutionised the understanding of the ecology of our sites and their environs. The study of animal bones on a much increased scale is beginning to build up more reliable pictures of the development of domestication and of food habits, while more sophisticated examination of human bones is shedding light not only on the incidence of diseases, but on the relationships of blood groups among populations, information which, if extended, may solve many problems of invasion, diffusion, immigration and integration. In addition, analysis of metals, pottery clays with their inclusions, glazes, and other manufacturing materials throws light, often unexpected, on methods of manufacture and on patterns of trade.

Two indispensable conspectuses of archaeologically-orientated scientific tech-niques will be found in Brothwell and Higgs (1969) and Sherratt, ed. 1980. To these must be added the Council for British Archaeology's *Handbook of Scientific Aids and Evidence for Archaeologists,* 1970. This is a handlist in loose leaf form which deals with 'artefacts and other material providing evidence' together with 'instrumental techniques (analytical, dating and geophysical)' and which contains bibliographical references for each technique. Recent work and technical advances are described in the journal *Archaeometry* and the *Journal of Archaeological Science.* To these should be added more specialised text-books such as Dimbleby, 1967 and Fleming, 1976.

Since these publications are readily accessible there is no need to repeat here the information given in them, but rather to urge that they, and the other more specialized text-books referred to, be studied by all directors of excavations.

There are two chief problems in the use of scientific aids. One is the necessity for the excavator to comprehend the processes involved, some of which are highly technical. Unless he understands at least the basic theory behind each process it will be impossible for him to use the results with the necessary degrees of caution and flexibility, or even to discuss the method intelligently with the scientist concerned. It is certainly not enough to accept a bare statement about the origin of pottery inclusions, or a thermo-luminescent date, and use it blindly in a report. Even if we are not capable of carrying out the techniques involved ourselves, we must appreciate their possibilities and limitations or we are likely to compound errors of all kinds. There is no doubt that the present-day excavation director is required to have an increasingly wide understanding of disciplines ranging from nuclear physics to the history of painting. He cannot simply be a technician who digs competently, takes samples, and then receives a mass of information from a battery of experts which he welds into a conglomerate of unrelated facts embed-ded in archaeological jargon.

The other problem facing the excavator who seeks scientific help is the cost of such help and, more particularly, the comparative rarity of scientists able and willing to provide *ad hoc* services. State-financed excavations are in the strongest position, being serviced by the Inspectorate of Ancient Monuments Laboratory which can arrange for a great variety of scientific help. This service is being strengthened by a series of research fellowships in a range of specialised disciplines sponsored by the Department of the Environment throughout the country. In some cases these fellowships will be able to offer help on a national basis. In addition, some of the major units now being developed have their own environmental and scientific staff.

For the director of non-State-aided excavations scientific help may be difficult to obtain, often being dependent on local personnel and facilities in museums and universities. The larger museums may have at their disposal a comprehensive range of techniques; others will be only able to offer a minimal service with access to other facilities in urgent and important cases. Universities offer a wide but variable range of scientific aids to the excavations which they run or with which they are associated. It is, at the moment, largely up to the director to arrange what facilities he can within the comparatively restricted network of specialists, an unsatisfactory situation, but one unlikely to be improved in the immediate future. As a result, many excavations suffer from a partial or total lack of scientific and specialist help and as a result the full potential of the excavated evidence is not realized. Sometimes the aid of scientific amateurs can be enlisted. They will obviously vary in the quality and accuracy of their techniques, and considerable tact may be needed, first to persuade them to allow their work to be assessed by a professional, and then, perhaps, to dissuade them from carrying on. A veterinary surgeon may not be a zoological anatomist, and an industrial chemist may not be the man to ask to analyse your soil samples. In addition, they may not use techniques and criteria which are compatible with those used by the leading specialists in the field, so that their work cannot be readily assessed and compared with data from other excavations. It should be added that such difficulties also exist between professional specialists, though moves are being made to establish common criteria and methods in a number of the more widely used techniques of analysis, such as that of animal bones and the characteristics of pottery.

The battery of scientific information potentially available to the excavator is formidable, but, if it is to be fully exploited, requires a greater understanding of and sympathy with scientific method than has often been the case in the past.

Relationships between excavators and scientific specialists have often been bedevilled by difficulties arising from the lack of mutual understanding of each other's problems, and from the essentially part-time nature of much scientific involvement in archaeology. The problems have been succinctly described by Mrs D. S.Wilson in an open letter to archaeologists (Wilson, 1973) which incorporates many valuable suggestions to archaeologists on the ways in which scientists should be treated. Equally, any scientist who is anxious to make the fullest contribution to an excavation should learn the scope and limitations of the techniques involved, ideally by taking part himself. It is far more satisfactory if a scientist can take his own samples, rather than receive them in a laboratory, even if they are accompanied by drawings and photographs of their contexts. The more understanding each has of the other's techniques, problems, and limitations, the greater will be the value of the joint work which they produce.

The use of scientific evidence

Excavators have tended either to seize on pieces of scientific evidence and give them undue weight in the support of their theories, or to relegate them to appendices, printed in the report beyond the acknowledgements, as if they bore little relevance to what was dug up. Pressure from the more forward-looking archaeologists and from scientists themselves, who see the potential of the information they can extract, has now made it *de rigueur* to send samples of all kinds for analysis, often without great thought of the relevance of the information which is likely to come from them. For instance, identification of a scatter of charcoal samples from the occupation layers of a medieval site is unlikely to add much to our knowledge of the arboreal flora of medieval Britain, and will only give a broad and diffuse picture of the trees growing in the vicinity and used for firewood. The information from these scraps of charcoal is, in most circumstances, not worth the considerable labour involved in identifying them. A large quantity of charcoal, clearly part of the structure of a burnt building, will be of more interest, especially if it can be shown that the sample comes from floor planking or weather-boarding, since the types of wood used for subsidiary structural elements are not well known.

The identification and analysis of a scatter of unstratified or poorly stratified mollusc shells, animal bones, mortar fragments or lumps of slag may simply not be worth the time it will undoubtedly take. Under these circumstances it is wise to ask the specialist to assess the probable importance of the material in the context of the excavation, rather than to collect it and send it, regardless, for analysis. This necessitates the specialist visiting the site, or at least being kept fully informed about the nature of the excavation and the contexts of any samples. This in itself would be a step forward from the situation in which the specialist never sees the site and perhaps does not even know it is being dug until the samples land on his desk. Only if the scientist, whether an environmentalist, a soil scientist, or an expert in mortars, slags, window glass or other materials, can discuss on the site the problems raised by the samples can he be expected to give a full appraisal of their significance rather than a mere identification and tentative interpretation. This is asking a lot. Since there are many excavations, all bristling with problems spanning the whole spectrum of scientific expertise, and few archaeological scientists, it is imperative that excavators help scientists to give the most effective service by prior consultation and by pruning requests for identification and analysis to those subjects and samples which are most relevant to the excavation, or the archaeology of the region, or which the scientist himself wants as comparative material.

It may be argued that an accumulation of small samples of apparently irrelevant material might eventually be synthesised in the manner of a large sample, but this is a decision to be made by the specialist in the discipline concerned. It is always possible, too, that a small sample may provide unequivocal evidence of something quite unexpected; the bones of an exotic animal, a vital fragment of a wall-painting or proof of an otherwise undetectable industrial process. But, in general, it is the large well-stratified samples that are likely to be the most useful, and to yield the most valid results.

If scientific reports on excavated material are to be comparable with one another it is important that the same criteria are used in the assessment and measurement of the samples.

This again, is ultimately a matter for the specialists concerned, but archaeologists should be aware of the problems, and should perhaps initiate discussions aimed at solving them.

Excavators are as prone to simplifying scientific evidence as historians are to simplifying archaeological evidence. A prime example is in the use of radio- carbon dates, where too often the central date of what is, in fact, a bell-curve stretching over maybe two centuries, is taken as the most probable date for the sample, and a historical argument built on this assumption. There is no doubt that a long series of determinations can be the basis for revolutionary reassessments of conventional dating (see Renfrew (ed.), 1974) but a single radio-carbon date is beset by too many uncertainties to justify its use as more than a suggestion of the range within which the true date falls (see Mackie et al., 1971). If the central radio-carbon date happens to coincide with the excavator's nascent theories, it is tempting not to point out in the report that the real date might be far from the central one.

Many other scientific dating techniques such as thermo-luminescence and remanent magnetism share the same lack of precision, and they should not be made to carry a greater weight of argument than they can bear. Dendrochronology can, under optimum conditions, give a fairly precise date for the felling of a tree for timber. But it would be unwise to date a whole building on the evidence of one of its beams, which might have been reused from an earlier building. Here again, the larger the number of samples the more reliable the conclusions which can be drawn from them.

The arts and sciences which converge in an excavation are all imprecise in varying degrees. The wider the areas from which we draw our evidence, the more detailed our digging and recording, the more samples we take, the more techniques we deploy, the nearer we shall get to the truth about the site in the periods which concern us.

Excavation and environment

In the past the study of the environment relating to archaeological sites has often been peripheral to the excavation of structures, the recovery of a dating sequence or a series of pottery types. In many cases the environment in which the site developed was completely ignored. These attitudes are now changing and with techniques for recovering and interpreting environmental evidence being rapidly developed and multiplied ancient environments are seen to be crucial for the full understanding of the siting, the food economy, the exploitation of the surrounding countryside and in some cases the uses to which the site has been put.

Most excavated sites contain a wealth of biological evidence which, properly interpreted, can add another dimension to the understanding of the site and its region by producing otherwise unobtainable information about the contemporary flora and fauna, pests, diseases, climate and weather. Seeds, mollusca, insects, and the elusive bones of the smaller mammals, birds and fishes, are not so easily recovered as potsherds and food bones, but techniques of sieving, both wet and dry, can produce significant quantities of material from the majority of sites. The extraction of pollen is a more specialized technique which supplements the information given by seeds and other preserved plant remains.

A number of wet-sieving and froth-flotation methods for the recovery of organic remains have been developed recently. Some are quite simple; others, for use on large-scale excavations, are designed for the continual processing of large quantities of soil.

The simplest method is the use of sieves of various meshes through which the soil, made into a slurry, is passed. An even more basic method of recovering the larger fragments is to agitate a sieve full of the deposit in a barrow filled with water. Various more sophisticated mechanical flotation and sieving machines have been developed. Their chief attribute is cheapness achieved by the ingenious use of scrap machinery. A number of plans have been published, among them the machine used by David Williams at Siraf (Williams, 1973), a mechanical sieve developed in Italy (Guerreschi, 1973) and the machine developed by the Marc 3 Unit in Hampshire (Lapinskas, 1975). To these must be added the Ankara and Cambridge machines described in Renfrew, Monk, and Murphy, 1976.

Some environmentalists believe that flotation machines should be used with reservation, since they are apt to distort the sample due to some of the specimens floating while others of the same species do not. Tiny snail shells full of silt, for example, may sink, while those that happen to be empty float. There is a case for recovering the complete evidence from some large samples of the material by washing and sieving everything, including the sediments in which the organic remains are embedded. Only in this way will control samples be recovered, samples which will monitor the recovery rate from the flotation of very large quantities of deposits.

As in all other sampling techniques the larger and more representative the samples the more valid the results are likely to be. If possible, the samples should be taken by the specialist himself. They should not simply be derived from the pits, ditches, floors, or other structures in which we are particularly interested, but from a wide variety of contexts (if not the whole site), in order to provide controls and comparanda.

The nature of the soil, as well as its degree of waterlogging will affect the survival of bones, or seeds, or pollen. Any assessment of environmental evidence must take this into account, and no doubt the specialist consulted will do so, but it is important that the precise nature of the soil and the conditions under which samples were taken should be made clear so that valid comparisons can be made with other sites.

The analysis of preserved organic materials, of pollen, seeds, insects, snails and the microscopic remains of plants has implications which are only just beginning to be realized. As an example, work on the silt from a Roman sewer system in York has provided a spectacular demonstration of the information to be inferred from microscopic remains. The presence of sewerage flies, human intestinal parasites, and sponge spicules (derived from toilet sponges imported from the Mediterranean) in some of the channels contrasted with entirely different assemblages from other channels. One of the other systems contained grain beetles and grain weevils, derived in all probability from a grain storage building, while another series contained molluscs, water beetles, pollen, and other evidence which suggests that it drained a closed, artificially heated baths building. Thus the presence of long-destroyed buildings can be postulated on the microscopic evi- dence alone (Buckland, 1974).

Recent work on past climates has shown that there is now sufficient evidence from glaciology, environmental archaeology, and historical records to justify postulating climatic reasons for some of the major changes in agriculture and population movements over the last 10-15,000 years (Lamb, 1972, esp. 170-95). For example the well-attested increase in ploughland in the twelfth-thirteenth centuries AD with its corresponding increase in population and the expansion and creation of villages and towns, followed by the contraction of the fourteenth and fifteenth centuries, can be attributed, at least in part, to slight but significant shifts in the levels of temperature and rainfall. An earlier and more dramatic dissimilarity from our present climate is well attested in the Bronze Age between the 6th millennium BC, and the 3rd millennium BC, when average land temperatures were 2°-3°C higher than today's figures and the sea was 2°C warmer. As a result oak, elm and lime trees were growing in Britain up to 1000 feet higher than the present limit. (The drop in the average temperature is about 3°C per 1000 feet of height). Clearly, such considerations are vital in the interpretation of our excavated sites and the understanding of their economy, the character of housing and the recreation of life on and around the site.

The changes in the flora and particularly in woodland species may record the clearance of forest and the expansion of agriculture, changes which may be reflected in the composition of the buried soils of the site. Such changes may be paralleled and supported by an increase in domesticated animal bones, a corresponding decrease in the bones of wild species and the first appearance of querns on the site. Conversely, an increase in woodland or scrub species in the pollen spectrum may indicate a reversion to forest, paralleling shrinkage or temporary abandonment of the settlement.

An introduction to pollen analysis will be found in Brothwell and Higgs, 1969, Chapter 14 and RESCUE has recently published a booklet *First Aid for Seeds* (Renfrew, Monk and Murphy, 1976) which concisely describes the preservation of seeds in archaeological deposits, sampling, flotation and the storage for specialist analysis. It is essential reading for excavators.

Analysis of the animal bones from a site will, of course, give information about the meat eaten by the inhabitants, but it may go further and throw an unexpected light on the marketing of the meat, or, by implication, the comparative poverty of the consumers. For instance, if all the meat bones are from butcher's joints it is probable that the animals were slaughtered elsewhere, as is the practice today; but if the remains include horns, skulls, hooves and so on, the animals probably came into the settlement or town 'on the hoof'. Sometimes a change in the practice can be observed. For example, the meat sold in the centre of a Roman town in its heyday may all be butchered, with the horns going elsewhere in the town to be made into handles, the hooves to be made into glue, the hides into leather and so forth. Later, in the town's decline, contracted and with a changed economy, live animals may well be sold, perhaps bartered, in the market. The poorer a community, the more it will exploit every scrap of the animal, just as in recent times, no part of the family pig was wasted, and the evidence will appear in the rubbish pits. Sometimes variations of the animal contents of rubbish pits within communities can point to differing social strata. On the site of the Black- friars in Worcester three pits, all datable by pottery to the period 1480-1560, showed marked variations in their bone content, one of them containing bones from older animals, whose meat would be tougher and less palatable, together with less variety of species. Though the deductions cannot be certain, the implications are that the households using this pit were poorer or had, at least, less attractive meat, than the families using the other two pits (Chaplin in Barker et al., 1970). Such analysis and reasoning can of course be extended into much wider fields.

The character of animal diseases detectable in surviving bone is also of great interest, though here again, the more samples which can be examined from the region the sounder will be the conclusions drawn from them—one could hardly postulate a disastrous murrain from two individuals.

In a long and well-stratified sample the introduction of new strains of animals may be detected. Does this reflect an immigrant community, or simply good husbandry? Here other varieties of evidence would have to be brought to bear. If the introduction of the new variety coincided with the introduction of a new type of pottery the case for immigrants would be strengthened; and so on. Clearly, once again, the larger and more carefully dug and recorded the sample, the more valid and illuminating will be the deductions which can be drawn from it.

Many of these scientific disciplines are still in the data-collecting stages, since it is only recently that their potential has been realised by archaeologists. It is incumbent on those of us who dig to help to develop and refine these techniques through the closest possible cooperation with their practitioners.

The study of building materials

Many archaeological sites, particularly, though not exclusively, in towns, consist of or contain large areas of hard-core foundations, pebble surfaces, rubble spreads, clay floors, post-sockets and other remnants of former structures. The study of these layers and features from the structural point of view is an unexploited source of information supplementing that obtained from the study of the soils formed naturally in and around the site. For example, it may be very difficult to determine the length of time that a pebble floor was in use, especially in aceramic periods. Exhaustive tests on the wearing capacity of surfaces of all kinds made in the course of research into road construction enable close estimates to be made of the length of time taken to wear facets on pebbles of varying hardness. Equally, long term experiments on the wear of paving stones, stone stair treads and thresholds make close estimates of wear-time on these features available. While there will always, in archaeological terms, be imponderables, such as the estimated numbers of persons using a surface per day, any experimentally proven figures are better than guess-work as a basis for argument. Similarly, an analysis of the load-bearing capacity of the various surfaces assumed to be foundations may avoid interpretations which are impractical or even ludicrous.

On the other hand, a half-metre thick layer of make-up on one of the sites at Wroxeter was shown by the materials engineer who was consulted to have been laid wet, as a slurry, rather like pre-mixed concrete. In this form, its load-bearing capacity would be considerably increased, so that it can be assumed that it was laid as a deliberate foundation for the timber structure subsequently built on it, and not as an accumulation of soil and debris fortuitously used.

When a post or a sill-beam supporting a building rests on the ground, the area under and round the timber becomes permanently compacted. This compaction can be measured by simple methods dependent upon the differential penetration of the surface by a probe. In this way the existence of former buildings may be demonstrated (see the forthcoming report on the excavation of the Baths Basilica at Wroxeter).

Another example of the sort of information which may be sought from the study of the behaviour of materials is one from the same excavation at Wroxeter, where a large fragment of masonry, apparently part of a window embrasure, had fallen from one of the walls of the baths basilica, apparently that of the clerestory, and embedded itself in a sequence of sandy and pebble floors. By measuring the degree of compaction at a number of points under and around the fallen masonry, and then by weighing the fragment, it is hoped to be able to calculate the height from which it fell. As it is part of a window this should give the approximate height of the clerestory windows above the ground.

Though the information supplied by the study of the materials used on our sites may not always be very precise, this approach, coupled with that of the natural soil scientist (exemplified in Limbrey, 1975), should add considerably to our understanding of their stratigraphic development and the intentions of past builders.

Synthesis: The History of the Site

Introduction

It should be clear from the writings included in this collection that archaeology is of necessity a synthetic discipline utilizing diverse techniques and modes of enquiry. Pulling together the data gathered and recorded to create a model of the site's history forms a grand synthesis when all aspects of the site are considered from the sequence of levels to the features and finds. Here scientific modeling might be employed in order to create and test a number of alternative interpretations based on varying interpretations of the data. Using an example of his own excavation at Hen Domen, Barker shows how a combination of the study of adjacent fields with the creation of a contour map, analysis of flora (using pollen analysis of samples), scientific dating (Carbon 14), finds, and documentary evidence, produced together a coherent model of a sequence of events. Further sources of evidence which may be applied at the synthesizing stage are a study of local history, which may bear on aspects of the site where available in documentary form, and art history, which may supply imagery related to the site or relevant to the interpretation of topography or buildings.

T he ultimate aim of an excavation is to draw together the very varied strands of evidence into a coherent whole: the sequence of structural and natural events which have taken place on the site from the earliest occupation (or before) up to the present day. To this structural framework is added all the converging cultural, economic, domestic and environmental evidence which can be detected and assessed.

It has been suggested in Chapter 5 that we shall approach the truth about the site more closely if we attempt to identify and explain the origin of every observable feature. In doing so we impose on ourselves a discipline that prevents us from ignoring awkward or inconvenient features. Similarly the use of a formal matrix or graph, such as that described on pp. 198-199, compels us to consider the relative positions of all layers and features and not simply to take a broad view of the more important or extensive.

Another exercise, which helps to clarify thinking at the later, synthetic stage of the excavation, is to take at random, or at 50 to 100 year intervals, a number of dates which fall within the known period of occupation of the site and to write descriptions or, better, make sketches of the *whole* site at those times. This ensures that every part of the site will be considered as part of the continuum of occupation and not just those structures which can be given relatively firm dates. There will, inevitably, be a good deal of uncertainty about the nature of the open spaces round buildings, and, more particularly, the survival of old buildings when new ones are erected. Usually, we tend to simplify and rationalise the periods of occupation of our sites, partly because it is easier to describe and particularly to illustrate these periods as a series of complete rebuildings across the site. However, as an almost cursory glance at a group of farm buildings, a small village, or an area in a town centre, will show, the situation is in reality kaleidoscopic, with single buildings being replaced while older buildings on each side remain, and with the infilling of gardens or vacant plots, the demolition of old buildings and their sites left open, to say nothing of repairs and extensions, such as kitchens or garages, to existing buildings, and more ephemeral structures, like garden sheds, coming and going at even shorter intervals.

Such a kaleidoscopic, one might almost say contrapuntal, interpretation of an excavation is not easy to achieve, mainly due to the limitations of our ability to date precisely the building and demolition of structures. Another major cause of difficulty in phasing is the impossibility of demonstrating horizontal relationships unambiguously across the site. For example one may be able to say that both Buildings IV and V are earlier than 111, and demonstrate this by means of a feature matrix, but one may not be able to demonstrate the chronological relationship of IV and V to each other, if they have no common horizontal stratigraphy beyond their mutual relationship to 111. Under these circumstances, alternative phase diagrams and plans would be necessary. However, if the site contains dozens of buildings, the permutations and combinations, all possible but none demonstrable, might be endless, and difficult to describe and illustrate without an unwieldy proliferation of phases and sub-phases. This detailed illustration would not only be tedious and poteritially confusing, but also exceedingly costly. Yet what is the alternative? Certainly not simplification in the name of tidiness or economy. If we are to approach a true description of the site (and this must be the first aim of any excavation) we must interpret and present the evidence as fully as we can, even if this means the loss of a strong story line such as the celebrated narrative introduction to the Maiden Castle report (Wheeler, 1943).

Archaeological evidence and historical documents

The relationship between archaeology and documented history has been the subject of a good deal of heart-searching in recent years. Perhaps the two most thoughtful and cogent discussions of the subject are Wainwright's (1962) and Dymond's (1974). There is no room here to summarize their arguments and the reader is referred to the books as a whole.

The establishment of the relationships between the archaeological evidence from an excavated site and historical documents relating to that site is full of pitfalls and must be approached with caution. It is only too easy to equate drastic changes in the archaeological evidence, such as rebuilding after burning, or abandonment of the site, with well-documented historical incidents. However, not every fire in south-eastern Britain in the mid-first century was due to Boudicca, nor every fourteenth-century village abandonment to the Black Death. On many sites; it would be very difficult indeed to detect the date and impact of the Norman Conquest. Building techniques, house styles and pottery types remain the same, or change progressively throughout the period. Perhaps only on defensive sites such as Sulgrave (B. K. Davison, personal communication) where a ring-work is imposed on an apparently undefended domestic complex, could a sudden and radical political change be postulated, though the cumulative evidence from fieldwork and excavation of castles would undoubtedly point to a new intensity in fortification and a change in military structures. However, as Davison has pointed out (1969) it cannot be shown that the new types of fortification (motte and bailey castles) were introduced from elsewhere, so that on purely archaeological grounds one could postulate an English conquest of Normandy (or a conquest of England and Normandy by a third party).

Perhaps the most thoroughly integrated study of a settlement by excavation and by examination of the documentary sources is that of Store Valby (Steensberg, 1975), where a mass of evidence relating not only to the excavated farms, their buildings and their furniture has been adduced, but where, by a close study of the registers of births, marriages and deaths, ownership, tenancies and the relationships and social standing of generations of farmers have been correlated with the buildings they lived in and worked from. In this case, as in that of so many deserted village sites, the archaeological evidence was often tenuous and ambiguous, and here the documentary descriptions of the farms at various periods illuminated the fieldwork and enabled more well-founded interpretations to be made than could have emerged with either form of evidence alone. The weakness of the excavation, as the author admits, was the paucity of environmental evidence and the summary treatment of the animal bones, of which there were insufficient for a full statistical analysis. The work remains a model of its kind, however, as yet unequalled by any British excavation.

A model interpretation

Another most illuminating interpretative study of a settlement site is that of the Glastonbury Lake Village by D. L. Clarke (1972). In this reconsideration of Bulleid and Gray's excavations carried out between 1892 and 1907 (published 1911 and 1917) the objective was 'simply to explore the old data in new ways' (*ibid,* 802). The method used was 'the erection of a set of alternative models, explicitly justified and derived from many sources, embodying alternative reasonable assumptions and then the explicit testing between the alternatives of their consequences for predictive accuracy and goodness of fit, by using skilfully devised experiments in the field or upon the recorded observations' (*ibid,* 801).

It is significant that the excavation chosen by Clarke is not only one of the few of a *complete* settlement available, but that in addition, being waterlogged, the retrieval of organic material and objects was very high, supplementing by many whole factors the information which would have been achieved if the site had been dry. The same study carried out on a partial excavation of a mucheroded or otherwise damaged site would have started with so much less information that the potential results would have been a good deal less trustworthy. As Clarke himself said: 'No archaeological study can be any better than the reliability of the observations upon which it is based and the assumptions that frame the development of its analysis and interpretation.' To my mind, the reliability of evidence from settlement sites depends on quantity and the size of the sample, as well as on the accuracy of the observations made on the spot.

Another distinct advantage that the Glastonbury site has for analysis and study of this kind is that the settlement was a multiple of structures which were repeatedly reproduced. There were none of the more or less violent changes of occupation and use which characterize many sites or parts of sites. On the one hand, we have the type of site which, by reason of the comparative homogeneity of its development, allows the stages of that development to be more easily compared one with another, and its relationships with its economic and cultural territory to be more confidently predicted.

Such sites include some deserted medieval villages (Wharram Percy will, eventually, no doubt, provide a classic example for the Glastonbury type of analysis): extensively excavated Saxon settlement sites, such as Chalton (Addyman, Leigh and Hughes, 1972) and Mucking (Jones, 1974), and prehistoric sites such as hill-forts where one of the most pressing problems is the relationship of defended settlements to their contemporary valley counter parts. In a slightly varied way cemeteries excavated on a large scale would also lend themselves to statistical analysis and model building. On the other hand, towns, whether Roman or later, are more difficult, because of the multiplicity of structural types, the constant destruction of earlier deposits by later building and the consequent losses of artefacts as well as structural evidence. Nevertheless, at Novgorod, the area of the town excavated in the 1950s and '60s was more or less homogeneous in its development and would allow just the sort of analysis demonstrated by Clarke (Thompson, 1967).

Clarke's Glastonbury paper, which is more concerned with the direct results of excavations than many of the other applications of analytical archaeology, is essential reading for would-be directors.

The convergence of varying kinds of evidence: an example

This example, again taken from the motte and bailey castle site at Hen Domen, Montgomery, demonstrates in a microcosm how a number of different techniques can be made to converge on one problem, each, in its own way, reinforcing the others.

It had been noticed that the outer ditches and ramparts of the castle bailey apparently overlay (and were therefore later than) slight traces of ridge and furrow in the field north of the site (A on fig. 7). Since even relatively datable early ridge and furrow is rare, especially on the Welsh border, the possibility that this field system was pre-Norman was of great interest. When trowelling of a small area under the rampart revealed a buried soil which itself covered plough furrows cut into the undisturbed boulder clay, it was decided to contour survey the adjacent field and to examine the evidence buried under the rampart. At the same time, the documentary evidence was re-examined.

The various techniques used are here listed for convenience:

Field work: the field adjacent to the site was photographed in various lights, including car headlights, in order to observe the slight undulations of the ground in the greatest detail. It was then contour surveyed on a grid with 1 metre intervals and the contours were drawn at 20cm. vertical intervals. The visible ridges and furrows were plotted by interpolation.

Computer print out: the grid of readings was fed into a computer which was programmed to draw the resultant contours in a three-dimensional print-out.

This was more objective than drawing by eye, and necessary because there was some scepticism about the existence of the field system (fig. 6). *Excavation:* a 20m. length of the rampart was trowelled down to the buried soil and its surface contour surveyed at 2cm. vertical intervals. This demonstrated the existence of ridge and furrow buried under the rampart. The buried soil was removed and the visible plough furrows plotted. Amorphous holes dug through the buried soil and into the underlying subsoil were interpreted as places where bushes or small trees had been removed.

Pollen analysis: samples of the soil buried under the rampart were sent for pollen analysis. The botanist concerned was not told at the time the implications of what he might find. As a result of the analysis he deduced that the pollen indicated that the area in which the rampart was built was open land, which had been used for arable agriculture, perhaps for cereals. The abandonment had been of several years' duration and the area had perhaps been used for rough grazing.

Carbon 14 dating: A sample of charcoal from the buried soil was dated by the laboratory at Birmingham to AD 980 ± 290.

Finds: the only find from the buried soil was a fragment of Roman pottery carved into an amulet (?) and incised with what appears to be a letter A. As pottery was virtually unknown on the Welsh border between c. AD 400 and c. AD 1100, the Roman sherd would have been an object of considerable curiosity, worthy, in an aceramic period, of being carved into an amulet.

Documentary evidence: Domesday Book (fol. 254, a, 1.) is explicit that Roger, Earl of Shrewsbury, built a castle, which he called Montgomery, in an area of waste which had formerly contained 22 vills but which, in the time of Edward the Confessor, had been a hunting ground for three Saxon thegns. Roger was made Earl of Shrewsbury in 1070 or 1071, so that the castle (which can be shown to be Hen Domen) was built then or shortly afterwards.

It will be seen that any one or two facets of this evidence, taken independently, would be suggestive but not conclusive, whereas together they provide incontrovertible proof of a ridged field system, probably belonging to a Saxon vill, and abandoned before the Norman Conquest. The evidence is published in full in Barker and Lawson, 1971.

The more varied the forms of evidence which can be adduced in our investigations the richer and more unequivocal will be the results. There is now an enormous variety of aids at our disposal. By understanding their potential through discussion with the specialists who use them and by prior planning we must learn to deploy these techniques to the greatest advantage.

A much more intensive, and perhaps the best, example of intergrated landscape archaeology is C.C. Taylor's study of Whiteparish in Wiltshire (Taylor, 1967), which the reader is urged to study.

All excavations are local history

However widespread the remifications of an excavation may ultimately prove to be, initially it is a piece of local history, embedded in the immediate landscape, and relating to the area around it. Even sites of the remoter prehistoric periods were settled by men influenced by at least some, and perhaps many, of the factors which influenced Anglo-Savon farmers and medieval traders. The gulf which separates so many local historians from archaeologists (and archaeologists from local historians) is regrettable and unhelpful to both. The undocumented and the documented history of a parish or a district must be seen as a continuum from geological times to the present, and though we may be interested in one period more than others, we shall stultify our work if we do not see it in its broadest context. The excavator has therefore to see his site from two points of view, one vertically though time as part of the development of settlement, agriculture, industry, religion or architecture—the cultural pattern of the area; and the other horizontally through space, when the site is seen as one of a contemporary group or series of related groups, which may cover the whole of a continent. The legionary fortresses at Gloucester or Lincoln are facets of the local histories of those cities, they are also examples of a type of fortification which once covered most of the known world. These are obvious examples, and the excavators of these cities see their fortresses in both contexts. But how many pagan Saxon cemeteries, or open Iron-Age settlements are related by their excavators to the siting of the nearby medieval village or its Saxon predecessor, or the expansion and contraction of settlement in the periods before and after those being dug?

Another element of landscape study often neglected by archaeologists is the geographical development of the area, whether natural or influenced by man. For example, the rise or fall of the water table due to deforestation or afforestation, to a programme of land drainage or the development of bog may be crucial in the siting of villages and their wells and springs, or in the pattern or character of their agriculture. Similarly, the study of the courses of rivers and streams may be of the utmost importance to the archaeologist. Until comparatively recently, the Roman city of Wroxeter was thought to have lost as much as a quarter of its area through erosion by the River Severn. A geographer, David Pannett, working independently of archaeology, has shown that the river has hardly changed its course in the last 5000 years, so that the remains of the city are intact. Recent excavation on the eastern defences overlooking the river strongly supports this view, which has revolutionary implications for the siting of the legionary fortresses which underlie the civil settlement, for the siting of the Roman river crossing, the ultimate size of the city, and many other problems.

There is little doubt that consultation with local historians and geographers could add yet another dimension to the understanding of an excavation.

Works of art as archaeological evidence

From the sculpture and cave-paintings of Palaeolithic times onwards, works of art can be of great assistance in the interpretation of contemporary archaeological evidence. There is little need to stress the value of Egyptian tomb-painting, Greek sculpture or

Roman wall painting in the understanding of the material remans of these civilisations. There are fewer survivals of art from very early times, in north- western Europe, but medieval and later drawings and paintings of towns with their defences, individual buildings, markets, workshops, fields, animals and implements can all be helpful in the understanding of excavated remains, while figure paintings and carvings, in particular those on tombs, can elucidate problems of dress ornament and detail.

The chief difficulty in the use of works of art as interpretative evidence is to determine whether or not the depiction is contemporary with the incident depicted, it it makes use of traditional forms, or alternatively, whether the work sets a traditional scene in dress and surroundings contemporary with the artist. Many Anglo-Saxon illuminated manuscripts use architectural backgrounds which can be traced back to Byzantine or Roman models, so that it would be unwise to use them as evidence for Anglo-Saxon building styles. Conversely, it was common practice for later painters from Masaccio onward to set Biblical scenes in their own landscapes, towns, and buildings, so that the soldiers guarding Christ's tomb in a painting by Mantegna are a better guide to fifteenth-century Italian uniform than to first-century Roman, and the dresses in a Nottingham alabaster, the alter vases shown in a fifteenth-century alterpiece, or the farming practices in a book of hours or on a misericord are likely to be up-to-date rather than historical.

On the other hand, tomb effigies may be added much later than the burials of the persons they commemorate. The effigy, in Shrewsbury Abbey, of Roger de Montgomery, who died in 1094, is dressed in the armour of a thirteenth-century knight. If we did not know this from the external evidence of many other thirteenth-century carvings we might well take this sculpture as evidence of Roger's dress.

In the later Renaissance and in the seventeenth and eighteenth centuries, painting became increasingly naturalistic, culminating in Canaletto's use of the *camera obscura*. As a result, the paintings and drawings of these centuries arc a rich source of information on contemporary buildings, dress, furniture and pottery.

Figure 69   Giulio Campagnola (1482-c.1515), The Old Shepherd engraving (Ashmolean Museum, Oxford).

As an example fig. 69 is a remarkable sixteenth century engraving which seems seems to show a timber castle standing on a motte or natural mound surrounded by a ditch. If this is so, it is one of the few realistic contemporary representations of a timber castle. The Bayeux Tapestry castles straddle the dividing line between the descriptive and the decorative, while most other illustrations of castles such as the magnificent series in *Les Très Riches Heures du Duc de Berry*, are of stone buildings.

The engraving shows a somewhat ramshackle, perhaps roofed, bridge leading from a gate tower over the ditch to a complex of buildings which includes a great hall, ? two towers (the second just appearing over the roof of the hall) and other roofed buildings, one with a louvred smoke outlet, perhaps surrounding an inner courtyard. The construction throughout is of vertical timbers which appear to have rotted characteristically at their lower ends. The buildings are of two storeys, with the upper storeys jettied. There is a suggestion of a postern towards the right hand side of the nearest building and perhaps a garde-robe structure at the opposite end. The hall has two chimneys. On the extreme right is a complicated jettied structure apparently built out over a valley.

The question is, of course, how fanciful is this drawing, and how far can it be used as a guide in the interpretation of a timber castle excavation? On the one hand, the careful realism of the shepherd, dressed in contemporary clothes, inspires confidence in the castle's authenticity. On the other hand, some of the structural details are dubious and impractical. The impression given is that the castle is not imaginary, or derived from a long line of other background drawings, but is of a building known to the artist, though drawn, as buildings so often are, without an understanding of structural principles, so that it does not stand up too well to architectural scrutiny. Nevertheless, since we have so little to guide us, it should not be discarded altogether. The general layout, with its piling of buildings together on the mound, is borne out by surviving stone castles and the excavated evidence, so far as it goes, of timber castles. (For example, the bailey at Hen Domen was crowded with buildings, some of them certainly of two storeys.)

Such a drawing may suggest solutions to otherwise intractable interpretative problems, though the dangers of arguing from one individual example to another are obvious, and it may be contended that a timber castle in Italy is minimally relevant to one in England or Wales.

Used critically, however, contemporary illustrations can be another and otherwise unparalleled form of evidence, especially helpful in areas where the written evidence fails.

A recent and most interesting example of the use of sculpture and painting in the interpretation of excavated evidence will be found in 'The Trelleborg House Reconsidered' (Schmidt, 1973).

Neo-evolutionism and the New Archaeology

Introduction

In this outline of more recent concepts in archaeology, we return to Bruce Trigger's account. Archaeology and Anthropology were transformed after the Second World War, a period with a renewed interest in social evolution, which was treated at this time with a certain confidence in the ability to make sense of change in the patterns perceived in the studies of past and present human society. Theories were largely materialistic and based on determining factors such as technology and environment and their interrelation.

Around 1960, an approach which came to be called the New Archeology was promoted by Lewis Binford and others. Utilizing new and improved sources of data in areas such as ecological study and settlement patterns, this movement followed a longstanding interest in cultural processes with a faith in the investigator's ability to interpret correctly patterns and individual artifacts in cultures over time. External factors were generally considered as determining agencies, change or equilibrium in the culture being the result of cultural adjustments. For Binford, how an artifact might be interpreted was related to cultural subsystems: technomic, sociotechnic and ideotechnic, that is, how it was used as a tool, what value it might have in the social system, and what ideological meaning it might have. As anthropologist, Binford naturally felt that the concerns and methods of anthropology and archaeology were the same, and his methods and approach attempted to respond to the interpretive needs of this discipline. The attempts to understand cultural change led to the development and widespread use of a General Systems Theory, which treated a society or culture as a system in which parts interacted.   Further, the mechanism was optimistically conceived of as universal, providing explanations of behavior for any system, even non-social. The implications were that change was a response, not related to individual choices within a culture, and that outside forces as the environment were constraints on behavior rather than being simply causal.

We can predict the transience of the New Archaeology itself—
but we should not confuse transience with insignificance.

D. L. Clarke, *Analytical Archaeologist* (1979), p.101

T he two decades following World War II were an era of unrivalled economic prosperity and unchallenged political hegemony for the United States. Despite the threat of nuclear war, this was a time of great optimism and self-confidence for most middle-class Americans. As had happened in Britain and Western Europe in the middle of the nineteenth century, this self-confidence encouraged a relatively materialistic outlook and a readiness to believe both that there was a pattern to human history and that technological progress was the key to human betterment. In American anthropology these trends were manifested in the revival of an interest in cultural evolutionism. While evolutionism did not become the predominant trend in American anthropology, it greatly increased in popularity in the 1950s and 1960s and exerted a significant influence throughout the discipline.

Neo-evolutionism

The neo-evolutionism that developed in the United States in the 1960s was yet another attempt by anthropologists living in a politically dominant country to 'naturalize' their situation by demonstrating it to be the inevitable outcome of an evolutionary process that allowed human beings to acquire greater control over their environment and greater freedom from nature. Yet neo-evolutionism differed in certain crucial features from the unilinear evolutionism of the nineteenth century. Its ecological, demographic, or technological determinism left no room for the idea that cultural change occurred because gifted individuals used their intelligence and leisure time to devise ways to control nature more effectively and thus improve the quality of human life. Instead neo-evolutionists argued, as diffusionists and social anthropologists had done, that human beings sought to preserve a familiar style of life unless change was forced on them by factors that were beyond their control. This position, which was rationalized in terms of ecosystemics, embodied views about human behaviour being naturally conservative that were far removed from the individual creativity that had been lauded by Spencer or that most nineteenth century evolutionists had used to explain cultural change. This alteration appears to reflect the difference between an early stage in the development of capitalism, when individual initiative was still highly valued, and a more developed phase dominated by multi national corporations, when the individual is no longer idealized as a major factor bringing about economic growth.

The two principal exponents of neo-evolutionism in the 1950s were the ethnologists Leslie White (1900-75) and Julian Steward (1902-72) (see White 1949, 1959; Steward 1955). White regarded himself as the intellectual heir of L. H. Morgan and of the indigenous, evolutionary tradition of American anthropology. He rejected the historical particularism, psychological reductionism, and belief in free will inherent in Boasian anthropology. In their place he offered the concept of 'General Evolution', which treated progress as a characteristic of culture in general, although not necessarily of every individual culture. White deliberately ignored the influence of environments and of one culture upon another and concentrated on explaining the main line of cultural development, which was marked by the most advanced culture of each successive period regardless of their historical relationship. He argued that this approach was justified because in the long run cultures that failed to keep ahead were superseded and absorbed by more progressive ones. Hence from an evolutionary point of view they are irrelevant.

White defined cultures as elaborate thermodynamic systems. In his early writings he argued that they functioned to make human life more secure and enduring, although later he rejected that view as anthropocentric and claimed that they evolved to serve their own needs (White 1975: 8-13). His perception of cultural change was materialistic and narrowly deterministic. He maintained that cultural systems are composed of techno-economic, social, and ideological components and that 'social systems are . . . determined by technological systems, and philosophies and the arts express experience as it is defined by technology and refracted by social systems' (White 1949: 390-1) He formulated his concept of technological determinism in terms of a 'basic law of evolution' which stated that, all things being equal, culture evolves as the amount of energy harnessed per capita increases, or as the efficiency of putting energy to work is increased. This law is summarized in the formula

Culture = Energy x Technology (C = E x T).

Despite the sweeping claims that White sometimes made for his theories, he stressed that, while they account for the general outlines of cultural development, they cannot be used to infer the specific features of individual cultures (White 1945: 346).

Although White's technological determinism has often been stated to be of Marxist origin, conceptually it has nothing in common with Marxism except a general materialist orientation. Instead, it reflects one of the principal themes of American social science scholarship, which has been described as privileging the relationship between technology and society at the expense of other kinds of relations, such as those between self and society (Kroker 1984: 12).

Steward championed an alternative multilinear, ecological, and more empirical approach to the study of cultural evolution. He assumed that there were significant regularities in cultural development and that ecological adaptation was crucial for determining the limits of variation in cultural systems. He sought by means of comparative studies to determine the different ways in which cultures had developed in different types of natural environments, believing that they would tend to assume the same forms and follow similar developmental trajectories in similar natural settings. These similarities constituted the 'cultural core', which consisted of those features of a culture that were most closely related to subsistence activities. The core embraced economic, political, and religious patterns that could be empirically determined to have major adaptive significance. Steward argued that the aim of evolutionary anthropology should be to explain the common features of cultures at similar levels of development rather than 'unique, exotic, and non-recurrent particulars' which can be attributed to historical accidents (Steward 1955: 209).

M. D. Sahlins and E. R. Service (1960) tried to reconcile these two approaches by differentiating between general and specific evolution. These were defined as being concerned with progress and adaptation respectively. Although the concept of evolution was thereby dissociated from automatically implying progress, in later studies Sahlins (1968) and Service (1962, 1975) used ethnographic data to construct speculative and highly generalized sequences of unilinear development, employing concepts such as band, tribe, chiefdom, and state. Implicit in their approaches, and in the scheme of political evolution developed by Morton Fried (1967), was the assumption that the greater selective fitness of technologically advanced societies ensured that progress characterized cultural change as a general feature of human history.

The most theoretically sophisticated approach of this sort is Marvin Harris' (1979) cultural materialism. He assigns a privileged role in shaping cultural systems to an array of material conditions, including technology, demography, and economic relations, and seeks to explain all sociocultural phenomena in terms of the relative costs and benefits of alternative strategies, as measured in terms of these criteria. Much of his work has been directed towards trying to explain the origin of food taboos, religious beliefs, and other cultural esoterica in terms of the relations that these customs have to basic economic considerations (Harris 1974,1977). While overtly less concerned with delineating evolutionary sequences than were Sahlins, Service, and Fried, Harris' approach is no less evolutionary than theirs.

What distinguished the various materialist approaches that developed in American anthropology in the 1960s from the evolutionary schemes of the nineteenth century was their view of causality. White adopted a very narrow form of technological determinism that reflected faith in technology as a source of social progress, while Steward embraced a less restrictive ecological and Harris a still broader economic determinism. Judged by Marxist standards all of these approaches are examples of vulgar materialism, because they view human behaviour as shaped more or less exclusively by non human constraints. Marxism, by contrast, includes humanly arranged relations of production in the economic base that determines social change.

Already by the middle of the nineteenth century some archaeologists were constructing sequences to describe the development of native cultures in the New World (Wilson 1862). These approaches, which located the main centres of development in Mesoamerica and Peru, did not disappear following the adoption of a culture-historical approach. In *Ancient Civilizations of Mexico and Central America H. J.* Spinden (1928) distinguished three levels of development, Nomadic (hunting and gathering), Archaic (agriculture), and Civilization; while in *Method and Theory in American Archaeology,* Willey and Phillips (1958) assigned all Cultures to five stages of increasing complexity: Lithic (big-game hunting), Archaic (intensive collecting), Formative (village agriculture), Classic (early civilizations), and Post-Classic (later prehispanic civilizations). Despite their evolutionary appearance these formulations sought to describe, rather than to account for, cultural change in developmental terms. They also relied as heavily on diffusionist explanations as did other culture-historical formulations.

Yet, with their growing interest in functionalist and processual explanations of the archaeological record, many American archaeologists were predisposed to be receptive to neo-evolutionary concepts, which emphasized regularities in culture. They noted that many of the key variables that White and Steward posited as major causes of cultural change were relatively accessible for archaeological study, unlike the idealist explanations of the Boasians. Because of their lack of direct information concerning human behaviour and beliefs, archaeologists were also less inclined to be critical of the shortcomings of neo-evolutionary theory than were ethnologists. Only a few objected that neo-evolutionism encouraged simplistic explanations and did not rule out adequately the possibility of alternative ones (Lamberg-Karlovsky 1975: 342-3) Neo-evolutionary anthropology intensified and gave new directions to trends already at work in prehistoric archaeology.

One of the first applications of neo-evolutionary theory to archaeology was B. J. Meggers' 'The law of cultural evolution as a practical research tool' (1960). She argued that because of the absence of non human sources of energy in small-scale societies, White's law, as it applied to them, could be rewritten in the following fashion:

Culture = Environment x Technology.

This suggested that any archaeologist who was able to reconstruct the technology and environment of a prehistoric culture should be able on the basis of that information to determine what the key features of the rest of the culture were like. Furthermore, any shortcomings were not the responsibility of archaeology but resulted from the failure of ethnologists to elaborate adequate theories relating technology and environment to the rest of culture. Meggers believed it to be an advantage that archaeologists were 'forced to deal with culture artificially separated from human beings' (Meggers 1955:129) and that her formulation placed so much emphasis on techno-environmental determinism that it saw no need to use archaeological data to study non-material aspects of cultural systems. Her attitude towards the use of ethnographic analogy resembled that of many nineteenth-century evolutionary anthropologists. Her position was, however, too lacking in direct application to attract significant support among archaeologists. Likewise, White's treatment of technology as an independent variable bringing about change too closely resembled Montelius' view of change occurring as a result of the desire of human beings to control nature more effectively. To a growing number of archaeologists, who were becoming aware of cultural ecology and were anxious to provide a materialist explanation of what factors promoted or discouraged technological innovations, White's views seemed old-fashioned, idealist, and teleological. Nevertheless, some archaeologists admired his deductive approach to understanding cultural change (Binford 1972: 110-11).

The New Archaeology

In 1959 Joseph Caldwell published an article in Science titled 'The new American archeology'. In it he surveyed major trends that he saw transforming archaeology. He cited growing interest in ecology and settlement patterns as evidence of a new concern with cultural process. Archaeological cultures were no longer regarded merely as the sum total of their preserved artifact types, each of which can be treated in a stylistic fashion as independent and equally significant. Instead they have to be analysed, as Taylor had proposed, as configurations or even as functionally integrated systems. He also supported the neo-evolutionary belief that behind the infinite variety of cultural facts and specific historical situations is a finite number of general historical processes. Finally he adopted the neo-evolutionary position that not all cultural facts are of equal importance in bringing about change. The primary aim of archaeologists must be to explain changes in archaeological cultures in terms of cultural processes.

Caldwell's paper reveals that during the decade following the publication of Taylor's *A Study of Archeology* the concept of processual change within cultural systems had achieved a new level of importance in American archaeology. While this was encouraged by developments within archaeology, in particular the study of ecology and settlement patterns, it was also promoted by the growing popularity of neo-evolutionary anthropology, with its emphasis on cultural regularities. The essential and enduring elements of the New Archaeology were the collective creation of a considerable number of American archaeologists during the 1950s.

These concepts were popularized among the younger generation of American archaeologists by Lewis Binford, who added new elements to create the approach that since the 1960s has been recognized around the world as the American New Archaeology. Binford engaged in a series of vigorous polemics in which he sought to demonstrate the advantages of the New Archaeology over traditional approaches, which he identified primarily with the modified form of the Midwestern Taxonomic Method practised at the University of Michigan while he had been a graduate student there in the 1950s. The resulting polarization made the New Archaeology appear to be a dramatic break with the past rather than a continuation and intensification of the functionalist and processual trends that had been developing in American and Western European archaeology since the 1930s. Although there was considerable passive support for old-fashioned culture-historical archaeology, many so-called 'traditional' archaeologists were adherents of these recent trends who merely objected to particular facets of Binford's programme. The rapid adoption of the New Archaeology thus reflected the predisposing tendencies at work in the 1950s, while Binford's polemics disguised a considerable degree of consensus about the general direction in which American archaeology should evolve.

Binford outlined the programme of the New Archaeology in two papers: 'Archaeology as anthropology' (1962) and 'Archaeological systematics and the study of culture process' (1965). He identified the goal of archaeology as being the same as that traditionally assigned to anthropology: to explain the full range of similarities and differences in cultural behaviour. He also maintained that archaeological data were particularly useful for studying changes that occurred over long periods of time. These explanations were seen as taking the form of generalizations about systemic change and cultural evolution. As a student of Leslie White, Binford was predisposed to believe that there were strong regularities in human behaviour and that there was little difference between explaining a single instance of social change and a whole class of similar changes. Hence his main concern was to account for cultural similarities rather than differences. Throughout his career he has devoted himself to explaining problems such as increasing complexity in hunter-gatherer societies, the development of agriculture, and to a much lesser degree the evolution of civilization (Binford 1983b).

Like Grahame Clark, Binford viewed cultures as humanity's extrasomatic means of adaptation. Changes in all aspects of cultural systems were therefore interpreted as adaptive responses to alterations in the natural environment or in adjacent and competing cultural systems. Binford described evolution as 'a process operative at the interface of a living system and its field' (1972: 106). This ecosystemic view essentially ruled out human inventiveness and innovation within cultural traditions as independent forces capable of bringing about major changes. It also treated cultures as normally tending towards equilibrium or homeostasis, with change being induced by external factors.

Although Binford viewed cultural change as being initiated by non-cultural or external factors causing perturbations in what would otherwise tend to be homeostatic systems, he insisted, as Clark and Taylor already had done, that it had to be understood in terms of the responses that occurred within cultural systems. He thus shared the tendency, already evident in settlement archaeology, to concentrate on understanding cultural change from an internal point of view. This approach emphasized systemic relations and therefore continuities in change as opposed to the discontinuities brought about by migration and diffusion. Within the general context of neo-evolutionism there was a growing tendency to believe in the capacity of human beings to invent and reinvent new forms of technology, social behaviour, and beliefs and values, as these were required by evolving social systems. Steward (1955: 182) had argued that every cultural borrowing might be construed as an 'independent recurrence of cause and effect' and Harris (1968: 377-8) had dismissed diffusion as a 'nonprinciple'. Chang (1962: 190-1) maintained that, if in the course of its development Chinese civilization had been unable to borrow new technological processes from the outside, the Chinese would have invented the same processes or ones of similar economic and social significance. Thus Binford differed from traditional American archaeologists by emphasizing humanity's capacity for innovation at the same time that he agreed with them in viewing undisturbed cultures as normally static.

Like Caldwell, Binford stressed the internal differentiation and systemic integration of cultures. He objected to the established normative view, which regarded cultures as collections of ideas held in common and transmitted over generations by members of particular social groups. In some of his writings his objections to views of culture as a mental phenomenon appear to rule out White's concept of culture as being symbolic in nature, although he otherwise praises White's views (Binford 1972: 105-13).

Like Caldwell, he also objected to each item of culture being regarded as equal in significance to all others and the percentage of similarities and differences in artifact types being treated as a measurement of the amount of effective communication between groups. He maintained that traditional archaeology attributed differences between cultures to geographical barriers or resistant value systems, while it viewed ideas as being spread from one culture to another by diffusion and migration. Although this description may have represented accurately the views about cultures held by traditional culture-historical archaeologists working in the midwestern United States or even those of Walter Taylor, it did not take account of the views of a growing number of functionalist archaeologists in the United States or of Clark and Childe in Britain. As early as 1925 Childe had employed a functionalist view of culture to facilitate his culture historical analyses when he distinguished between ethnic traits, which did not diffuse readily, and technological ones, which did.

Binford argued that cultures were not internally homogeneous. All of them were differentiated at least according to age and sex roles and the degree to which they were internally shared by individuals varied inversely with their complexity. Individuals always participated in cultures differentially, making a total cultural system a set of functionally interrelated roles. Because of this, it was wrong for archaeologists to treat artifacts as equal and comparable traits. Instead they must try to determine the roles they had played within living cultural systems. This necessitated an effort to achieve a relatively holistic view of these systems.

At this point Binford could have attempted, as Willey (1953), Childe (1958a), and various settlement archaeologists had done, to reconstruct social systems. This approach concentrated on delineating patterns of human interaction and determining the functional relationship of cultural traits to social systems. Instead he followed White in viewing cultures as adaptive systems composed of three interrelated subsystems: technology, social organization, and ideology. Thus he supported the view that human behaviour was determined by forces of which human beings are largely unaware and which frequently are located in the natural realm.

Binford argued that material items do not interact within a single subsystem of culture but reflect all three subsystems. Technomic aspects of artifacts reflect how they were used to cope with the environment; sociotechnic ones have their primary context in the social system; and ideotechnic ones relate to the ideological realm. In 1962 he suggested that each type of artifact might be interpreted as relating primarily to one of these classes, but by 1965 he noted that individual artifacts frequently encoded information about all three. A knife might be used for cutting, but its gold handle could denote the upper-class social status of its owner and a symbol engraved on the blade might invoke divine protection for him.

Binford went further than either Clark or Taylor had done in arguing that, because artifacts have primary contexts in all sub systems of culture, formal artifact assemblages and their contexts can yield a systematic and understandable picture of total extinct cultures. He maintained that the archaeologist's primary duty is to explain the relations that are extant in the archaeological record. In particular he repudiated the idea that it was inherently more difficult to reconstruct social organization or religious beliefs than it was to infer economic behaviour. The idea that archaeologists could study any problem that ethnologists could, and over much longer periods of time, won support among many young archaeologists who were frustrated by the artifact-centred, culture-historical approach that still continued to pervade much American archaeology in the early 1960s. They were anxious to demonstrate that ethnologists were wrong when they smugly proclaimed that archaeology was 'doomed always to be the lesser part of anthropology' (Hoebel 1949: 436).

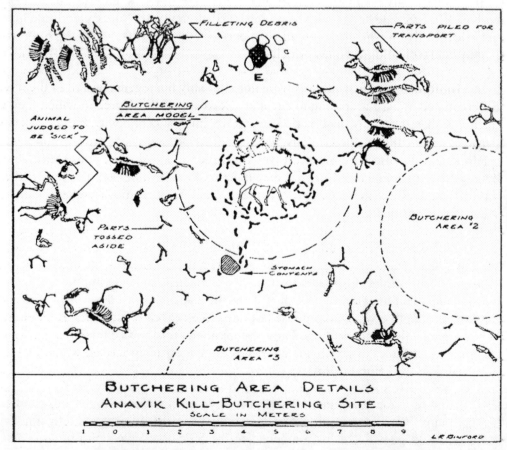

Figure 42   Binford's plan of a modern Nunamiut butchery area at Anavik Springs, Alaska, showing where caribou were dismembered and waste products were disposed

Binford observed that archaeologists had already made significant progress in using knowledge derived from the physical and biological sciences to interpret those aspects of the archaeological record relating to technomic behaviour, especially subsistence patterns and technological practices. On the other hand, anthropologists did not know enough about correlations between social behaviour or beliefs and material culture to infer much sociotechnic or ideotechnic information from the archaeological record. Only after such correlations had been established and archaeologists had acquired a holistic knowledge of the structural and functional characteristics of cultural systems could they begin to investigate problems of evolutionary changes in social systems and ideology. Binford argued that in order to establish such correlations archaeologists must be trained as ethnologists. Only by studying living situations in which behaviour and ideas can be observed in conjunction with material culture was it possible to establish correlations that could be used to infer social behaviour and ideology reliably from the archaeological record. Binford saw this as a promising approach to understanding the past because, as a neo-evolutionist, he believed that there was a high degree of regularity in human behaviour which comparative ethnographic studies could reveal. These regularities could then be used to infer many aspects of prehistoric cultures that were not directly observable in the archaeological record. If human behaviour were less regular than he assumed, such correlations would be fewer in number and less useful for reconstructing prehistoric cultures and understanding change.

Some of the principal early applications of the New Archaeology were attempts to use ceramics to infer the residence patterns of prehistoric communities. It was assumed that, if women made the pottery used by their families, design elements would tend to cluster where knowledge of pottery making was transmitted from mothers to daughters in matrilocal societies but would become randomized in patrilocal ones where female potters from different lineages lived adjacent to one another (Deetz 1965; Whallon 1968; Hill 1970; Longacre 1970). The sex of potters was determined by applying the direct historical method rather than by means of forensic evidence as Tret'yakov had done in the 1930s. In these early studies the alternative possibility that some pottery was professionally made and exchanged over long distances was not examined, nor were the conditions under which broken pottery was discarded (S. Plog 1980). These pioneering efforts by American archaeologists to infer social organization from archaeological evidence therefore did not reach the high standards Binford had set for such work. They also may have provided a misleading impression of the kind of operations that were required by the deductive approach.

Among Binford's principal original contributions at this time was his insistence that the correlations used to infer human behaviour from archaeological data had to be based on the demonstration of a constant articulation of specific variables in a system. Only if a particular behavioural trait could be shown always to correlate with a specific item of material culture, wherever both could be observed, could such behaviour be inferred from the occurrence of that item in the archaeological record. This in turn necessitated a deductive approach in which relations between variables that are archeologically observable can be observed. Only by means of such measurement of concomitant variation can regularities be established that are useful for understanding prehistoric cultural systems. Analogies are merely a source of hypotheses to be tested in this manner

(Binford 1972:33-51). Binford championed the positivist view that explanation and prediction are equivalent and that both rest upon the demonstration of a positivist approach was seen as eliminating subjective elements and establishing a basis for the objective, scientific interpretation of archaeological data. To achieve this level or rigour, however, archaeologists had to adhere to deductive canons which utilized well-established correlations, as outlined by Carl Hempel (1962,1965) in his covering-law model of explanation. From this perspective the most useful correlations are present. Since then archaeologists have realized that, because of the complexity of human behaviour, most correlations are statistical rather than absolute in nature and that most statistical correlations are of a lower rather than a higher degree of magnitude, a problem that ethnologists engaged in cross-cultural studies have long had to contend with (Textor 1967). Under these circumstances the problem of equifinality, or different causes producing the same effect, becomes increasingly troublesome, as archaeologists engaged in simulation studies have realized (Hodder 1978; Sabloff 1981). Yet Binford has continued to pay much less attention to deductive—statistical than to deductive—nomologcal explanations (M. Salmon 1982:120-2).

The extension of the covering-law method to the explanation of cultural change tended to exclude consideration of all but situations of notable regularity. This correlated with Binford and his followers repudiating historical studies, which they equated with chronology, description, and a preoccupation with accidental occurrences (Binford 1967b: 235; 1968b). This line of reasoning had been introduced to American archaeologists by the ethnologist Clyde Kluckhohn (1940) when he wrote that Mesoamerican archaeologists had to choose between historical studies that sought to recreate unique events in all of their idiosyncratic detail and scientific research that addressed significant trends and uniformities in cultural change. This invidious dichotomy between history and science, which paralleled the distinction that American anthropologists drew between history and evolution, was reinforced by Taylor (1948: 156-7) and Willey and Phillips (1958: 5-6), who regarded culture-historical integration as an objective that was inferior to formulating general rules of cultural behaviour. Binford viewed archaeologists' efforts to explain particular historical events as inductive behaviour that would doom archaeology to remain a particularistic, non generalizing field. He argued that archaeologists instead must seek to formulate laws of cultural dynamics. While in historical retrospect this position can be seen as reflecting the belief that human history is governed by strong regularities, it deflected archaeological interest from significant aspects of cultural change that do not display such regularities.

Binford also denied the relevance of psychological factors for understanding prehistory. He identified the use of such concepts with Boasian idealism and the culture-historical approach and argued that they had no explanatory value for an ecological interpretation of culture and cultural change. On the contrary, within an ecological framework specific psychological factors could be viewed as an epiphenomenal aspect of human behaviour that arose as a consequence of ecological adaptation. He also argued that archaeologists are poorly trained to function as palaeopsychologists (Binford 1972: 198).

New Archaeologists have continued to condemn explanations of change that invoke either conscious or unconscious psychological factors. Instead they have identified relations between technology and the environment as the key factors determining cultural systems and, through them, human behaviour. In this respect they clearly differ from Marxists who see individual and collective perceptions of self-interest as a major cause of change. On the other hand this rejection of perceptions is shared by many other Western social scientists. It seems to reflect a tendency that has its roots in Christian theology to equate reason and volition with free will. If human behaviour is to be explained it must therefore be shown to be determined by something other than reason. This factor has been variously identified as culture (Tylor, Kroeber), society (Durkheim), subconscious drives (Freud), or ecosystems (Steward).

Systems theory

Binford's ideas quickly attracted a large following among American archaeologists, especially younger ones. At least one senior scholar, Paul Martin (1971), rallied publicly to his support. Binford's work also influenced Colin Renfrew (1979,1984), an English archaeologist who taught for a time in the United States, and had much in common with the formulations of David Clarke (1968), another Englishman who was, however, independently influenced by the locational analysis and general systems approaches of the New Geography that had developed at Cambridge University (Chorley and Haggett 1967). In America also attempts were soon made to account for cultural change in terms of General Systems Theory. This was a body of concepts that the biologist Ludwig von Bertalanffy began to develop in the 1940s, which sought to delineate the underlying rules that govern the behaviour of entities as diverse as thermostats, digital computers, glaciers, living organisms, and sociocultural systems. It was assumed that all of these could be conceptualized as systems made up of interacting parts and that rules could be formulated that described how significant aspects of any system functioned, regardless of its specific nature (Bertalanffy 1969; Laszlo 1972a, b, c). Systems theory allowed archaeologists to transcend the limitations of traditional social anthropological analyses of static structures by studying not only structure-maintaining but also structure-elaborating (or morphogenetic) processes. Many of the most important of these studies were based on cybernetics, which sought to account for how systems functioned by mapping feedback between their various parts. Negative feedback maintains a system in an essentially steady state in the face of fluctuating external inputs, while positive feedback brings about irreversible changes in the structure of the system. The concept of feedback offered archaeologists a more precise, and potentially quantifiable, mechanism for interrelating the various components of a changing cultural system than did the essentially static social anthropological concept of functional integration (Watson *et al.* 1971: 61-87).

There was, however, no agreement about how feedback was to be measured. It has been identified with goods, energy, or information, and with all three combined. The concept of energy was especially congenial to ecological approaches. In an influential pioneering study Kent Flannery (1968) argued that favourable genetic changes in maize and beans encouraged Mesoamerican hunter-gatherers to reschedule their food procurement patterns in order to increase their dependence on these two plants, thus setting in motion systemic changes that did not stop until maize and beans had become the principal foci of intensive agriculture. Soon after, the concept of information processing became central to a discussion of the development of social hierarchies and complex societies. This theorizing drew upon and helped to elaborate a body of propositions derived from General Systems Theory concerning disproportional growth. These propositions attempted to explain the effects of increasing scale on the evolution of new institutions for collecting information and making decisions (Flannery 1972; Rathje 1975; Johnson 1978, 1981). While archaeologists were rarely able to apply General Systems Theory in a rigorous mathematical fashion, it has provided a model for studying cultural change that gave new meaning to Binford's call to do this in terms of systemic analyses.

The development of an internal view of cultural change was greatly assisted by radiocarbon dating, which was invented by Willard Libby in the late 1940s and immediately applied to dating archaeological material (Libby 1955). This new technique reduced the need for archaeologists to rely on seriation and cross-cultural trait distributions to construct cultural chronologies. It also became possible for the first time to date sites around the world in relationship to one another and to assign calendrical dates rather than only relative ones to prehistoric sites. Archaeologists were thus able to study rates as well as sequences of change. Renfrew's (1973a, 1979) reinterpretation of European prehistory was based almost entirely on calibrated radiocarbon dates, which he used to demonstrate that Neolithic and Bronze Age sites north and west of the Aegean were considerably older than Montelius and Childe had determined on the basis of cross-dating.

Radiocarbon dating had a similar effect on the study of North American prehistory. There, everywhere except in the Southwest, where calendrical dates for sites back to the beginning of the Christian era had been derived dendrochronologically since the 1920s, radiocarbon chronologies revealed that cultural sequences had developed over longer periods and far more slowly than had previously been believed (cf. Ritchie 1944, 1965). By greatly slowing the rate of cultural change in the eastern United States and Western Europe, radiocarbon dating made it easier for archaeologists to credit the possibility that major changes had come about as a result of internal changes rather than attributing them to diffusion and migration as they had previously done.

Although the New Archaeologists agreed that the main causes of cultural change were not to be found within sociocultural systems or identified with human volition, they did not agree about either the specific causes of change or the degree to which social behaviour was shaped by these factors. Ecological explanations of change continued to be very important, although unicausal theories, such as those that attributed the origins of civilization to the development of complex irrigation systems, were gradually abandoned (Hunt 1972). Ecological factors once again came to be viewed more as a constraint upon human behaviour than as an explanation of the specific forms that human behaviour has taken. At the same time other causal factors were considered. Ester Boserup's *The Conditions* of *Agricultural Growth* (1965) revived an interest in speculations dating back to the eighteenth century that gradual population increase could be a major independent variable bringing about cultural change. Although her theory had been devised to explain the development of more intensive forms of agriculture, archaeologists applied it to explain the origins of agriculture (P. Smith 1976) and civilization (Young 1972), and finally the totality of cultural change (M. Cohen 1977). While it provided a major stimulus for palaeodemographic studies, the results were rarely sufficiently detailed or comprehensive to permit a substantial test of the theory. In due course archaeologists began to stress the cultural and biological factors that influence the rate of population growth and demographic factors have ceased to be widely regarded as independent causes of change (Cowgill 1975; Binford and Chasko 1976).

Robert Dunnell and some of his students opted for a different sort of systemic approach, that uses biological ('scientific') evolutionary theory to explain cultural as well as biological variability (Dunnell 1980a; Wenke 1981; Rindos 1984). They argue that traditional cultural evolutionism has failed to internalize such key tenets of scientific evolutionism as random variation and natural selection. While admitting that mechanisms of trait transmission are more varied and the stability of the units on which selection operates is less so with respect to cultural than to biological phenomena (both issues that Kroeber [1952] and other anthropologists discussed long ago), they maintain that an approach based on general principles of scientific evolutionism can offer explanations of human behaviour that are superior to those offered by cultural evolutionary approaches. This often involves the radical reformulation of traditional questions. For example, David Rindos (1984: 143) has defined domestication as a mutualistic relation of varying degrees between different species. He does not view the adaptation of plants and animals to human needs as different in nature from the adaptation of human beings to the needs of plants and animals. This approach carries to an extreme the denial that consciousness and intentionality play a significant role in shaping human behaviour.

Although systems theory inspired some highly specific explanations of cultural change, such as Flannery's hypothesis concerning the development of plant domestication in Mesoamerica, in the long run it encouraged archaeologists to note the complex ramifications of cultural processes. This stimulated identification of the numerous interlinking factors that brought about cultural change and led some archaeologists to recognize that even key variables might have played a less important role in shaping cultural systems than they had hitherto believed. This in turn has led many archaeologists to adopt a more inductive approach to explaining causality. It was also recognized that because of the complexity of cultural systems the same factors might have different effects or different ones the same effect depending on individual circumstances. Flannery (1972) suggested that explanations of cultural development should concentrate less on the conditions bringing about cultural change than on the types of systemic changes that could be observed in the archaeological record. He offered, as examples of evolutionary mechanisms, 'promotion' and 'linearization'. Promotion involved established institutions rising in a developing hierarchy of control to assume transformed and more far-reaching roles. Linearization occurred when higher-order controls cut past and eliminated traditional lower-order ones after the latter had failed to function in a more complex setting.

Flannery's approach was extremely valuable for gaining an understanding of change from a social-structural point of view. It also drew attention to a source of constraint on human behaviour that was different from, and seemingly independent of, the ecological constraints that American archaeologists previously had been considering. If social and political systems could only assume a limited number of general forms (a point

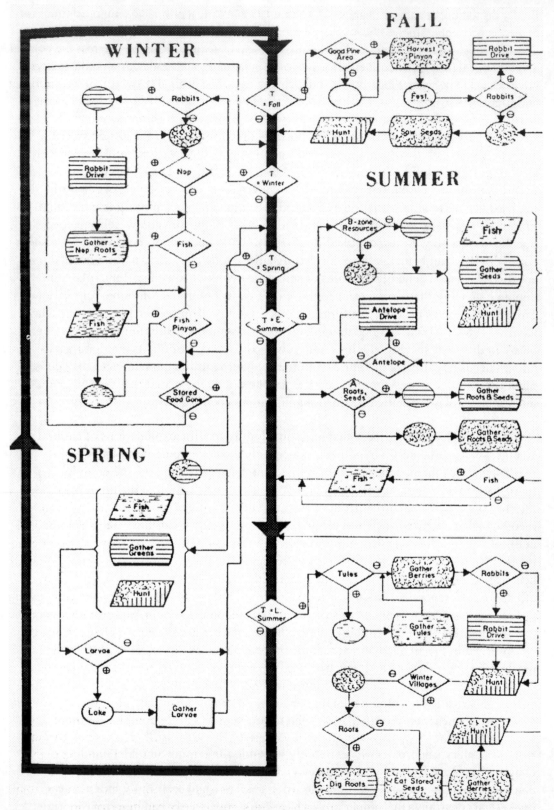

Figure 43   System flow chart for Shoshonean Indian subsistence cycle, by D. H. Thomas, 1972

Archaeologists soon began to move further away from rather than nearer to a consensus about factors governing sociocultural change. Working within a neo-evolutionary tradition, processual archaeologists tried hard to demonstrate that a limited number of ecological and demographic variables played a predominant role in shaping sociocultural systems. Yet the regularity in these systems consistently turned out to be less than neo-evolutionary theory predicted. It was also more difficult than neo-evolutionary theory suggested for archaeologists to infer one aspect of sociocultural systems from known characteristics of another part, especially features of social organization and ideology from knowledge of the economy. Stuart Struever (1968) argued, for example, that the means by which a population derives its subsistence from the environment plays such an important role in shaping the entire cultural system that the nature of settlement patterns can be predicted and hence explained in terms of technology and the natural environment. He viewed settlement patterns as 'an essential corollary of subsistence' and interpreted 'variations between cultures [as] responses to differing adaptive requirements of specific environments' (p. 133-5) He therefore believed that archaeological settlement patterns only served to confirm that relationship. Yet a growing understanding of settlement patterns has indicated that prediction is not so simple and that significant factors other than technology and environment shape their development (Trigger 1968b; Clarke 1977). Under these circumstances an inductive systems approach offered a growing number of archaeologists a methodology that seemed more productive of insights into the causes of variation than did the narrowly deterministic explanations suggested by neo-evolutionists. These archaeologists either implicitly or explicitly rejected the rigidly deductive approach originally advocated by the New Archaeology.

The New Archaeology promoted a more sophisticated and productive view of sampling by revealing the often unconscious biases that had governed traditional archaeological research and the inadequacies of these approaches for understanding prehistoric cultures as systems. Prior to the development of settlement archaeology, the excavations of urban centres had concentrated on ceremonial precincts and palaces, while generally ignoring how ordinary people had lived. Regional investigations often paid little attention to the seasonality of hunter—gatherer sites and ignored low-level sites, such as peasant hamlets, in hierarchical societies. Settlement studies, such as Gordon Willey's systematic investigation of peasant hamlets in the Belize Valley (Willey *et al.* 1965) had already begun to correct these biases. New Archaeologists advocated the use of sampling strategies to guide both surveys and excavations and economize on the time and labour needed to carry out research. Underlying this advocacy was their belief that, because strong regularities were inherent in cultural systems, a small part of a system could be representative of the whole. Now, however, it was no longer a single site, but some portion of a site network that was thought to be typical of the whole.

Various forms of sampling helped archaeologists to recover a more representative selection of the material to be found in large heterogeneous sites. Yet random sampling has come to be seen as an initial excavation strategy that must be supplemented in the later stages of research by an increasing number of judgmental decisions about what areas should be excavated (Redman 1986). Studies of early civilizations based upon total regional surveys have provided the data to allow simulated examinations of the representativeness of various sampling strategies. Sanders, Parsons, and Santley's (1979:

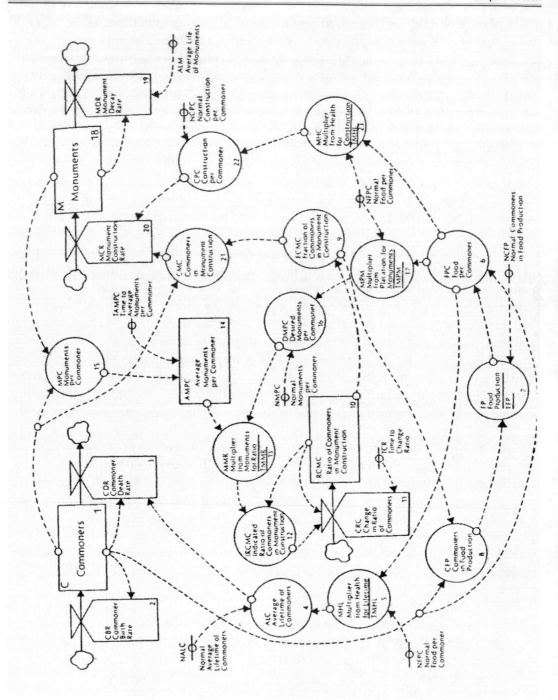

491-532) survey of the Valley of Mexico revealed marked diversity in local patterns of development and also the need to study the entire region in order to understand what was happening in its various parts. For example, the massive increase in population and growth of urbanism in the Teotihuacan Valley early in the Christian era can only be understood when it is realized that similar population growth was not occurring elsewhere in the Valley of Mexico, but on the contrary the population of those areas was declining at that time. Robert Adams (1981) has shown similar local diversity in his studies of

Mesopotamian settlement patterns. These findings have severely challenged the belief that patterns from one area are necessarily representative of a whole region. As a result it is now agreed that much larger samples than had hitherto been thought necessary are required before they are representative of a whole and that the study of changes over long periods requires something approaching total samples. These changes in views of sampling correlated with the realization that regularities in cultural systems had been over-estimated during the initial stages of the New Archaeology.

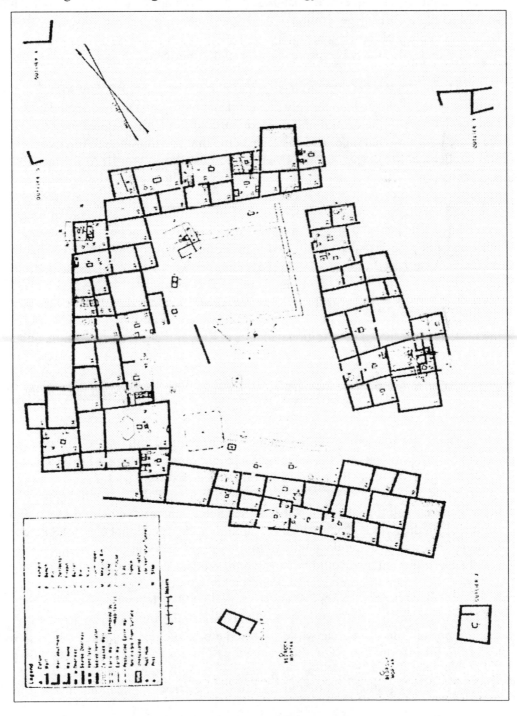

Anti-historicism

Critics have argued that the New Archaeology represented a revolution in the technical and methodological spheres rather than in archaeological theory (Meltzer 1979). Yet the stand that Binford took against the still influential culture-historical approach in the United States was no less a break with that past in terms of high-level theory than it was methodologically. The questions that must be answered are why did his approach appeal so powerfully to a rising generation of American archaeologists and why, apart from Binford's undeniable charismatic qualities, was he able so quickly to popularize views that until then had only slowly been spreading through American archaeology?

Thomas Patterson (1986a) has argued that the majority of New Archaeologists were recruited from the increasingly powerful and nationalistically oriented middle class that has its base in the central and western parts of the United States rather than from the more internationally inclined east-coast elite that had dominated American economic and intellectual life during the early years following World War II. At the most basic level the nomothetic orientation of the New Archaeology appealed to the tendencies of these Americans to value what was technologically useful at the same time that they remained suspicious of pure science because of what they saw as its elitist tendencies, as well as its suspected disregard for conventional religious beliefs. The contempt for what was not practical also manifested itself in the low respect accorded to historical studies in America (Bronowski 1971: 195), an opinion epitomized in the industrialist Henry Ford's remark that 'History is . . . bunk' (Lowenthal 1985: 244). The low value accorded to history further reflected the 'present-mindedness' of American society, which romantically viewed itself as having prospered by throwing off the shackles of the past, as represented by traditional claims of descent, class, and tradition, and creating a new society rationally designed to serve the interests of the enterprising individual (Kroker 1984: 8). Even though prehistoric archaeology was a branch of anthropology, its culture-historical approach reduced its prestige and led it to be regarded as a dilettantish pursuit by the American public and by other anthropologists.

The New Archaeology followed the lead of the generalizing social sciences, such as economics, political science, sociology, and ethnology by claiming to be able to produce objective, ethically neutral generalizations that were useful for the management of modern societies. This desire to conform to a more prestigious model of scholarly behaviour was reinforced as the National Science Foundation emerged as a major source of funding for archaeological research. It was argued that archaeology could provide information about the nature of long-term interactions between human groups and the environment that would be of value for modern economic planning (Fritz 1973), a view shared even by some archaeologists who rejected the general philosophy and methodology of the New Archaeology (Dymond 1974). The study of prehistoric irrigation systems in Arizona might reveal unsuspected problems associated with modern ones in the same area, while stratified archaeological sites in California were looked to for information about the frequency of major earthquakes that could help to decide whether or not atomic-energy generators should be installed nearby (F. Plog 1982). These suggestions are reminiscent of the practical applications that were used to justify Soviet archaeology in the 1930s and later by Childe (1944b) as a practical reason for public support of archaeological research. In *TheArchaeology of Arizona* Paul Martin and Fred Plog (1973: 364-8) argued that generalizations about human reactions to stress derived from ecological studies of prehistoric Arizona might help to explain the behaviour of underprivileged black and hispanic groups living in the ghettos of modern American cities.

This emphasis on the possible practical applications of their research encouraged social scientists to abandon holistic attempts to understand human behaviour, and instead led them to seek solutions to problems conceived in limited technical terms (Wolf 1982: ix). Such research was endowed with further scientific credentials by positivist claims of ethical neutrality. To produce 'relevant' findings that would justify an honoured place for archaeology in a society in which 'technocratic efficiency is considered as the supreme value' (Kolakowski 1976: 229)' many American archaeologists saw themselves having to turn away from a historical understanding of the past to create the generalizations about human behaviour that were the hallmark of successful social scientists. It is within this context that we must understand Binford's (1967b: 235) claim that historical interpretation is unsuited to play more than a 'role in the general education of the public'. He was not the first archaeologist to promote the idea that such generalizations were to be regarded as archaeology's supreme achievement. Kidder (1935: 14) had argued that the ultimate goal of archaeological research should be to establish generalizations about human behaviour, while Taylor (1948: 151) and Willey and Phillips (1958: 5-6) saw them as constituting a common anthropological focus for archaeological and ethnological research.

The anti-historical bias of the New Archaeology can also be viewed as an ideological reflection of the increasing economic and political interventionism of the United States on a global scale after World War II. Its emphasis on nomothetic generalizations was accompanied by the obvious implication that the study of any national tradition as an end in itself was of trivial importance. Richard Ford (1973) called into question the legitimacy of 'political archaeology' and of any correlation between archaeology and nationalism, asking archaeologists instead to embrace a 'universal humanism'. By denying the worth of such studies the New Archaeology suggested the unimportance of national traditions themselves and of anything that stood in the way of American economic activity and political influence. The corrosive effects of similar arguments in other fields upon the national traditions of neighbouring Western countries have been well described for this period (G. Grant 1965). In particular, it has been documented how the American promotion after World War II of abstract expressionist art as the dominant international style resulted in the disintegration or trivialization of many national and regional traditions of painting. There is also strong evidence that the promotion of this art style was carried out deliberately and with financial support from the United States government as well as from private foundations (Lord 1974: 198-215; Fuller 1980: 114-15). While New Archaeologists may not have been conscious agents in the promotion of United States political and economic hegemony, their programme appears to have accorded with that policy.

The most striking impact of this anti-historical viewpoint was exhibited in relation to native North American prehistory. By making the explanation of internal changes central to its interpretation of archaeological data, the New Archaeology stressed the creativity of native North Americans to a much greater extent than diffusionist explanations had done and for the first time placed native people on an equal footing in this respect with Europeans and other ethnic groups. Only amateur archaeologists, such as Barry Fell (1976, 1982) R. A. Jairazbhoy (1974, 1976) and Irvan van Sertima (1977), have continued to belittle native people by attributing major elements of their cultural heritage to prehistoric visitors from the Old World. The New Archaeology thus implicitly ended over a century of condescending and often overtly racist interpretations of native prehistory by white archaeologists. Yet from the beginning processual archaeologists ignored the significance of their achievement as a result of their insistence that generalizations were the principal goal of their discipline and by studying ecological adaptation at the expense of historically specific artistic traditions and religious beliefs.

By doing this, New Archaeologists used data concerning the heritage of native North Americans to formulate generalizations that they claimed were relevant for understanding Euro-American society. This tendency to use data about native North American prehistory as a basis for generalizing about human behaviour suggested that for the most part the significance of native people for archaeologists had not changed. Despite some involvement on behalf of Indians in land-claims cases, most processual archaeologists remained as spiritually alienated from native North Americans as their predecessors had been in the nineteenth century. This alienation has proved increasingly costly to the interests of archaeologists at a time when the native population of North America is rapidly growing and native people are becoming militant in their struggle to control their own social, economic, and political destiny. Efforts by native people to forbid or regulate access to prehistoric sites have resulted in a growing number of legal confrontations between archaeologists and native people and only limited and often ineffectual efforts at accommodation (Meighan 1984). While some native groups, such as the Pueblo of Zuñi, have sponsored their own programmes of archaeological research in an effort to achieve a more detailed and accurate view of their history (E. Adams 1984; Ferguson 1984), most native people have been repelled by the negative attitudes toward them that traditionally have been reflected in interpretations of archaeological data and in particular by the refusal of archaeologists to study the past as a record of native American history and culture.

British archaeologists who were influenced by the New Archaeology did not adopt the anti-historical attitudes of their American counterparts. David Clarke, a highly original thinker who was even more deeply influenced by the systemic approach of the New Geography than by Binford, was rightly critical of the intuitive manner in which many British archaeologists sought to compose 'historical narratives' without first analysing archaeological data in a rigorous manner in order to extract as much behavioural information as possible from them. Yet he did not condemn the historical analysis of archaeological data. After the publication of *Analytical Archaeology* (1968), which brought a host of quantitative methods pioneered by other social and biological sciences to bear on problems of archaeological classification and explaining cultural change, he returned to the study of European prehistory. His later papers dealing with this subject are characterized by a concern for the ecological basis of cultural development, attention to the social milieu in which economic transactions occurred, and a balanced interest in local development and regional networks of interaction. In 'The economic context of trade and industry in barbarian Europe till Roman times' (Clarke 1979: 263-331), which he wrote for *The Cambridge Economic History,* he attempted to summarize the relevant archaeological data in the light of Karl Polanyi's theories concerning the social embeddedness of primitive economies. This paper has been described as 'a great advance on previous work in its discussion of the social functions of artefact-types and its inference of the circulation-systems of which they are the fossilized remains' (Sherratt 1979: 197). His more detailed studies addressed such central issues of European prehistory as a reinterpretation of the social organization and economy of the late Iron Age settlement at Glastonbury (Clarke 1972b) and a survey, taking account of ecological, ethnographic, demographic, and economic, as well as archaeological data to counteract the traditional faunally oriented interpretations of the Mesolithic economies of Europe (Clarke 1979: 206-62). Colin Renfrew (1979) has also devoted his career to studying European prehistory. In addition to a major revision of the continent's chronology, he has used techniques introduced by the New Archaeology to address problems of trade, political development, and changing social organization in prehistoric times.

While American archaeologists, traditional and New, have tended to equate history with the study of chronology and idiosyncratic events, Clarke and Renfrew, who were trained in a European tradition that views prehistory as an extension of historical enquiry into periods that lack written records, were familiar with historiography and therefore recognized the unrealistic nature of the dichotomy that American anthropologists (and formerly British social anthropologists as well) drew between history and science. The British historian E. H. Carr (1967: 117) observed that 'Every historical argument revolves around the question of the priority of causes'. The American archaeologist A. C. Spaulding's (1968) claim that the chief distinction between science and history is the latter's overwhelming dependence on common-sense explanations did a grave injustice to the work of many twentieth-century historians, in whose writings interpretations of an impressionistic sort have been replaced by ones based on solid bodies of social-science theory. While the extent of the role played by chance factors in shaping historical events is a subject for debate, historians agree that individual behaviour is not random and must be viewed in relation to a social and cultural matrix that can be explained, if not predicted, by rules (Carr 1967: 113-43). Clarke, in particular, was willing in trying to explain complex historical situations to move beyond Binford's Hempelian logico-deductive positivism, which he was aware was already considered outmoded by most philosophers. He also maintained the necessity to compare alternative explanations and that 'speculation is both essential and productive if it obeys the cardinal injunctions that it must predict and that some of those predictions must ultimately be testable' (Clarke 1979: 259). The early work of Clarke and Renfrew has provided strong evidence, as have more recent contributions by other Western European archaeologists (Renfrew and Shennan 1982), that historical interpretation and evolutionary generalization are not antithetical approaches but instead may proceed concurrently and to their mutual advantage in archaeology.

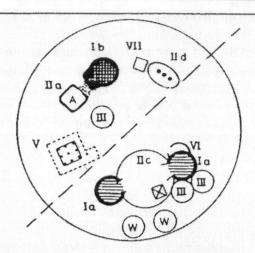

FIG. 21.1. The modular unit – the social and architectural building block of which the settlement is a multiple. The analyses of vertical and horizontal spatial relationships, structural attributes and artefact distributions convergently define a distinct range of structures (I–VII) repeatedly reproduced on the site. Each replication of the unit appears to be a particular transformation of an otherwise standardized set of relationships between each structural category and every other category. The basic division between the pair of major houses (Ia) and their satellites, and the minor house (Ib) and its ancillaries may be tentatively identified with a division between a major familial, multi-role and activity area on one hand and a minor, largely female and domestic area (see Fig. 21.6).

Below: the iconic symbols used to identify the structures in the schematic site models, Figs. 21.2–21.5.

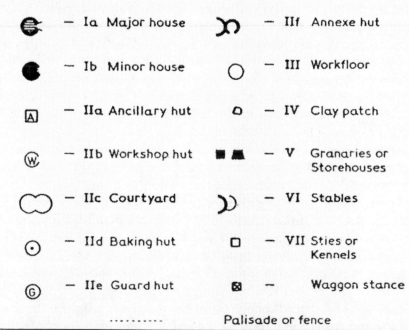

– Ia Major house		– IIf Annexe hut	
– Ib Minor house		– III Workfloor	
– IIa Ancillary hut		– IV Clay patch	
– IIb Workshop hut		– V Granaries or Storehouses	
– IIc Courtyard		– VI Stables	
– IId Baking hut		– VII Sties or Kennels	
– IIe Guard hut		– Waggon stance	

Palisade or fence

Figure 46   Modular housing unit at Glastonbury Iron Age site, as identified by D. L. Clarke

Cataclysmic archaeology

Beginning in the 1970s the cultural-evolutionary paradigm that guided the high-level interpretations of the New Archaeology underwent a major change. Since the late 1950s the optimism and security of the middle classes in the United States had been seriously eroded by a succession of chronic and deepening economic crises that were exacerbated by repeated failures of foreign policy, especially in Vietnam. These events produced a marked decline of faith in the benefits to be derived from technological development. This in turn spawned a proliferation of middle-class protest movements. While these movements consistently have avoided addressing the crucial economic and political problems of American society, they have profoundly altered social values and influenced the social sciences.

The oldest of these is the ecology movement, which views unrestrained technological development as poisoning and gradually destroying the world ecosystem. Its beginnings were signalled by the publication of Rachel Carson's *Silent Spring* (1962). It has since promoted awareness of an immediate danger to public health from a broad array of technological processes and warned that in the long term even more catastrophic consequences may result from the continuing pollution of the environment. The second movement, to promote a conserver society, stresses that certain natural resources essential for industrial processes are available only in finite quantities in nature; hence the world is rapidly reaching a point where further industrial expansion may become impossible. It is predicted that the exhaustion of key resources will result in declining living standards, or even the collapse of civilization. Hitherto it had generally been assumed that new raw materials or sources of energy would be found before old ones became depleted. Paul Ehrlich's *The Population Bomb* (1968) drew attention to yet another cause of anxiety. He argued that if unprecedented population growth were not checked, the results would be disastrous in the near future. As a result of these movements, social scientists and the general public became increasingly sceptical about the benefits of technological progress. As their political and economic insecurity increased, they, like the late nineteenth-century European middle classes, came to view cultural evolution as a source of danger and perhaps ultimately of disaster. Even rapid cultural change was condemned for producing dysfunctional 'future shock' (Toffler 1970).

These shifting attitudes laid the groundwork for a conceptual reorientation of archaeology that was as dramatic as the late nineteenth-century shift from unilinear evolutionism to the culture historical paradigm had been. The new paradigm marked yet another retreat from the optimistic view of change formulated during the Enlightenment and intensified neo-evolutionism's rejection of the belief that technological innovation was the result of a process of rational self-improvement and the driving force promoting cultural change. Two specific developments in economics and social anthropology served as a catalyst for this shift.

Boserup (1965) had argued that while increasingly labour intensive modes of agriculture yielded more food per unit of land, they required more labour for each unit of food produced. Therefore only the necessity to support slowly but inevitably increasing population densities would have led groups to adopt such systems. Her thesis was construed as evidence that developments which previous generations of archaeologists had interpreted as desirable results of humanity's ability to solve problems and make life easier and more fulfilling were in fact responses to forces beyond human control. Throughout history these forces had compelled people to work harder, suffer increasing exploitation, and degrade their environments.

The demonstration by Richard Lee and Irven DeVore (1968) that hunter-gatherer economies could support a low population density with less effort than was required by even the least demanding forms of food production not only was interpreted as support for Boserup's position but also led archaeologists to adopt new interpretations of prehistoric hunter-gatherers. Instead of being viewed as living on the brink of starvation, they were portrayed as leisured groups with plenty of spare time to devote to religious or intellectual pursuits. Even relatively conservative archaeologists began to idealize the more egalitarian prehistoric cultures as examples of 'conserving societies' that provided models of how we ourselves should behave in relation to the environment (Cunliffe 1974: 27). Some archaeologists questioned the evidence on which these formulations were based and their general applicability (Bronson 1972; Cowgill 1975; Harris 1979: 87-8). Yet the rapid and relatively unchallenged way in which these studies came to influence the interpretation of archaeological data, often in the absence of adequate measures of prehistoric population size or even of relative population change, suggests the degree to which they accorded with the spirit of the time.

Archaeologists also began to express reservations about conventional neo-evolutionary theories that analysed change as if it occurred in slow, gradual trajectories of the sort that Braidwood and MacNeish had documented in their studies of the origins of agriculture in the Near East and Mesoamerica. Robert Adams (1974: 248-9) pointed out that there were abrupt shifts in the development of early civilizations, sometimes separated by long periods when relatively few changes occurred. Soon after Renfrew (1978) attempted to use catastrophe theory, which had been invented by the French mathematician Renè Thom, to explain changes in the archaeological record. Catastrophe theory treats the question of how, as the result of particular conjunctions of internal states, a set of fluctuating variables can produce discontinuous effects (Saunders 1980). While it remains to be demonstrated how rigorously Thom's mathematics, which can treat only four variables at once, can be used to explain social behaviour, the concept attracted considerable attention among archaeologists in Britain and America (Renfrew and Cooke 1979). Although Thom and Renfrew were both interested in 'catastrophes' that produced more complex as well as simpler states, the ready acceptance of catastrophe theory as an analogue of social process reflected widespread fears that Western societies might be sliding towards a catastrophe in the conventional as well as the mathematical sense. Finally archaeologists have sought to imbue the concept of discontinuous cultural change with additional scientific prestige by drawing parallels between it and that of punctuated equilibrium being promoted by some evolutionary biologists (S. Gould 1980; Eldredge 1982). These views of cultural change have made archaeologists more aware of the need to distinguish varying rates of change in the archaeological record, sometimes over relatively short periods of time. Gaps are also being recognized in the archaeological record that in the past would have been filled by unwarrantedly projecting known cultures backwards and forwards in time or hypothesizing undiscovered intermediary forms. This has challenged archaeologists to acquire ever greater control over cultural chronologies. It has also reinforced the belief that cultures are more fragile and cultural change more fraught with dangers than archaeologists had believed hitherto.

These new ideas about the nature of cultural change have promoted a pessimistic and even tragic version of cultural evolution that interprets demographic, ecological, and economic factors as constraining change to occur along lines that most human beings do not regard as desirable but which they are unable to control. This eschatological materialism implies that the future is always likely to be worse than the present and that humanity is journeying from a primitive Eden, filled with happy hunter-gatherers, to a hell of thermonuclear annihilation. We have already noted that neo-evolutionism differed from nineteenth-century evolutionism in its rejection of the belief that cultural change occurred as the result of rational and willing action by human beings who sought to acquire greater control over their environment. This new cataclysmic evolutionism also differed from previous disillusionment about progress, which had resulted in diffusionists denying that there was any natural order to human history. Instead of denying that there was such an order, cataclysmic evolutionists stressed a fixed process of change that at best human beings might hope to slow or halt, but which otherwise would result in their ruin (Trigger 1981a). Only a few archaeologists who see trouble ahead for their own society continue to argue that it is possible to learn from the past how to 'adjust and cope' (J. Bradley 1987: 7).

Cataclysmic evolutionism, with its curious resemblances to the medieval view of history, but with God replaced by an evolutionary process that renders human beings the victims of forces beyond their control, seems to be the product of an advanced capitalist society that is not performing to the satisfaction of large numbers of the middle classes. Significantly, neither evolutionary archaeologists nor most of the opponents of environmental pollution, unchecked population growth, and the wastage of natural resources treat these problems as ones that can be resolved by means of concerted economic and political reforms carried out on the national and international levels. Instead they mystify these problems by locating their causes in a general evolutionary framework and seek when possible to ameliorate them in discrete, piecemeal ways. By exculpating leading industrial societies of explicit political responsibility for what is happening, cataclysmic archaeology helps to reaffirm the expansionist goals of American society in the midst of a growing international economic and ecological crisis. It also seeks to promote social solidarity by denying the political origins of social conflict. On the downswing of a long cycle, cataclysmic evolution attributes the shortcomings of a world economy to largely immutable evolutionary forces rather than to specific and alterable political and economic conditions that have evolved under American hegemony. This explanation has attracted a willing audience amongst the insecure middle classes of other Western nations, who are as anxious as are their American counterparts to believe that they are not responsible for the fate that they fear is overtaking them.

While the origin of ideas has no necessary bearing on whether or not they are correct, it is fairly obvious that the high-level evolutionary theories that guided the interpretation of archaeological evidence in the 1970s reflected a serious and prolonged economic, political, and social crisis in which the interests of the dominant middle classes were perceived as deeply threatened. It is also evident that these high-level views influenced the expectations of archaeologists concerning how the archaeological record might best be interpreted. All of this seriously calls into question the objectivity that the New Archaeology claimed on the basis of its positivist methodology.

A number of archaeologists, especially among those doing research or employed in the southwestern United States, have proposed interpretations of the archaeological record that closely approximate the central values of conservative American political ideology. In *The Archaeology of Arizona* Martin and Plog (1973) viewed cultures as adaptive systems and argued that those possessing the greatest amount of random variation were best fitted to survive when confronted by environmental or demographic challenges or competition from neighbouring groups. Dunnell (1980a) and Cordell and Plog (1979) also assume that there is present in every society a broad spectrum of alternative behavioural patterns on which the cultural equivalent of natural selection can operate. This viewpoint emphasizes the adaptive value of individual choice in a manner analogous to economic free-market theories. William Rathje (1975) utilized certain principles concerning disproportional growth to construct a scheme that seeks to account for how expanding early civilizations coped with the problem of processing increasing amounts of information. He proposed that in the early stages increasing complexity was managed by employing greater numbers of officials to process information and make decisions. Later an attempt was made to forestall the growth of bureaucracy beyond economically acceptable limits by resorting to greater standardization. The development of uniform system-wide codes (such as fixed weights and measures) decreased the amount of accounting that was necessary. Still later, efficiencies were attempted by encouraging greater autonomy at lower levels, while the whole society was integrated as a series of economically interdependent regional components. Blanton *et al.* (1981) have applied the basic ideas of this scheme to the evolution of complex societies in highland Mesoamerica. They argue that, while the economies of the earlier Classic civilizations were deeply embedded in the political organizations of the region, later economies were more entrepreneurial and functioned more independently of state control than ever before. The archaeologically attested results of such *laissez-faire* arrangements are said to have been a vast increase in the quality of goods available to most people. Other archaeologists have argued that, on the contrary, in late prehispanic times the economy of the Valley of Mexico was strongly controlled by the Aztecs, who used their military power to centralize lucrative craft production in their capital Tenochtitlan (Parsons *et al.* 1982; Hassig 1985). Peter Wells (1984) has assigned a major role to entrepreneurs coming from outside the established local elites in bringing about social change in Iron Age Europe, thus making this period an exemplar of 'Thatcherite enterprise culture' (Champion 1986).

While these interpretations look like rationalizations of American and British *laissez-faire* idealism, many of them have sought theoretical justification at the highest possible levels. Martin and Plog grounded their discussion in ecological theory and Rathje related his to General Systems Theory. Yet no specific attempts were made to adapt these theories to the archaeological study of human behaviour. The advantage of random variation was presented as a universally valid principle without any attempt to inventory the extent of such diversity empirically or to identify the factors that determine its range. This is a weakness paralleling the lack of concern for factors causing variability in rates of population growth in theories that invoked this factor as an independent cause of cultural change. Nor did the exponents of intracultural diversity take account of the requirements that the necessity for the safe and effective deployment of increasingly powerful technologies might generate for planning and consensus. Likewise Rathje did not consider the possibility that, unlike modern states, the rulers of early civilizations might have limited the interventions of their cumbersome data-processing systems into the affairs of ordinary people to those matters that related directly to securing the goods and services required to achieve their own specific goals. The development of Near Eastern civilization suggests a gradual but continuing increase in bureaucracy and the use of military force rather than the reverse. What is most interesting about their theories is that, despite their potential overt attraction to American archaeologists, who generally tend to be conservative, they have aroused less interest than has cataclysmic evolution. The appeal of explanations that disguise or naturalize stressful economic and political relations seems to be greater than that of ones that express a conservative ideology more directly.

A conservative ideology may, however, be exerting a more powerful influence on interpretations of prehistory with respect to the study of fossil hominids. Under the direct or indirect influence of sociobiology, there is a growing tendency to stress evidence of biological and behavioural differences and to treat these differences as correlated. This in turn leads to growing suspicion of interpretations of the behaviour of Lower Palaeolithic hominids that are based on analogies with modern hunter-gatherer societies. We are informed that the Australopithecines were more like specialized apes and that the technological and behavioural capacities of early *Homo* increasingly appear to have been unlike our own (Cartmill *et al* 1986: 419). While former tendencies to emphasize the human-like qualities of early hominids are interpreted as an ideological overreaction to Nazism, no attention is paid to the possible ideological basis of currently popular alternative explanations.

Conclusions

Both Soviet (Klejn 1977) and American (Davis 1983: 407) archaeologists have drawn attention to some striking similarities between the New Archaeology and the archaeology created in the Soviet Union in the early 1930s. These parallels are the more interesting because all but a handful of American archaeologists remained almost completely unaware of the strengths and weaknesses of Soviet archaeology until the late 1970s. Both approaches were based on an evolutionary view of cultural change and sought to understand the regularities exhibited by that process. They agreed that these regularities were strong and could be studied by using a materialist framework. Migration and diffusion were played down in favour of trying to explain the changes that occurred within cultural systems over long periods of time. Traditional typological studies that sought to elucidate chronologies and spatial variations in material culture were regarded as old-fashioned and there was a corresponding increase in functional interpretations of archaeological data.

Yet, despite these similarities, there was a marked difference in the high-level theories that guided the interpretation of archaeological data. The New Archaeology embraced various forms of ecological and demographic determinism, which located the major factors bringing about change outside the cultural system and treated human beings as the passive victims of forces that mostly lie beyond their understanding and control. On the other hand, dialectical materialism, while not denying the importance of ecological factors as constraints on human behaviour or minimizing the role they played, especially in the early stages of cultural development, locates the major cause of cultural transformations squarely within the social realm, where it takes the form of competition to control wealth and power between different groups within the same society. Even in its most mechanistic and evolutionary formulations, such as prevailed in the Soviet Union in the 1930s, Marxism accords a central role to human beings pursuing their self-interest as members of social groups. What was most striking about the New Archaeology was its unwillingness to accord human consciousness or volition any role in bringing about cultural change. Marxists could argue that neo-evolutionism's denial of a creative role for human beings reflects the dehumanizing effects of the growth of corporate capitalism, which effectively has destroyed the concept of an economic system built upon individual initiative that was the ideal of the middle classes in the nineteenth century.

Although the New Archaeology advocated studying all aspects of cultural systems, archaeological publications indicate that most New Archaeologists concentrated on subsistence patterns, trade, and to a lesser degree social organization. Binford's own research largely has been concerned with technology and subsistence patterns as they relate to ecological adaptations. Major aspects of human behaviour, such as religious beliefs, aesthetics, and scientific knowledge, received little attention. The scope of the New Archaeology does not appear to have expanded beyond that already embraced by the ecological and settlement-pattern approaches that developed in the 1950s. The fields investigated by the New Archaeology also fall within the lower echelons of Hawkes' hierarchy, although Binford rejected the claim that this hierarchy established inevitable restrictions on the archaeological study of any aspect of human behaviour.

The explanation for this failure to study all aspects of human behaviour lies with the ecological approach. The New Archaeology shared the neo-evolutionary belief that cultural systems were characterized by a high degree of uniformity and that it was possible to account for this uniformity by identifying the ecological constraints that shaped human behaviour. Yet it now appears that, while whole cultural systems can be viewed as constrained to some degree by the nature of their adaptation to the ecosystem, the constraints exercised on the technology and economy are far stronger and more immediately recognizable than are the ones on social organization, and these in turn are greater than are the constraints on specific beliefs and values. Hence the techniques adopted by the New Archaeology work best when dealing with those aspects of culture that are subject to the greatest restraint. The New Archaeologists appear to have erred in assuming that ecological constraints would exert the same degree of influence on all aspects of culture and hence in feeling justified when they ignored alternative factors that shaped the archaeological record. Paul Tolstoy (1969:558) was correct when he stated that determinists consider worthy of attention only those traits with which their theories appear equipped to deal.

Yet, almost from the beginning, doubts were expressed about the adequacy of this formulation, especially by those who attempted a systemic approach. In the 1970s and 1980s growing awareness of these weaknesses challenged some Western archaeologists, including ones who had played a key role in establishing the New Archaeology, to rethink their basic assumptions about human behaviour and how the archaeological record should be interpreted. This also led a growing number of archaeologists to recognize for the first time that the ideological underpinnings of archaeological interpretations were something other than the mistaken notions of the past and to challenge the positivist pretence of ethical neutrality.

CHAPTER

16

Contextual Archaeology

Introduction

Trigger continues his analysis of recent archaeology with shifts away from the New Archaeology, led to an extent by Ian Hodder (whose work appears in Chapters 17 and 18). The approach of the New Archaeology, in which the character of material culture is viewed as a system and process that adjusts and adapts to change, is replaced by analysis that takes into account all manner of social dynamics having to do with families, legitimization, dominant and competing groups. It is, therefore, strongly contextual, requiring "a comprehensive internal study of archaeological cultures." (p. 305) The archaeologist has the daunting task of considering that the culture being studied needs to be examined in a greater depth, taking into consideration its complexity in areas such as art and religious beliefs, which are not to be considered the results of responses in a system, but take a more active role in which volition, even the volition of an individual, might be crucial. In this chapter, Trigger suggests that the practice of archaeology needs to be distinguished in its methods and objectives from history and other social sciences, this being most telling in the study of prehistoric cultures for which we have only material remains. The nature and extent of preservation of archaeological record needs also to be examined more critically. And, ultimately, one must be conscious of the limitations of investigators: their resources, research interests, and abilities.

Although Ian Hodder has participated in and even inspired many of the trends noted above, his contextual approach to archaeology stands apart from them in certain respects and is now recognized as the principal challenge and rival paradigm to processual archaeology (Binford 1986, 1987). Basic to contextualism is Hodder's ethnographically well-documented claim that material culture is not merely a reflection of ecological adaptation or sociopolitical organization but also an active element in group relations that can be used to disguise as well as to reflect social relations. Overtly competing groups may use material culture to emphasize their dissimilarities, while an ethnic group wishing to use another's resources may attempt to minimize the material manifestations of such differences. High-status groups actively use material culture to legitimize their authority (Hodder 1982b: 119-22), while in some African cultures calabash and age-graded spear styles, which cut across ethnic boundaries that are marked in terms of other aspects of material culture, signal the general opposition of women and young men to dominant elders (ibid. 58-74). Even tensions within certain extended families have been shown to be expressed and reinforced by variations in pottery decoration (ibid. 122-4). Hodder's view that material culture is used as an active element in social interaction contradicts the carefully developed arguments of processual archaeologists that the relative elaboration of graves within a society accurately mirrors the degree of social differentiation (Saxe 1970; J. Brown 1971; O'Shea 1984). Research by Hodder and his students has shown that complex ideas relating to religion, hygiene, and status rivalry also play significant roles in influencing burial customs (M. Pearson 1982). In some societies simple burials reflect a social ideal of egalitarianism that is not effectively put into practice in everyday life (Huntington and Metcalf 1979: 122). Thus to determine the social significance of burial customs archaeologists have to examine other aspects of the archaeological record, such as settlement patterns. As a result of such research, it may quickly become apparent that a particular society with simple burial customs was not egalitarian in practice and this in turn will reveal the ideological status of these customs.

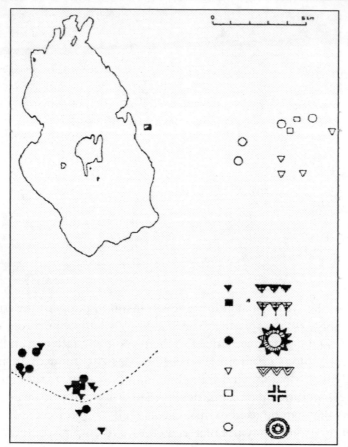

Figure 47

Hodder's recording of ethnographics distribution of shield types

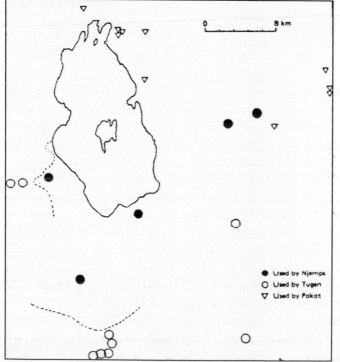

Figure 48

Calabash motifs among different ethnic groups in the Baringo are of Kenya, 1982.

The contextual approach is based upon the conviction that archaeologists need to examine all possible aspects of an archaeological culture in order to understand the significance of each part of it. It is assumed that in the case cited above the discrepancy between burial and settlement patterns would reveal the ideological colouration of the burials, provided that archaeologists were convinced that burials representing all social classes had been found. By drawing attention to properties of material culture that hitherto had been ignored, Hodder has revealed the dangers inherent in interpretations of archaeological evidence that is analyzed in isolation from its broader cultural context. He has also demonstrated material culture to have dynamic symbolic properties that accord better with a Marxist or historical particularist interpretation of culture than they do with a neo-evolutionary one. By arguing that an archaeological culture cannot be interpreted adequately in a piecemeal fashion, Hodder places new demands on archaeologists for a comprehensive internal study of archaeological cultures, which complement the demands of world-system advocates for broader regional coverages. This is very different from the belief of processual archaeologists that a few selected variables can be studied at a single site to answer a specific archaeological problem (Brown and Struever 1973).

Contextual archaeology also rejects the validity of the neo-evolutionary distinction between what is culturally specific and cross-culturally general that was the basis of Steward's dichotomy between science and history. This validates an interest in culturally specific cosmologies, astronomical lore, art styles, religious beliefs, and other topics that lingered on the fringes of processual archaeology in the 1960s and 1970s. As Dunnell (1982a: 521) has observed, the ecological and evolutionary approaches borrowed from the biological sciences were not designed to explain motivational and symbolic systems. Hodder encourages archaeologists once again to take account of the complexities of human phenomena and to realize that universal generalizations do not exhaust the regularities that characterize human behaviour. They are urged to look for order within individual cultures or historically related ones both in terms of specific cultural categories, such as the canons governing artistic productions, and in the way different cultural categories relate to one another (Bradley 1984).

The study of patterning in material culture has been influenced strongly by Claude Lévi-Strauss' structural approach, especially his investigation of the symbolic patterns underlying native American mythology. Basic to this form of analysis is the conviction that where the richness and variability of the archaeological record is too great to be explained only as a response to environmental constraints or stimuli, factors internal to the system must also be considered (Wylie 1982: 41). Ernest Gellner (1985: 149-51) has elegantly contrasted ecology and economics, which study the regularities resulting from a scarcity of resources, and structural approaches, which study the order that human beings impose on those areas of their lives that, because of their symbolic nature, are not subject to any form of scarcity. Yet the relationship of the symbolic order to economic and adaptive forms of behaviour still remains to be defined. It is no longer possible to maintain that symbolic aspects of material culture are merely a passive reflection of more pragmatic behaviour. Yet how can the archaeologist determine in specific cases, except pragmatically, whether the relationship is one of reflection, inversion, or contradiction? Furthermore, linguistic analogies suggest that the relationship between material culture and its symbolic meaning may be essentially arbitrary (Gallay 1986: 197).

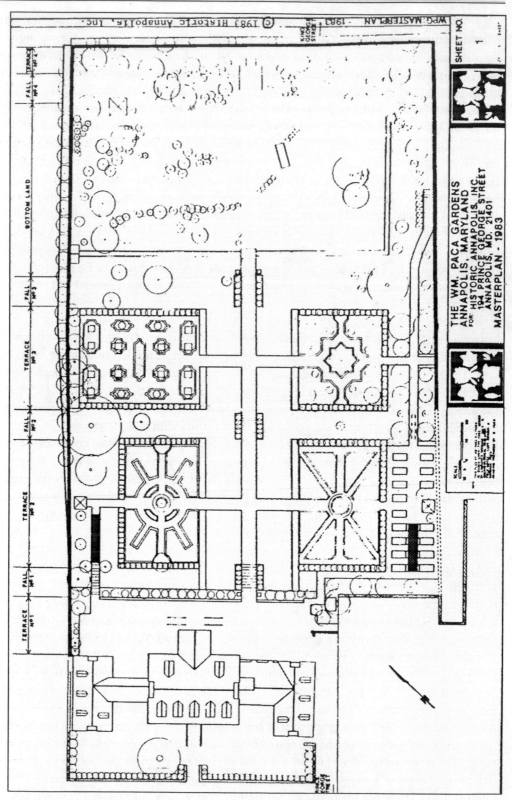

Figure 49   Eighteenth-century William Paca Garden. Annapolis, Maryland; the outlines
                    of the garden are archaeologically determined

Structural archaeologists express admiration for the pioneering work of André Leroi-Gourhan (1968), who documented patterns in the locations and associations of the different animal species represented in Upper Palaeolithic caves in Western Europe and interpreted these as referring to myths dealing with the relations between male and female principles, as well as for Alexander Marshack's (1972) demonstration of seasonal patterns in associated mobiliary art. These works encouraged the discovery and exploration of further patterning in the archaeological record that had been ignored by processual archaeologists, such as the orientation of Neolithic tombs in Sweden (Tilley 1984) and similarities in the patterning of Neolithic tombs and houses in Western Europe (Hodder 1984a). Yet so far no archaeologist has discovered how to get beyond speculation in interpreting the cultural meaning of such regularities for early prehistoric times. Gallay (1986: 198-200, 281) has argued that no way can be found to demonstrate an isometric relation between our ideas about the past and ideas that were actually held in the past.

Archaeologists have had more success in relating the designs of houses and gardens in colonial Virginia and New England to class values and attitudes that are documented in the written records of that period (Glassie 1975; Deetz 1977; Isaac 1982; Leone 1982). This experience is similar to that of art historians who can find order in the themes and styles of Greek statuary as it changed over time. Yet, while they can relate this to a definable, changing aesthetic, they cannot understand the significance of that aesthetic in verbal terms without written records. Hodder (1982b: 192-3; 1982d) has been interested in seeing if cross-cultural regularities can be discovered in attitudes toward dirt or the elaboration of pottery designs. If such regularities could be found, they would probably have a basis in human psychology. They would also indicate patterning in human behaviour that cross-cuts both of the levels (adaptive and stylistic) that Gellner has identified. Such relationships remain, however, problematical.

The study of the symbolic meaning of material remains during recent millennia has been facilitated by the direct historical approach. R. L. Hall (1979) has drawn upon ethnographic and ethnohistorical material concerning native religious beliefs and symbolism collected in eastern North America since the seventeenth century to explain the structure of Adena burial mounds in that region over 1,500 years earlier, as well as why certain classes of artifacts were included in later Middle Woodland burials. George Hamell (1983) has used regularities in historically recorded Iroquoian, Algonkian, and Siouan myths to explain the significance of the inclusion of natural crystals, objects made from marine shell and native copper, and certain other materials in eastern North American burial contexts for over 6,000 years, from late Archaic times into the historical period. Both of these anthropologists offer detailed symbolic explanations of regularities in burial customs for which no cross-cultural generalizations could account. The main problem that is posed by this work is that of verifiability. In the cases of Hall and Hamell, proof rests upon the applicability of analogies drawn between ethnographic and archaeological data that there are sound reasons to believe are historically related. Hamell's evidence is particularly convincing because there is strong proof in the archaeological record of continuity in the use of these materials from their earliest appearance into the historical period. In recent years San ethnography has been used to indicate the shamanistic significance of much southern African rock art and the meaning of specific symbols, such as the eland (Schrire *et al.* 1986: 128). Yet in his study of *Jewish Symbols in the Greco-Roman Period* Erwin Goodenough (1953-68) has demonstrated the fallacy of assuming that continuities in iconography necessarily indicate continuity in mythology, since the significance accorded to representations is as likely to change over time as are the ways beliefs are symbolized (Goff 1963: xxxv). Yet a general continuity in cultural context and in a total symbol system argues strongly in favour of a continuity in meaning (Vastokas 1987).

Hodder, like Childe, further stresses the importance of cultural traditions as factors playing an active role in structuring cultural change. These traditions supply most of the knowledge, beliefs, and values that simultaneously influence economic and social change and are reshaped by that change. They can also play an active role in resisting or promoting specific changes. This corresponds with Marx's observation that 'human beings make their own history . . . not under circumstances chosen by themselves . . . but directly encountered, given, and transmitted from the past' (Kohl 1981b: 112). It is not possible to predict either the content of a cultural tradition in all of its specific detail or the detailed trajectories of cultural change. Yet when these trajectories are known from the archaeological record they increase the archaeologist's ability to account for what has happened in the past.

Both the Marxist-inspired versions of archaeological interpretation and contextual archaeology began as semi-peripheral, and specifically British, critiques of the imperialist pretensions of American processual archaeology. These critiques have been adopted by a growing number of American archaeologists who have become aware of some of the contradictions between rhetoric and reality in their own society, as it has grown increasingly reactionary and defensive in recent years. Exposure to Marxist ideas, usually at second or third hand, has helped to reveal the mechanistic strictures of neo-evolutionary theory, which treats human beings as passive instruments rather than the makers of history. There is a growing awareness of the complexity of cultural change, of the need to view this process in its totality, and of the inadequacy of the dichotomy between history and evolution. New interpretations generally have moved in the direction of greater idealism and express growing doubts that anything approaching an objective understanding of the past is possible.

Ironically these developments appear to reflect yet a further stage in the growing despair that it is possible to do anything to change the direction in which American society is moving by those who might like to see it changed. Many of he self-style Marxists perceive the ideological factors buttressing the structures of capitalism and seem to believe that ides alone may bring about or prevent social change. Orthodox Marxism claims that such as naive idealism dooms its exponents to political importance. This trend towards idealism in archaeology may be viewed as a secular equivalent of the increasing preoccupation with religion in middle-class American society in general and therefore as marking a further stage in the disintegration of the self-confidence of this class (Harris 1981). Long ago Engels postulated a positive correlation between the self-confidence of the middle classes and their propensity to adopt a materialist outlook (Marx and Engels 1957: 250-80).

While these idealist archaeologists recognize that a variety of mental symbolic, and social factors bring about sociocultural change, they are unwilling to accept the Enlightenment view that planning and intentionality also play a significant role in doing so, even if it is admitted that the effects of change are often not the ones that were foreseen. Yet, as Leach (1973: 763-4) has observed, our capacity for 'original speech creativity' is closely linked with nonverbal forms of creativity as well as with human consciousness. This, he added, implies that human beings are not just part of a world governed by 'natural law' but have a unique ability to engage in 'work' (praxis) that allows them to alter their surroundings intentionally. Given that foresight and planning are characteristics of human behaviour, there is no reason why these features should not be assigned a significant role in any account of social change, even though the constraints that channel and select behaviour cannot be ignored. The principal error of Enlightenment philosophers and nineteen-century unilinear evolutionists was the autonomous role they assigned to human creativity. In the future a major subject of debate may be between materialists who identify the principal endogenous locus of change with relations of production and idealists who identify it with pure internationality. A dichotomous treatment is not, however inherent in these concepts.

In North America, prehistoric archaeology as a whole still has not moved far enough away from neo-evolutionsim to see itself as constituting, not merely a branch of anthropology, but also a technique for studying the past within a broader discipline of prehistory. The latter position is commonly held in Europe and in the past has been discussed sympathetically by a few American archaeologists such as Irving Rouse (1972). There is growing recognition that the human skeletal evidence studied by physical anthropologists may tell us as much about prehistoric diet as do floral and faunal analyses (Cohen and Armelagos 1984) and even more about band exogamy than does the study of artifact styles (Kennedy 1981). Yet there is little general awareness of the value of combining the study of archaeological data with that of historical linguistics, oral traditions, historical ethnography, and historical records, although it is clear that many archaeological problems can be resolved in this way. In American studies of African prehistory, there is a strong tradition of such interdisciplinary studies (Murdock rg1959a; D. McCall 1964). The same is true of Polynesia (Jennings 1979) and Joyce Marcus (1983b) follows J. E. S. Thompson (1898-1975) in arguing the benefits of such an approach for Mayan research. The resistance seems to come from the view, widely held by processual archaeologists, that their discipline must be based as exclusively as possible on the study of material culture. Even though most of them agree that the ultimate goal of archaeology is to understand human behaviour and cultural change, they seek maximum disciplinary autonomy by relying only on universal generalizations about relations between material culture and human behaviour to translate archaeological data into information about such behaviour. This desire to push the interpretative potential of archaeology as far as possible without relying on other disciplines for information about the past is partly justified by the fear that interdisciplinary approaches can degenerate into an exercise in dilettantism. Such concerns do not, however, nullify the value of interdisciplinary research, provided that it is understood that such studies must exploit the historical potential of each discipline to the greatest extent possible, using its own data and methods before comparisons of findings are attempted.

Growing realization that many aspects of past human behaviour can be understood through correlations of a more culturally specific nature eventually should suggest the limitations of a purely archaeological approach and encourage archaeologists to seek to discover how other types of information can be combined with archaeological data to promote a better understanding of the past. The result will be a still broader and more enriched version of contextualism. Implementing this sort of approach requires cultivating a wider range of cultural interests than have been associated with processual archaeology. In their book on the Inca town of Huánuco Pampa, Craig Morris and Donald Thompson (1985: 58-9) are content to describe the *ushanu* or platform in the center of the town as a structure related to aspects of ceremonial life. While they discuss its use in state ceremonies they do not note that the *ushnu* was symbolically the place where the powers of heaven and earth met and that control of these powers was a central claim of the state (Gasparini and Margolies 1980: 264-80).

Archaeology as itself

In mainstream Western archaeology there has been a growing awareness of the distinctive qualities of archaeological data and of the need to understand these qualities if archaeology is to provide reliable information about human bevaviour. In England this has taken the form of an enhanced awareness of the differences between archaeological and historical methods (Clarke 1968: 12-14) and in America a growing conviction that archaeology is different from ethnology and the other social sciences. The most obvious difference is than prehistoric archaeology is the only social science that has no direct access to information about human behaviour. Unlike economists, political scientists, sociologists, and ethnologists, archaeologists cannot talk to the people they study or observe their human beings thought or did in prehistoric times. That must be inferred as far as this is possible from the remains of what they made and used.

It has long been recognized that the archaeological record normally contains a far from complete sample of the material remain of the past. In 1923, John Myres (1923a:2) observed that it consisted of the equipment which the people 'of each generation were discarding.' In *Archaeology and Society*, Grahame Clark (1939) examined in great detail factors that influence the preservation of archeological data. In their initial enthusiasm, New Archaeologists tended to assume that the archaeological record, if adequately interpreted, offered a relatively complete and undistorted picture of the societies that had produced it. Gradually, however, following Robert Ascher (1961:324), these archaeologists became aware that artifacts were made, used, and frequently discarded in different contexts, not all of which were equally represented in the archaeological record. Archaeological sites were distorted or destroyed by subsequent human activities and natural processes, and finally the recovery of archaeological information was dependent upon the knowledge, interests, and resources of individual archaeologists. Knowing what happened at each of these stages was vital for understanding the limitations and significance of the archaeological record.

The first major step towards formalizing such knowledge was taken by David Clarke in 1973 in a paper entitled 'Archaeology: the loss of innocence' (Clarke 1979: 83-103). He argued that archaeology would remain 'an irresponsible art form' unless a body of theory was systematized that related archaeological remains to human behaviour. The basis for such systematization was the recognition that archaeologists possessed only an attenuated sample of what they proposed to study. This observation was encapsulated in Clarke's memorable comment that archaeology was 'the discipline with the theory and practice for the recovery of unobservable hominid behaviour patterns from indirect traces in bad samples' (p.100). The scientific interpretation of archaeological data depends on recognizing that, of the full range of hominid activity patterns and social and environmental processes that occurred in the past, archaeologists have access only to the sample of associated material remains that in turn have been deposited in the archaeological record, survived to be recovered, and actually been recovered. Clarke defined five bodies of theory that archaeologists intuitively employ in their interpretive leaps from excavated data to final report. The first of these was pre-depositional and depositional theory, covering the relations of human activities, social patterns, and environmental factors with each other and with the samples and traces that are deposited in the archaeological record. Post-depositional theory treats the natural and human processes that affect the archaeological record, such as erosion, decay, ground movement, plundering, ploughing, and the reuse of land. Retrieval theory deals with the relations between what survives in the archaeological record and what is recovered. It is largely a theory of sampling, excavation procedures, and flexible response strategies. Analytical theory deals with the operational treatment of recovered data including classification, modelling, testing, and experimental studies. Finally, interpretive theory deals with relations between the archaeological patterns established at the analytical level and directly unobservable ancient behavioural and environmental patterns. Thus interpretive theory infers the processes that pre-depositional theory explains. Clarke believed that the challenge for archaeologists was to develop a corpus of theory appropriate for each of these categories. Only a small portion, mainly relating to the pre-depositional and interpretive levels, could be derived from the social sciences. The rest had to come from the biological and physical sciences. The totality of this theory, together with metaphysical epistemological, and logical theory relating to archaeological operations, was necessary to create a scientific discipline of archaeology.

In the United States, Michael Schiffer (1976) independently pioneered an analogous but less inclusive approach (in that it did not embrace Clarke's analytical level), which he called 'behavioral archeology'. He proposed that archaeological data consisted of materials in static relations that have been produced by cultural systems and subjected to the operation of non-cultural processes. Because of these two sets of processes the archaeological record is 'a distorted reflection of a past behavioral system' (p. 12). The challenge is for archaeologists to eliminate this distortion in order to gain an accurate understanding of past behaviour. Schiffer was optimistic that this could be done provided that three sets of factors were controlled. The first are 'correlates', which relate material objects or spatial relations in archaeological contexts to specific types of human behaviour. Correlates allow archaeologists to infer how artifacts were made, distributed, used, and recycled, often in exceedingly complex ways, in living societies. If a cultural system were frozen at a specific moment in time, as to some extent happened to the city of Pompeii as a result of being buried under the ash of Mount Vesuvius in A.D. 79, and perfectly preserved, no additional factors would have to be taken into account in order to understand life at that moment. The interpretation of archaeological sites normally, however, requires archaeologists to take account of site-formation processes, which involves determining how material was transferred from a systemic to an archaeological context and what happened to that material in the archaeological record. The first of these are 'cultural formation processes', or C-transforms, which attempt to understand the processes by which items are discarded in the normal operation of a cultural system. Through the detailed study of discard rates, discard locations, loss probabilities, and burial practices, C-transforms can predict the materials that will or will not be deposited by a social system in the archaeological record and thus establish a set of relations that will permit the cultural system to be inferred more accurately from its remains. Ethnographic research on problems of this sort suggests that artifacts and artifact debris are more likely to be abandoned in the localities where they were used in temporary hunter-gatherer sites than in larger and more sedentary ones, where the disposal of waste material was much more highly organized (Murray 1980).

The realization that large numbers of artifacts are found in contexts of disposal rather than those of manufacture or use has stimulated much ethnoarchaeological research that aims to discover regularities in patterns of the disposal of refuse. It has also prompted observations that archaeology may of necessity be primarily a science of garbage. J. A. Moore and A. S. Keene (1983: 17) have pronounced studies of site formation processes to be 'the archaeological agenda for the 1980s'. Other studies seek to determine the transformations that artifacts undergo in the course of usage. Stone tools are likely to be curated and reused much more intensively in sites lacking easy access to sources of raw material than in ones close to such sources (Binford 1983a: 269-86). C-transforms also include post-depositional human activities, such as ploughing and looting, that may distort the archaeological record. This may often happen in predictable ways, such as the greater likelihood that robbers will remove gold objects rather than commonplace ones from graves. Finally non-cultural formation processes, or N-transforms, allow archaeologists to determine the interactions between cultural materials and aspects of the non-cultural environment from which they are recovered. Schiffer argues that by accounting for the ways in which archaeological data functioned in systemic contexts, entered the archaeological record, and were transformed by it, archaeologists should be able to eliminate the 'distortions' caused by formation processes and infer the original systemic context in which the functioned. This can be done by formulating laws about the between material culture on the one hand and human behaviour and natural forces on the other. These laws include many low-level empirical generalizations. This had led Binford (1983a: 237) to describe Schiffer as being primarily an inductivist.

Binford (1983a: 235) has challenged Schiffer's view by arguing that the archaeological record cannot be 'a distortion of its own reality'. He maintains that the challenge of archaeological interpretation is to understand the 'distorted' material as a significant part of the record and that most of Schiffer's C-transforms, such as periodically cleaning out hearths, were everyday activities. Yet, since Schiffer seeks to understand processes, it seems unreasonable to suggest that he treats past cultural systems as frozen in time. What Binford does demonstrate is that it is naive to believe that archaeologists can totally purge the archaeological record of the various disorganizing processes that controlled its formation and, having done that, reconstruct the cultural system as Schiffer hopes to do. Schiffer's approach has helped to stimulate much research that has resulted in a more sophisticated understanding of the behavioural significance of archaeological data. Previously factors such as discard rates were barely considered by archaeologists except in assessing the significance of animal bones. It is now increasingly recognized that many cultural processes are so complex and varied and that the chances of equifinality are so great that the neutralization of distorting influences cannot produce a complete interpretation of the archaeological record from a behavioural point of view (von Gernet 1985; P. Watson 1986: 450). As belief in neo-evolutionism wanes and the diversity of human behaviour increasingly is accepted, this limitation tends to be acknowledged as inherent in the data rather than as a methodological weakness. Hence, while archaeologists continue to apply Schiffer's approach profitably, many of them do not expect his full programme to be realized.

Binford (1977, 1981) has also contributed to a growing awareness of the distinctiveness of archaeology from anthropology with his emphasis on middle-range theory. He argues that the dependence of archaeological knowledge of human behaviour in the past on inference rather than direct observation often renders the independence of observations and explanations suspect and leads to the fallacy of 'confirming the consequent' (1981: 29). From this he concludes that archaeologists cannot use the archaeological record or the inferred past to test their premises and assumptions. To develop reliable means for knowing the past they must engage in middle-range research, which consists of actualistic studies designed to control for the relations between the dynamic properties of the past, about which they seek knowledge, and the static material properties common to past and present. As in his earlier work, Binford sees the key for understanding archaeological data from a positivist perspective as lying in the establishment of valid correlations between material culture, which archaeologists can observe, and behaviour, which they cannot. His present formulation clearly distinguishes, however, between general theory, which seeks to explain human behaviour, and middle-range theory, which is concerned with inferring such behaviour from archaeological data. Middle-range theory is therefore of interest exclusively to archaeology, as opposed to general theory, which is the common concern of all the social sciences.

Middle-range theory embraces acts of identification, such as distinguishing different classes of habitations, hide scrapers, or base camps, as well as diagnosing the economic, social, and ideological functions of artifacts. It also includes identifying patterns of human behaviour as these may relate to family organization, village structure, and political relations, although in this case growing respect is shown for the observation made long ago by David Aberle (1968) that concepts that are very useful for ethnographic interpretation may not be well suited for interpreting archaeological data. For example, archaeologists find it easier to deal with behavioural categories, such as matrilocal residence, than with jural concepts, such as matrilineal descent. Middle-range theory also subsumes the study of cultural and natural site-formation processes. It thus embraces the study of regularities in physical processes as well as in cultural behaviour. Much of Binford's (1984) most important research in recent years has involved using arguments about natural site-formation processes to challenge the human origin of many of the patterns observed in the archaeological record for Lower Palaeolithic times. He has shown that many of the data interpreted as evidence of big-game hunting or even major scavenging at that time could be merely natural distributions of bone in incidental association with traces of human activity. While this issue is far from settled, Binford's research has called into question the validity of some long-standing interpretations of early hominid behaviour. He has also demonstrated that, in their support of particular theories about hominid behaviour, archaeologists have failed to consider possible alternatives or to analyze the data sufficiently thoroughly.

Binford's concept of middle-range theory has stimulated an increasing amount of ethnoarchaeological research as well as experiments that duplicate the manufacture and use of prehistoric artifacts. Ruth Tringham (1978) has discussed how these two approaches can be combined to their mutual advantage, thereby carrying forward an argument originally advanced by Sven Nilsson 150 years earlier. Binford's (1978) own work exemplifies the careful application of ethnoarchaeological research to archaeological problems. His desire to understand the behavioural significance of the well-documented variability in the Mousterian assemblages of Western Europe led him to carry out fieldwork among modern hunting groups in Alaska. He has since applied what he learned about their economic and spatial behaviour to a whole series of problems relating to Old-World Palaeolithic archaeology (Binford 1983b).

At least two major difficulties have been identified with the use of middle-range theory. The first objection is that ethnoarchaeological studies are 'theory dependent' and 'paradigm relative' (Wylie 1989). Just as in archaeology, what is accepted as a valid correlation is partly influenced by the presuppositions of the investigator. The principal advantage of ethnoarchaeology, or any ethnographic study, is that behaviour is observed, not inferred, hence the opportunities for speculations to multiply are more limited.

A second and related problem is the relevance of middle-range theory for archaeological interpretations. Binford is aware that using present regularities to explain the past involves uniformitarian assumptions and argues that these claims must be warranted by supporting arguments. He suggests, for example, that the ecological and anatomical characteristics of still extant species which ancient human beings exploited are 'enduring objects for which uniformitarian assumptions might be securely warranted' (Binford 1981: 28) and expresses the hope that other domains can be elaborated as research progresses. Other archaeologists see these uniformitarian assumptions as involving as great a leap of faith as those Binford suggests affirm the consequent (P. Watson 1986: 447-8). Uniformitarian assumptions have their dangers. One of these is ignorance of what is happening at the present time. Scientists may misunderstand the past because they fail to take account of long-term processes, as was the case with geology prior to the recognition of plate tectonics and continental drift. Another problem is that social scientists may consider to be universal, characteristics of human behaviour that are specific to a particular stage of cultural development. Marxists, who believe that human nature is substantially altered by evolutionary change, are less willing to invoke universal features of human behaviour than are archaeologists who assume, along with the philosophers of the Enlightenment, that human behaviour remains unaltered by social change. Problems can also rise in applying analogies, because archaeologists are unable to distinguish what is characteristic of humanity in general (or of a particular mode of production) and what is specific only to historically related cultures. Anthropologists remain unable to distinguish on theoretical grounds between analogies, resulting from convergent evolution, and homologies, that owe their similarity to historical relations. Instead, they must do so empirically, using historical or archaeological evidence. The variety of forces bringing about social change also complicates the question of what modern societies can serve as true analogies of prehistoric ones. We have already noted that, while Binford found that the settlernent patterns of hunter-gatherers in high latitudes shared many features that distinguished them from hunter-gatherer patterns in warmer climates, all of these northern societies were engaged in trapping and selling furs to Europeans long before they were studied by anthropologists. We do not know whether the common features Binford described represent an ecological adaptation extending back thousands of years or had developed in recent centuries as a consequence of new economic rclations. In this case archaeological data about prehistoric settlement patterns are essential to provide insights into the developmental significance of modern behavioural patterns and produce convincing warranting arguments. Yet, despite such cautionary tales, a blanket rejection of uniformitarianism may be far more dangerous for the development of archaeology than its opposite. Despite this problem, middle-range theory is a very useful device for interpreting archaeological data.

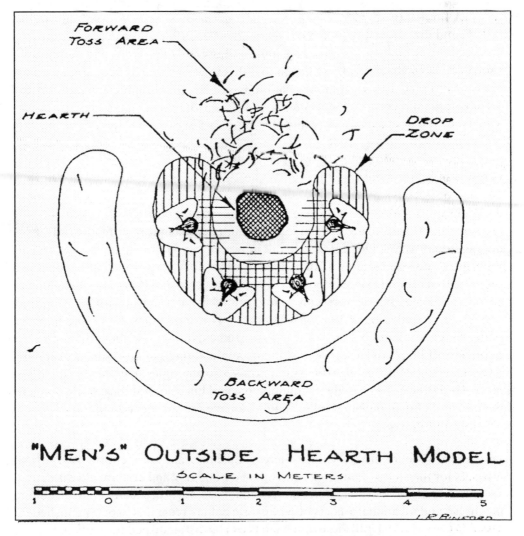

Figure 50   Model of drop and toss zones, as developed by Binford from his ethnoarchaeological study of the Nunamiut of Alaska

A more important limitation appears to be that human behaviour is considerably less uniform than Binford, as a neo-evolutionist, continues to believe. Much more ethnographic documentation is needed before we can agree with his assertion that all hunter-gatherers use their camp space in much the same way, producing easily recognizable features such as bedding areas, drop zones, toss zones, and aggregate dumping areas, and proceed to interpret all Palaeolithic archaeological sites in terms of models derived from the Bushmen and Nunamiut (Binford 1983b: 144-92). Even if the use of camp space can be proved to be relatively uniform, there are many aspects of human behaviour that cannot be accounted for in terms of universal generalizations, whether these concern behaviour in general or societies at specific levels of development (Watson *et al*. 1984: 264). Hence more culturally specific explanations, such as have been proposed by Hodder and other structuralist archaeologists, are likely to play an important role in explaining archaeological data alongside Binford's middle-range theory (von Gernet and Timmins 1987).

A final, more narrowly empiricist approach advocated by André Leroi-Gourhan (1968) and more recently by Robert Dunnell (1971, 1982b) seeks to separate archaeology from its ties with social anthropology and ethnology, and perhaps with the social sciences generally. It is alleged that this relationship has encouraged a flawed approach to archaeological interpretation, based on ethnographic analogy. Instead the archaeological record must be understood on its own terms. While Dunnell allows that aspects of the archaeological record that represent style rather than function cannot be encompassed by this approach, he believes that it facilitates the study of the evolutionarily significant portions of archaeological data, which are seen as explainable in terms of biophysical variables (cf. Wylie 1985b; Watson 1986: 444-6). Other archaeologists have proposed to explain archaeological data by employing principles derived from sociobiology (Nash and Whitlam 1985), a position that Dunnell (1980a: 60-6) specifically has repudiated. Both approaches require an arbitrary delineation of what is important and not important about human behaviour and also the ignoring of unique features of such behaviour that have developed in the course of biological evolution. More importantly, however, it has not been demonstrated that the empirical data of archaeology can be interpreted behaviourally without recourse to some sort of analogies (P. Watson 1986: 446). However much experimental work is done, for example in the form of use-wear studies, inferences about human behaviour permeate all levels of such research and its application to interpreting archaeological data. The danger is that uncritical common-sense analogies may unwarrantedly replace more disciplined ones based on ethnographic and historical studies. Valid concerns about the dangers of using ethnographic analogies have not succeeded in producing a credible alternative.

There is currently very little interest in the relevance of the formal classifications of artifacts for the study of problems other than chronology and cultural classification. The significance of formal variation for understanding ecological, social, political, ethnic, symbolic, and ideational aspects of prehistoric cultures remains to be established (Gardin 1980; C.Carr 1985). Until these dimensions can be distinguished formally in the archaeological record, a major techique for bridging the gap between the archaeological and behavioural spheres will remain unexploited.

Conclusions

The growing realization that archaeology is methodologically differentiated from the other social sciences because of its inability to observe human behaviour or speech first hand, particularly as represented by Binford's middle-range theory, closely parallels the arguments advanced by Klejn and his associates in the Soviet Union that archaeological data first must be understood in their own right before they can be used to study historical problems. In both cases the question arises whether a body of strictly archaeological theory that is concerned with inferring human behaviour from archaeological data can be more objective than high-level theories that are concerned with explaining human behaviour and are demonstrably influenced by archaeologists' responses to contemporary social issues. That archaeologists around the world, regardless of their political orientation, appear to be able to adopt each other's interpretive innovations while maintaining different high-level views of human behaviour, suggests that to some degree middle-range theory and the operations used to infer human behaviour from archaeological data may be relatively uninfluenced by social biases. Yet the formulation of middle-range theory involves the use of concepts that acquire their significance in social settings. This indicates that the differentiation between middle-range and general theory may not be as great in that respect as many archaeologists believe.

Although a few archaeologists maintain that deterministic forms of evolutionism are 'returning to center stage' (Dunnell in Rindos 1984: ix), most American and Western European ones seem to be increasingly convinced that human behaviour is complex and that accounting for its development requires nothing less than explaining the course of human history in all of its bewildering diversity and specificity. In their more extreme manifestations, these developments are moving in the direction of historical particularism, a doctrine that is in accord with the intellectual obfuscation and despair about effecting constructive change that are currently rampant in American popular culture. Yet most American archaeologists seem unlikely to reject the accomplishments of the last 30 years to embrace a form of neo-Boasianism, even if they judge the neo-evolutionism of the 1960s to be no longer tenable. They appear to be abandoning the idea that only aspects of culture that recur cross-culturally are worth understanding, to be trying to understand specific sequences of development in their historical complexity, and to be abandoning the proposition that prediction is the only form of explanation. At the same time archaeologists are likely to remain concerned with delineating and explaining cross-cultural regularities in human behaviour and to use these explanations, where they are appropriate, to understand specific sequences of development (P. Watson 1986: 442-3) In the future, evolutionary theory probably will be concerned not only with the regularities that societies exhibit as they develop from one level to another but equally with how adjacent interacting societies at different stages of development influence one another. For the first time we will have an evolutionary theory that is able to take account of colonial relations past and present and hence of some of the basic processes that have led to the development of anthropology and prehistoric archaeology. Finally Western archaeologists are likely to become increasingly aware of the relations between individuals and groups who study the past and how they view it, an awareness that should also reveal more clearly to archaeologists the nature of the contemporary Western societies in which they live.

The future perception of causality is harder to predict. There is good reason to believe that, if a respectable emphasis on understanding cross-cultural regularities persists, archaeologists will continue to regard material factors as significant constraints on human behaviour and therefore as major influences shaping cultural development. In all probability there will be less emphasis on specific technological and ecological factors and more on broader economic relations, as well as on constraints on social and political organizations provided by general systems theory. Ideologies, beliefs, and cultural traditions generally will be seen as part of the context in which economic change comes about. What is unclear is the importance that will be accorded to these factors and whether they will be interpreted as operating within the constraints set by economic and social conditions or as promoting major cultural changes in a more independent fashion. It is unlikely there will be unanimity on this topic. It is also uncertain whether concepts, such as planning, intentionality, and foresight, will play a significant role in understanding cultural change within either a materialist or a non-materialist framework, since they are theoretically compatible with both. For them to do so, archaeologists will have to adopt a much more critical role with respect to their social milieu than is currently the case.

Whatever happens, the growing sense of the unity and complementarity of historicism and evolutionism in Western archaeology should allow archaeological explanation to move beyond the vulgar materialism of processual archaeology, the sterile idealism of historical particularism, and the ersatz Marxism of the critical and structuralist approaches. This moderate shift, following a short period when neo-evolutionism was in the ascendant, would contrast with the radical swing from unilinear evolutionism to historical particularism at the end of the nineteenth century and the long periods during which each of these two extreme positions was dominant. If a similar radical swing does not occur today, it is at least partly because archaeologists have learned from experience the unproductiveness of these dichotomous and extreme views of human behaviour. This suggests that a body of procedures for inferring human behaviour has developed within Western archaeology that is now sufficiently mature to influence how it interprets its data, sometimes in opposition to external beliefs and values.

The Use of Analogy

Introduction

With this chapter, we encounter the writings of Ian Hodder directly. Hodder (1948-) may be considered one of the theoretical leaders In anthropological archaeology; as we have seen in Chapter 16, he is at the forefront of postprocessualist theory. Turning to a practice of field archaeologist, he became director of the Neolithic site of Çatalhöyük in Turkey.

Many artifacts can be identified by comparison with known examples that have the same or very similar form; this may seem easiest when dealing with utilitarian objects such as tools. With stone tools, for instance, the anthropologist may be able to make comparisons with recent or living cultures that use such objects. Scientific study, such as the examination of cutting edges, may confirm or refute the value of such comparisons. It may be argued that cross-cultural comparisons are our best method of identification, but using analogy becomes questionable in the case social/religious practices such as burial. How are we to use analogy in a more critical and reliable way? Based on distinctions made by philosophers of science, Hodder presents ways to make reliable inferences using analogy by considering first whether analogies are formal (sharing common properties), or relational (if there is a "natural link or cultural link between the between the different aspects of the analogy" (p. 323)). This means that more similarities of the aspects of the analogies make the assumption of a relationship more likely, and one might be more attentive to aspects that are dissimilar. Above all, Hodder considers the importance of context and

PRESENT PAST :AN INTRODUCTION TO ANTHROPOLOGY FOR ARCHAEOLOGISTS by HODDER, IAN. Copyright 1982 by PICA PRESS.

illustrates this with the evidence of disposing of waste materials, here addressing not only economy, technology, and environment, but value systems: what attitudes toward filth might a culture have?

W hen an archaeologist digs an object out of the ground and says 'this is an axe', how does he know? He may have dated the site from which the object comes to millenia before the first written records, so how does he know it is an axe? The answer is, really, that he doesn't. All he can do is make a reasonable guess based on the fact that the object he has in his hand from the past looks like axes he has seen in his own or in other contemporary societies. In the first half of the nineteenth century, the Danish scientist P.W. Lund sent back polished stone axes from Brazil to be compared with Danish antiquities (*fig. 1a*). This information supported early Scandinavian archaeologists such as Nilsson in their notion that similar artifacts found on their soil were indeed 'primitive' axes. Polished stone objects found widely in Europe (*fig. 1b*) have the shapes of axes with sharp edges; they are called axes on analogy with modern objects.

To support the axe interpretation the archaeologist might examine the edge of the artifact with a microscope to show that it has traces of wear from cutting; he might conduct experiments to show that it is possible to cut down a tree with such an object; and he could conduct pollen studies of the environment of the prehistoric site where the object was found to show that trees had been cut down in the vicinity. Yet all these subsidiary studies are developed to support or weaken the initial analogy.

Much the same could be said for nearly every other interpretation that the archaeologist makes about the past. He is rarely shown directly what prehistoric objects were used for. He has to guess, using analogies. So, when he finds a circle of post holes in the ground and says 'this is a house', he is influenced by evidence of modern round houses lived in by many Africans and American Indians (*fig. 2*).

Many such interpretations may seem obvious to the archaeologist and he may be unaware that he is using an analogy at all. It needs no specialist knowledge to describe an object as an axe, pin, dagger, sword, shield or helmet. And the notion that circles of post-holes indicate houses is so deeply enshrined in archaeological teaching that the archaeologist may not question the ethnographic origin of the idea. Other uses of ethnographic analogies are more conscious and calculated. When an attempt is made to reconstruct from fragments of archaeological evidence the organization of prehistoric social relations, exchange, burial ritual and ideologies, the archaeologist searches among traditional societies today, in Africa, Asia and America, or in historic Europe, for suitable parallels and analogies.

Figure 1

Archaeological and ethnographic stone axes.

A: **Polished axes from Brazil sent by Lund to the Royal Society of Northern Antiquaries in Copenhagen (Klindt-Jensen 1976).**

So, in nearly every interpretation he makes of the past, the archaeologist has to draw on knowledge of his own or other contemporary societies in order to clothe the skeleton remains from the past in the flesh and blood of living, functioning and acting people. The drawing of analogies would thus seem to play a central role in archaeological reasoning. Yet recently, many archaeologists have tried to diminish the use of analogies because they are unreliable, unscientific and limiting. Why is this?

Problems with analogies

An interpretation of the past using an analogy is thought to be unreliable because, if things and societies in the present and past are similar in some aspects, this does not necessarily mean they are similar in others. As an example of this difficulty we might take Grahame Clark's (1954) reconstruction of life at the Mesolithic site of Star Carr in Yorkshire, England. Clark suggests (1954, 10-12) that the evidence of skin-working at Star Carr argues for the presence of women on analogy with the hunting peoples of North America and Greenland. Amongst the Caribou Eskimos women are mainly responsible for flaying the kill and preparing the skins for use, and Clark suggests the same for his Mesolithic hunter-gatherers from Yorkshire. On the basis of the presence of women, Clark further postulates the number of people living at Star Carr, and the form of subdivision of labor. The environment, technology and hunting-gathering economy of the

Star Carr inhabitants and the Eskimos are, very vaguely and broadly, comparable. But are these general similarities in some spheres sufficient to allow us to infer correlations in others? There seems no reason to suppose that skin working amongst modern Eskimos and at 7200 BC Star Carr was carried out by the same sex just because they both had broadly the same economy and environment. Clark's interpretation seems highly unreliable.

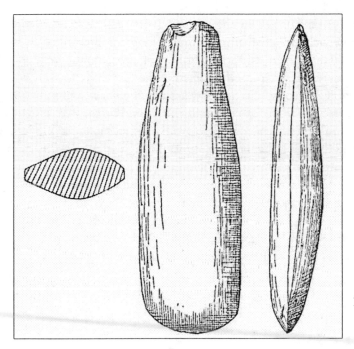

B: **Neolithic stone axe from Cambridgeshire, England**

Clark, in the Star Carr example, seems to be assuming a deterministic 'uniformitarianism'; he supposes that societies and cultures similar in some aspects are uniformly similar. Such a view is unreliable, especially given the great spans of time over which the comparisons are being made and given the great diversity of present-day cultural forms. Clark happened to use the North American Eskimos, but he could have chosen other societies where men prepare the skins.

If analogies are unreliable, they must also be unscientific. Or so the argument goes. It has been implied by many archaeologists recently that we can never check or prove analogies because we can always find alternative analogies which would fit the data from the past equally well. Because similarities in some aspects do not necessarily, certainly or logically imply similarities in others, we can never prove interpretations such as Grahame Clark's at Star Carr. Such archaeological interpretation is seen as subjective story-writing, pure speculation without any scientific basis.

While it will be explained below why charges of unreliability and anti-science are only really relevant to the misuse of analogy, a charge that analogical reasoning limits and restricts our knowledge of the past also needs to be considered. It seems logically to be the case that, if we interpret the past by analogy to the present, we can never find out about forms of society and culture which do not exist today (Dalton 1981). We are limited in our interpretation to our knowledge of present-day societies. Since these societies, industrialized and non-industrialized, represent a highly specialized set of interlinked economic, social and cultural adaptations, it seems unlikely that they adequately represent the full range of social forms that existed in the past. So we would never be able to understand the full variety of prehistoric societies. Anyway, what would be the point of repeating our knowledge of contemporary societies by tagging labels on to societies in the past?

The various criticisms of the use of analogy in archaeology have led to some extreme statements rejecting analogical reasoning in archaeological interpretation. Freeman (1968, 262) claimed that 'the most serious failings in present models for interpreting archaeological evidence are directly related to the fact that they incorporate numerous analogies with modern groups'. While few archaeologists would now go as far as Freeman, it is widely accepted that the use of analogies should be limited. Ucko (1969) has indicated the possible pitfalls in interpreting past burial practices using analogies, and Binford (1967) has indicated that analogical reasoning is of little value unless associated with a rigorous, scientific testing procedure. Tringham (1978, 185) also suggests that we should try and move away from discovering analogies which can be fitted to archaeological data, while Gould (1978a) has attempted to move 'beyond analogy'. I will try to show that these assessments of the value of analogy in archaeology are clouded by a misconception of the nature and proper use of analogy. It will then be possible to reassess the supposed unreliable, unscientific and limiting features of analogies.

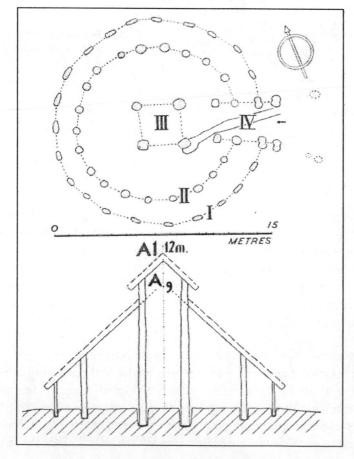

Figure 2

Circles of post-holes and round houses.

A: Circles of post holes from the Iron Age site of Little Woodbury, England, reconstructed by Bersu (1940).

B: A modern round house in Kenya

The proper use of analogy

As a form of inference, 'analogy' can be defined as the 'transportation of information from one object to another on the basis of some relation of comparability between them' (Umeov 1970; Wylie 1980). The proper use of such analogies has been discussed by philosophers of science (Hesse 1974;Copi 1954;Umeov 1970) and from their work we can draw some general conclusions (see Wylie 1980).

A distinction can be made between *formal* and *relational* analogies. According to a formal analogy it is suggested that, if two objects or situations have some common properties, they probably also have other similarities. Such analogies are weak in that the observed association of characteristics of the objects or situations may be fortuitous or accidental. So other analogies, of the relational kind, seek to determine some natural or cultural link between the different aspects in the analogy. The various things associated within the analogy are said to be interdependent and not accidentally linked.

There is in fact a continuum of variation from the more formal to the more relational analogy. Unfortunately, most archaeological uses of analogy have tended to cluster at the more formal end of the scale. Clark's interpretation at Star Carr is really a formal analogy in that the Mesolithic site and the Eskimos are said to be similar in certain aspects (environment, technology and economy) and are 'therefore' similar in other aspects (women do the skin preparation). No link is suggested by Clark between the two parts of his analogy; we are not told why females prepare skins in such environments, technologies and economies. Other examples abound. In the late Iron Age in southern England, four or six post-holes are frequently found on hillforts and settlement sites arranged in a square averaging 3m by 3m. Analogies with contemporary and recent societies suggested to Bersu (1940) that these post-holes contained posts holding up granaries with raised floors (*fig. 3*). The formal similarity in the square of posts in past and present agricultural societies was taken as indicating a similar above-ground function.

Figure 3   **The interpretation of four-post arrangements as granaries.**

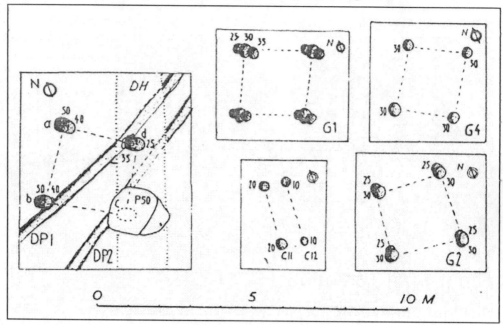

A: **Arrangements of four post-holes at the Iron Age site at Little Woodbury, England (Bersu 1940).**

B: **A modern raised granary and store of the Tugen in Kenya. For other modern examples *see fig. 30*.**

How can such formal analogies be strengthened? Most obviously, the more similarities that can be identified between the two situations being compared, the more likely are other similarities to be expected. A formal analogy becomes more reasonable as the number of similarities increases. At some point, the volume and detail of comparable points become so great that it is unreasonable to suppose differences in the few aspects for which comparability is unknown. So, in the Star Carr example, if we could list a very large number of ways in which the prehistoric site was a replica of a modern Eskimo site, similarities in the 'unknowns', including who prepared the skins, might be thought to be expected. Similarities between the 'squareness' of post-hole arrangements in past and present sites could be augmented by examining the detailed dimensions of the post-holes, their widths and depths, by considering the soil conditions, the presence of vermin and damp which might cause the above-ground storage of grain to be necessary, and by searching for evidence of grain in the post- holes. As the number of similarities between past post-hole arrangements and present above-ground granaries increases, the interpretation of the Iron Age feature in terms of a granary becomes more acceptable

One way in which the number of formal similarities between a past and present situation can be increased is by comparing a recent archaeological site with modern sites in the same area. Thus, in North America it is sometimes possible to interpret prehistoric palaeo-Indian sites on the basis of analogy with modern or historically recorded surviving Indian groups in the same vicinity. In Africa, also, continuity between archaeological and ethnographic data can frequently be assumed. Such comparisons make up what is called the *direct historical approach* in archaeology. Where continuity between the past and present can be assumed, it is easier to acknowledge many formal similarities between the information being compared.

If the direct historical approach cannot be followed, formal analogies can be further strengthened by a very different strategy. Rather than simply increasing the number of similarities between the source and the subject of the analogy, the range of instances in which various characteristics of the analogy are associated can be emphasized. Thus, if it could be shown that, whatever the environment or economy, skin working was always carried out by women, then Clark's interpretation at Star Carr would have greater validity. Similarly, if it could be shown that patterns of post-holes with particular detailed dimensions were, in modern and historical examples, always associated with above-ground granaries, then the Iron Age interpretation would be more believable. In fact, neither of these two correlations can be made. Yet it remains possible to substantiate the use of an analogy by demonstrating its wide range. In recent archaeology, such wide-ranging statements, valid across different cultures and environments, have sometimes been declared *cross-cultural laws.*

Schiffer, one of the main exponents of the development of cross- cultural laws, or 'correlates', has provided many examples. He describes (1978, 233) the law taken from Yellen's detailed ethnographic studies that the diversity of maintenance activities performed at a settlement varies directly with the length of occupation'. Thus the 'law', which in this case is little more than an expression of association, states that the longer a group of people stays in the same place, the more different types of activities it will perform. Schiffer (ibid., 244) shows that this observation has been made independently in a range of very different situations. In suggesting the credibility of the analogy, appeal is made to the great range of societies and cultures where the suggested relationship between length of occupation and number of activities holds true.

A third aspect of the strengthening of formal analogies can be identified. The conclusions drawn from the analogy should not be too ambitious in relation to the number of similarities between the source and subject. In Clark's example, very little attention is paid to listing the similarities between Star Carr and Eskimo hunters and yet the interpretations made are highly ambitious. However, a cautious and modest interpretation based on a large number of correspondences may be seen to be more acceptable.

However much we might reinforce our analogies by increasing the number and range of similarities between past and present objects and situations, comparisons made at the formal end of the scale will always remain shrouded in unreliability and will always remain easy prey for ridicule and for charges of anti-science. In particular, it will always be possible to provide examples where the suggested association or correlation breaks down. The depressing tone of Ucko's (1969) article on analogies for the interpretation of burial remains derives from the ease with which he can show that various aspects of burial, such as cremation, the body lying looking to the east, or the presence of rich graves, may mean very different things in different societies. The recent archaeological literature abounds with 'cautionary tales' which show how easily archaeologists can make mistakes in using particular analogies since alternative interpretations can be found. Archaeologists have delighted in visiting recently abandoned camps, interpreting the remains as archaeologists, and then asking the inhabitants of the site what actually occurred there. Invariably, the archaeologists' interpretations are shown to be wrong.

All such pessimism and caution derive from an overemphasis on formal as opposed to relational analogies. Of course, different analogies can be found to fit the same set of archaeological data if we simply look for formal similarities in the arrangement of post-holes and if we simply list associations of traits. Analogies, from wherever they are derived, must be deemed to be relevant to the subject of study in the past. I have applied Central Place Theory, derived from modern locational studies of the arrangement of towns in Germany, to Roman Britain. This use of analogy has been rightly criticized (Hodder 1975) because it is irrelevant to pre-industrialised societies such as existed in Roman Britain.

Relational analogies are thus concerned to demonstrate that similarities between past and present situations are relevant to the 'unknowns' that are being interpreted, whereas the differences that can be observed do not really matter; they are not really relevant because there is little link between what is different and what is suggested as being the same. Archaeological uses of analogy often do imply, although they rarely state, some necessary relationship between the various aspects of the analogies. But the relationships that are suggested are nearly always functional. Examination of four-post above-ground granaries indicates that they may function to keep out vermin and to keep the grain dry. The longer a site is occupied, the more functions are necessarily carried out there and so a wider range of debris and waste products is found.

The attempts which have been made in archaeology to use and develop relational analogies have aimed to define the contexts in which different properties of societies and cultures are functionally interdependent. It is thought to be possible to demonstrate that 'in certain conditions C, if A, then necessarily B'. The supposition is made that the material culture which the archaeologist digs up functioned in a particular way. So if, in the past, a group of people had a certain style of life, then material culture was used in particular ways; material culture patterning can be predicted because of its functional relationships with other aspects of life.

For many, the existence of such predictable functional links has meant that analogies can be scientifically tested against archaeological data. It is suggested (e.g. Gould 1978; Tringham 1978) that we can find present-day analogies for our data from the past, but that the unreliability of these analogies can be decreased by 'testing' their consequences in the material remains. This widely held illusion that the charge of anti-science can be avoided by a particular form of 'testing' of analogy against data derives from Binford's much quoted example of the use of analogy in archaeology. It is worth briefly considering Binford's (1967) account in order to demonstrate the false character of the claims for the 'hypothetico-deductive' testing of analogies and in order to show the nature of relational analogies.

Binford discusses the interpretation of 'smudge pits', 'caches', small pits filled with carbonised corncobs in Mississipian sites and dated from AD 470 until recent times. He describes their archaeological distribution, shape and size, and he then lists ethnographic examples of similar pits which are used for smoking hides. He demonstrates that the archaeological and ethnographic pits occur in approximately the same region in North America, that they have the same form, and that there is possible continuity between the archaeological and ethnographic examples (so the direct historical approach is being used). Binford proposes that the archaeological pits were used for hide smoking.

It is of interest to note that, up to this point in Binford' analysis, he has used a largely formal analogy. The relationship between the archaeological pits and hide smoking is based on the formal similarity of he sizes, shapes and contents of the ethnographic pits, on the formal similarity in their distribution, and presumably on other similarities implied by the continuity of societies through time. But Binford then says that he can 'test' his interpretation by drawing deductively a set of secondary expectations.

The deductive predictions are based on functional links between hide smoking and other aspects of life. Binford suggests that other activities involved in hide smoking might be identified archaeologically in the vicinity of the 'smudge pits'. He notes that, ethnographically, hide smoking was carried out in a spring and summer 'base camp' so that the 'smudge pits' should occur, archaeologically, in sites occupied during these seasons. In addition, in the ethnographic cases, hide smoking was women's work, so stylistic variation in 'smudge pits' should vary directly with variation in other female-produced items such as pots.

Binford presents his secondary predictions as testable hypotheses within the framework of a scientific deductive and positivist explanation, breaking away from subjective interpretations which use analogies. But in view of the discussion above it is apparent that Binford, in the second part of his analysis, has simply shown how the formal analogy could be supported by increasing the number of similarities. It could also be claimed that various functional links are being assumed between hide smoking and other activities. By searching for such additional and functionally relevant similarities between the past and present situations which are being compared, Binford strengthens his interpretation and moves towards a relational analogy.

Binford's interpretation of 'smudge pits' is not a good example of the use of the hypothetico-deductive method. If a true deductive argument had been followed there would have to be some logically necessary link (Binford 1972, 70 calls it a logico-deductive argument) between his predictions and the use of 'smudge pits' as hide smoking facilities. But no such logical necessity can be demonstrated in this instance. For example, it does not seem at all logical to me that all artifacts, including 'smudge pits', associated with women should show the same stylistic variation. It would need to be explained to me *why* pots made by women should be linked in an argument to 'smudge pits' made by women. In other words, I would search for a relational analogy which examined more adequately the relevant causal links between the different parts of the analogy. When archaeologists claim a 'logically deduced' argument, they are usually simply imposing their own assumptions on the data. In a relational analogy all the linking arguments must be examined in relation to a clearly defined and explained cultural context, in which the various functional activities take their place. More generally, archaeologists need to examine why one variable (such as pot variation) is relevant to another (such as smudge pits) when using an analogy. There must be greater concern with causal relationships rather than simply with associations. But our assessment of cause and relevance is always likely to be influenced by our own cultural and personal preconceptions. The use by archaeologists of the hypothetico-deductive method recognized this problem of subjectivity and tried to overcome the biasses by rigorous testing of hypotheses against data. But this notion is misconstrued because, as well as considering the data, we consider or assume causal relationships lying behind the data.

If Binford was really using a logico-deductive argument, we would expect the secondary predictions to lead to valid independent tests of the initial proposition that 'smudge pits' were used for hide smoking. In fact, the second tests of data are not independent of the first. The identification of other activities involved in hide smoking near the 'smudge pits' would support the analogy, but they do not 'test' the proposition. The archaeologists' interpretation of tools as used for hide smoking activities may itself be influenced by the proposition that is to be tested. In addition, no matter how many times pits and tools are found in association, the pits may still have been used for some other purpose, with the hide smoking activities carried out around them. We need to know much more of the cultural framework within which these various activities were carried out and why they were associated together. The analogy can be supported by examining the cultural interdependence between the different aspects of data, but it cannot be 'tested' on independent data. The whole process of inference is one of building up an edifice of hypotheses, adding one to another and moving beyond the data in order to explain them. In such a procedure there is always the possibility of error, incorrect assumptions, faulty logic, biassed observation and so on. We cannot prove or disprove, partly because our predictions and expectations (the 'test') may themselves be incorrectly construed, but also because there are no independent data, and a great deal of subjectivity is involved.

I have discussed little the disproof of theories, and yet refutation is seen by many archaeologists as an important aspect of their scientific methods, derived from Karl Popper. But in my view one cannot disprove in an absolute sense in archaeology any more than one can prove. I have shown how we can support a hypothesis by considering (a) relevance, (b) generality, (c) goodness-of-fit (number of similarities between object and analogy). Many archaeologists would agree that one cannot prove a hypothesis because other hypothetical processes could produce the same observed pattern. But they would say we can disprove a hypothesis if the predictions of the hypothesis are not verified in empirical data. However, the prediction is itself based on a hypothesis which may be incorrect. Any disproof is itself a hypothesis. For example, say I have made the hypothesis that, on analogy with modern societies and environments, a past shell-collecting society concentrated on the larger and more nutritious shell type A in order to maximise the resource potential in the environment. Consider the situation in which I find that on the prehistoric site there is mostly the smaller shell type B and few shells of type A. Can I say I have disproved the maximisation hypothesis? Clearly not, since there may be other reasons why few type A shells were found on the site. Type A shells may have been discarded elsewhere even though they were the most abundant species collected. The general problem here is that the predictions are not necessary outcomes of the behavioral hypothesis. In Binford's smudge pit example, if the styles of pots made by women do not correlate with the styles of pits, the hypothesis that the pits were used for hide smoking is not disproved. The hypothesis may, if the reader accepts Binford's assumptions about the causes of stylistic variability, be weakened but not disproved since the hypotheses (that the pits were for hide smoking and that women made the pits and the pots) may be correct but the prediction (that the styles of pits and pots should correlate) may be incorrect. The archaeologist can never test the validity of the predictions themselves because there are no data available from the past concerning the relationship between material culture and human activity. In the shell-collecting example, we could never be certain that shells of a certain type had been deposited in such a way that archaeologists would find them. So, although we can support or weaken hypotheses by arguments of relevance, generality and goodness-of-fit, we cannot test or refute in any absolute or final way.

The 'smudge pits' example does illustrate that it would be possible to be rigorous in the use of analogies if the number and range of similarities are great and if relationships between the different aspects of the analogy could be adequately specified. After the publication of Binford's interpretation of the pits as for hide smoking, Munsen (1969) suggested an alternative hypothesis that they were used in the smudging of ceramics. In his reply to Munsen's suggestion, Binford (1972) rightly indicated that it would be possible to differentiate between the two interpretations by examining other linked aspects of the use of the pits for the two alternative functions. Thus, by examining the causal relationships in a particular cultural context between the pits and other activities which also might be identifiable in the archaeological record, it becomes possible to differentiate between competing analogies.

Relational analogies and the notion of the context of the things being compared can now be seen to be essential aspects of the proper use of analogy in archaeology. We can avoid the charges of unreliability and anti-science by increasing the number and range of points of comparison between past and present, but also by identifying the relevance of the comparisons. We have to understand the variables which are relevant to the interpretation of particular features of cultural evidence; we must have a better idea of the links between the properties we are interested in and their context. As I have already indicated, the links and the contexts in which archaeologists have recently been most interested concern function. What I wish to do now is develop the idea, to be examined more fully later in this book, that the notion of context must include not only function, but also the ideational realm.

Context

It may be helpful to begin with an example. We shall see in Chapters 3 and 5 that many archaeologists have recently attempted to make generalizations about the way people living in settlements organize and deposit their refuse. Schiffer (1976) and Binford (1978), for example, have suggested several cross-cultural relationships between discard behavior and size of site, length of occupation, amount of effort put into making a tool, and so on. For example, it has been suggested that, with longer and more intense occupation on a site, there is more secondary removal and clearance of refuse away from activity areas. This is a functional relationship concerned with the need to keep areas habitable and clean, and with the likelihood of secondary kicking and removal as population densities increase. Now, while the theoretical statements concerning such cross-cultural generalizations do note the importance of describing the conditions under which the relationship holds, in practice the conditions, the context, are not well defined. The 'law' is supposed to be universal, or the context is simply pushed off to the side under the heading 'other things being equal' (Binford 1976). There is rarely any analysis of what the 'other things' might be except in so far as analysis is made of technological, economic and environmental constraints. We have already seen how dangerous it is to assume that aspects of the material environment are sufficient to define a context for the relationship between variables.

In the studies of refuse, no emphasis has been placed on how peoples' attitudes to dirt and rubbish might affect the functional relationships between discard patterns and site size and occupation intensity. Yet there are many anthropological studies, which will be discussed in Chapter 5, that demonstrate how our conceptions of what is dirt and our concern with keeping things clean are very much dependent on local frameworks of meaning. Attitudes to refuse vary from society to society, and from group to group within societies; just consider the dirt and rubbish piling up around a gypsy camp site in England and the offence that is given to many of the hygienic, sparkling pillars of non-gypsy society; or the contrived dirtiness and dishevelled aspect of hippies breaking away from the attitudes, standards and interests of their middle-class parents who are concerned with tidiness, manners and impeccably clean self-presentation. There can be no simple functional links between refuse and types of site, lengths of occupation or forms of society, because attitudes and conceptions intervene.

The notion of context, then, must concern both functional and ideological aspects of life. In developing the use of analogy in archaeology the emphasis must be on examining *all* the different aspects of context which might impinge upon particular characteristics of material culture. But this more developed notion of context implies that every context is unique. The framework of meaning within which we carry out day-to-day actions is a unique combination of ideas, strategies and attitudes. And the symbolism given to material culture within such a meaningful context is likely to be peculiar to that context.

In the discussion of relational analogies it was suggested that it is possible to answer the criticisms that analogies are unreliable and unscientific. But a third problem with analogies was also identified in the first part of this chapter: analogies from the present limit our understanding of the past. The emphasis on the unique nature of each context aggravates the problem. If each context in which material culture is used represents a peculiar arrangement of meanings and ideas and personal strategies, how can we ever use a present context to interpret evidence from the past?

This is not such a difficult question to answer as it might seem at first sight. The problem of the contextual nature of material culture patterning can be examined in two ways. First, each unique cultural context is assembled from general principles of meaning and symbolism, which are often used in comparable ways. Thus, in many societies dirt is used as a symbol of rejection of the control and authority of dominant groups. So, Gypsies use dirt to contradict the non-Gypsy society in which they live in much the same way as hippies use dirt and disorder to defy the generation and society of their parents. One aim of the development of the use of analogies is to increase our understanding of how aspects of material culture patterning such as dirt and disorder can be used in personal and group strategies. The general principles of material symbolism must be examined. But in developing generalizations about symbolism it is essential to pay particular attention to the links with other variables, and to the conditions under which a particular type of symbolism might be used. Clearly not all minority groups use dirt as a part of their rejection of authority. We need to examine carefully what other factors are relevant and how they are linked. If we know a lot about how aspects of material culture (such as dirt or burial) are used and given meaning, if we know a lot about the links between material culture and its functional and meaningful context, then we can interpret new situations, unique cultural arrangements beyond present-day experience. We can interpret how the new cultural 'whole' has been assembled from general principles which are well understood.

Second, in all uses of analogy it is necessary to define what aspects of the things being compared are similar, disimilar or of uncertain likeness. The aim is to throw light on what is not known (the uncertain likeness) by demonstrating the strength and relevance of the positive analogy, while showing that the negative likenesses are of limited consequence. So, all analogical reasoning accepts that there will be some differences between the things being compared. We can set the past beside the present even if some aspects of the contexts do differ. Indeed, Gould (1978) has suggested a 'contrastive' approach which moves 'beyond analogy'. He indicates that we can use modern situations as base lines *against* which to compare evidence from the past. In fact Gould's contrasts do not lead to a different approach; they are an integral part of the use of analogy.

It is important, then, to be able to decide whether the differences between a past and present situation are enough to invalidate the use of a particular positive analogy. In making such a decision it is essential to understand the factors which link variables of material culture to their context, as suggested in the first point above. For example, I have compared the use of material culture to mark ethnic group distinctions in modern Kenya and Iron Age Britain (Blackmore, Braithwaite and Hodder 1979) even though the pattern of annual rainfall differs considerably in the two places. I feel it is valid to make such a comparison because my studies of ethnic group expression identified no direct link to rainfall patterns. However, it would be invalid to draw analogies from the Kenyan area in order to interpret Iron Age farming practices in Britain, since rainfall regime and agricultural systems are closely linked. Depending on the analogy being made, different aspects of context are more, or less, relevant to an assessment of the validity of the analogy and interpretation.

It is possible to interpret the manipulation of material items in a unique context in the past by (a) referring to general principles of symbolism and to generalisations about the links between those principles and the context in which they are used, and by (b) carefully using selected analogies for different aspects of the evidence, identifying similarities and differences, and gradually building up from bits and pieces to an understanding of how the whole picture is composed.

In my answer to the problem of how to use analogies if each situation, past and present, is unique, it has become evident that two types of analogy are necessary; (a) it is valid to suggest general theories about the relationship between material culture and social and economic aspects of life as long as the links to context are understood; (b) with that general theoretical knowledge, it is possible to assess which aspects of each particular analogy are relevant. The use of relational analogies depends on a good theoretical framework within which one can identify what is relevant in a particular case.

Examples of the peculiar and particular nature of modern material culture patterning are important as archaeologists carefully select analogies to build up, from bits and pieces, to an assessment of the whole in each context. An interest in the particular as opposed to the general is also essential since the traditional societies that remain for us to study today are often highly specialized to particular environments and ways of life. Indeed it is probable that types of society which were common in the past are represented by only one or a few examples today. Particular modes of manipulation of material culture may be extremely rare today. There will always be a place for the unique and the odd, even if only to provide a contrast.

Conclusion

On the whole the criticisms that have been made of the use of analogy in archaeology should be restricted to its misuse. Interpretation with the aid of analogies is unreliable and non-rigorous when the similarities between the things being compared are few in number and when the relevance of the comparison cannot be adequately demonstrated. The proper use of analogy in archaeology must pay special attention to context; that is, to the functional and ideological framework within which material items are used in everyday life. Most recent discussions of analogy in archaeology have considered cross-cultural laws which note the co-occurrence of different aspects of material culture and society. Such studies pay too little attention to when and why covariation occurs. It is necessary to examine not only the *existence* and *strength* of covariation, but also its *nature* and cause. It is only when archaeologists understand more fully the conditions and context in which certain things hold true that the use of analogies can be seen to be reliable and rigorous.

Several archaeologists have recently attempted to diminish the role of analogies by suggesting that analogies should simply be used for the forming of propositions about the past. The real guts of a scientific archaeology is then said to be in the deduction of the consequences of the proposition and in the testing of those implications in independent archaeological evidence. In fact, the nearest the archaeologist can get to a rigorous method is the careful use of a relational analogy. The analogy is situated within its relevant context.

For the moment it is difficult to see how archaeologists might break away from their dependence on analogies with the present; or why they should want to do so. I have tried to show in this chapter the importance of analogy in archaeology, and I have attempted to demonstrate that the use of present analogies does not entirely limit our interpretations of the past. While it is true that all our interpretations of human behavior and thought are affected by the society in which we live, it is also true that we can comprehend different societies, cultures and economies in other parts of the world, and that we can use this additional information in describing and explaining the past. As archaeologists our dependence on other societies, other behaviour and ways of thought always has been, and remains, immense. The links with ethnography and anthropology are close, as Chapter 2 shows.

CHAPTER 18

Ethnoarchaeology

Introduction

Hodder's espousal of the use of ethnoarchaeology, that is, researching present societies for comparison with archaeological interpretation, looking broadly in terms of cultural uses and mechanisms, and more narrowly, to understand the employment of an artifact and values attached to it by the society that uses it. The stress is on "the development of theories about the relationships between the characteristics of ethnic groups and why they change."(p. 335) A comparison is made between various forms of "experimental archaeology," in which situations resemble laboratory experiments in which variables can be controlled to help determine the feasibility of interpretation: in this way archaeological interpretations might be "tested." Hodder considers this "experimental" method most useful or most valid in showing how something is likely to have been made, but is less helpful in suggesting why it occurs.

PRESENT PAST :AN INTRODUCTION TO ANTHROPOLOGY FOR ARCHAEOLOGISTS by HODDER, IAN. Copyright 1982 by PICA PRESS.

An important source of analogies, although as we shall see not the only source, is difficult to label since almost every word which is commonly used brings with it offence. But I hope that, if I talk of traditional, less-industrialised contemporary societies, my meaning will be understood. In the last 25 years archaeologists have begun to carry out field studies amongst traditional societies in order to answer questions of archaeological interpretation and in order to develop and examine analogies. It is this type of work which is called ethnoarchaeology.

First, some definitions. Although the word 'ethnoarchaeology' was used in 1900 by Fewkes, it has only recently become a popular term. Yet there is a divergence of opinion as to its meaning. Gould (1978b) and Stiles (1977) define it as the comparison of ethnographic and archaeological data. This definition seems hopelessly broad, especially if one accepts that all archaeological interpretation involves making analogies with present-day societies. Nearly all archaeological interpretation could then be described as ethnoarchaeology. Stanislawski (1974), on the other hand, defines ethnoarchaeology as being a field study and it is easier to concur with such a viewpoint. Ethnoarchaeology is the collection of original ethnographic data in order to aid archaeological interpretation. This second definition coincides more closely with current usage than does the first. The armchair archaeologist leafing through ethnographic tomes is less likely to retort 'I am doing some ethnoarchaeology', than is an archaeologist conducting his own ethnographic field research.

There is often confusion about the relationship between ethnography, ethnology and anthropology and it is perhaps necessary to clarify these terms. Ethnography is the analytical study of contemporary ethnic groups; an examination of their material, social and linguistic characteristics. Ethnology, on the other hand, is the development of theories about the relationships between the characteristics of ethnic groups and about why they change. Ethnology has tended to be concerned with simpler, non-literate peoples, so leaving the more complex industrialised societies to sociology, geography, etc. Anthropology is a wider set of sciences, which in North America includes archaeology, but which in Britain does not, concerned with the study of man, usually simpler, less industrialised man. It is a generalising discipline which includes both ethnography and ethnology. For further definitions and distinctions between European and American terminologies the reader is referred to Rouse (1972)

Relations with experimental approaches in archaeology

Contemporary traditional societies are not the only source of analogies for the archaeologist. Analogies can also be derived from studies of material culture in our own, highly industrialised societies as will be shown in Chapter 9, and such work is also called ethnoarchaeology. But in our own societies archaeologists can also set up artificial experiments in order to draw further analogies with the past. Both experimental archaeology (Coles 1973; 1979) and computer simulation (Hodder 1978b) are concerned to test the feasibility of particular archaeological interpretations. They differ from ethnoarchaeology in several ways. In the first place, an experiment such as firing pots in a kiln in order to see what methods and kilns could have been used in the past can be truly experimental in that different trials can be made, the conditions and temperature in the kiln can be accurately monitored and recorded, and variables can be controlled. The simulation of a hypothesised process of prehistoric exchange on the computer can be even more carefully controlled, with huge numbers of different trials being 'run' and the effects of different variables carefully examined and experimented with. In an ethnoarchaeological study, on the other hand, there is little experimental control. One is above all an observer and an asker of questions; one cannot try this and that and see what happens.

What ethnoarchaeology loses in experimental control it gains in 'realism'. The ethnoarchaeologist does not study an artificial environment that he has created (although we shall see in the discussion of field methods that some qualification is needed here). He can fit the firing of pottery in a kiln into its total social, cultural and economic context, and he can observe all the possibly relevant variables. The experimental archaeologist, on the other hand, has created an artificial situation, even though trying to duplicate as closely as possible the prehistoric information. The experimental archaeologist tries to learn and implement craft techniques to which he is unaccustomed and which his society has long forgotten. Apart from these practical difficulties, the experiment is carried out in a vacuum so that links with the social, cultural and ideological aspects of life are difficult to identify. While he may be able to examine the effects of technological and natural variables in his experiments, the experimental archaeologist is at a loss to assess the broader context which, in Chapter 1, was suggested as being of such importance. Computer simulation is totally artificial. Any analogies that derive from such work depend entirely on the assumptions that the archaeologist has fed into the computer. The working of the computed model depends on the second-hand ethnographic and experimental information.

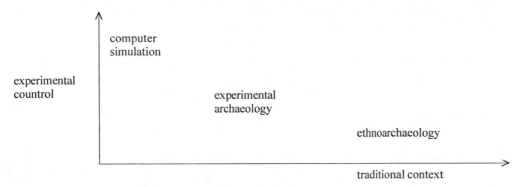

Figure 4   **Some aspects of the relationship between computer simulation, experimental archaeology and ethnoarchaeology**

Experimental archaeology involves the carrying out of experiments in order to test beliefs about archaeological data. We have seen that it is less realistic, but more controlled than ethnoarchaeology. But ethnoarchaeology has one possible additional advantage over its rival. It can be claimed to be less ethnocentric. Any experiment carried out within our own society is bound by the assumptions and knowledge of that society. The extent to which we can broaden our ideas about the past by conducting experiments in modern Western society is limited. Ethnoarchaeology, on the other hand, is able more radically to confront the Western archaeologist with alternative behavior. The ethnocentric bias can more readily be broken. However, there is a danger that we substitute one type of ethnocentricism with another, and I have already shown in Chapter 1 that analogies must not be taken over wholesale from one modern traditional society to a prehistoric society. There is a need for careful selection and control of analogies.

Attempts have been made by some archaeologists to combine the advantages of ethnoarchaeology and experimental archaeology by carrying out limited but controlled experiments in traditional contexts. One example is the experiment conducted by White and Thomas (1972) in which native New Guineans were asked to carry out experiments in stone tool manufacture. Duna-speaking people from the Central Highlands of Papua-New Guinea were asked by the ethnoarchaeologists to make traditional stone tools and the variation in form of the tools made by men in different parishes could then be analysed. Such an experiment carried out by ethnoarchaeologists has the advantage that the analysis, and the discovery of the variables which are thought to have most affect on tool variation, can be controlled and sufficiently large samples can be obtained. But there are also disadvantages. In particular, the ethnoarchaeologist is no longer an observer of traditional behavior. He isolates activities from their context and he intrudes himself starkly onto the scene. He brings an artificiality and the context, normally such an important constituent of ethnoarchaeological work, is eroded. We end up knowing very little about the conditions under which the relationships identified by White and Thomas might hold true, so that it is difficult to use their results in other contexts.

Experimental archaeology is of greatest value in understanding how things could have been made and used, and in identifying the natural properties of materials such as flint when flaked by man or stone when used to cut down trees. But in answering 'why' questions which seek to relate technologies and economies to broader social and cultural contexts, the approach is limited.

History of the use of ethnographic analogies in archaeology

Ethnoarchaeology has been given a more restricted definition than the general use of ethnographic analogies. But it is necessary to chart, even if sketchily, the history of the use made by archaeologists of ethnography and anthropology in order to assess the present importance and purpose of ethnoarchaeology. The past use of ethnographic analogies can be followed in both Europe and America.

In Europe, the Renaissance revival of interest in the Classical world and its literature led to an awareness of ancient societies existing prior to literary civilizations. Indeed the earliest ethnographies which were to prove of service to archaeologists may well have been the accounts of Caesar and Tacitus, who in *De Bello Gallico* and the *Germania* described the native inhabitants of France, England and the lower Rhine area. But at the same time as the increasing interest in early ethnographies led to a picture of a barbarous past, pictures of a very different kind from the contemporary world were also arousing attention.

Explorations beyond the known world introduced the sixteenth-century European to altogether novel cultures. John White, the Elizabethan explorer in Virginia, described and illustrated the villages, ceremonies, arrowhead manufacture and the hunting and farming activities of the Indians of Pomeiock. Some of his watercolors were printed in de Bry's (1590) edition of Harriot's *Brief and true report of the new found land of Virginia.* But de Bry also attached to the volume the first representation of past Britons as other than Tudors, Romans or mythical heroes. The pictures were accompanied by the following caption. 'The painter of whow I have had the first of the Inhabitants of Virginia, give me allso thees 5 Figures fallowinge, fownde as hy did assured my in a colld English cronicle, the which I wold well sett to the ende of thees first Figures, for to showe how that the Inhabitants of the great Bretannie have been in times past as sauuage as those of Virginia' (from Orme 1973, 488). So here an ethnographic parallel was used in order to add information to what was known about the past. In 1611 John Speed referred to the Virginians in supporting his theory that the Ancient Britons went naked. Again ethnography was used to shock the civilized members of seventeenth-century society about their primitive past.

Another instance in which ethnography was used to change romantic and mythical interpretations of the past was in the debate about early stone implements. In the mid-seventeenth century Aldrovandus described stone tools as 'due to an admixture of a certain exhalation of thunder and lightening with metallic matter, chiefly in dark clouds, which is coagulated by the circumfused moisture and conglutinated into a mass (like flour with water) and subsequently indurated by heat, like a brick', and at about the same time Tollius suggested that chipped flints were 'generated in the sky by a fulgurous exhalation conglobed in a cloud by the circumposed humour' (Daniel 1950, 26). Other interpretations of early stone tools were that they were thunderbolts or elf arrows. Such theories were put to an end in Oxford by Dr Robert Plot and his father-in-law Dugdale and his assistant Lhwyd in 1686, 1656 and 1713 respectively, incorporating the aid of ethnographic parallels. By 1800, John Frere could describe Palaeolithic hand axes as 'weapons of war'.

In the eighteenth century many parallels were built between ethnographies and the European past, as is clear from the titles of J.T. Lafitau's 1724 Paris publication *Moeurs des Sauvages Amériquains, Comparées aux Moeurs des Premiers Temps,* and J.Kraft's 1760 Copenhagen publication *Brief account of the principal institutions, customs and ideas of the Savage Peoples illustrating the human origin and evolution generally* (Klindt – Jensen 1976). Lafitau had been a French missionary in Canada and he drew parallels between Indians and the Bible and classical literature. Kraft's more general work was translated into German and Dutch, but remained largely unnoticed by archaeologists. He explicitly drew parallels between stone tools found in the soil in Europe, and primitive stages of man, on analogy with existing primitive societies.

All these instances of the use of ethnographic parallels in the sixteenth to eighteenth centuries were concerned with making simple formal analogies for the immediate purposes of clarification and for the derivation of alternative interpretations A lack of concern with the dangers of ethnographic parallels continued in the nineteenth century with the exception of such archaeologists as Nilsson in Denmark and Pitt Rivers in England.

Nilsson in *Primitive Inhabitants of Scandinavia* (1843) used a 'comparative method' by which prehistoric artifacts were compared with formally and functionally identical objects used by modern peoples. He claimed that by using the comparative method archaeology ought to be able 'to collect the remains of human races long since passed away, and of the works which they have left behind, to draw a parallel between them and similar ones which still exist on earth, and thus cut out a way to the knowledge of the circumstances which have been, by comparing them with those which still exist'. But he also noted that care was needed in the use of ethnographic analogies. 'Similarities such as the presence of similar stone arrows in Scania and Tierra del Fuego do not always prove one and the same origin' (quoted by Daniel 1950, 49). The same caution is evident in Pitt Rivers' important and independent development of the use of ethnographic comparisons. General Pitt Rivers' involvement in the army led to an interest in the development and improvement of the rifle. His careful classification of categories and forms of rifle was followed by careful collections of a wide range of weapons, boats, musical instruments, religious symbols and so on. In arranging his material, Pitt Rivers was more concerned with types than their country of origin. Archaeological and ethnographic material could be compared, side by side. Yet, like Nilsson, he was wary of discussing only formal parallels. In making an analogy it was necessary to demonstrate functional as well as formal identity. This concern with function extends the context of the formal similarity and moves towards a relational analogy. Orme (1973, 487) suggests that the work of Wilson (1851), Evans (1860), Christy and Lartet (1875) in recognising and identifying artifacts used comparisons with the material culture of contemporary traditional groups, while the more general interpretations of Lubbock (1865) and Tylor (1865) also relied heavily on ethnography. In 1870, Sir John Lubbock wrote in *The Origin of Civilization and the Primitive Condition of Man* that 'the weapons and implements now used by the lower races of men throw much light on the signification and use of those discovered in ancient tumuli, or in the drift gravels: . . . a knowledge of modern savages and their modes of life enables us more accurately to picture, and more vividly to conceive, the manners and customs of our ancestors in bygone ages'. The influence of ethnography on archaeology in the second half of the nineteenth century increased as part of two additional developments. The first was the reference, in interpretations of the past, to the folklore survivals of 'primitive' antecedants (Daniel 1950, 185). Second, the 'culture' concept began to replace the previous emphasis on dividing archaeological material into epochs. The European school of 'anthropogeographers' started by Ratzel and his pupil Frobenius described cultural areas in West Africa and in Melanesia. The work of German ethnologists came to have a great impact on the development of the culture concept in archaeology as it was later to be adopted by Childe. Indeed, Daniel (1950, 246) has described the organization of prehistory into cultures as the anthropological attitude to prehistory.

Though the debt to ethnography and anthropology in the second half of the nineteenth century was large, the cautions of Nilsson and Pitt Rivers went generally unheeded. Formal parallels were applied with little attention to context and the dangers were little discussed.

The trend of increasing links with anthropology continued in the first half of the twentieth century with, for example, the journal *Annals of Archaeology and Anthropology* first issued in 1908 under the auspices of the University of Liverpool Institute of Archaeology, but the increase in quantity was not always associated with an increase in quality.

The first issue of *Antiquity* (1927) included an article by Raymond Firth on Maori hillforts which was intended to aid British prehistorians in the interpretation of their own Iron Age earthworks. While the place of hillforts in Maori society is well discussed, comparisons with English hillforts are scanty and formal, based on such features as the size and shape of ramparts. Thomson, in his 1939 study of the Wik Munkan Aborigines of the Cape York Peninsula of Australia, recognized that the archaeologist would be confused and possibly misled by the surviving material culture. The Aborigines lead such different lives in the different seasons of the year that the archaeologist might be fooled into thinking the different assemblages were produced by separate peoples. In addition, Thomson noted that very little would survive to be found by archaeologists anyway. This is the first example of a pessimistic, negative type of analogy which became common later as 'cautionary tales'. Most such cautions have the characteristic that they are little concerned with the context which leads to the particular material remains: in the Australian example the context is highly specialized and generalization would be difficult (see discussion in Chapter 5).

Parallels with societies closer at hand seemed to avoid some of these problems. In his report of the excavations at Skara Brae, a Neolithic settlement on the Orkney Islands, Childe (1931) used analogies with recent inhabitants of the northern isles in his interpretation of the functions of beds and other features inside the huts. Clark (1952) also used a wealth of information from recent and modern Scandinavian societies in order to provide formal analogies for prehistoric tools. But in the same book many formal comparisons were made over great distances to the Eskimos and tribes of Canada and North America, as was also seen (Chapter 1) in his account of the Star Carr site. More recently, a visit by Grahame Clark to Australasia led to an article (1965) comparing, with some concern for context and relevance, the axe trade there with the distribution of Neolithic axes in Britain. It was suggested, on the basis of the similarities of the axes, their very wide distributions, and the simple level of societies, that the Neolithic axes were traded by ceremonial gift exchange, much the same as in New Guinea and Australia.

An increasing concern with relevance and context has continued in the careful and informed analogies drawn in the more recent work of, for example, David (1971; 1972) and Rowlands (1971; 1976). But the emphasis on formal comparisons still remains. Clarke (1968) used evidence from Californian Indians to suggest that links could be set up between the forms of regional artifact distributions and linguistic groupings, while other formal comparisons of cultural distributions have been made by Hodder (1978a). Such formal studies are now decreasing in frequency as warnings are made (e.g. Ucko 1969) and assessments published (Orme 1973; 1974; 1981). The strength of the link between archaeology, anthropology and ethnography has now reached a new peak in England and continental Europe with ethnographic archaeology posts in three departments of archaeology in English universities, several archaeology and anthropology joint degrees, numerous courses, and a host of articles, many of which will be referenced in the pages which follow. Nevertheless the fuss over the conscious rapprochment between archaeology and anthropology in Britain is slight when compared with the call to arms that has emanated from North American publications over the last 25 years. Indeed much of the recently increased popularity of ethnography for archaeologists in England and Europe must be seen as a result of influence from the other side of the Atlantic.

In America, the presence of living Indian societies in areas where excavations were being undertaken helped to make archaeologists aware of the possibilities of using the present to interpret the past. In a much more direct way than in Europe, American archaeologists have always been able to make use of ethnohistory and modern ethnographic accounts. An example of the early use of ethnography in America is provided by the resolution of the 'moundbuilders' controversy. By the late eighteenth century, a large number of mounds or ruins had been discovered in Ohio and in other frontier areas. Any idea that these monuments could have been built by the Indian 'savages' was rejected, and a 'lost race' was imagined which had been replaced by the Indians. The nature and origin of the lost race of moundbuilders were the subject of much fanciful speculation until finally, in the late nineteenth century, the myth was laid to rest by the work of Cyrus Thomas. Major John Wesley Powell (the first explorer to descend the Grand Canyon rapids of the Colorado River in a boat; see *fig. 6)* was Director of the Bureau of Ethnology and he picked Thomas to carry out research into the mounds in the 1880s and 1890s. Through Thomas' excavations and comparisons of the excavated material with contemporary Indian material culture in the same areas, Powell and Thomas were able to suggest that the moundbuilders were the same people as the modern 'savages'.

This direct historical approach, used by Thomas to throw light on archaeological information, was part of a more general emphasis on continuity. Around the turn of the century a number of studies (Fewkes 1893; Hodge 1897; Kroeber 1916) tried to use archaeological evidence to test Indian oral traditions or to find sites associated with particular clan myths. Analogies based on continuity in local areas were an important part of the ethnic identification of cultural complexes throughout the early part of the twentieth century in North America. In particular, W.D. Strong (1935) and J.H. Steward (1942) developed the direct historical approach as a distinct procedure within archaeological interpretation.

Figure 5   **An important early European view of the south-eastern American Indians is provided in the illustrations of Jacques Le Moyne, who accompanied the French settlers to north-eastern Florida in the 1560s. This drawing shows a burial ceremony with the grave or small burial mound outlined in arrows and topped by a conch-shell drinking vessel. The mourners surround the mound, and in the background is a palisaded village. Pictures such as this were either unknown to or ignored by early writers on the Moundbuilder controversy (Willey and Sabloff 1974)**

Although the same emphasis on using continuity to support analogies is still seen in more recent American work (for example in the 'smudge pit' study discussed in Chapter 1), there has been an increasing concern over the last 30 years with generalization, as part of the conscious expansion of what came to be termed 'anthropological archaeology'. In 1948 (p. 6) Taylor described the archaeologist as a 'Jekyll and Hyde, claiming to "do" history but "be" an anthropologist'. The use of direct, continuous analogies was more clearly associated with a historical emphasis, and the new concern with making general statements about man, society, ecological relationships and systems which has lasted to the present day, eschewed emphases on historical frameworks and sought to embrace more closely the generalizing science of man. Associated with this development has been a decreasing concern with causal relationships within particular contexts when using ethnographic analogies. The aim has been to build and use general comparative analogies. Interpretations of the past are obtained through broadly comparative and quasi-universal generalizations about human cultural behavior, rather than being confined to a specific historical context (Willey and Sabloff 1974,207). But this view has not gone without its critics in America. According to Anderson (1969), 'logical analysis of form depends as much on perception of the object, which is conditioned by cultural background, as by any universal principles'. Those recent studies which do examine context and which use relational analogies have been more concerned with the functional and ecological context than with the realm of ideas.

Figure 6

Major John Wesley Powell consulting an Indian on the Kaibab Plateau, near the Grand Canyon of the Colorado River in northern Arizona (Willey and Sabloff 1974)

It was in this more recent period, as 'anthropological archaeology' became taken up as the battle cry of the 'new archaeologists' (Meggers 1968; Longacre 1970) that ethnoarchaeology became defined as a distinct area of research. We have already seen that the word was used as early as 1900 by Fewkes, but it was in the '50s and '60s that the main development occurred. Various definitions and outlines of ethnoarchaeology and the equivalent terms 'action' or 'living' archaeology were suggested by Kleindienst and Watson (1956) and Ascher (1962) and specific studies appeared (Thompson 1958, Oswalt and Van Stone 1967). The *Man the Hunter* symposium (Lee and De Vore 1968) was important in bringing a large amount of information and general statements about hunter-gatherers to the notice of archaeologists, while in the same year the collection of essays edited by the Binfords included important ethnoarchaeological studies (e.g by Longacre and Ayres). Since then the number of studies, definitions and books has greatly increased (Donnan and Clewlow 1974; Stiles 1977; Yellen 1977; Ingersoll, Yellen and MacDonald 1977, Gould 1978b; 1980; Binford 1978; Kramer 1979). But it is important to realize that this rash of ethnoarchaeological work is not characterized by a uniformity of approach. Variation in views on definitions was described at the beginning of this chapter. There is also still considerable variation in the emphasis placed on context and relevance. For example, Wilmsen's (1979; 1980) careful study of the particular Bushman cultural and historical context and the patterning of material remains contrasts with Schiffer's (1978) call for the generation of cross-cultural 'laws'. While some studies are interested in only the ecological and functionally adaptive context within which material residues are produced (e.g Binford 1978), others are concerned to examine the cognitive basis of behavior (e.g. Hardin 1979).

There is also variation in views about the part played by ethnographic analogies in archaeological interpretation. Oddly, much of the recent ethnoarchaeological fervor has occurred at a time when the dominant consensus among American archaeologists has been that the role of analogy should be limited. Several archaeologists have emphasized that explanation should proceed by the testing of deductive hypotheses. The analogy derived from ethnoarchaeology is seen as playing only a small initial role in suggesting the hypothesis. In Chapter 1 we saw why this view is misleading. In fact, archaeologists do and can proceed rigorously by the careful use of relational analogies and it is not necessary to set up this procedure as 'hypothetico-deductive'.

The increase in ethnoarchaeology is a product of the anthropological emphasis in American archaeology, and of the growing interest in the formulation of cross-cultural generalizations about human behavior. Ethnoarchaeology is also seen to provide particular hypotheses to be tested deductively against archaeological data. Whether carried out by Americans or Europeans, and however it is used, ethnoarchaeology now has a number of important functions. First, it became clear, as archaeologists turned more and more to social anthropologists for advice and inspiration, that existing ethnographic studies were inadequate. Ethnographers had rarely collected the type of data on material residues that is most relevant for archaeologists. They had concentrated on aspects of social and linguistic variability, and on general accounts of cultural material. Few ethnographic studies provided detailed information on the locations of settlements, size and shape variation of artifacts, or disposal processes. In particular, questions concerning the depositional and postdepositional processes which result in distributions of artifacts and features on archaeological sites could not be answered using existing ethnographic studies. The increased interest in such questions in the last ten years (e.g. Schiffer 1976) has been one further factor encouraging the recent rise to importance of ethnoarchaeology. It became necessary for the archaeologist to collect his own ethnographic information, and in fact most ethnoarchaeology is today carried out by people trained as archaeologists, not by ethnographers or social anthropologists.

A second important function that ethnoarchaeology provides is to salvage relevant information from forms of society which are fast disappearing. The colonial destruction of numerous peoples from Tasmania to North America was as horrifyingly efficient as it was speedy. The technique of flint-knapping used by the last Californian Indian, Ishi, was recorded by Nelson (1916), but such information was usually lost or badly recorded. What we have left now are the remnants of our slaughter. The traditional societies which did survive are fast becoming incorporated into world-wide economies. Wobst (1978) notes that most ethnoarchaeologists now mainly consider the local adaptive aspects of hunter-gatherer groups. Regional and interregional links are sifted out because they are 'modern', 'post-contact' and 'distorting'. If we do think it is important to examine traditional societies, ethnoarchaeology must not lose time in placing them in their modern world context.

The desire to study traditional, less industrialised societies is understandable for those archaeologists who wish to examine flint-knapping and other techniques which are no longer to be found in Western society. Yet there is a possibility that, after having overrun and pillaged Australian, African and American peoples militarily, economically and socially, we follow this up by an 'intellectual colonialism'. I have said that ethnoarchaeology is important in that it helps to break away from a Western ethnocentricism. But there is a terrible risk that in examining 'primitive' societies we are really just repeating that ethnocentricism in a new and more sinister form. We assume that our own 'developed' society is less relevant in finding analogies for Neolithic Europe in 6000 BC than are 'undeveloped' Africans or Australians. But 'primitive' Africans might not see it in the same light. They are not devolved, reverted or stagnant societies. There is a potential danger in 'dressing up' European Neolithic society like Kenyan tribesmen, in the same way that in the eighteenth century Ancient Britons were dressed like Virginians. This form of intellectual ethnocentricism is part of the evolutionary perspective which has gripped archaeology throughout this century. Breaking away from such biases leads to the third function of ethnoarchaeology today.

Ethnoarchaeological studies in Western industrialised societies are as equally valid as studies in the less industrialised world if the importance of a control over context is accepted. I have tried to show that the drawing of analogies for the prehistoric past must move away from formal cross-cultural studies, to a more careful consideration of the links between material patterning and its functional and ideational context. We need to understand *why* material is patterned in a particular way in each cultural milieu. This emphasis on the links themselves means that Western society is as good a source for analogies as are less industrialised peoples. If we can understand all the functional and ideological factors which cause variation in how we bury our dead in modern England, that is if we understand the links between burial and its context, then we can assess whether the modern information is relevant to a particular prehistoric situation. While technological studies of particular, fast dying-out, activities such as flint-knapping remain important, the more generally applicable 'contextual' studies do not depend on finding 'primitive' societies. Rather there is a need to consider all forms of society in their own terms.

The third function of ethnoarchaeology, and in my view the most important, is to develop ethnographic analogies which concern the principles which relate material patterning to adaptive and cultural contexts. But in saying this it also becomes apparent that a change is needed in ethnoarchaeological methodology. For the moment nearly all the ethnoarchaeological studies of which I know have been carried out by people trained as archaeologists and I have already suggested why this should be so. Ethnoarchaeology simply involves the archaeologist going off to do a bit of ethnoarchaeology, often as a sideline or second interest. The archaeologist treats the ethnographic data as if they were archaeological data and he uses archaeological methods (sampling, recording, etc.). As far as I am aware, there is no detailed account in the ethnoarchaeological literature of field methods, interview techniques, and the problems of sampling live populations. This remarkable lack results from what Gould (1978b) has called the 'materialist' emphasis of ethnoarchaeology. There is an assumption that the ethnoarchaeologist is concerned with the actual products of behavior, with plotting material remains and with objective descriptions. But as soon as it is accepted that the context of material activities is the major concern, then anthropological field methods take on a real importance. It we are to find out the social and cultural framework which informs the making of a pot or the knapping of a flint blade, then we must understand the limitations, difficulties and problems of interviewing, observing and understanding members of other societies and their material products. We shall see that not only people but even pots can lie.

Ethnoarchaeological field methods

Various published sources of world ethnographic data are listed by Stiles (1977), but since I have defined ethnoarchaeology more narrowly than the general use of ethnographic analogy, as a field study, I will examine here only field methods. For more general accounts of anthropological methodology see, for example, Naroll and Cohen (1973) and Brim and Spain (1974).

Perhaps the major problem to confront any ethnoarchaeologist working in a contemporary society is that what people do may bear little relation to what they say. For example, in my initial work in the Baringo District in Kenya, I was told that many of the clay pots in use in houses and compounds were up to 80 years old. In fact in *Man* (1977) I published several maps containing such information. In subsequent years, after talking to anthropologists who had worked longer in the region than I had, and after talking to the potters and observing the frequency of pot breakage, I realized that it was extremely rare for any pot to last more than eight years. Similarly, I was told by a number of informants that a group of pots came from a particular source. After measuring the pots it became clear that the information was almost certainly incorrect.

In modern western society individuals often mislead when asked questions concerning various aspects of material culture. For example, many may be embarrassed or ashamed to answer correctly questions concerning the amount of different types of refuse that they produce. Work in Tucson, Arizona and in Milwaukee has demonstrated that estimates of garbage disposal rates based on verbal information were often severely misjudged (Rathje 1979).

Perhaps the most widely discussed instance of a lack of correspondence between verbal information and actual behavior concerns the notion of the 'type'. Are the categories and types of artifacts identified by the archaeologist purely of his own making, or do they correspond to a 'native' classification? Ford (1954) saw types as archaeological and imposed, while Spaulding (1953) suggested that native categories could be inferred by using various statistical techniques. There are now a large number of examples such as those given by Gould (1974), Hardin (1979) and White & Thomas

(1972) which show that archaeological and native categories do not coincide. White and Thomas, for example, note that the primary archaeological division of stone artifacts into cores and flakes is not made by native New Guinea highlanders. Clearly, in studying the cultural context and ideological basis of material culture patterning, we may be examining meaningful behavior which is not expressed at a particular verbal level. What are the reasons for this?

There is a wide range of factors which may cause a disjunction between what people do and say. One reason is that there is a real difference between verbal and non-discursive knowledge. For example, we may know how to speak without being able to explain the grammatical rules of the language. So, in material culture, we may know what to do even if we cannot explain it verbally. This appears to be the case in modern western society where what people say about material culture is probably less thought out than their views on religion, sex, politics and the like. Material, everyday knowledge is not and need not be an area of discursive knowledge.

In some cases this undiscussed, hidden meaning of material things can be used strategically in social relations. For example, women may be able to make subtle and effective statements about their social position by using everyday artifacts which are not consciously discussed and regulated by dominant male members of society. But it is difficult to generalise. In other societies, true knowledge about the meaning of things and their spatial arrangements in settlements may be controlled by an elite minority. This dominant group may maintain its position partly by a withholding of knowledge about how the world is put together and the members of that group may intentionally mislead the uninitiated (cf Barth 1975). How difficult it is going to be, in such a situation, for the ethnoarchaeologist to penetrate the relationship between what is said and what is done.

Much of the confusion may, however, result from simple and direct lying where the informant seeks immediate gain from the ethnoarchaeologist. For example, in my Baringo example, it is probable that the ages of pots were grossly exaggerated because it was thought that I might want to buy pots (in the footsteps of the anthropologists who had worked in the area before me). It became important to be known in the area as someone who did not have purchase in mind. Other reasons for intentional misleading are extremely numerous and include the possibility that the researcher is an inappropriate sex or age, that the area has had a history of maltreatment by white colonial powers, that missionaries have encouraged a feeling of guilt in relation to traditional activities, that the interpreter is not respected, or simply that the ethnoarchaeologist, wishing to measure pots and refuse, is perceived as a fool, unworthy of attention.

A further reason for a lack of correspondence between what is seen and heard may result from problems of comprehension. Whether the researcher is trying to learn the language or is using an interpreter, there may be many misunderstandings. In fact, the informant with the best will in the world may be unable to understand and comply with the questions asked. Binford (1978) records that, in retrospect, his initial questions of the Nunamiut Eskimos could not be answered in a straightforward way, however much this frustrated him at the time.

The very presence of the ethnoarchaeologist may mean that people behave in a different way so that what they say and do may be different from what is observed. The outsider always changes the situation that is being observed. Yellen (1977, 289) discusses how food is distributed within a society, but this includes food distributed to an anthropologist. The ambiguous position and standing of the outsider may cause entirely novel ways of distributing food and of acting within the home environment.

Given that the verbal and non-verbal often do not coincide, and that the degree of coincidence varies with culture and context, we need to examine models which link the ideal and the actual together. Yellen (1977) provides an example from his work amongst the !Kung Bushmen. In practice, !Kung individuals move widely and social ties are loosely organized, but the !Kung see themselves as a series of loosely defined territorial groups. Yellen (ibid., pp. 48-9) suggests a model according to which these two contradictory aspects are part of the same system. The formal band territorial model provides a mental framework for deciding on and justifying varying courses of individual action and for predicting in a loose way what others will do. But in the !Kung environment there is a need to be able to adapt rapidly and flexibly. So, over the long term, there is a practice of individual changes and movements in order to rearrange the demographic map.

During the chapters which follow, other examples will be given of the structured way in which idea and practice may not correspond. But, as Bloch (1971) demonstrates in his analysis of the ideal component of Madagascan burial which contrasts with the practice of daily life, it is incorrect to assume that the material world is more or less 'real' than the non-material. Both aspects are organized in relation to each other, as complementary components in a cultural unit.

Given the pervasive 'problem' that spoken and observed information may not coincide, for whatever reason, some archaeologists have suggested the particular 'solution' that was mentioned earlier (p.40). The 'problem' is 'solved' if we accept Gould's materialist position. Wobst (1978) notes that ethnography involves the study of recorded behavior, while archaeologists study actual behavior. In a more extreme view, Schiffer (1978, 235) suggests that ethnoarchaeologists should only observe actual behavior, and not study word-of-mouth reports. Such an approach would first of all be impossible since, as has been suggested, the very presence of the ethnoarchaeologist in a living situation affects and changes behavior. The more the ethnoarchaeologist remains a remote outsider the more he/she changes what he/she observes. Also such a materialistic approach limits scientific research because it is difficult to find out basic questions concerning the observed data, such as where and when and by whom a pot was made, or who is the brother of the potter. Equally, it is impossible to examine the all-important two-way relationship between discursive and non-discursive knowledge, and to examine material behavior within a social, ideological and cultural context.

The ethnoarchaeologist' must not duck the issue and play at part-time anthropology. While the ethnoarchaeologist does bring to anthropology the training to observe behavior and its products, there will be few research problems for which such observation is sufficient. The ethnoarchaeologist must also face the issues of how to examine what is said, thought and explained by informants.

One procedure would be to arrive in the field with a questionnaire worked out in advance with advice from sociologists and others trained in interviewing techniques. Such an approach would frequently involve filling in forms with yes/no answers. While there may be some research questions and cultures in which this approach would be adequate, there are considerable dangers involved. For example, in many countries informants will answer yes or no depending on the tone of the question; the main concern of the informant may be to provide a pleasing answer rather than a correct one. Such problems could be countered by introducing cross-checks in the questionnaire. But it may be difficult to assess all the biases of age, sex, colour and so on mentioned above with such an inflexible technique.

In many cases the informant will find the questions ambiguous or unclear. This is especially the case in an alien culture where there may be many subtle differences in meaning which cannot be accounted for in a prepared checklist. Perhaps the most serious disadvantage of the questionnaire technique is that the researcher cannot be led down new avenues. By far the best way to find out about the unknown is to listen and learn.

One extreme, but highly effective, example of this was used by Guilbert Lewis (1980) in his work among the Gnau of New Guinea. Even though one might use a tape recorder, the anthropologist is usually present, intruding into the scene. Lewis placed his tape recorder by groups of people talking and left. The people being studied had, by then, got used to the technical device being around and carried on their conservations and rituals regardless. The ethnoarchaeologist will usually want to record visual information, and since it will be impractical to film continuously and remotely, greater intrusion must occur. Indeed, there are many advantages in participating and becoming accepted, in so far as it is possible, within the study group. Understanding may come with closer contact, there will be time to learn the language, initial distrust may be allayed. During a long stay in which some participation is achieved, it is possible to use a variety of recording procedures; tape recordings of undirected discussion, notes or tape recordings of partially directed discussion in which questions from the researcher focus the informants on a particular topic, direct observation and recording.

Clearly the degree to which participant observation is used depends to a considerable extent on the nature of the research problem. Those interested in regional settlement patterns in relation to environmental features may have less need to understand verbal information than those concerned with the meaning of ritual. However, I find it difficult to envisage topics that could successfully be completed without any reference to the explanations of the individuals themselves. It is sheer cultural and intellectual snobbery to allow no reality to informants' analyses of their own situation. It is important to examine the relationship between the spoken causes of events and the outsider's identification of correlations and interactions.

As much as the interview technique depends on the research questions being asked, so does the sampling design. How many villages, areas, houses, pots or people should be studied depends on the aspects of behaviour that the analyst is interested in and the degree of certainty that is required in the conclusions. If the questions are fairly straightforward, such as the relationship between size of settlement and duration of occupation, there are numerous equations in sampling theory (Mueller 1975 : Cherry, Gamble, Shennan 1978) which can be applied in order to determine an adequate random sample (for example, of settlements). Usually, however, there will be numerous questions and variables to be examined and a more subjective assessment of sample size will be required.

Major problems in the sampling design may concern the differences between an archaeological and a living settlement plan. In the living situation artifacts, and even houses, are constantly being moved and it may (although this depends on the particular culture) be impossible to produce a map of the settlement 'frozen' at one moment. The ethnoarchaeologist may be particularly interested in this mobility but his recording may be confounded not only by the speed and frequency of moves, but by changes in functions of artifacts, removals from the village, re-use of houses and so on. 'Tagging' of artifacts may often be impractical or prevented by informants. For the moment there are few guidelines available to the ethnoarchaeologists faced with such problems. The particular solution will depend on the questions being asked and the circumstances and ease of work.

In all societies there is likely to be great variation in activities and use of artifacts at different times of the day, season and year. There may also be variations at longer intervals related to environmental and climatic fluctuations and historical and external political events. The archaeologist may be particularly interested in recording these various ranges of behaviour so that the resulting palimpsest can be compared with an archaeological composite pattern. Long and repeated visits to the study area are, therefore, necessary and are in any case implied by the need to participate and learn languages for which no grammar or dictionary may have been published. In practical terms, the ethnoarchaeologist may have arrived in a study area at a time when women are busy in the fields so that they cannot talk easily and domestic tools and crafts cannot be observed. It will be desirable for the ethnoarchaeologist to spend a total of at least one year in the study area.

Various other practical aspects of conducting ethnoarchaeological fieldwork in a foreign country are so contingent on the laws of that country and its particular relations with the home country that little of a general nature can be prescribed. It is, of course, legally and ethically important to obtain the necessary research and travel permits, and embassies will often be a good starting point here. For many third world countries, applications may now take six months to a year to be processed, and the outcome may well be unsuccessful. Plans must, therefore, commence early and alternatives prepared. Many countries are now, understandably, highly sensitive to the attentions of anthropologists seeking a traditional 'primitiveness'. Success in applications is best assured through those already working in an area, and by a clear and honest statement of research aims.

In conclusion, in undertaking ethnoarchaeological fieldwork the archaeologist is aware of responsibilities to the country and people studied and to the anthropologists who, in the future, will wish to work in the same or similar areas. Their work depends on the good relations set up by earlier researchers.

Involvement in ethnoarchaeological fieldwork also requires recognition of the peculiarity of the task. One has to be more than an anthropologist and more than an archaeologist. The differences from archaeology are clear. There are also differences from anthropology. First, there is a particular concern with material culture. While the materially constructed world, including everything from fine painting to hearths, is a hopelessly broad category about which to generalise, there are certain aspects such as the ambiguity of material as opposed to verbal symbols, and the non-discursive nature of much material organization, which do allow material culture to be defined as a distinct area of analysis (for further discussion of this point see Chapter 10). Second, ethnoarchaeology includes and focuses attention on everyday mundane behavior, not just the rituals and myths of societies. Third, as has already been noted, the ethnoarchaeologist is trained to observe behavior which he/she can then compare with written and spoken information. In all these, and probably many other ways, ethnoarchaeology is a distinctive area of field research with particular problems of its own. As well as being versed in anthropological field techniques, the ethnoarchaeologist must also be aware of additional problems, some of which I have tried to outline in this chapter. It is only as further ethnoarchaeology is completed that a full text of appropriate field techniques and biases can be written.